100 GREAT OPERAS
AND THEIR STORIES

December 1993

My dear friend Wes,

May this book add to your enjoyment of fine music as you pursue your dreams and happiness in the journey of life.

With much love and admiration,

Benjamin Stephen Kerschberg

100 GREAT OPERAS
AND THEIR STORIES

HENRY W. SIMON

A new revised and abridged
edition of *Festival of Opera*

ANCHOR BOOKS
DOUBLEDAY
NEW YORK   LONDON   TORONTO   SYDNEY   AUCKLAND

An Anchor Book

PUBLISHED BY DOUBLEDAY

a division of Bantam Doubleday Dell Publishing Group, Inc.
666 Fifth Avenue, New York, New York 10103

Anchor Books, Doubleday, and the portrayal of an anchor
are trademarks of Doubleday, a division of Bantam Doubleday
Dell Publishing Group, Inc.

100 Great Operas was originally published as *Festival of Opera*
by Doubleday in 1957.
The Anchor Books edition is published by arrangement
with Doubleday.

Library of Congress Cataloging-in-Publication Data
Simon, Henry W. (Henry William), 1901–1970.
100 great operas and their stories / by Henry W. Simon.
—A new rev. and abridged ed., 1st Anchor Books ed.
    p. cm.
    Rev. and abridged ed. of: Festival of opera. 1957.
    1. Operas—Stories, plots, etc.   I. Simon, Henry W.
(Henry William), 1901–1970. Festival of opera.   II. Title.
III. Title: One hundred great operas and their stories.
MT95.S59   1989   88-36697
782.1'3—dc19   CIP
                  MN

5   7   9   10   8   6

FOR ROZ

CONTENTS

Contents

Contents

Contents

PREFACE

AN APOLOGY FOR SMILING

Every one of the stories in this book is—or, at least, once was—good. I say this with confidence because no composer who ever lived would take the time and trouble to write a score for a story he knew to be bad. In fact, most opera composers, today as in the past, spend a large part of their time and care looking for a good story to set—and composers are men with outsize I.Q.'s. If they weren't, they could never master the intricacies of writing a score.

Why, then, should there be so prevalent a conviction among our literate population that practically the lowest form of literature is the opera libretto and that there is nothing quite so ludicrous as an opera story? For there is no getting away from the fact that many of the stories in this book include basic or incidental absurdities.

Here, then, is the explanation. There are, first of all, a number of opera stories, like *Pelleas and Melisande* or *Gianni Schicchi*, which not only were good to begin with but remain good in the operatic telling. Then there are great stories from mythology, like the Orpheus, the Electra, and the Trojan War legends; there are Bible stories, like Samson's and Salome's; there are historical stories like Godounoff's and King Gustave's; there are stories based on great plays like Goethe's *Faust* and Shakespeare's *Othello*; there are stories derived from stage hits like Sardou's *Tosca* and Belasco's *Butterfly*; and there are even a few entirely original tales written by the composers themselves, like Leoncavallo's *Pagliacci* and Menotti's *Amahl*.

But some operatic stories have, with time, come to seem hopelessly old-fashioned; others have been ruined for us by the vagaries of stage life and even of political life. Thus, the story of Camille (*La Traviata*) once seemed so violent and realistic an attack on sexual morals as to shock our British grand- or great-grandfathers a hundred years ago into banning it, whereas today it strikes us as a sentimental or at best a quietly touching romance; while the libretto of A *Masked Ball* struck Verdi's original censors as so forceful a lesson in regicide that they fastened magnificent absurdities upon it even before the musical score was completed.

In retelling these stories for this book, I have tried, in my introductory notes and in the telling of the stories themselves, to explain some of these absurdities, even to highlight them when doing so might suggest to the reader a greater sympathy with the work of art he is asked to consider. For these operas are all works of art which (with a few exceptions) have had the vitality to survive on the stage whether or not a modern audience can take the story as seriously as the composer must have before he set the words to music. Under the spell of great music well performed, the willing suspension of disbelief that Coleridge demanded for poetry is more easily come by when whatever nonsense may occur on the stage has already been forgiven and when one can throw oneself under the spell of the words, the action, the scenery and the music in the way the composer could have wished.

H.W.S.

100 GREAT OPERAS
AND THEIR STORIES

THE ABDUCTION FROM THE SERAGLIO

(*Die Entführung aus dem Serail*)

Opera in three acts by Wolfgang Amadeus Mozart with libretto in German by Gottlob Stephanie based on a play by Christoph Friedrich Bretzner

KONSTANZE, *a Spanish lady*	*Soprano*
BLONDCHEN, *her English maid*	*Soprano*
BELMONTE, *a Spanish nobleman*	*Tenor*
PEDRILLO, *his servant*	*Tenor*
SELIM PASHA	*Speaking part*
OSMIN, *overseer of his harem*	*Bass*

Time: 16th century
Place: Turkey
First performance at Vienna, July 16, 1782

Mozart composed *The Abduction from the Seraglio* at one of the happiest times in his short life. He was barely twenty-six; he was very much in love with Konstanze Weber; he was engaged to marry her and, in fact, he did so just a little over three weeks after the opera's premiere. In addition, the first name of his fiancée was the name of the heroine of the story of the opera. All this delight, I like to think, is reflected in the music of the opera.

It isn't really so much an opera as what the Viennese of the time called a *Singspiel*, that is, a gay play with music. All of the action is carried on with spoken dialogue, and the characters break into song only to express strong emotions, seldom to further the story. One important character, the Pasha, does not sing at all but only speaks.

The Abduction from the Seraglio

Eighteenth-century Vienna was crazy about Turks. There were Turkish dress styles, Turkish hair-dos, Turkish stories, and a great deal of Turkish music—or what the Viennese thought was Turkish music. Some of the pianos even had tiny drum and bell attachments to make "Turkish effects." The story and music of *The Abduction* were part of this Turkish fad. It concerns a high-minded Pasha of the sixteenth century, who captures a beautiful English maiden, Konstanze, and her maid Blondchen (meaning "little blonde"), and also Pedrillo, the servant of a young Spanish nobleman named Belmonte.

OVERTURE

The overture, a familiar piece in concert halls, reflects the contemporary Turkish fad: it makes prominent use of both the triangle and the bass drum. Gay in mood, as the overture to any *Singspiel* should be, it offers a moment of sweet sadness by including, in a minor key, the young hero's opening aria.

ACT I

Without waiting for a conclusion to the overture, the curtain rises on Belmonte, the noble young Spanish hero of the story. He has reached a seaside plaza outside the palace of the Pasha, and he sings of his hope of finding Konstanze there (*Hier soll ich dich denn sehen, Konstanze*—"Here may I hope to find you, Konstanze"). An unpleasant old fellow named Osmin appears. He is picking figs in the garden and singing a ditty about unreliable sweethearts (*Wer ein Liebschen hat gefunden*—"Whoever has found a sweetheart"). Now, Osmin is the Pasha's overseer, and when Belmonte asks about his friend Pedrillo, he receives a very scurvy welcome. Osmin, it seems, is in love with Blondchen, but so is Pedrillo, and the girl favors the young Spaniard. When Osmin has disappeared, Pedrillo himself comes out and tells his old master that he is a favorite of the Pasha. Immediately they begin to scheme to get the two girls away.

A chorus of Janissaries, welcoming the Pasha, interrupts them, and a scene between the Pasha and the lovely Konstanze tells us how things are going. The high-minded Turk loves the lady, but he will not force his suit on her. She, for her part, still pines for her old love, Belmonte, and frankly tells her captor so. It is a fine, brilliant coloratura aria she has there (*Ach, ich liebte—*"Ah, I was in love"). When she has left, Pedrillo introduces Belmonte to the Pasha as a visiting architect. The Pasha is most cordial, but when he has left, old Osmin tries to keep the two friends from entering the palace. An amusing trio follows (*Marsch, marsch, marsch—*"March!"); and as the act ends, the two men push Osmin aside and rush in.

ACT II

So far we have not met the most engaging lady in the cast —Blondchen; but in the very opening of Act II, which takes place within the palace, she really tells old Osmin off. English girls can't be ordered around, she says, not even in Turkey; and before she gets rid of him, she offers to scratch the fellow's eyes out and to get him beaten. It's quite a scene. But Konstanze is more tragically disposed. Belmonte has (she thinks) failed to rescue her, and now the Pasha demands that she love him tomorrow. This state of affairs she reveals to Blondchen in the aria *Durch Zärtlichkeit—*"Through tenderness." The Pasha enters at this point and demands her love at once—even threatening torture. This is the occasion for her wonderful aria of defiance called *Martern aller Arten—*"All kinds of martyrs." Then there follows a scene between little Blondchen and Pedrillo. He tells his girl the great news: Belmonte has arrived. In fact, he is in the palace as an architect; he has a ship anchored in the bay; and they will all elope at midnight! As for the ever-suspicious Osmin, he will have to be taken care of by a well-prepared drink.

Almost at once Pedrillo has his chance. Osmin comes in and it does not take a long argument for Pedrillo to overcome his Mohammedan scruples about alcohol. The old fellow drinks himself silly and is dragged off sound asleep. The act ends with a perfectly delightful quartet by the four lovers. The Spanish men are at first a little suspicious about the faithfulness of the two girls; but they are quickly convinced, and the plans to elope that night are confirmed.

ACT III

Scene 1 begins at midnight. Belmonte and Pedrillo, outside the palace, are ready to abduct Konstanze and Blondchen in the approved romantic fashion—that is, with ladders and serenades. They begin properly enough, and Belmonte gets away with his Konstanze. Unfortunately, it is a rather noisy business, and the jealous Osmin recovers from his drunken stupor just in time to catch the runaways. They are all brought in under guard; the Pasha is summoned; and the culprits are condemned to an immediate and hideous death. Yet there is time for a lovely duet, of farewell and of courage, between Belmonte and Konstanze, and also for a rather fiendish aria of revenge by Osmin (*Ha! wie will ich triumphiren*—"Ha! how I shall triumph o'er you").

Scene 2 Then, within the palace, comes the surprise ending. It turns out that Belmonte's father had been the Pasha's worst enemy and had treated him most harshly. The high-minded Turk wishes to teach the Europeans a lesson in forbearance. He pardons Belmonte and presents him with his own beloved Konstanze, and he forgives Pedrillo and Blondchen even over the protests of Osmin. Naturally, everyone except Osmin is thoroughly delighted, and the opera ends with a concerted number in which all join in praising the Selim Pasha.

As you see, the enthusiasm for things Turkish extended even to the character of the Mohammedan nobility. Variations on this theme may be found further on in this book, both in Rossini's *Italian in Algiers* and in Weber's *Oberon*.

L'AFRICAINE

(*The African Maid*)

Opera in five acts by Giacomo Meyerbeer with libretto in French by Eugène Scribe. Often sung in Italian as *L'Africana*.

DON PEDRO, *President of the Royal Council*	Bass
DON ALVAR, *member of the Council*	Tenor
DON DIEGO, *another*	Bass
INEZ, *his daughter*	Soprano
ANNA, *her attendant*	Mezzo-soprano
VASCO DA GAMA, *an officer in the Portuguese Navy*	Tenor
SELIKA, *an Indian slave*	Soprano
NELUSKO, *another*	Baritone
THE GRAND INQUISITOR	Bass
THE HIGH PRIEST OF BRAHMA	Baritone

Time: about 1500
Places: Lisbon, Hindustan, and the oceans between
First performance at Paris, April 28, 1865

Every once in a while in the history of opera there comes a composer whose work seems to dominate the whole repertoire. So it was with Handel in England; so it was with Spontini in Germany; so it was with Meyerbeer in all Western Europe and in America. Then, virtually in one season, as with Handel and Spontini, their works disappear from the stage, seldom if ever to be resurrected. Meyerbeer's work has disappeared more slowly. It was at its height in popularity when the composer died (his last opera, *L'Africaine*, having its premiere a year after his death); and a season without *Les Hu-*

guenots, *Le prophète, Dinorah,* or *L'Africaine* was still all but
unthinkable for a great opera house in the time of our grand-
parents. By the middle thirties, however, he had completely
disappeared from the stage of the Metropolitan and many
other houses; and while he still is performed in the French
opera museums and given an occasional revival in Germany,
his vogue is long past. The operas of many far more obscure
composers have been accorded semi-permanent immortality
by grace of complete recordings; but as of this writing, not a
single one of Meyerbeer's once extremely popular works can
be purchased in this form.

One can only speculate on the reason for this neglect. My
speculation is that Meyerbeer was so much a man of the theater, so much a showman, that once the fashion for his elaborate spectacles had worn out, they seemed too tinselly and
artificial for even the broad and tolerant tastes of opera lovers.
His scores are full of fine, effective numbers; but they are
spotty, calculated for stage effect; and one or two real gems,
like *L'Africaine's* O *paradis,* are not enough to make them
viable as a whole. Perhaps at some future date they will seem
old and interesting enough to warrant resuscitation in some
form. The glories of Handel's operatic scores are gradually being rediscovered through concert and phonograph performances, though his stage style is still too classically stiff to be
successfully employed. Even Spontini is listened to with interest on phonograph records. Men who appealed strongly to
their own age must have some vitality for ours, and I believe
that Meyerbeer's unquestionably great gifts will one day
again be appreciated in some form or other.

ACT I

Shortly before a meeting of the Royal Council of Portugal at
Lisbon, the daughter of one of the councilors, Inez, confides,
in an aria, her hopes to her attendant, Anna, that the fleet of
the explorer Bartolomeu Diaz may return soon in safety, for
she is in love with Vasco da Gama, a young officer on this
voyage.

L'Africaine

Inez's father, Don Diego, brings her her first bit of bad news: the King has decided that she is to marry Don Pedro, President of the Council, a man she thoroughly detests. Furthermore, Don Diego likes the match. The second bit of bad news comes from Don Pedro himself, who reports that the fleet of Diaz has been lost with virtually every member of the cruise. And the worst news of all comes when, in answer to the lady's inquiry, he scans the list of missing officers and says that Da Gama is one of those who perished. A trio follows in which, on one side of the stage, Don Diego tries to comfort his sorrowing daughter while warning her not to arouse her new fiancé's suspicions, while Don Pedro, on the other side of the stage, gives voice to those very suspicions.

Now, in full panoply, the Council enters the chamber and, as a sort of opening ceremony, sings a vigorous male chorus in honor of the Grand Inquisitor, leader of conservative thought in Portugal. The first business of the Council is to decide whether, after the failure of the great Diaz expedition, any more should be undertaken. The Grand Inquisitor is scornfully opposed to any further such waste of money and effort; Don Pedro, claiming the King's backing, argues for an effort to find the remains of the Diaz company; and Don Alvar, one of the younger councilors, creates a sensation by reporting that a member of that company waits without.

This survivor turns out to be the intrepid young Vasco da Gama, who demands that he be allowed to lead an expedition for the honor of Portugal. The argument continues, with the negative approach of the Grand Inquisitor about to get the upper hand when Vasco plays his trump cards. These are introduced in the shape of two very dark and dignified handsome young foreigners, Selika and Nelusko. Actually, despite the title of the opera, Selika is an Indian queen, Nelusko a member of her court who is in love with her. They have been taken as captive slaves in the neighborhood of the Cape of Storms, but beyond this bit of information Selika will vouchsafe nothing. Yet her glances at Vasco, and Nelusko's rage when he notices them, inform the audience clearly enough who is in love with whom. Meantime, Vasco makes the telling

17

point that these captives prove the fact that there is a land beyond Africa, and that it is worth an expedition.

The Council continues its angry deliberations, quiets down with a prayer for divine guidance, and finally comes to the conclusion, as announced by the Grand Inquisitor, that Vasco is mad, and his request is turned down. Vasco's angry answer is that Columbus was also considered mad, and the argument waxes furious all over again. Finally the Grand Inquisitor can take no more. In the name of the Pope, he sends Vasco to prison. The two Indians are taken along with him.

ACT II

In the Inquisition prison to which Vasco and his two Indian slaves have been consigned he lies asleep, while Selika sings a lovely aria that begins as a lullaby but develops into a passionate avowal of love before it ends (*Sur mes genous*—"On my knees"). Nelusko slinks in at the end of the aria and attempts to murder the sleeping man, only to have Selika hold back his dagger hand. She points out that Vasco had saved their lives by buying them in the slave market, and that, furthermore, a man of such a proud race as Nelusko's should never stoop to murdering a defenseless sleeper. In an aria of considerable power (*Fille des rois*—"Daughter of kings") he acknowledges his loyalty, but his hatred of Christians and his love for Selika overpower him. It becomes necessary, then, for Selika to save Vasco's life from a second attack, waking him up.

A lesson in geography follows. There is a large map conveniently located on the wall of the cell, and as Vasco tries to trace a route to India upon it, Selika shows him the proper way to get there. So delighted is Vasco with this information (it was just what he suspected all along, he says), that he embraces the Indian girl, inspiring in her great satisfaction, not unmixed with fear.

At this moment they are interrupted by four visitors—Don Pedro, Don Alvar, Inez, and Anna—and the stage is set for a long, effective, and partially unaccompanied septet. What transpires from the singers is that Inez has purchased Vasco's freedom through marrying Don Pedro, that Pedro has received permission to lead the expedition which Vasco had hoped to undertake, that Selika and Nelusko will be taken on the expedition along with Inez, and that everyone excepting Don Pedro couldn't be unhappier about the way things have turned out.

ACT III

An unusually elaborate set is called for in this act, which takes place aboard the flagship of Don Pedro's flotilla in search of an Eastern passage to India. On top, where almost all the action takes place, is the main deck; below is shown a cross-section of the ship, with the cabins of the various passengers.

Early in the morning of a fine day in mid-ocean Inez is lolling on a couch, sunning herself, as Selika and the rest of her female attendants entertain her with a chorus about their swift and easy-sailing vessel. Don Pedro makes some fatuous comments on his own talents as a navigator; the male chorus of sailors obliges with a chanty; and all the vocal and orchestral forces join in a fine prayer to St. Dominic, patron saint of sailors.

Nelusko has been taken along on this trip in the role of pilot: it was he who stole Vasco da Gama's maps and presented them to Don Pedro. Don Alvar warns Pedro that the Indian is apparently not to be trusted, reminding him that two ships have already been lost; but the blustering captain insists on permitting Nelusko to change the course. It was Adamastor, the god of storms, who destroyed those two ships, explains the Indian, and he describes the doings of this dread deity in a ballad sung for the benefit of the crew (*Adamastor, roi des vagues profondes*—"Adamastor, king of the depthless waves").

As a matter of fact, Nelusko is steering a course directly for the reefs that had destroyed the ships of Diaz, and he fears that his plans may be upset when a ship bearing the Portuguese flag is sighted and a boat is sent with a messenger. This messenger turns out to be Vasco himself with precisely the warning that Nelusko had feared. Furthermore, he warns Don Pedro, once the vessel has been beached, a horde of savages is waiting to complete the disaster for the Portuguese. Pedro, however, suspects that Vasco's motives may have something to do with the presence of Inez aboard the ship; and when Vasco admits it, he is ordered to be bound to a mast at once and shot.

Inez and Selika, hearing the noise above, rush from their cabins and beg for the life of the man they love, Selika even threatening Pedro with a dagger. In a passage that is customarily cut in performance, Pedro then orders the Indian girl bound to the mast and flogged, a fascinating bit of stage business that is interrupted with warnings of an approaching storm. Before Pedro can get his rival executed, the winds blow the ship on the reef and, almost at once, Indian warriors board her and begin to butcher the men as the women engage in futile prayer. With the male chorus of Indians singing a triumphant chorus in praise of Brahma, the action-packed scene comes to an end.

ACT IV

Before a Hindu temple in Hindustan, a procession of the priests of Brahma passes, a ballet is danced, and Selika, the Queen, is welcomed home. Instructed by the High Priest, she swears to uphold the local laws and allow no foreigner on the sacred Hindustani soil. But off-stage the Portuguese women are being tortured, and Selika wonders fearfully over the fate of Vasco.

Nelusko does not add to his beloved Queen's cheer by telling her that all the Portuguese men have been slain; but a moment later news comes that there is one who has survived, and Nelusko, fearing it may be Vasco, orders him executed forthwith. With practically everyone else in the temple, Vasco is led in by the soldiers but seems to be quite unaware of his sentence. Instead, he is rapturously impressed with the beauty of the land he now sees, and he sings by far the most familiar number in the opera, the tenor aria *O paradis*. It is not merely the nature-lover in him that draws forth this eloquent melody: Vasco dreams of the glory that will be Portugal's when she has gained this earthly paradise—and he shall be the donor.

Even when the soldiers terminate his reverie with the unwelcome information that he is to die, he demands instead that he be given a ship—or at least a messenger—to tell Portugal the great news. The soldiers raise their weapons threateningly, and at that point the services in the temple are over. As Selika emerges, he calls her by name; and when Nelusko, the High Priest, and the others demand his immediate execution, she declares that Vasco is her husband, and that he saved her at a slave market and gave her her freedom. Nelusko, of course, knows that this story is partly untrue; but in an aside she tells him that unless he vouches for the marriage, she shall die along with her beloved Portuguese officer. In a stormy aria, with choral background, Nelusko expresses his despair (*L'avoir tant adorée*—"To have adored her so much"), but he finally swears the great falsehood on the holy Brahman Golden Book. As this marriage must be duly solemnized, the priests now return to the temple to prepare for it and leave their Queen alone with the man who is to be their King.

Selika tells Vasco of the sentence of death that has been passed on Inez and the other women, and she fears now that he will leave her, as he is free to do. Vasco, however, appears to be almost in a trance, and as he returns to his senses, he falls in love with Selika. After a passionate love duet, the High Priest and others return and invoke the blessings of the gods on the happy couple. But heard off-stage, during the chorus of rejoicing, are the sad voices of Inez and the other doomed women intoning a mournful farewell to the beautiful Tagus River of Portugal. As Vasco hears the voice of Inez singing the melody of her first-act aria, he attempts to rush off to her, but he is pushed toward the temple and his Indian queen by all the singers and the dancers.

ACT V

Scene 1 (which is often omitted) is devoted chiefly to a duet, in Selika's garden, between her and Inez. Although she had originally planned to have Inez slain, Selika gradually realizes that their loves for Vasco are equally great and that he prefers his countrywoman. Thereupon Selika calls Nelusko and the soldiers, orders that Vasco and Inez be put on a ship bound for Portugal, and tells Nelusko to meet her at the end of a certain promontory to watch the departing sails.

Scene 2 On that promontory Selika addresses first the sea, which is no deeper than her misery, and then the manchineel tree, whose poison is to bring her misery to an end. She gathers up a few blossoms, inhales the deadly perfume, and in a trance imagines herself once more in Vasco's arms. Nelusko, arriving too late, sees what has happened, seizes some of the poisonous blossoms for himself, and dies contentedly in the arms of the woman he loved. Off-stage a chorus intones the beauties of love in the afterlife.

Postscript for the historically curious: As all books on explorers tell us, Vasco da Gama was the leader of the first Portuguese expedition to reach India by sea. That was in 1498, and he had the assistance of an Indian pilot. Subsequently a second expedition under one Don Pedro Cabral (who accidentally discovered Brazil on the way) made the same trip, and left some Portuguese there to establish a factory. They were all massacred by the Indians. In 1502, Vasco returned to the scene, took a fearful revenge, returned home, and married a girl named not Inez but Catarina.

But it would be as unkind as it is unnecessary to criticize the talented librettist Scribe for his cavalier way with history. He gave Meyerbeer the original libretto in 1838, when it did deal with an African and not an Indian girl. Three years later Meyerbeer had composed the score and found himself dissatisfied with both his own work and Scribe's. After considerable bickering Scribe revised everything, and only now was Vasco da Gama introduced as a character. Meyerbeer thereupon took another eight years revising both score and libretto, and still another four making changes in detail. Finally, on May 1, 1864, the last copying and changes were completed, and the next day the composer died. This was still not the end of the changes, for scenes and orchestration were further amended by friends of Meyerbeer before the first production. No one, however, seems to have thought of correcting the name of the opera.

AÏDA

Opera in four acts by Giuseppe Verdi with libretto in Italian by Antonio Ghislanzoni, based on a French prose version by Camille du Locle, based, in turn, on a plot by François Auguste Ferdinand Mariette, with the composer lending a considerable hand in both the prose and the versified versions

THE KING OF EGYPT	*Bass*
AMNERIS, *his daughter*	*Contralto*
AMONASRO, *King of Ethiopia*	*Baritone*
AÏDA, *his daughter and slave of Amneris*	*Soprano*
RADAMES, *an Egyptian officer*	*Tenor*
RAMPHIS, *High Priest of Egypt*	*Bass*
A MESSENGER	*Tenor*

Time: period of the Pharaohs' power
Place: Memphis and Thebes
First performance at Cairo, December 24, 1871

I should like to introduce this great masterpiece of art with a few words about money, just to show that serious composers are not always poor, struggling, unappreciated fellows, but that they are sometimes rewarded for their work in a really princely fashion. The fact is that Verdi asked for—and received without any effort at bargaining—the sum of $30,000 for *Aïda*. The contract was signed before the composer had written a single note, and all that the purchaser got for his 150,000 francs was one copy of the score and the right to produce it first in Cairo, Egypt—and in Cairo only. Verdi retained all the other rights, and these included royalties from performances everywhere else in the world and publication of the score and the libretto. When one remembers that, in the Europe of 1870, $30,000 would be worth at least $200,000 today—and also that there was no income tax—one can see that the Khedive of Egypt, who paid the money, set a high value on musical genius.

I do not mean to imply that Verdi was a money-grabber. He really didn't need money, in the first place. It took a great deal of persuasion to get him to write an opera at all; and when he did undertake *Aïda*, he paid his librettist generously —and also contributed a portion of the advance to the sufferers in the siege of Paris. He worked hard and conscientiously, too. He took a four-page outline of the story by the Egyptologist Mariette Bey and, with his French friend Camille du Locle, worked out a four-act libretto. Then he engaged the Italian poet Ghislanzoni to transform it into an Italian libretto, and he worked over every detail of that libretto, even writing some of the lines himself. As for the music, he composed that within four months.

The world premiere in Cairo on Christmas Eve of 1871 was a huge, international success, with distinguished visitors from all over the world—not including, however, Giuseppe Verdi. But he was present, forty-six days later, at the Italian premiere in Milan. This was an equally great success, and *Aïda* has been the pet showpiece of practically every opera company in the world ever since.

PRELUDE

For the Milan premiere Verdi composed a special overture, but, conscientious artist that he was, he did not like it when it was done. It remains in manuscript, and no one has ever performed it so far as I know. At Milan they performed the eloquent but more modest prelude heard first in Egypt. It remains one of the many glories of the score. It begins softly, in the violins, with the tense but restrained theme of Aïda

herself, which is developed symphonically in contrast with the
ominous theme of the high priests.

ACT I

The story supplied by Mariette was based, he said, on a
historical incident; but he never did say when the incident
occurred, except "in the time of the Pharaohs." As the Pharaohs ruled—by Mariette's own estimate—from 5004 B.C. to
A.D. 381 that gives us quite a stretch. Whenever it was, then,
there was trouble between Egypt and Ethiopia.

Scene 1 In the hall of the King's palace in Memphis, the
Egyptian High Priest, Ramphis, tells a young officer named
Radames that the Ethiopians are again on the warpath and
that a general is to be chosen. Left alone, Radames hopes he
may be that general, and then sings of how he also hopes
someday to marry the beautiful Ethiopian slave Aïda and
bring her back to her own country. This, of course, is the
familiar aria *Celeste Aïda*.

Unfortunately, the King's daughter, Amneris, is in love with
Radames and, on finding him alone, virtually tells him so.
But when Aïda joins them, Amneris correctly interprets the
warm but despairing glances exchanged by the tenor and soprano. Aïda justifies her tears—with good reason—on the
grounds of the prospect of war with her own people, and a
dramatic trio follows, each character expressing his own emotions simultaneously.

Now Ramphis, the King, and the whole court come in. They
hear an alarming report from a messenger: the Ethiopians are
already invading, led by a fierce warrior named Amonasro. The
King then announces that Radames has been chosen to lead
the Egyptians in battle, and there is a vigorous, martial choral
number, calling on all Egyptians to defend the sacred Nile
River. At its close Amneris turns to Radames and proudly
instructs him: *Ritorna vincitor!*—"Return as conqueror!" Then
they all march out.

All, that is, excepting Aïda. She repeats Amneris's line ironically, then prays for the safety of her father, then remembers

that his victory would mean the defeat of her beloved Radames, and finally ends her great aria with a pitiful, almost whispered prayer for the gods to have mercy on her.

Scene 2 takes place in the dimly lighted Temple of Vulcan. The priests are gathered for the ceremony of anointing Radames as General of the Egyptian armies. Off-stage, a solo priestess and a chorus intone a prayer, and on-stage other priestesses perform a ritual dance before the altar. A silver veil is placed over Radames, and Ramphis presents him with a sword. The priest then intones a solemn prayer for the protection of Egypt's sacred soil. Radames joins in the prayer; so do all the other priests; and the ceremony ends with an invocation to the Egyptian God, the "Almighty Ptah."

ACT II

Scene 1　On a terrace of the palace in Thebes, Princess Amneris reclines voluptuously on a couch. Her female slaves beautify her, the while singing the praises of Radames, who has led the Egyptian armies to victory. Further entertainment is supplied by a troupe of Moorish slaves, who execute an eccentric dance.

Then follows the great scene between Amneris and her Ethiopian handmaiden, Aïda. The Princess pretends sympathy for the girl because her people have been defeated, but her real purpose is to find out whether Aïda is her rival for the love of Radames. This she does by announcing his death in battle. Aïda's cry of anguish convinces the Princess of what she has suspected. She accuses Aïda and announces that Radames is really alive after all. Aïda's rapturous cry of "Thank God!" brings their rivalry out into the open. The slave begs for pity, but the Princess is passionately bitter about it. Suddenly their powerful duet is interrupted by off-stage trumpets and a chorus of triumph. Instructing her slave to follow her to the triumphal ceremonies, Amneris sweeps out, leaving Aïda to repeat the pitiful prayer she had voiced at the end of the opening scene.

Scene 2 is the stirring *Triumphal Scene.* On a great avenue

at the entrance to the city of Thebes, crowds are gathered
about the throne. Warriors come in, then priests and dancers.
There is a ballet and general rejoicing. The King mounts the
open-air throne, and his daughter is seated beside him. Finally
the returning hero, Radames, is welcomed, and the great
Triumphal March—so familiar with its stentorian trumpets—
is played just before he is drawn in on a chariot. When the
King offers him anything that he wants, his first request is
to have the captives brought forth. A miserable band of Ethiopians is brought on, in chains, led by Amonasro, their King.
He manages to instruct Aïda secretly not to betray his true
identity; and when he is asked to speak, he says that Amonasro
has been killed, and he is himself a simple warrior. With great
dignity he asks for mercy. The priests are against this, but
Radames and the populace plead for the prisoners. A compromise is reached: all will be freed but this warrior, who is
their leader. He, it seems, is put under something like house
arrest.

Then, without consulting the young man as to his wishes,
the King announces that Radames shall marry the Princess
Amneris. She, of course, is delighted; Aïda and Radames are
filled with consternation; Amonasro tells Aïda that he still has
hopes for their fatherland; and everyone else sings loudly and
joyfully. It makes a grand concerted climax.

The opening music suggests the scene vividly. It is a hot
summer night on the banks of the Nile, near the Temple of
Isis. A boat glides up, and the High Priest Ramphis and Princess Amneris step out and enter the temple; for it is the eve
of her wedding to Radames, and she must pray.

When they have disappeared, Aïda, heavily veiled, comes
for a last rendezvous with her lover. If, she says, it is only to
bid farewell, then she must drown herself in the Nile; and
she sings her second great aria of the opera (*O patria mia*),
in which she gives voice to her longing for her native land.

But before her lover keeps his engagement, her father finds

her. At first they sing warmly of their country, but Amonasro has more serious business on his mind. Their armies have reformed. All he needs to know is where to attack the Egyptians —and Aïda must get this information out of her lover. She recoils in horror, but Amonasro is so eloquent in describing what defeat will mean for her own people that finally she agrees.

As Radames approaches, Amonasro hides himself. The lovers greet each other rapturously. Radames hopes that the new battle that is pending may delay his wedding to Amneris, while Aïda is all for his deserting now. She sings him a ravishing description of her country, but Radames refuses to turn traitor. Then Aïda turns on him and tells him to marry Amneris and forget her. At this he begins to weaken. He agrees to run away with her; he even tells her where the soldiers are whom they must avoid. This is what Amonasro has been waiting for. He rushes out, to the horror of Radames, and tries to drag the young soldier off with him. But suddenly Amneris and the priest issue from the temple. Amonasro and Aïda make good their escape, but the bitterly disillusioned Radames refuses to go along and, with a dramatic gesture, he surrenders his sword to the priest.

ACT IV

Scene 1 is the big scene for Amneris. Radames is about to be tried for treason. She waits in a passage near his cell and demands that he be brought forth. When he comes, she pleads to be allowed to save him. All she requires is that he give up Aïda and marry herself. Even when he learns that Aïda has escaped (though Amonasro has been killed), Radames turns down her offer of life with stoic scorn. He is led off by his guards.

As the priests, solemnly chanting, file past to go to the dungeon where the trial will take place, Amneris reviles herself. Her jealousy, she says, will bring death to her beloved. Down below, the trial begins. Radames is charged by the priests with deserting camp before battle, with betraying his country, his

King, and his honor. Though called on to do so, he makes no defense. Sentence is then pronounced: Radames is to be buried alive beneath the altar of the god he has failed to honor.

When the priests have filed back from the dungeon of justice, Amneris curses them as "infamous tigers" and an "impious lot." They remain unmoved, and even after they have passed by her, she continues to hear them repeat their condemnation of Radames. As the scene closes, she works herself up into a wild fury of frustration.

Scene 2 takes place on two levels. This was Verdi's own idea. Above is the interior of the Temple of Vulcan, where two priests set into place a stone to cover the opening. Through that opening Radames had been thrust into the crypt below. There he is awaiting death, and he utters a soft wish that Aïda may be happy wherever she is, and never hear of his dreadful end. But a moment later he sees a figure approaching him in the dimness. It is Aïda. She has managed to get into the tomb, knowing what would happen to Radames, and she has been awaiting him for three days.* With a cry of anguish Radames tries to lift the heavy stone, for he cannot bear the thought of Aïda's dying, so young and so beautiful. But death is already coming over her. She sings her last farewell to earth (O *terra, addio*), and Radames joins in with her. Above, Amneris has entered. She has prostrated herself on the floor above the crypt, and she moans a prayer for Radames, who holds her dying rival in his arms. And as she prays, and as the priests chant a prayer, and the lovers sing their final farewell below, the curtain slowly falls.

* This explanation of Aïda's moribund state appeared in an early version of the libretto only.

ALCESTE

(*Alcestis*)

Opera in three acts by Christoph Willibald
Gluck with libretto in Italian by Raniero da
Calzabigi based on Greek legend as told in the
tragedy by Euripides

ADMETUS, *King of Pharae*	*Tenor*
ALCESTIS, *his wife*	*Soprano*
HERCULES, *the legendary strong man*	*Bass*
EVANDER, *a royal messenger*	*Tenor*
APOLLO, *god of many things*	*Baritone*
THANATOS, *god of death*	*Bass*
HIGH PRIEST	*Bass*

Time: legendary
Place: Thessaly
First performances at Vienna, December 26, 1767 (in Italian), and at Paris, April 23, 1776 (in French)

Gluck's operas—especially *Orfeo* and *Alceste*—meet the
test of being classics better than any other composer's. By this
I mean that they are the oldest operas to receive repeated
productions even today. *Alceste*, for instance, is nine years
older than the American Revolution, and yet it is still part
of the repertoire of almost every great opera house in the
world. An opera really has to have something to survive so
long, and so vigorously.

And this is what *Alceste* has: it has noble melodies and
striking arias; it has vigorous and dramatic choruses—plenty
of them, too; it has strong, striking orchestration, not just
plunkety-plunk accompaniments like so many older operas;

and above all, it tells its great old story with dramatic and musical integrity. That great old story is based on the popular dramatic theme of a love that is faithful unto death. It is a part of classical Greek mythology which you will find in your Bulfinch and in Euripides.

When Gluck composed the opera, he was engaging in a sensational aesthetic war. He was trying to purge opera of some of those excesses that he believed made Italian opera absurd; and he made a special point of saying that the music should serve the drama, not get in its way. The arguments are clearly set forth in the famous preface to the published score, which is required reading for all serious students of the opera. (Actually, it was written by the librettist, Calzabigi, and only signed by Gluck.)

The opera was a huge success in Vienna, where it was given in Italian. For Paris, ten years later, Gluck made a drastically different version, one which stuck closer to his announced principles and which is the one always given today. It was a failure. Gluck took it philosophically and wrote: "*Alceste* can only displease when it is new. It has not yet had time. I say that it will please in two hundred years . . ." For once, an artist was right when he made such a prediction. At least, I hope that he was right. The prediction has less than twenty years to run.

ACT I

In the first act the people of the city-state of Thessaly are already mourning their good King, Admetus, who is on the point of death. They pray to Apollo, for the King had once done Apollo a great service. Queen Alcestis and her children are announced by the messenger, Evander. She joins in the prayer, singing the fine aria *Grands dieux du destin*, but it takes some time to get an answer. Finally, after the elaborate offering of sacrifices and a stately ballet, the High Priest announces the decision of the oracle of Apollo's temple. Yes, he proclaims, Admetus may be saved, but someone must offer to take his place in death. No one is devoted enough to do this, and all his subjects flee from the temple, leaving Alcestis alone. It is then that she has her greatest moment (and, incidentally, her greatest aria, *Divinités du Styx*). She decides that she cannot live without Admetus, and that she herself must make the sacrifice and take his place with Death. It is on this noble note that Act I ends.

ACT II

The second act begins with the rejoicing of the people, for their beloved King Admetus is well again, spared by the gods. They sing; they dance; they rejoice; and Admetus joins in the thanksgiving. Yet he knows that *someone* must have laid down his life to meet the conditions of the gods, and he is troubled by the absence of his wife, Queen Alcestis. Presently she comes in and tries to join in the general tone of rejoicing; but as Admetus questions her, the truth slowly dawns on him. Finally she admits it: Alcestis has offered herself to the gods to take the place of Admetus. Horrified, he reproaches her, for he cannot think of life without Alcestis any more than she could think of it without him. But—as Alcestis points out—the decision is made: the gods have accepted her sacrifice; and, as the act ends, she starts on her way to the realms of Hades, of Death.

ACT III

Scene 1   Like the first act, the last one begins with the populace mourning. But this time the people of Thessaly are mourning the loss of their Queen Alcestis instead of their King Admetus. Now, in comes a new and refreshing figure. He is Hercules, the strong man, who has just finished the twelfth and last of his Herculean labors. An old friend of the family, he is profoundly shocked when Evander informs him of what has happened. Immediately he resolves to try to get Alcestis back from Hades. (His last labor, though he is too polite to refer to it, had been getting Cerberus back out of Hades. It may therefore be assumed that he feels well trained for his new task.)

Scene 2   This scene takes us to the gates of Hades. Alcestis wishes to enter at once—to die; but the specters of Hades tell her she must not enter before nightfall. Admetus, who has followed his wife, now comes in, hoping to take her place, but Alcestis nobly refuses. The god of death, Thanatos, appears and gives Alcestis the chance to renounce her vow, to remain on earth, alive, and let Admetus take her place. Still Alcestis remains firm.

And now night begins to fall, and the specters of Hades call upon Alcestis to enter the gates. She is about to do so, when stout Hercules appears. He struggles against all the specters and appears at last to be triumphant, when the great god Apollo himself intervenes. So deeply impressed is Apollo with the devotion of husband and wife and with the valorous friendship of Hercules that he pronounces a happy ending to the tragedy. Hercules is given immortality, and Alcestis and Admetus are to return to earth, the models for all happily married people. The gates of Hades vanish; a host of people comes in; and the opera ends with a chorus of rejoicing led by Admetus, and with a grave and dignified, but happy, ballet.

AMAHL AND THE NIGHT VISITORS

Opera in one act by Gian-Carlo Menotti with
libretto in English by the composer

AMAHL, *a crippled boy*		Boy Soprano
HIS MOTHER		Soprano
KASPAR		Tenor
MELCHIOR	} *the three kings*	Baritone
BALTHASAR		Baritone
PAGE TO THE KINGS		Baritone

Time: the first Christmas Eve
Place: on the road to Bethlehem
*First performance telecast from New York, December 24,
1951*
First stage performance at New York, April 27, 1952

Amahl and the Night Visitors is the first opera ever commissioned for television. The National Broadcasting Company
telecast its premiere on Christmas Eve of 1951, and it elicited
such a warm response that the performance has become an
annual event. The effort has been made to retain the original
cast year after year; but as the leading role is that of a boy
soprano, certain obvious difficulties have arisen. Nevertheless,
its audience for each of these performances has been esti-
mated at several million; and thus *Amahl* has probably been
heard by more Americans than any other opera—certainly
more than any other American opera.

The story takes place on the first Christmas Eve. In a small
hut live an impoverished widow and her crippled son Amahl.

He hobbles on a crutch and loves to play his shepherd's pipe. He is also very imaginative—always seeing things. That is why his mother does not believe him at first when he says there are three kings calling on them. He is also a very curious child. That is why he asks the kings quite personal questions—such as whether they have blue blood and what is in that box they are carrying. And the kings are very simple and honest men. That is why they give Amahl very simple and honest answers. And that is why they are very much pleased when the shepherds (Amahl's neighbors) come and bring them simple gifts. The nicest gift of all turns out to be a shepherd's dance.

The kings are also kindly and warmhearted. That is why they do not mind when they catch Amahl's mother trying to steal their gold in the night. They decide that the child *they* are going to see (who is the Christ child, of course) does not need the gold. And that also is why they are so much pleased when the miracle happens and Amahl suddenly finds that he can walk.

Amahl and his mother love each other dearly. That is why Amahl, though crippled, attacks the kings' page when he catches her stealing. And that is why, when the child leaves with the kings, you truly believe the mother and son as they sing their simple duet: "I shall miss you very much."

As Amahl goes up the road with the three kings, he again plays his pipe—just as he had played it when the curtain went up.

L'AMORE DEI TRE RE

(*The Love of Three Kings*)

Opera in three acts by Italo Montemezzi with libretto in Italian by Sem Benelli, based on Benelli's play of the same name

ARCHIBALDO, *King of Altura*	Bass
MANFREDO, *his son*	Baritone
FIORA, *wife of Manfredo*	Soprano
AVITO, *a former prince of Altura*	Tenor
FLAMINIO, *a castle guard*	Tenor

Time: 10th century
Place: Italy
First performance at Milan, April 10, 1913

Once, during the last years of his life, which he spent in California, Italo Montemezzi set down his musical credo. Music without melody, he said, is inconceivable. Neither academic formality nor "realism" in music, he said, appealed to him. All he wanted to do was to clothe the characters in his operas in a musical atmosphere where they could live and express themselves.

It sounds like a modest enough ambition, but it is one that only the most sensitive composers have ever realized. In *The Love of Three Kings* he realized it with stunning success. It tells a violently dramatic story with a dignity and subtlety seldom reached by the more realistic "realism" of the verists, with whom he is sometimes classified. Yet it does not lose an ounce of dramatic impact thereby.

Oddly enough, his masterwork has been more generally appreciated in his adopted country, the United States, than in his native Italy. Here he was invited to conduct performances repeatedly, and to coach the leading singers in their parts. He was a modest gentleman whom everyone liked as a human being and respected as a musical poet of unimpeachable integrity.

ACT I

Forty years before the action begins, Archibaldo had invaded Italy from the north and made himself King of Altura. As part of the peace pact, he had insisted that the beautiful Fiora, affianced to the local Prince Avito of Altura, should become the bride of his own son, Manfredo.

So it was done; and now Archibaldo, a blind old man, continues to live in the royal castle, suspicious of his daughter-in-law, and, despite his handicap, keenly sensitive in every other sense and nerve to what goes on about him.

When the opera opens, it is night in a hall of the castle. Manfredo is away at war, and old Archibaldo is uneasily hoping for his return. There is a lighted lantern for Manfredo, and after speaking with a guard, Flaminio, about the events of forty years back he instructs him to put out the light: Manfredo will not return tonight. Flaminio, who is faithful in the service of the new King, is yet a patriotic Alturan even after all these years. As dawn is approaching and he hears the sound of a rustic flute in the distance, he leads the blind old man uneasily away; for he knows the significance of the sound.

Almost as soon as they are gone, Fiora and Avito come into the hall from her room. Their guilty love is something that Archibaldo has seemed to sense, and Avito is made all the more uneasy when he notes that the light has been extinguished: someone, he feels, may have been spying on them. Fiora tries to reassure him; there is a short but passionate love scene; and suddenly the cry of "Fiora! Fiora! Fiora!" is heard off-stage. Avito makes good his escape just before Archibaldo returns. She, too, tries to take advantage of the old man's blindness, but he guesses her presence; he hears her heavy breathing; he demands to know to whom she has been speaking.

Blandly she lies to him: there has been no one, she says, but she senses, too, that he does not believe her. Fortunately, they are interrupted by Flaminio, who reports the approach of Manfredo. The uxorious warrior has left the war to spend a night with his wife. She greets him with more politeness than warmth, tells him that she has been waiting up for him (as Archibaldo will corroborate, says she), and takes him to her room. As they leave, the old man mutters to himself a bitter prayer: "O God, since Thou hast taken away my eyes, let me indeed be blind!"

ACT II

The next day Manfredo must bid farewell to Fiora and return to the siege. On a terrace, high on the castle walls, he asks for some token of her affection, but in vain. Then he pleads only that she wave a scarf to him till he is out of sight. She is moved—more by pity than by love—and when he has left, she takes a scarf from a servant and waves from the battlement. But when Avito comes, the weary waving ceases. He, too, wishes to leave, and forever, but their passion overpowers them; and in the midst of their duet Archibaldo returns with Flaminio. He cannot, of course, see Avito, who begins to attack him with a dagger. But Flaminio silently intervenes; Fiora signals him to leave; and he goes off.

Now the old man menacingly accuses Fiora of having been with a lover. Frightened but still in proud control of herself, she at first denies it. He takes hold of her, and in a powerful seizure of desperate pride she tells him yes, she does have a lover, and she taunts the old man with it. Repeatedly he demands his name; repeatedly she refuses it. Finally he pushes her back on a bench and, with cold hatred, chokes her to death.

Manfredo, who has seen the waving stop and fears that Fiora may have fallen from the parapet, returns a moment later. His father tells him what he has done and why; and Manfredo's feeling is one of deep pity for a beautiful woman who could feel such love, though not for him. Archibaldo picks up the body of Fiora, slings it over his still-powerful shoulders, and follows his grieving son off the stage.

ACT III

The body of Fiora has been laid in the crypt of the castle. Off-stage a choir is heard singing a dirge. On-stage is a group of Alturans, who bemoan the loss of their Princess and cry for vengeance on the murderer.

When Avito enters, they depart respectfully. He speaks to her; he weeps in despair; and finally he bends over to kiss her lips. A poison begins to overpower him, and Manfredo, coming in at that moment, tells him that her lips were a trap to catch the lover whose name she so well guarded. But Avito is happy to die for love of Fiora, while Manfredo again feels only sorrow that so great a love as hers could not have been for himself, who loved her equally well. He, too, bends over to drink from her lips the deadly poison.

When the blind Archibaldo gropes his way toward the bier and seizes on the man lying at his feet as the guilty lover, it is Manfredo whom he touches. From his dying son he learns how tragically his fatal plan has overwhelmed him.

ANDREA CHÉNIER

Opera in four acts by Umberto Giordano with libretto in Italian by Luigi Illica based, roughly, on the life of the poet André de Chénier

ANDREA CHÉNIER, *a poet*	Tenor
COUNTESS DE COIGNY, *an aristocrat*	Mezzo-soprano
MADELEINE DE COIGNY, *her daughter*	Soprano
BERSI, *Madeleine's mulatto maid*	Mezzo-soprano
CHARLES GÉRARD, *another servant*	Baritone
INCREDIBILE, *a spy*	Tenor
MATHIEU, *a waiter*	Baritone
ROUCHER, *a friend of Chénier's*	Bass
MADELON, *an old woman*	Mezzo-soprano
DUMAS, *president of the Revolutionary Tribunal*	Baritone
SCHMIDT, *jailer at St. Lazare Prison*	Baritone

Time: Act I shortly before the French Revolution
       Acts II–IV, 1794
Place: Paris
First performance at Milan, March 28, 1896

The true story of André de Chénier might have furnished an operatic plot quite as romantic as the imaginary one provided by Luigi Illica. Chénier was born, of a French aristocrat and a Greek mother, in Constantinople. As a young man, he led a rather wild life in France, took early to writing verse, at one time began, in poetry, a whole encyclopedia of universal knowledge, had a brief career as a diplomat in England, espoused the ideals of the French Revolution, but became revolted at its excesses. He wrote bitter satires on the subject,

but was quite safe till one evening, when visiting an aristocratic friend in the country, he was picked up by the police,
who were looking for someone else. It was not a case of mis-
taken identity: they just didn't want to go back empty-handed.
In the 140 days of his imprisonment he composed poetry of
such magnificence that it earned him a permanent and important place in the history of French literature. In fact, it
was only after his death that much of his earlier work, which
had gone unpublished, was dug up here and there and became the subject of such serious study and criticism as is given
only to great dead men.

His brother Joseph, the revolution's leading dramatist,
might have had the political influence to save him, but he
thought that André's best chance for coming out alive lay in
remaining quietly in prison till he was forgotten. Joseph mis-
calculated. At the age of thirty-two André went to the guillotine. The last detail is almost the only one that Illica used
accurately, though the general character of the young man
would seem to be faithfully enough projected.

Andrea Chénier was Giordano's fourth operatic score. He
composed it while still a comparatively obscure young man of
twenty-seven, seated in a warehouse in Milan full of grave-
stones and other funeral statuary. (I mention this as an odd
fact of no particular significance.) From the night of its premiere, March 28, 1896, he was a famous man, and remained
one till he died in 1948 even though he never quite equaled
that success. It was a career not dissimilar to those of his fellow "verists," Mascagni and Leoncavallo, each of whom composed an extremely popular opera in his twenties but never
managed to repeat.

ACT I

In the ballroom of the Countess de Coigny, some of the
Parisian nobility is having its last fling before the tumbrels of
the French Revolution begin to roll. Servants are moving the
furniture preparatory to the big evening party. Among them
is Gérard—the heavy baritone lead of this opera. In his open-

Andrea Chénier

ing aria he expresses his hopeless love for Madeleine, the daughter of his mistress; he commiserates with his aged father for having to work so hard; and he predicts that one day his class will rise and ruin this house, which he hates. Then the Countess de Coigny comes in with her daughter, Madeleine, an excessively pretty blonde. She discusses dresses with her maid-in-waiting, Bersi, and the Countess makes sure that everything is ready for the party. Presently the guests arrive. There is a lot of frivolous talk about politics, and there is singing by professional entertainers.

Among the guests there comes the poet Andrea Chénier, and Madeleine lightly asks him to recite some verses. At first he refuses. Then, beginning with elaborate compliments to the lady, he ends his poem with a protest against the way the lower classes are treated in his beloved France. No upper-class lady like Madeleine, he concludes, could really understand love. It is quite a discourse—and quite a fine tenor aria, generally known as the *Improvviso*. Everyone at that aristocratic party is duly shocked, and, to cover the embarrassment, the Countess orders the musicians to begin the gavotte. But scarcely has the dancing begun when a chorus of paupers enters the room led by Gérard, who vigorously denounces his employers and symbolically tears the livery off his old father's back. Quickly he and the paupers are hustled out, and Chénier follows them. Then, when peace and propriety are once more restored, the dancing can begin again. The aristocrats have clearly failed to see the handwriting on the wall.

ACT II

Several years have passed: the Bastille has been taken, and the revolution rules. One of its leaders is Gérard, the former lackey. The poet, Andrea Chénier, has also helped, but now he is under suspicion as a counterrevolutionary. As for the Coigny aristocrats, their château has been burned to the ground, and only Madeleine survives.

The act takes place outside a café in Paris. Bersi, Madeleine's former maid and now a jolly revolutionary, is talking with a man who boasts the incredible name of Incredibile. A spy for Gérard, he knows Bersi is still on intimate terms with an aristocratic lady (that's Madeleine, of course) and asks whether she isn't afraid. In a devil-may-care aria Bersi proclaims the happiness of being a revolutionary.

Now Roucher, a good friend of Chénier's, meets him at the café. He has brought the poet a passport so that he may flee the country, but Chénier refuses. He has been receiving mysterious and anonymous letters from a lady, and like a true romantic poet, he has fallen in love with her. Then a crowd passes by with Gérard at their head. Still in love with Madeleine, he describes her to Incredibile, and the spy promises to find her that very night. Off he goes, with Bersi, but a little later he observes that young woman talking to Chénier. Bersi is telling him that the mysterious lady of the letters is about to meet him, and the spy is still lurking about when Madeleine comes in. A duet naturally develops at this point for tenor and soprano, and at its climax Chénier and Madeleine are pledged to each other. Incredibile has meantime run off to get his master, Gérard, and as the two men face each other, Roucher manages to spirit the lady away to safety. Gérard and Chénier draw swords, but the former lackey is no match for the former aristocrat, and the revolutionary leader falls, slightly wounded. Lying on the ground, Gérard recalls their earlier friendship and whispers to Chénier that his name is on the death list. As a crowd gathers, Chénier manages his escape.

ACT III

Act III takes place in the Revolutionary Tribunal in Paris, where so many men and women were hastily judged or misjudged. The ominous chords of the opening suggest the cruel heartlessness of the proceedings.

To begin the session, Mathieu (formerly a waiter) growlingly demands more funds from the crowds. He gets nothing. Gérard, the former lackey, tries next, and with an impassioned plea for France, he gets contributions of gold and jewels. A blind old woman even offers up her fifteen-year-old grandson. His father had been killed storming the Bastille, she says; his elder brother at Valmy. And now her last support is gratefully accepted by the revolution. The crowd thereupon sings the *Carmagnole*—the revolutionary dance-song performed so often at jolly ceremonies, such as guillotinings.

Then, as the crowd disperses, in slinks the sinister figure of Incredibile, the spy. He reports to his employer, Gérard, that Chénier has been arrested and that Madeleine will doubtless follow him here at once, and he urges Gérard to write out a denunciation of Chénier. Now Gérard has his great *scena* (*Nemico della patria?*—"An enemy of the fatherland?"). He begins to pen the denunciation; he shrinks from so base an action against a patriot and former friend; he wonders at his own change from patriot to murderer; he bitterly acknowledges that love for Madeleine has led him to this; and he finally writes the fatal document and hands it to Incredibile.

When Madeleine arrives, Gérard tells her how he has had her lured there and urges on her his long-standing devotion and love. Madeleine tries to escape, and when Gérard blocks her path, she screams. But suddenly she is quiet again. In a moving aria (*La mamma morta*—"My mother dead") she speaks of her mother's terrible death by fire when her house was burned by the mob, and offers her own fair body in payment for Chénier's life. Gérard is won over. He now says he will try to save Chénier; but it is too late. He receives the message that Chénier is already there and about to be tried. The court files in; several prisoners are quickly disposed of by the court; and finally Gérard's recently penned denunciation of Chénier is brought against him. In vain Gérard tries to save him. He protests that his own denunciation is nothing but lies, but the court and the crowd believe he has been bribed. Chénier (unlike the others) is allowed to defend himself, and he sings a ringing aria (*Sì, fui soldato*) full of courage and patriotism.

But even Gérard's attacking the justice of this court is no help. The jury files out, and during the brief wait Chénier is heartened by the sight of Madeleine. The verdict is, of course, the one that crowd and court want to hear—*Guilty*, and the sentence is *Death*. As Madeleine despairingly cries out the name of Chénier, the poet is led off to his death cell.

The short last act takes place in the courtyard of St. Lazare Prison in Paris. Shortly before the dawn of the day he is to be executed, Chénier sits writing at a table. He is visited by his friend Roucher, and after the jailer has left, he reads Roucher what he has been writing. It is a beautiful set of verses—the farewell to life of a poet (*Come un bel dì di maggio*—"Like a beautiful day in May").

Now Roucher must leave, and as Chénier is led back to his cell, his old friend and rival Gérard comes in leading his beloved Madeleine. Madeleine bribes the jailer to let her take the place of a condemned woman named Idia Legray so that she may be with Chénier to the end. Deeply moved, Gérard leaves to try to appeal to Robespierre, the most powerful man in France at the moment. (The opera does not tell us this, but it is a fact that, three days after the death of Chénier, Robespierre himself was executed, and *then* Chénier might have been saved.)

The jailer brings back Chénier, and there follows the ecstatic, almost exultant, final love duet, as Madeleine and Chénier look forward to being united in death. At its close the guards come in; the names of Andrea Chénier and Idia Legray are called out; and, hand in hand, the lovers walk out for their appointment with the guillotine.

ARABELLA

Opera in three acts by Richard Strauss with libretto in German by Hugo von Hofmannsthal

COUNT WALDNER	Bass
ADELAIDE, *his wife*	Mezzo-soprano
ARABELLA ⎫ *their daughters*	Soprano
ZDENKA ⎭	Soprano
MANDRYKA, *a wealthy gentleman*	Baritone
MATTEO, *an officer* ⎫	Tenor
COUNT ELEMER ⎪ *suitors of Arabella*	Tenor
COUNT DOMINIK ⎬	Baritone
COUNT LAMORAL ⎭	Bass
THE "FIAKERMILLI"	Soprano
A FORTUNETELLER	Soprano

Time: 1860
Place: Vienna
First performance at Dresden, July 1, 1933

It is often said that late Richard Strauss is not so good as early or middle Richard Strauss. For instance, *Der Rosenkavalier*, produced in 1911, when the composer was forty-seven, is his greatest operatic success. *Arabella*, produced twenty-one years later, is not nearly so popular. A comparison is inevitable, for both operas are comedies, both are laid in Vienna (though almost one hundred years apart in time), both deal with what we may call upper-middle-class love, both are famous for waltzes, and both call for a pretty soprano to dress up as a young man. Yet *Rosenkavalier* is popular, *Arabella* is not. Why? Had the old maestro lost his cunning at sixty-eight? I think not. Most people will agree, I believe, that the best of *Arabella* is on a par with the best of *Rosenkavalier*. Only there isn't too much of "the best." Let us admit there are large dull stretches in *Arabella*. But the best of it is very well worth hearing and cherishing.

ACT I

The story takes place in the Vienna of 1860. An impoverished ex-army officer, Count Waldner, has brought his family to a hotel suite in Vienna, hoping that by gambling or by marrying off his elder daughter advantageously he may recoup his fortune. This elder daughter is Arabella, and it takes money to keep her in clothes and to exhibit her at dances. That is why the younger daughter, Zdenka, is disguised as a boy and known as Zdenko. It's cheaper that way.

All this necessary background we learn during the opening domestic scene that takes place in the living room of the expensively furnished hotel suite occupied by the Waldner family. The Count's wife, Adelaide, is having her fortune told, and little Zdenka skillfully handles some dunning tradesmen.

When Zdenka is left alone, one of Arabella's most eligible and most ardent suitors comes to call. His name is Matteo, a gallant Italian officer, and he confides in the girl he would like to think of as his future sister-in-law. He tells her that if he had not had a truly wonderful letter from Arabella a couple of days ago, he would be on the verge of suicide. Arabella, it seems, has not even looked at him for days on end. He leaves a bouquet of flowers for his beloved, and when he is gone, we learn the true state of affairs from Zdenka's soliloquy. Secretly she is herself in love with Matteo, and it is she who has written that "truly wonderful" letter to him, letting him think it came from her sister.

But Matteo is clearly not the "right man" for Arabella. We learn her thoughts on this subject—and several others—in a long duet between the two sisters, one of the finest passages in the score. She thinks, rather, that the right man may be a mysterious fellow she has never met but only seen a number of times around the hotel. Zdenka loyally urges the suit of Matteo, and Arabella, just as loyally, urges Zdenka to doff her disguise and get herself a man. Then Arabella muses about *really* falling in love. "And when the right one comes . . . neither of us will doubt it for a moment," sings Arabella. Her tune (an old Croatian one) starts with the four notes of the familiar tune we know as "How Dry I Am." After the duet the girls leave to get Arabella ready for a sleigh ride.

Now, their father, Count Waldner, has had no luck with his gambling. As a last resort he has written a letter to a wealthy old friend, a bachelor named Mandryka. He hopes Mandryka will come through with a loan, and, as a sort of encouragement, he has enclosed a picture of Arabella. What Waldner does not know is that his old friend is dead and that his name and all his wealth have gone to a nephew, a tall, dark, handsome young man. This younger Mandryka has fallen in love with Arabella's picture, has come to Vienna to meet her, and is about to call on her papa.

Mandryka, a strange, formal sort of gentleman, tells Waldner he has sold a forest for this journey; he implies that he is practically ready to marry Arabella; and he offers—in the politest way possible—to lend Waldner a couple of thousand-florin notes. He then retires, saying that he will call formally upon the ladies later in the day. Waldner is delighted; he can scarcely believe his good luck; he shows off his new-found wealth, first to a waiter of the hotel and then to little Zdenka.

Arabella is now ready for her sleigh ride, and she thinks over the men she does *not* want to marry—including the fellow who is about to take her out. And (as the orchestra plays the melody of "the right man") she thinks about the mysterious stranger. He is—as the listener might guess, but as Arabella has no way of knowing—none other than Mandryka. Meantime, Arabella thinks of the ball at which she will be queen tonight. The strains of a Viennese waltz are heard, and the act closes as she goes off with her sister, Zdenka.

Arabella

ACT II

The second act takes place the same evening, at a big ball. Arabella is the queen of that ball, turning down suitor after suitor who asks for a dance. But then she meets Mandryka. At once she recognizes him as "the right man," and he proposes marriage even more promptly than Romeo did to Juliet. In fact, their meeting at a ball, their falling in love at first sight, and their ardent first duet are in many ways parallel to the great passage from Shakespeare.

After their duet Arabella leaves Mandryka for the time being, claiming that she wishes to say farewell to her youth, to all the things that made up her girlhood. Together with an overdressed coquette known as the "Fiakermilli" (who sings her a brilliant polka) Arabella is the cynosure of all eyes. She bids farewell to each of three noble suitors, but the fourth suitor, Matteo, is desperate. Zdenka, still disguised as a boy, fears that her loved one may commit suicide, as he has threatened. She therefore presents him a key, with the implication that it comes from Arabella; and she says definitely that it will admit him to the room of the one who sent it. Mandryka, unfortunately, overhears this conversation, and he believes that Arabella is already planning to betray him. Cynically he calls for wine and gaiety; he flirts with the Fiakermilli; he invites the coachman to drink champagne; and at the end of the act he leaves angrily for his hotel.

ACT III

Back at the hotel Matteo discovers he has been tricked. His rendezvous has been with Zdenka, not with Arabella. But when he sees Zdenka—now with her hair down, a beautiful girl, and one who really loves him—he is happy. He forgets Arabella.

As for Mandryka and Arabella—well, that misunderstanding is now also cleared up. She offers him a drink. If he smashes the glass, that is a symbol of their engagement. Of course, he does smash it; of course, he takes her in his arms; and of course, they kiss. As the curtain goes down, she breaks away from him and trips up to her room. Tomorrow is another day.

50

ARIADNE AUF NAXOS

(Ariadne on Naxos)

Opera in prologue and one act by Richard Strauss with libretto in German by Hugo von Hofmannsthal

CHARACTERS IN THE PROLOGUE

THE MAJOR-DOMO	Speaking Role
MUSIC MASTER	Baritone
THE COMPOSER	Soprano
THE TENOR (later Bacchus)	Tenor
AN OFFICER	Tenor
THE DANCING MASTER	Tenor
THE WIGMAKER	Bass
A LACKEY	Bass
ZERBINETTA	Soprano
PRIMA DONNA (later Ariadne)	Soprano
HARLEQUIN	Baritone
SCARAMUCCIO	Tenor
TRUFFALDINO	Bass
BRIGHELLA	Tenor

CHARACTERS IN THE OPERA

ARIADNE		Soprano
BACCHUS		Tenor
NAIAD		Soprano
DRYAD	Three nymphs	Contralto
ECHO		Soprano
ZERBINETTA		Soprano
HARLEQUIN		Baritone
SCARAMUCCIO		Tenor
TRUFFALDINO		Bass
BRIGHELLA		Tenor

Time: 18th century
Place: Vienna
First performance in original version at Stuttgart, October 25, 1912
First performance in "new" version at Vienna, October 1916

Ariadne auf Naxos, partly classical mythology, partly *commedia dell'arte*, and partly eighteenth-century Viennese satire, was first thought of, by Strauss and Von Hofmannsthal, as a little gift. The gift was for Max Reinhardt, the great stage director, who had stepped in and saved the premiere of *Der Rosenkavalier*. In its original version *Ariadne* was intended to be the special entertainment given by Monsieur Jourdain for his guests in the Molière comedy *Le bourgeois gentilhomme*. So that the evening would not be too long, a good half of Molière had to be sacrificed. The resulting entertainment was, nevertheless, still very long, rather inconclusive in its effect, and very expensive to put on. It required, not only a whole opera company, but a whole dramatic company as well.

At any rate, the mixture was not considered successful, wherefore Molière was dropped completely, a prologue was written and composed, and the opera slightly changed. It is this revised version that is generally given today and described in the following paragraphs.

PROLOGUE

The prologue takes the place of the Molière story, but the scene is now in the home of a very wealthy Viennese bourgeois gentleman of the eighteenth century. This anonymous gentleman is planning an elaborate entertainment for his guests, and the various artists involved are having troubles backstage. For instance, immediately after the orchestral prelude, a pompous major-domo tells the Music Master that a comedy is to follow the opera. And when the Music Master has to tell this to his pupil and protégé, the Composer, that young fellow is quite distraught. It is not his only trouble. He wants a rehearsal with the leading lady; he wants one with the tenor; and he even thinks of new and lovely tunes to put into the work at the last moment. Meantime he meets the leading comedienne, Zerbinetta, and is at once smitten with her. For a moment he is almost reconciled, but now the Major-Domo comes back with a really shocking rearrangement. The master does not want the comedy to follow the opera; he wants them played simultaneously! And they mustn't take longer than the opera would have taken alone.

In a great hurry—and with considerable confusion—a compromise is worked out so that both things can go on at once. Just how this is done will be seen in the description of the opera itself. Meantime, however, the Composer is more and more attracted to the coquettish Zerbinetta, and there is a very attractive love duet between them. But it is time for the show to go on. The Music Master summons everyone; the Composer sings a happy hymn to music, and comes down to earth only at the last moment. He sees the vulgar comedians preparing to ruin his opera, and he runs off in despair.

THE OPERA

In Greek mythology we are told that Ariadne, Princess of Crete, had helped Theseus slay the Minotaur. Naturally, she therefore fell in love with the hero; and, equally naturally, he carried her off with him. According to one legend (the one followed in this work), he unceremoniously abandoned her on the island of Naxos. Here we find her when the opera begins. She is watched over by three so-called "elementary beings," Naiad, Dryad, and Echo, who marvel over her beauty. She sleeps a good deal, but when she is awake, she yearns, in fine Wagnerian fashion, for Death, expecting somehow, to be carried off by Death as though by her lover, Theseus.

The coquettish, comical, earthy Zerbinetta and her friends try to cheer the neurotic demigoddess. These friends, who come directly out of the *commedia dell'arte*, are a male quartet named Harlequin, Scaramuccio, Truffaldino, and Brighella. First Harlequin (the baritone of the quartet) tries—to no avail. Then all four try, with both dance and song. Still no luck. Finally Zerbinetta joins them. And here she has a long recitative and aria—the most difficult music, bar none, ever composed for a coloratura. She tries—gaily, melodiously—to teach Ariadne her own philosophy of life and love, which is always to feel in love with and faithful to one man, but at the same time welcoming the next. It has been this way with a whole list of men, some of whom she names, and sometimes she has carried on with two of them at once. Her aria, with its wide jumps and decorative roulades, is pure nymphomaniacal coloratura. Ariadne remains uninterested; in fact, she retires into her cave before the aria is over. And at its end the unembarrassed Zerbinetta gaily acts out her philosophy of love. She flirts outrageously with three of the men at once— only to abandon them all and take up with the fourth.

Now Ariadne's three attendant nymphs come on. They have seen a beautiful god approaching, and they summon Ariadne from her cave. Off-stage is heard the voice of the young god Bacchus. He has just escaped from the enchantress Circe and is singing of this triumph. Ariadne at once hails him, taking him for the long-awaited messenger of Death. Bacchus, however, is anything but that: he is the god of wine. Ariadne and he fall in love at once; they sing a long and powerful love duet; and they retire, at its end, into the cave. (Eventually, we are told by mythology, they were married.)

But just before Bacchus utters his final words of love, from within the cave, Zerbinetta appears for a brief moment and reminds us that when a new man—or god—comes along, ladies are likely to find him pretty wonderful.

THE BARBER OF SEVILLE

(Il barbiere di Siviglia)

Opera in two acts by Gioacchino Antonio Rossini with libretto in Italian by Cesare Sterbini, based on the comedy of the same name by Pierre Augustin Caron de Beaumarchais

DR. BARTOLO	Bass
BERTA, *his housekeeper*	Mezzo-soprano
ROSINA, *his ward*	Mezzo-soprano
BASILIO, *her music teacher*	Bass
FIGARO, *a barber*	Baritone
COUNT ALMAVIVA	Tenor
FIORELLO, *his servant*	Bass

Time: 17th century
Place: Seville
First performance at Rome, February 20, 1816

The Barber of Seville was not the original title of this opera, though it was of the Beaumarchais play on which it is based. It was *Almaviva, ossia l'inutile precauzione* (*Almaviva, or the Futile Precaution*). The reason Rossini took the futile precaution of retitling the work was that a *Barber of Seville* set to music by Giovanni Paisiello had been popular on the operatic stage for more than thirty years, and Rossini did not wish to offend the respected and irascible composer of over a hundred operas, who was then seventy-five years old.

Despite the precaution, Paisiello's followers (some say inspired by the old man) set up such a din of shouting and catcalls at the premiere of Rossini's work that it was a bad failure. Rossini, who had conducted, slunk out of the theater;

55

but when his leading lady later called to console him, she reported that he was imperturbably asleep in bed.

The second and subsequent performances that week went better; but the initial failure made for a slow start for the long and wide popularity of this work. As for Paisiello, he died three and a half months later and never knew that Rossini's work would completely overshadow his own. As a matter of fact, when Paisiello's work is occasionally put on today by some opera workshop, one is struck by the many outward similarities; yet the vigor, the vitality, the musical humor that have made the younger man's work survive many thousands of performances are found in much smaller quantities in the Paisiello score. Rossini's won not only the love of millions but the genuine respect and affection of such utterly differently oriented composers as Beethoven, Wagner, and Brahms.

OVERTURE

The overture that we always hear nowadays was not the original overture to the opera, which consisted of a mélange of popular Spanish tunes. That one, somehow or other, managed to get lost soon after the first performance. Rossini, a notably lazy fellow, thereupon dug up an old overture from his trunk, one that he had composed seven years earlier for a forgotten tidbit named *L'Equivoco stravagante*. It had also been useful when he ran short of overtures for two other operas, *Aureliano in Palmira* and *Elizabeth, Queen of England*. And though its gay, tripping tunes would scarcely seem to serve well for a tragedy about the Queen of England, it serves so well for *The Barber of Seville* that certain musical commentators have imagined they saw in it musical portraits of Rosina, Figaro, and Lord knows what else.

ACT I

Scene 1   On a street in Seville a hired band of musicians gathers to accompany young Count Almaviva as he serenades his lovely Sevillian inamorata, Rosina. It's a very pretty, florid

serenade the Count delivers (*Ecco ridente*). No use, though;
the music fails to summon Rosina, who is closely watched by
her old guardian Dr. Bartolo. The musicians are dismissed
with considerable trouble by the Count and his servant, Fi-
orello, and presently a jolly baritone is heard tra-la-la-ing off-
stage. It is Figaro, the barber, sounding off in praise of himself and telling us how indispensable he is to everyone in town.
This self-endorsement is, of course, the delightful *Largo al
factotum*. It quickly turns out that Figaro has known the
Count a long time. (There aren't many people around town
he does *not* know.) The Count—with the aid of a bit of ready
cash—enlists Figaro in his purpose to marry Rosina, and they
begin to make plans. But they are interrupted by Dr. Bartolo,
who leaves his house muttering that he plans to marry Rosina
himself that very day.

Now the two conspirators have to act quickly. With Bartolo
gone from the house, Almaviva tries another serenade, and
this time he identifies himself as Lindoro. Also this time he
gets a response. Rosina begins to answer favorably from the
balcony, when she is forcibly drawn back by someone inside.
The quick brain of Figaro at once hatches a plot. Almaviva
shall disguise himself as a drunken soldier and gain entrance
into the house by saying that the army has billeted him there.
The idea appeals to the Count, and the scene ends with a jolly
duet as the lover expresses his delight over the prospects of
success while the barber expresses *his* delight over the prospect
of getting paid.

Scene 2 Things happen pretty fast and furiously in the
second scene, which takes place in Dr. Bartolo's house. Perhaps the best way to keep them in mind is to make special
note of the big arias and concerted numbers. First, then, there
is the famous coloratura aria *Una voce poco fa*. In it Rosina
first admits her love for the unknown serenader Lindoro, then
vows to marry him despite her guardian, and goes on to tell
what a fine, docile wife she could make until thwarted. Under
such circumstances she can be as devilish as any other shrew.
(Usually, in modern performances, this role is sung by a coloratura soprano. That, however, is not the way Rossini wrote

it. He intended it for a coloratura *mezzo*-soprano, a rather rare phenomenon in the twentieth century.) After her aria she has a cordial little talk with Figaro, the barber, and a less cordial one with Dr. Bartolo.

The next big aria is known as *La calunnia*—in praise of calumny or vicious gossip. Don Basilio, a music master, reports to his old friend Dr. Bartolo that Count Almaviva has arrived in town, and that he is Rosina's mysterious lover. How is he to be discredited? Why, says Basilio, by calumny. And that is the occasion for the aria, in which evil whispers are graphically described as developing into a veritable storm of disapprobation. Following this comes a long and rather coy dialogue between Figaro and Rosina in which the barber tells the girl that a poor young man named Lindoro is in love with her and she had better write him a note. Rosina, as a matter of fact, has already written the note, and she gives it to the barber to be delivered. There is then another dialogue—a short one—in which Rosina tries to mislead her old guardian with a half a dozen lies, all of which he sees through.

Roused to fury by these attacks on his dignity, Dr. Bartolo has the third big aria of this scene (*A un dottor della mia sorte*). A professional man of his standing, he says, can't be treated like that—and he orders Rosina locked up in her chamber.

Soon after this enters Count Almaviva according to plan— that is, disguised as a drunken soldier who claims to be billeted in the doctor's house. None of the doctor's protests can help him: the apparently drunken soldier disregards his evidence of exemption, threatens him with his sword, shouts and curses—but also manages, *sub rosa*, to let Rosina know he is Lindoro. Everything develops into a terrific uproar as, one by one, the servant Berta, the barber Figaro, and the music master Basilio join in. Finally the police break up the row. The Count is about to be arrested, when he privately shows the police officer his true rank, and the act ends with a brilliant nine-part chorus in which everyone agrees that the whole situation is quite insane.

ACT II

With the beginning of the second act confusion is even worse confounded. Count Almaviva comes to Bartolo's house in a new disguise—the black cloak and shovel hat of the seventeenth-century professor. He says he is substituting for Don Basilio, who is sick, and he insists on giving Rosina a music lesson. During that lesson (in most modern opera houses) the leading soprano usually interpolates anything from "Home Sweet Home" to the most elaborate coloratura aria. But for the original score Rossini provided a song called *L'Inutile precauzione*—"The Vain Precaution"—which was the original subtitle to the opera. Dr. Bartolo doesn't like this "modern music," as he calls it, and obliges in his turn with a silly, old-fashioned ditty.

A moment later Figaro enters and insists on shaving the doctor; and while the old fellow is handicapped with a face full of lather, arrangements are made by the lovers for an elopement that evening. But things are just a little too clear to satisfy the authors of this opera, and so Don Basilio enters. He is, of course, not sick at all; but in a very amusing quintet everyone persuades him that he has scarlet fever, and he is packed off to bed. All these unusual developments have aroused Dr. Bartolo's suspicions, and at the end of another amusing concerted number, he shoos everyone out. Then, by way of contrast, there is a cute little song for Berta, the maid, who remarks on the idiocy of every old fool's wanting to get married.

At this point, the orchestra paints a vivid storm to indicate what the weather is outside and also to suggest the passage of some time. (The music for this was borrowed by Rossini from his own opera *La pietra del paragone*.) Now—enter the Count and Figaro in cloaks, ready for the elopement. First, however, they must persuade Rosina that their intentions are honorable, for until this point she does not know that her Lindoro and the Count Almaviva are one and the same. They are soon ready, and are singing the elopement trio (*Zitti, zitti*) when they find the ladder gone! It turns out later that Dr. Bartolo

59

had taken it away as he went off to arrange his own marriage to Rosina.

And so, when Basilio and a notary arrive—sent by Bartolo —the Count bribes these newcomers to officiate at *his* wedding to Rosina. The hasty ceremony is scarcely over when Bartolo returns with police officers. Everything is now explained, and the doctor is even partially reconciled to his defeat when the Count assures him he may keep Rosina's dowry for himself. The comedy thus ends—as it should—with general rejoicing.

And if you want to find out what happened subsequently to these characters, turn to the account of Mozart's *The Marriage of Figaro*, which is based on Beaumarchais's sequel to his *Barber of Seville*.

THE BARTERED BRIDE

(*Prodaná Nevešta—Die verkaufte Braut*)

Opera in three acts by Bedřich Smetana with
libretto in Czech by Karel Sabina

KRUSCHINA, *a peasant*	*Baritone*
KATINKA, *his wife*	*Soprano*
MARIE, *their daughter*	*Soprano*
MISHA, *a wealthy landlord*	*Bass*
AGNES, *his wife*	*Mezzo-soprano*
WENZEL, *their son*	*Tenor*
HANS, *Misha's son by a first marriage*	*Tenor*
KEZAL, *a marriage broker*	*Bass*
SPRINGER, *manager of a circus*	*Bass*
ESMERELDA, *a dancer*	*Soprano*
MUFF, *a comedian*	*Tenor*

Time: 19th century
Place: a small Bohemian village
First performance at Prague, May 30, 1866

It was after Austria's defeat at the hands of Italy that
the Czechs, around 1860, began to cultivate their own arts in
a deliberate encouragement of nationalism. Franz Josef's government became less restrictive; national theaters started to
be built; and native art music was needed (the Czechs always
having had a fine native folk music). Smetana and, later,
Dvořák were the most prominent serious composers developed
under this nationalistic movement, and some of their orchestral music, at any rate, quickly was adopted by the whole
Western world. But the only nineteenth-century Czech opera
that has entered the repertoire of European and American

61

opera houses is *The Bartered Bride*, and this was not originally written as an opera but as an operetta. It had two acts, twenty musical numbers, and spoken dialogue. The requirements of foreign opera houses soon caused Smetana to make his score more ambitious. Three years after the premiere, for performance at the Opéra Comique of Paris, Smetana added an aria for the leading soprano as well as some dances, including the now famous *Polka* and *Furiant*; and the following year, for performance at St. Petersburg, the opera was divided into three acts and the spoken dialogue turned into recitative. It is in the final version that it is almost always played nowadays.

OVERTURE

Music lovers who have never heard *The Bartered Bride* in its entirety must still be quite familiar with the overture, as it has long been a standard part of the orchestral repertoire. Its themes are all heard a second time during the finale of Act II.

ACT I

On the main square of a small Bohemian village a chorus of countryfolk sets the tone of the whole opera by singing gaily in praise of spring and of youthful love—with an added note of warning about the dangers of marriage. The two young lovers, Marie and Hans, alone are feeling sad, and when the villagers leave, their reasons become clear in a duet. Marie is bothered for two reasons. First, she knows that her parents are arranging a wedding for her with some unknown. Second, she knows nothing about the life of Hans before he recently came to this village. Hans is of a more sanguine nature. He assures Marie that all she needs to do is to remain steadfast to him, and no unknown suitor can take her away. As for the second point, he tells her that he came of a wealthy home, but his father's second wife did not like him, and so he has come away to seek his own fortune. The two lovers swear eternal faith very prettily, but they are interrupted when three

older characters occupy the stage. These are Marie's parents—
Kruschina and Katinka—and a comic marriage broker named
Kezal. Their conversation reveals the fact that the parents are
practically ready to give away Marie in marriage to the son of
a rich man named Misha. Only the mother has some reserva-
tions. She thinks that Marie ought to be consulted.

When Marie hears of these plans, she firmly puts her foot
down, announcing that she has already promised to marry
Hans. The older folk are scandalized, and Father Kruschina
goes off to talk the matter over with Misha, while Kezal decides to tackle Hans.

Once more the countryfolk gather on the stage, and the
act closes with the very jolly *Polka*.

ACT II

The second act begins with a drinking song at the local inn.
It is punctuated with solos by the marriage broker, Kezal, in
praise of gold, and by the young lover, Hans, toasting (of
course) love. Then everyone joins in a dance.

Now, for the first time, we meet Wenzel, a pathetic figure
of a young man—the son of the wealthy Misha and the candidate for Marie's hand. The poor fellow stutters and is dreadfully shy. He has never met Marie, but Marie knows who he
is. And so, in a duet, she persuades him to give up the unknown Marie. That young woman, she says, has no use for
Wenzel, no respect for him; she will make his life miserable;
and, furthermore, there is a very pretty young girl in the village who is sighing her heart out for love of Wenzel. Finally
Marie makes Wenzel swear that he will never even come near
Marie. This number is followed by another long duet, a very
comic one, in which Kezal tries to persuade Hans to give up
Marie. Hans, he says, is too inexperienced to know that you
must have money to marry. Nor does he know how dreadful
women can become once they have caught their men. Better
to remain single! And then, with complete lack of logic, he
offers Hans a girl who has everything under the sun. He lists
each item, and Hans repeats every detail after him. Further-

more, Kezal is prepared to offer 100 . . . 200 . . . no—300 gulden for giving up Marie. Give her up—to whom? asks Hans. Why, to the son of Misha, of course.

Now, Hans himself is really a son of Misha by Misha's first marriage, but Kezal does not know this. Therefore, Hans is prepared to sign an agreement. He is to receive 300 gulden with the understanding that Marie must marry no one but the son of Misha. Everyone comes in to witness the signing of this document, and everyone is shocked that Hans should be willing to sell his fiancée. Only Hans knows that he will have the last laugh and that Marie will never be a "bartered bride."

ACT III

Alone on the town square, Wenzel bewails his failure to make love successfully in a comic aria marked *lamentoso*. Suddenly, with trumpets and drums, a circus troupe appears at the inn. Wenzel is childishly delighted. He hears Springer, the leader of the troupe, announce a performance that very afternoon, and he is enchanted—as is every audience—with the *Dance of the Comedians*. He also falls in love at first sight with Esmerelda, the pretty tightrope walker. But Muff, another member of the troupe, rushes in to announce that the fellow who plays the bear is hopelessly drunk. No one else of the right size can be found, and so Springer and the pretty Esmerelda persuade Wenzel to join the troupe—to learn to dance—and to be the bear!

Before he can go off with them, his parents interrupt. Agnes, Misha, and the marriage broker Kezal try to persuade Wenzel to sign the contract to marry Marie. But for once the boy knows his own mind: he absolutely refuses—and he runs off. Now it is Marie's turn to be persuaded to agree to the marriage. Even her own parents join in, and when they show her the paper that her lover Hans has signed, her heart is broken. Pitifully she asks a few minutes to think it over. In a lovely sextet, the older people agree to give her some time, but they will soon return.

Marie now has a mournful aria, and she is not at all cheered up by Hans, who joins her in an annoyingly cheerful frame of mind. He, of course, knows that everything will turn out all right, but he does not have time to explain it to his girl. In fact, he only makes matters rather worse in their brief duet. So, when Kezal offers him his money (according to the contract), he agrees readily, and everyone in the village is sure that Marie will make a lovely bride for Wenzel. At this point Wenzel's parents enter, see Hans for the first time, and greet him as Misha's long lost son. Thus everything is cleared up for the lovers, for the contract calls for Marie to marry Misha's son, and it doesn't say *which* son. Marie chooses Hans, and Kezal is laughed off the scene.

Now there are shouts: "Save yourselves! A bear's got loose!" But it is only Wenzel, disguised in his bear's suit. His mother drags him off; Misha blesses the happy young couple; and the opera ends as everyone joins in a chorus: *Hurray for the bartered bride!*

BASTIEN UND BASTIENNE

Light opera in one act by Wolfgang Amadeus
Mozart with libretto in German by F. W.
Weiskern, based on Marie Justine Benoîte
Favart's parody of Jean Jacques Rousseau's *Le
devin du village*

BASTIEN, *a shepherd*	Tenor
BASTIENNE, *a shepherdess*	Soprano
COLAS, *a magician*	Bass

Time: 18th century
Place: outside a European village
First performance at Vienna, probably in September 1768

Mozart, as everyone knows, was a child prodigy. He composed *Bastien und Bastienne* at the age of twelve. It was
commissioned by no less a personage than Dr. Anton Mesmer,
the inventor of mesmerism—a kind of hypnotism used for cur-
ing people of all sorts of diseases. Later on his mesmerism
came to be generally regarded as something like quackery, but
in 1768 the good doctor was a highly respected and wealthy
practitioner in Vienna, and *Bastien und Bastienne* was presented at a garden party he gave that fall. Its libretto was a
parody of another famous little musical work—*Le devin du
village*, by Jean Jacques Rousseau. Apparently *Bastien und
Bastienne* was not too great a success, for it was not given a
second performance till Mozart had been in his grave almost
a century. It was, therefore, impossible for Ludwig van Beethoven, born two years after Mesmer's party, to have heard
the overture. I mention this fact because the main theme of

Mozart's little opening music is almost note for note the same as the main theme of the great *Eroica* symphony. Just one of those amusing accidents.

The story of *Bastien und Bastienne* is about as simple as anything can be. Bastienne is a shepherdess in love with Bastien, a shepherd. She tells us about it in two short opening arias. Then there is some bagpipe-like music, and in comes the fortuneteller Colas. In a long scene she complains of Bastien's interest in a wealthy girl, while Colas advises her to act uninterested in Bastien's defection and to make believe she has other admirers. When Bastien appears on the scene, the shepherdess hides while Colas tells him of Bastienne's new interests. The shepherd, of course, really wants only his shepherdess, and in a couple of short arias Colas promises help through reading aloud from his book of magic. This is nothing but a lot of nonsense, and consists of magic words like *Diggidaggi* and *Schurry-murry*.

And so, when Bastien and Bastienne meet again, there is a lover's quarrel which ends in a duet of reconciliation. Then the little opera closes with a trio in praise of the beautiful weather and the arts of the magician Colas. Nothing could be more innocent or charming.

LA BOHÈME

(*The Bohemians*)

Opera in four acts by Giacomo Puccini with libretto in Italian by Giuseppe Giacosa and Luigi Illica with considerable assistance from Giulio Ricordi and the composer, based on incidents from Henri Murger's novel *Scènes de la vie de Bohème*

MIMI, *a seamstress*	*Soprano*
RODOLFO, *a poet*	*Tenor*
MARCELLO, *a painter*	*Baritone*
COLLINE, *a philosopher*	*Bass*
SCHAUNARD, *a musician*	*Baritone*
BENOIT, *a landlord*	*Bass*
ALCINDORO, *a state councilor and follower of Musetta*	*Bass*
PARPIGNOL, *an itinerant toy vendor*	*Tenor*
CUSTOM-HOUSE SERGEANT	*Bass*
MUSETTA, *a grisette*	*Soprano*

Time: about 1830
Place: Paris
First performance at Turin, February 1, 1896

It is the evening of February 1, 1896, in the opera house at Turin. A brilliant audience has gathered to hear the world premiere of the new opera by Giacomo Puccini, whose *Manon Lescaut* was a nationwide success. The conductor is Arturo Toscanini, aged twenty-eight, whose repute is already such that an American critic had written, after hearing him conduct *Die Götterdämmerung,* that he "was the only artist the city of New York should be proud to invite to conduct."

Under such auspices one might have expected the premiere of the most lovable of all Italian operas to be a resounding success. It wasn't. It wasn't a failure, either, but the public reception was little better than lukewarm, while the critics were far from unanimous in liking it. One of them went so far as to call it "empty and downright infantile." The Metropolitan premiere, in 1900, elicited some even worse epithets. "*La Bohème,*" said the *Tribune,* "is foul in subject and fulminant and futile in its music . . . Silly and inconsequential . . ."

By no means all the critics were this wide of the mark. Despite the opinions of many musicians, professional critics are proved far more often right than wrong by the general opinion of posterity. But in this particular case no one was so exactly right as Puccini's publisher, Giulio Ricordi. After working and worrying with the composer and his librettists for the entire three years that the opera was in the making, he wrote to Puccini three months before the premiere: "Dear Puccini, if this time you have not succeeded in hitting the nail squarely on the head, I will change my profession and sell salami!"

ACT I

The first act takes place in Paris on a Christmas Eve in the 1830's. It is in the attic apartment of Rodolfo and Marcello, members of a quartet of happy-go-lucky, poverty-stricken Bohemians. As the scene opens, Marcello, an artist, is complaining to his friend Rodolfo, a poet, of the terrible cold. The fireplace having long been without fuel, Rodolfo gets a brilliant idea: he will use for kindling the paper on which he has written a five-act tragedy. Presently Colline, the philosopher member, enters, and warms himself at the meager grate. And lastly we meet the fourth member, Schaunard, the musician, who has mysteriously come by the means to buy food and wine. The four are reveling and at the height of joy, when Benoit, the landlord, makes his appearance and demands some rent. He is, however, plied with wine and is soon pushed out rather roughly—and without his money. Schaunard, Marcello, and Colline thereupon depart for the Café Momus, leaving Rodolfo, who explains that he has an article to write.

A few moments later there is a timid knock at the door. It is a pretty young neighbor, whose candle has gone out. Rodolfo invites her to come in. Racked by a coughing spell, she sits down and has a sip of wine. Rodolfo relights her candle, and she leaves but returns a moment later because she seems to have dropped her key. Rodolfo gallantly searches for it; and as they grope in the darkness, the candles having gone out, Rodolfo grasps Mimi's hand. This is the signal for the beautiful aria *Che gelida manina*—"Thy tiny hand is frozen," in which he tells about his way of life and his work. When he has finished, the girl answers in her equally celebrated aria, *Mi chiamano Mimi*—"They call me Mimi," and goes on to describe her simple life as a seamstress. Rodolfo and Mimi are now quite in love, and when they hear their friends shouting to them from below, Rodolfo ceremoniously takes Mimi's arm, and they leave to join the others at the Café Momus.

ACT II

The second act takes place outside the Café Momus, where our Bohemian friends have taken a sidewalk table. A large part of the opening of this act is given over to a musical depiction of Gay Paree in the Latin Quarter on a Christmas Eve. Everyone is in a festive mood, and people are buying things they don't really want. Rodolfo introduces his new girl friend to his friends, and presently a rich gentleman, named Alcindoro, and his gaily overdressed companion enter and occupy a table nearby. Now, the girl Alcindoro has brought is Musetta, and Musetta is the ex-girl-friend of Marcello, the painter. She is bored to tears with her rich, elderly admirer and tries desperately to pick up her old companion. First he will have none of her, but then she sings her famous waltz song, *Quando m'en vo' soletta per la via*—a frankly self-adulatory bit—and Marcello is lost.

Suddenly Musetta screams: her shoe, she says, is pinching her—which is her device to get rid of Alcindoro for a few minutes. When he has hustled off to find another pair of shoes, she joins the Bohemians and has a fine time. Now a patrol marches by; street urchins follow behind them; and last of all, the procession is joined by the Bohemians and their two girlfriends. And so, when Alcindoro returns, he finds he has lost a girl and has inherited, in her place, the enormous bill the others have run up at the café.

ACT III

It is a bitter cold February morning at one of the gates of Paris. Workers demand—and finally get—admission from the police, and Puccini's excellent atmospheric music almost makes one shiver with the cold. Poor Mimi, very ill, summons Marcello from the inn where he lives with Musetta. She tells the painter piteously about her constant bickering with the jealous Rodolfo, who even now is in the tavern, having left Mimi after a quarrel. When he emerges, she hides behind a tree and overhears her lover tell Marcello how desperately ill Mimi is, and how it would be wise for them to separate. Suddenly he hears her cough and turns to her compassionately, while Marcello rushes indoors, for he hears Musetta laughing and suspects she is again flirting with another man. In her touching aria *Addio, senza rancor* Mimi bids Rodolfo farewell; and in the heartbreaking duet that follows they think that in the springtime they can be together again. But the duet grows into a quartet as Marcello and Musetta bring their quarrel out of doors. The contrasting notes of the quarreling couple and the sentimental one are worked up into a marvelous ending for the act—one of the finest quartets in all of Italian opera. And before it is over, Rodolfo and Mimi have decided to remain together, while the other couple is definitely separated.

ACT IV

In the final act we are once more in the attic studio of Marcello and Rodolfo. The painter is trying to paint, the poet to write. But it is no use. They cannot get their minds off Musetta and Mimi, from whom they are again separated, as they sing the duet *Ah, Mimi tu più non torni.* The whole atmosphere changes when their friends Colline and Schaunard turn up with a windfall of food. The four of them now act just like children: they play they are at a banquet; they dance comical dances; and two of them engage in a mock duel. But the merriment is just as suddenly stopped when Musetta enters. She has with her their old friend Mimi, and Mimi, she tells them, is obviously dying. Quickly the poor girl is brought in and laid gently on the bed. As she speaks quietly to Rodolfo, saying how cold she is, the others do their best to help. Musetta tells Marcello to sell her earrings to get a cordial and the services of a doctor. Colline, in a touching little aria (*Vecchia zimarra*), bids farewell to his overcoat, which he goes out to sell.

At last the two lovers are left alone, and they sing sadly of their former happiness. Mimi, weakening, goes to sleep, and when the others return, Musetta prepares some medicine and breathes a quiet, intense prayer. As Rodolfo goes to hang Mimi's cloak over the window to keep out the light, Schaunard examines her more closely and notes, horror-struck, that she is already dead. At first no one dares tell Rodolfo. But he sees the expressions on their faces, and with a despairing cry of "*Mimi, Mimi!*" he rushes across the room and flings himself down beside the body of the girl he had loved desperately.

Postscript for the historically curious: In an engaging essay entitled "The Original Bohemians," George Marek has identified the originals of the characters in the opera. Most of the following details are based on this essay.

Rodolfo—This was Henri Murger, author of the autobiographical novel *Scènes de la vie de Bohème,* which was published in 1848 and served as the source of the libretto. He was, as a young man, an unsuccessful scribbler very much like Rodolfo, who, at one point, shared not only his room with a fellow-Bohemian, but also a single pair of trousers. A play, written in collaboration with Barrière, on the basis of the novel, was so successful that Murger could afford to stop being a Bohemian, and did.

Mimi—The principal model was a sickly grisette named Lucile. As a matter of fact, Mimi in the opera tells us her real name is Lucia. She was pretty, had a rather unpleasant character, and died of consumption. The death occurred not in a garret but in a hospital, and Rodolfo-Murger did not hear of it in time to claim the body. It was dissected by medical students.

Marcello—He was a composite of two close friends of Murger's, both artists, one named Lazare and one Tabar. Lazare was very prosperous (for a Bohemian) and Tabar very talented. Maybe there is some moral in this.

Colline—Another merger of two characters, philosophical writers named Jean Wallon and Trapadoux. The latter was the one who went around in the costume usually affected on the stage by Colline—a tall hat and a long green surtout. But it was Wallon who was always carrying books, as Colline does in Act II of the opera.

Schaunard—His real name was Alexandre Schanne, part painter, part writer, part musician. (In the second act of the opera he buys a French horn.) His own autobiography, *Souvenirs de Schaunard,* identifies his Bohemian friends. By the time he wrote it, however, he had ceased being a Bohemian and had become a prosperous toy manufacturer.

Musetta—Modeled largely on a somewhat exhibitionistic model who, to quote Mr. Marek, "left the Latin Quarter and led an irregular life in regular fashion." Later on she was drowned in a ship crossing the Mediterranean.

Benoit was a landlord's real name. His house was in the Rue des Cannettes. Mimi-Lucile, not Rodolfo-Murger, was his tenant just before the girl died.

Café Momus was the real name of the favorite haunt of the real Bohemians. Its address was 15 Rue des Prêtres, St. Germain l'Auxerrois.

BORIS GODOUNOFF

Opera in prologue and four acts by Modest
Moussorgsky with libretto in Russian based on
Alexandre Sergevich Pushkin's play of the same
name and passages from Nikolai Mikhailovich
Karamzin's *History of the Russian Empire*

BORIS GODOUNOFF, *the Czar*	Bass
FEODOR, *his son*	Mezzo-soprano
XENIA, *his daughter*	Soprano
NURSE	Mezzo-soprano
TCHELKALOFF, *clerk of the Duma*	Baritone
PIMEN, *an old monk*	Bass
GRIGORI, *the false Dmitri*	Tenor
PRINCE SHUISKI, *adviser to Boris*	Tenor
MARINA, *daughter of the Voivode of Sandomir*	Mezzo-soprano
HOSTESS OF THE INN	Mezzo-soprano
VARLAAM ⎫ *vagabond monks*	Bass
MISSAIL ⎭	Tenor
RANGONI, *a Jesuit priest*	Baritone or Bass
POLICE OFFICER	Bass
IDIOT	Tenor

Time: 1598–1605
Place: Russia and Poland
First performance at St. Petersburg, February 8 (Russian-style
   January 27), 1874

There are half a dozen versions of this opera. Moussorgsky himself made two; his friend Rimsky-Korsakoff made two;
Shostakovich made one a few years ago for Russian opera

75

houses; and John Gutman and Karol Rathaus made still another for the Metropolitan Opera Company in 1953. Each of
them differs from the others in which scenes are and are not
included, and in the order of the scenes; and the last two
versions discarded Rimsky-Korsakoff's changes in orchestration
and general slicking up of Moussorgsky's original. But as the
second Rimsky version is the one that is still most often heard
in opera houses and on recordings, I shall follow that in my
description.

Actually, for the purpose of telling the story, it does not
make too much difference which one we follow. For, whatever
way the events are told, this is not a tight tragedy. Rather, it
is like a chronicle play—one of the Richard or Henry dramas
of Shakespeare. It is a series of scenes from Russian history,
and the Russian people themselves, as we see them in the
great choral scenes, make up one of the two principal characters, the other being, of course, Boris himself.

PROLOGUE

Scene 1 Russian history tells us that Czar Ivan the Terrible died in 1584 and that of his two sons one was a teen-age
half-wit and the other a small child. Boris Godounoff had been
the Czar's closest friend and adviser, and he was made Regent
while his sister married the half-wit. The little boy, placed in
a monastery, soon died, while Boris's feeble-minded brother-
in-law, for whom he was acting as regent, died seven years
later without having any children. Now the members of the
nobility, as well (some historians claim) as the people themselves, wished the ablest man in the country—Boris—to become
Czar. Faithful to the memory of his friend, he at first refused.
The first scene of the prologue shows the people, outside the
monastery of Novodevichy, being ordered to pray that Boris
take on the crown. The police order them to do this, and so
does Tchelkaloff, the clerk of the Duma—that is, Russia's
seventeenth-century equivalent of a parliament. Not that the
people are very clear about what they are supposed to do:
they have to be prompted by knouts and the example of some

passing monks. But it all doesn't work. Tchelkaloff has to come out on the steps of the monastery and tell them, at the end of the scene, that Boris remains obdurate.

Scene 2 But Boris did not remain obdurate forever, and the second scene of the prologue is devoted to his coronation. Here the libretto departs rather importantly from history, as many great dramatic chronicles (including Shakespeare's) frequently do. Boris, it now appears, has only made believe that he does not want to be crowned Czar of Russia. Like Shakespeare's King Richard III before him, he has plotted for this very end. Like Richard, he has created an artificial demand for his coronation; and, also like Richard, he has had the rightful monarch (the little boy) murdered for this purpose. Now he is about to be crowned. But, unlike Richard, his conscience bothers him. The scene takes place in Moscow in the courtyard of the Kremlin between the two great cathedrals of the Assumption and the Archangels. The people, urged on by Prince Shuiski, acclaim their hero. "Long live the Czar!" they cry. In a somber mood Boris appears. He prays to God for help, for he knows he is unworthy. (I should add here that Boris may not have ordered the murder of that little boy, but for the purpose of the opera we must assume, like Moussorgsky and Pushkin before him, that he did.) Anyway, the great bells acclaim him, the people join in a magnificent folk chorus, and the procession moves into the cathedral.

ACT I

Scene 1 takes place five years later in the monastery of Chudovo. A good old monk named Pimen is sitting in his cell, completing the chronicle of the Czars of Russia. A novice of the monastery lies near him, asleep. Presently Grigori, the novice, awakes. They converse a while, Grigori asking questions, Pimen answering them. Grigori's last question is: How old was the little Czarevitch Dmitri, whom Boris had murdered? And the answer is that he would have been exactly the age of Grigori had he lived. Just then a bell summons the monks to prayer. Off-stage, chanting is heard, and Pimen

leaves to join in the prayers. But Grigori remains. He has
conceived a desperate idea: he will leave the monastery, and
he will proclaim himself as the rightful heir to the throne—
the Czarevitch Dmitri!

Scene 2   Grigori has now started on his way to mount the
throne of Russia. On the border of Lithuania the jolly hostess
of an inn sings a folk song about a dove-colored drake. Presently two vagabond monks come in—Varlaam and Missail—
and young Grigori, dressed as a peasant, follows hard on their
heels. Already somewhat drunk, Varlaam sings a boisterous
song about how Czar Ivan had once killed 83,000 Tartars by
exploding mines in their midst. As Varlaam drinks more and
more, Grigori questions the hostess. She tells him that the
border of Lithuania is very close, and that the police are
searching for a man who has escaped. Soon the policemen
come in, bearing a warrant for the arrest of someone or other.
But, like any Russian police officer of the seventeenth century,
the chief one cannot read. Therefore Grigori offers to read
the warrant for him, and in doing so deliberately makes the
description of the fugitive fit Varlaam. That drunken fellow
insists there must be some mistake. With great effort, he himself spells out the description in the warrant, and, of course,
it is found to fit, not Varlaam, but Grigori. However, by that
time, in the general confusion, Grigori has escaped through
a window. They all chase out after him but are too late to
catch up.

ACT II

In the Kremlin at Moscow, where the Czars of Russia always lived, we find the two children of Boris with their old
nurse. The daughter is mourning the death of her fiancé, and
the nurse vainly tries to comfort her by singing a fable about
a couple of young lovers. Then she turns her attention to the
little boy, Feodor. She sings a song to him, too—about a gnat
who threw a stick at a flea and hurt himself so badly that he
died. Nurse and Feodor then play games together, clapping
their hands in time. But when Czar Boris comes in, the games

have to stop. Boris turns to the map of Russia that Feodor has been studying from, and it saddens the aging man. Here he has a great monologue. Things are going badly in Russia, both politically and economically. Everyone blames the Czar, who feels guilty, for he still remembers the murdered body of the little Czarevitch. A nobleman enters to whisper to Boris about dangerous intrigues at court, but the Czar dismisses him, turns once more to his son, and gets some comfort and pleasure from the silly story about a parrot that the boy tells him.

The comfort does not last long. Prince Shuiski now enters. He tells Boris about the growing success of a pretender who is raising an army. Boris demands to know whether it was really little Dmitri who had been murdered by his orders. The crafty Shuiski tells him that it was, but that the body did not decay, and that a smile continued to play on its face. The Czar dismisses Shuiski. Then, left alone, he is prey to all his superstitions. His conscience bothers him, and he imagines he sees the bloodstained body of the murdered boy. In an agony of fear, he cries for it to leave him in peace. And the act ends as he pitifully begs for God's forgiveness.

ACT III

Much of the music of this act—called "the Polish act"—was added by Moussorgsky in his second version. The criticism had been made that there wasn't enough music for a good leading lady. Moussorgsky agreed.

Scene 1 Dmitri has been making progress in his effort to overthrow Boris and supplant him. He has reached Poland; he has begun to raise an army of followers; and he has the support of certain Polish nobles, including the Voivode (roughly—Governor) of Sandomir. The Voivode's beautiful daughter Marina has ambitions to become the Czarina; and in the first scene, after being entertained by her ladies-in-waiting with songs about love, she tells them that tales of derring-do suit her better. After dismissing them, she sings an aria, in the rhythm of the Polish mazurka, indicating quite clearly that it is through Dmitri that she expects to realize her ambitions. Suddenly there appears in her apartment the rather sinister figure of Rangoni, a Jesuit priest, who lectures her sternly on her duty to convert Russia to the true church of Rome once she is Czarina. Marina is terrified.

Scene 2 takes place by a fountain in the romantic garden of the castle of Sandomir. The false Dmitri awaits a rendez-vous with his beloved Marina, for whom he once thought of giving up his ambitions. Rangoni appears to strengthen these ambitions, to assure him that Marina loves him despite certain snubs she has had to endure for his sake, and to ask only to be allowed to accompany them to Moscow and be his spiritual guide.

And now the garden is filled with fashionable guests, who dance a polonaise, paying court to and even flirting with Marina, as Dmitri jealously watches. The scene concludes with a long and melodious duet in which Marina alternately repulses and encourages the pretender. The false Dmitri ends by vowing to lead an army to Moscow, and to make Marina his Czarina. As they embrace, Rangoni steps out from behind his hiding place, while the music in the orchestra—no longer on the famous love theme—seems to signify that this victory will be, not Dmitri's or Marina's, but that of the Roman Catholic Church.

ACT IV

Scene 1 There are two scenes in the last act, and sometimes one is given first, sometimes the other. I shall start with the one usually given first in the Rimsky version. It shows how the people are rising to follow the false Dmitri in rebellion against the hated Czar Boris. In the dead of winter, in the forest of Kromy, a ragged crowd drags in a nobleman, bound and gagged. They mock this follower of the Czar, and they mock the Czar, too. The village idiot comes in, and a group of children mock him, for he sings a foolish ditty. Our old friends, the vagabond monks Varlaam and Missail, also join the crowd of rebels. But when two Jesuit priests come in, praying, the crowd turns on them. Led by Varlaam and Missail, the peasants attack the monks and drag them off, intending to hang them.

But now Grigori, the pretender, rides in on a fine horse. All bow to him; he promises to rid them of Boris; and, shouting their allegiance, they follow the false Dmitri. Only the fool is left on the stage. Sadly he sits down; the snow begins to fall; and he sings his prophecy:

> *The foe will come . . .*
> *Darkness will descend . . .*
> *Weep, weep, you hungry Russian people!*

Scene 2 takes place in the council hall of the Kremlin in the year 1605. The boyars—that is, the noblemen of the Czar's council—are discussing in a foolish way the revolt of the false Dmitri. When Prince Shuiski comes in, he tells them of the agony that he saw Czar Boris suffering a few days before, and he describes the scene in which Boris imagined he saw the murdered Czarevitch. The foolish boyars will not believe him. But suddenly Boris himself enters, deeply distraught. Shuiski calls in an old priest, who turns out to be Pimen, the monk who shared the cell with Grigori in Act I. Pimen tells Boris about the dream of a blind shepherd. He had seen the murdered boy Dmitri in that dream, and the boy had urged him to pray at his grave. So the blind shepherd had gone to the cathedral of Uglich and prayed there, and lo, he was cured of his blindness. Boris hears this tale with growing horror. At its end he cries for air and falls fainting into a chair. He dismisses the boyars and calls for his son, Feodor. The boyars and Boris himself now know that he is dying, and he sings a last and deeply touching farewell to little Feodor. He advises him how to be a good ruler and begs him to care for his sister, Xenia. Then he prays heaven to protect the boy and to guide him.

Off-stage the funeral bell begins to toll, and a sad chorus is heard. Presently a procession of boyars and monks files in, stunned into silence. The once mighty Boris rises to his full height. "I am still your Czar!" he cries, and then, more feebly, "God forgive me. There—there is your Czar." A last spasm overtakes him as he still points to little Feodor. And as he whispers, "Forgive me!" he falls back, dead, in his chair—or, as some of the more athletic bassos act it, rolling on the floor.

Postscript for the historically curious: The regency and reign of Boris were, historically, a very mixed blessing for Russia. Among his "reforms" was a law that prevented peasants from moving off their land, thus virtually creating serfdom in Russia. It was this law that inspired many peasants to join the standard of Dmitri, as is shown in the forest of Kromy scene.

The more experienced part of Dmitri's army included Poles, Cossacks, Hessians, and Russian exiles. They were virtually at the gates of Moscow when Boris died unexpectedly April 13, 1605. Dmitri, a well-educated, able man, had himself crowned Czar, executed the widow and son of Boris, bettered the lot of the peasants, formed a number of Western alliances, and saved the life, on one occasion, of the rather oily character Prince Shuiski of the opera. He was also received into the Roman Catholic Church by Rangoni.

On May 8, 1606, less than a year after his coronation, Dmitri married Marina, and nine days later, in a plot hatched by Shuiski, was assassinated. Thereupon Shuiski became Czar.

Grigori was not the only "false Dmitri." A second one was successful enough to raise an army of over 100,000, unseat Shuiski, and marry Marina, the widow of the first false Dmitri. He was murdered by a man whom he had ordered flogged. That was in 1610.

Two years later there was still another false Dmitri. This one succeeded in persuading the Cossacks to acknowledge him as Czar but reached Moscow only as a prisoner. There he was executed.

CAPRICCIO

Opera in one act by Richard Strauss with libretto in German by Clemens Krauss with the assistance of the composer

THE COUNTESS	Soprano
THE COUNT, *her brother*	Baritone
OLIVIER, *a poet*	Tenor
FLAMAND, *a musician*	Tenor
CLAIRON, *an actress*	Contralto
LA ROCHE, *director of a theater*	Bass
MONSIEUR TAUPE, *a tenor*	Tenor

Time: about 1775
Place: near Paris
First performance at Munich, October 28, 1942

In an opera, which is more important, the words or the music? Mozart plumped for the music, Gluck for the words. It is a favorite subject of discussion among composers and aestheticians, and Richard Strauss discussed it at length with his conductor, Clemens Krauss, in 1933 during the rehearsals for *Arabella*. Six years and several operas later, Strauss wrote to Krauss suggesting that they collaborate on the libretto of an opera on the subject. It was to be the last opera that Strauss completed.

Only one act, the work still takes almost two and a half hours to perform, and most of it is given over to the discussion of this very interesting but not very dramatic question of aesthetics. The discussion takes place in the home of a charming French Countess named Madeleine, who lives near Paris in the latter half of the eighteenth century. (This was about the time when Gluck was trying to get operas to make more sense by insisting that the words were more important than the music.) Among the guests of the Countess are Olivier, a poet; Flamand, a composer; Clairon, an actress; La Roche, a theatrical director; Taupe, a tenor; and the Countess's brother. The discussion is held in a civilized fashion; and before the guests leave for Paris, they agree that Olivier and Flamand shall write an opera on the subject in which each of those present will portray himself.

Olivier and Flamand are associated in another way, too: each is in love with the Countess (who admires both of them), and Olivier has written a sonnet to her which Flamand has set to music. And Madeleine has promised to decide, by eleven the next morning, which of the two she will marry.

The last scene finds Madeleine alone in her boudoir. (Strauss loved to write long scenes for sopranos alone—especially alone in their boudoirs.) One immediately thinks of the famous mirror monologue in Act I of *Der Rosenkavalier*. Well, there is a mirror in this one, too; and the general atmosphere of sweet and melancholy sentiment is not dissimilar.

"Tomorrow at eleven!" begins the soliloquy. Madeleine simply cannot make up her mind. Which art is more potent? Poetry or music? She goes to her harp and sings over the sonnet written to her—a fine, old-fashioned love sonnet. She feels herself a prisoner—a prisoner of the web of two arts. Choose one and not the other? Impossible! So she turns to her mirror to ask counsel. But the mirror has no answer either. And the opera ends without our finding out just who will be the lucky one tomorrow at eleven.

If you ask me—I think it will be the musician. His music seems to me to be so much more persuasive than that German sonnet! But then, that's only one man's opinion.

CARMEN

Opera in four acts by Georges Bizet with libretto by Henri Meilhac and Ludovic Halévy
based on the novel by Prosper Mérimée

CARMEN, *a gypsy*	*Soprano, Mezzo-soprano, or Contralto*
DON JOSÉ, *a corporal*	*Tenor*
ESCAMILLO, *the toreador*	*Baritone*
MICAELA, *a peasant*	*Soprano*
EL DANCAIRO ⎫ *smugglers*	*Baritone*
EL REMENDADO ⎭	*Tenor*
ZUNIGA, *José's captain*	*Bass*
MORALES, *an officer*	*Bass or Baritone*
FRASQUITA ⎫ *gypsies*	*Soprano*
MERCÉDÈS ⎭	*Soprano or Mezzo-soprano*

Time: about 1820
Place: Seville and thereabout
First performance at Paris, March 3, 1875

Carmen is, I believe, the most widely popular of all
operas. There is a legend that disappointment over the failure
of its premiere caused Bizet's death three months later. But
the fact is that the opera was more popularly received than
any music Bizet had composed before (it scored thirty-seven
performances at the Opéra Comique in its first season and
has been performed there more than three thousand times
since), and Bizet died, at thirty-seven, of a physical disease—
probably an embolism. It is now part of the repertory of every
opera company in every language—even the Japanese—and its
popularity is not confined to the opera stage. It has been made

into restaurant music, virtuoso piano transcriptions, and several movies; and the latest and most successful of the movie versions, *Carmen Jones,* is based on a Negro operetta version that was a huge Broadway hit.

It is not hard to see why it is popular. It has so many good tunes! It is so dramatic! It is so bright and clear! And all these characteristics can be heard in the prelude. It starts bright and clear—like a sunny day in Spain; it continues with the famous tune of the Toreador Song; and it becomes suddenly dramatic with the Fate theme—the one that suggests Carmen and her violent death.

ACT I

The prelude ends on a dramatic, dissonant chord, and the curtain rises on a midday scene in a public square in the city of Seville, 130-odd years ago. Soldiers, at rest, are commenting on the scene, which is just outside a cigarette factory. A country girl, Micaela, comes in search of her boy friend, the corporal Don José; and when she finds he isn't there, she gracefully resists the blandishments of his comrades-in-arms and retires. Now there is a change of the guard, during which a group of urchins imitates the soldiers. The new guard includes Don José and his commanding officer, Captain Zuniga, who briefly discuss the attractions of the factory girls. Apparently these young ladies have a fascinating reputation; for a group of young men (today we would call them drugstore cowboys) gathers outside the factory for the midday recess. The girls come out, smoking cigarettes—a pretty bold thing to do in the twenties of the last century! But the men are waiting primarily for the most attractive of all the girls—Carmen.

Heralded by a quick little version of her Fate theme, she makes her entrance, flirts with the boys, and then sings her famous *Habanera*. It is a frank warning that to love Carmen is a dangerous business. Don José (a bit of a prig, I always thought) pays her no attention—and so, at the end of her song, she wantonly throws a flower at him. Everyone laughs at his embarrassment as the girls return to work.

Micaela returns to give Don José greetings from his mother, which is the occasion for a very sweet duet. It is barely over before a terrific din breaks out among the factory girls and they come swarming from the factory. Captain Zuniga, trying to restore order, discovers that Carmen has caused the trouble by attacking one of the other girls. He orders Don José to arrest the culprit and leaves her in his charge while he makes up his mind, in the guardhouse, what should be done with her. Left alone with José, Carmen completes her conquest of the young soldier by singing the seductive *Seguidilla*. In it she promises to sing and dance for him—and to love him—at a certain disreputable inn run by her friend Lillas Pastia. And so it happens that when Zuniga comes out to order Carmen to prison, she is able to push Don José aside and make good her escape. As for the young corporal, he is placed under arrest.

ACT II

Each of *Carmen's* four acts is prefaced by a prelude or entr'acte of its own. The one that introduces Act II is based on a little soldier's song which, later in the act, is sung by Don José. When the curtain goes up, there is a lively party going on at the inn of Lillas Pastia as Carmen leads the merriment in a wild and swirling song known as the *Chanson Bohème*. Don José's old commanding officer, Captain Zuniga, is prominent among the guests, trying to ingratiate himself with Carmen. He does not have much luck, for, on the whole, she prefers less respectable company. However, she is delighted to hear that Don José has now served his sixty-day sentence for helping her escape.

Suddenly a popular athlete appears on the scene. He is Escamillo, the toreador; and, of course, he sings his *Toreador Song*, with everyone joining in the chorus. Like Zuniga, he is smitten with Carmen's bright eyes; and she, for her part, plays up to his opening gambits.

But it is late, and time for closing. Soon no one is left but Carmen and a quartet of gypsy smugglers: two girls named Frasquita and Mercédès, and a couple of ruffians called El

Dancairo and El Remendado. They join in a delightful patter
quintet, which celebrates the usefulness of girls in carrying out
smuggling raids—for smuggling is their business. But off-stage
sounds the voice of Don José singing the soldier's song, *Halte
là!*

Carmen shoos the others out and warmly welcomes Don
José back from jail. As she had promised, she begins to sing
and dance for him. In the midst of her dance the trumpet
sounds retreat in the distance, calling Don José to his duty.
He begins to depart, only to arouse Carmen's angry contempt. "Is this a way to treat a girl?" she cries. "You canary!"
Stung by her taunts, he brings out the flower she had flung
him, and, in the very moving *Flower Song*, tells her how it
inspired him throughout his days in prison. Impressed and
mollified, Carmen again begins to woo him. José's conscience,
however, is getting the better of him, when Zuniga saves the
day for romance by coming in unbidden and ordering Don
José to the barracks. This is too much for the youngster. He
draws his sword and is about to attack his superior officer
when the gypsies rush in and politely disarm the Captain.
Now José doesn't have much choice: he is practically forced
to give up his military career and join the smuggling gypsies
—just as Carmen had planned. And the act ends with a stirring chorus in praise of the free life. It is sung enthusiastically
by everyone but Zuniga.

ACT III

The flute solo that begins the entr'acte before Act III
sounds as if it were going to be "The Minstrel Boy," but it
turns into an even better tune—better for opera, anyway. The
act opens with a chorus of smugglers—the gang that Don José
has been forced to join. They are in a lonely spot in the mountains on professional nefarious business, and Carmen, who is
already growing tired of Don José, tells him he might be better off with his mother. A lighter note is introduced after their
quarrel, when Frasquita and Mercédès start telling their fortunes with cards. I must say that they deal themselves very

attractive fortunes: one is to find a passionate lover, the other a rich oldster intent on marriage. But Carmen joins in the pastime on a much more somber note, for she turns up the ace of spades, the card of death. "It is useless to try to escape one's fate," she mutters in her famous *Card* aria. But now the smugglers are called to duty—that is, to try to smuggle their goods over the border. (Their chorus at this point has always struck me as being remarkably noisy for criminals bent on so secretive a job.)

When they are gone, the village girl Micaela comes in search of Don José. She is very much frightened, and she asks the protection of the Lord in a touching aria (*Je dis que rien ne m'épouvante*). Suddenly José, who has been left on guard, fires a shot, and Micaela is frightened away. However, it is not Micaela he has aimed at, but Escamillo, who is there in search of Carmen. When José discovers what Escamillo is after, the two men start a fight with knives. José is getting the better of it, when Carmen gets back just in time to save the toreador. Gallantly thanking Carmen, he invites everyone to his next performance in Seville. As he starts down the mountainside, Micaela is found. She delivers her message: José's mother is dying and wishes to see him once more. Carmen contemptuously tells him he had better go. But before he goes, he turns furiously on her and warns her that they shall meet again— that only death can part them. Off-stage, the toreador's song is heard, and Carmen tries to rush to him. But José, turning back once more, hurls her violently to the ground—and finally leaves, as the orchestra quietly and ominously repeats the toreador's melody.

ACT IV

The last act is introduced by some of the most brilliant and pulse-beating music in the whole score. Everyone is in his best clothes; everyone is getting ready to watch the great Escamillo perform in the arena at Seville. A large and impressive parade of dignitaries enters the theater—all of it duly described by the chorus. Finally, in comes the toreador himself, and on his arm is Carmen, dressed in such finery as only a successful bullfighter could afford. They sing a brief and rather banal love duet, and then Escamillo disappears into the theater, everyone except Carmen following him. She is warned by her friends, Frasquita and Mercédès, that Don José has been lurking about. Defiantly she remains outside alone, saying she does not fear him.

Then Don José comes on, tattered and ragged, a pitiful contrast to Carmen in her holiday best. Pitifully he pleads to be taken back, but she shows him only contempt. The more pressingly he pleads, the more contempt she shows; and finally she throws the ring he had given her directly in his face. Off-stage the chorus is cheering the toreador, José's successful rival. Maddened by this and by Carmen's behavior, he threatens her with his knife. Desperately she attempts to rush past him into the theater; but just as the crowd shouts that Escamillo is victorious, he plunges the knife into his lost beloved. The crowd pours out, while Don José, brokenly cries: "You can arrest me . . . Oh, my Carmen!"

CAVALLERIA RUSTICANA

(*Rustic Chivalry*)

Opera in one act by Pietro Mascagni with libretto by Guido Menasci and Giovanni Targioni-Tozzetti based on a play by Giovanni Verga which is in turn based on his own prose tale of the same title

SANTUZZA, *a village girl*	*Soprano*
TURIDDU, *a young soldier*	*Tenor*
MAMMA LUCIA, *his mother*	*Contralto*
ALFIO, *the village teamster*	*Baritone*
LOLA, *his wife*	*Mezzo-soprano*

Time: an Easter Day in the late 19th century
Place: a village in Sicily
First performance at Rome, May 17, 1890

The title *Cavalleria rusticana* is usually translated as *Rustic Chivalry*. This is half ironic, as the behavior of most of the characters is anything but chivalrous. In fact, as Giovanni Verga originally wrote the story, it is downright barbarous—far more violent than in Mascagni's opera.

It is this quality—stark, naked passion, expressed in unabashed violence—that may partly account for the immediate success of the work. It is essentially, of course, a literary quality. Verga's novelette is regarded as a minor literary classic, and Duse and other actresses used to have great success with the tale given as a spoken drama. It was one of the first and most prominent successes, in both literature and music, of the school of *verismo*—"the theory that in art and literature the ugly and vulgar have their place on the grounds of truth and aesthetic value," to quote Webster.

The little work was the first of three winners in a prize contest held by the publisher Sonzogno, and it catapulted its completely unknown composer, then aged twenty-seven, into overnight fame. It was not a local fame. Even in New York there was a bitter fight for its premiere performance. Oscar Hammerstein, years before he built his great Manhattan Opera House, paid $3000 for the rights only to be anticipated by a rival manager named Aronson, who gave a so-called "public rehearsal" of the work on the afternoon of October 1, 1891. Hammerstein's performance took place the same evening. That was less than eighteen months after its Roman premiere. But before that all Italy had heard it, not to mention Stockholm, Madrid, Budapest, Hamburg, Prague, Buenos Aires, Moscow, Vienna, Bucharest, Philadelphia, Rio de Janeiro, Copenhagen, and Chicago, in the order named.

For well over half a century Mascagni lived on the fame and royalties won by this little masterpiece. He never composed another opera remotely approaching the success of *Cavalleria,* but he died in 1945 full of fame and honors.

PRELUDE

The story takes place in a Sicilian village at the end of the last century. The time is Easter Sunday, and the prelude begins with quiet music, like a prayer. Soon it becomes more dramatic, and in the middle of it is heard the voice of the leading tenor, off-stage, singing a love serenade—the *Siciliana.* He is the recently returned soldier Turiddu, and he is serenading his mistress, Lola.

THE OPERA

After the prelude, the orchestra and chorus set the scene for us by describing a fine Easter Sunday morning on the principal square of a Sicilian village. Presently the village girl, Santuzza, asks old Mamma Lucia about her son Turiddu.

Santuzza is badly worried because she is engaged to Turiddu, and some of his recent behavior has not been very fitting. The two women, however, are interrupted by the entrance of Alfio, a bluff, hearty, and popular young teamster, who sings a jolly song about his jolly life, as he cracks his whip (*Il cavallo scalpita*). He does not yet know that Turiddu has been making love to his pretty wife, Lola. A brief exchange with Mamma Lucia, in which he mentions that he had seen her son that morning near his house, makes Santuzza even more suspicious.

But now some organ music issues from the church. Off-stage, the choir sings. The villagers all kneel, and with Santuzza contributing a fine solo, they join in a beautiful prayer, the *Regina coeli*. A religious procession enters the church and the villagers follow, but Santuzza keeps old Lucia outside to tell her story. In the aria *Voi lo sapete* she tells how Turiddu, before he went to the Army, promised to marry her, how he returned and deserted her, and how he is now paying court to Lola. Lucia is shocked but promises no help. Therefore, when Turiddu himself comes in, Santuzza appeals to him directly. He offers unconvincing excuses, and he is growing very angry, when they are interrupted by the subject of the quarrel. Lola, very prettily dressed, comes in, on her way to church, singing a ditty about love; and when she has gone, the quarrel breaks out again with renewed violence. Finally, Turiddu will stand no more of it. He hurls Santuzza to the ground and storms into the church as she cries a curse after him.

The last one to come to church is Alfio. Santuzza stops him, too, and almost before she knows it, has told him of the goings-on between Lola and Turiddu. Santuzza's earnestness leaves no doubt in his mind that she is telling the truth. He runs off, swearing a terrible vengeance, and Santuzza, filled with remorse, follows him.

With the stage empty, the orchestra plays the lovely, devotional *Intermezzo*. It is an ironically peaceful comment on the murderous passions that have been aroused.

Now church is over, and the villagers pour happily out. Turiddu invites everyone to a drink and sings his gay *Brindisi*, or *Drinking Song*. But Alfio, in a menacing mood, comes on the scene and angrily refuses Turiddu's offer of a drink. The two men confront each other, a challenge is exchanged, and Alfio imperturbably answers Turiddu's violent threats by saying he will meet him in the orchard. It is now Turiddu's turn to be filled with remorse. He calls his mother, bids her take care of Santuzza, takes a tearful farewell, and runs off. The terror-stricken Santuzza rushes in with some frightened neighbors, and a moment later a woman screams that Turiddu has been murdered. Alfio has won his duel.

LA CENERENTOLA

(Cinderella)

Opera in two acts by Gioacchino Rossini with libretto in Italian by Jacopo Ferretti, based on Charles Guillaume Etienne's three-act French libretto *Cendrillon* for operas by Niccolò Isouard and Daniel Steibelt

DON RAMIRO, *Prince of Salerno*	*Tenor*
DANDINI, *his valet*	*Baritone or Bass*
ALIDORO, *professional philosopher serving the Prince*	*Bass*
DON MAGNIFICO, *Baron of Monte Fiascone*	*Bass*
CLORINDA ⎱ *his daughters*	*Soprano*
THISBE ⎰	*Mezzo-soprano*
CINDERELLA (*or* LA CENERENTOLA, *whose real name is Angelina*), *Don Magnifico's stepdaughter*	*Contralto*

Time: unspecified, but the manners and customs are those of the 18th century
Place: Salerno
First performance at Rome, January 25, 1817

Listen, my children (if there are any children listening to me), and you shall hear—the story of *Cinderella*. It is not the same story you have heard again and again. It is not quite the one told of old by Perrault, by the French Mother Goose—or even by our own Walt Disney. There are no glass slippers in our tale; there is no kind fairy godmother, and there is no unkind stepmother. But there *is* a handsome prince; there *are* two silly old stepsisters; and there *is*, of course, pretty Cinderella herself.

Perhaps if the opera had been written a hundred years earlier, it might have had a pumpkin changing into a coach, magically appearing and disappearing finery, and all the other delightful tricks of the fairy tale. At that time Italian opera houses had all the machinery to represent magic. But when Rossini started to write the music on Christmas Day of 1817, the Valle Theater of Rome was much more modestly equipped, and its manager concocted a simpler tale for the maestro. He was also in a great hurry to have the opera, and so the composer did as he often did—borrow a few numbers from other operas he had already composed. The really delightful overture, for instance, he took from *La Gazzetta,* which he had composed for Naples only a few months earlier. He worked so fast—and so did the cast—that the first performance took place a month later. Perhaps for this reason it failed at first. But it soon became a huge success and for many years ranked in popularity, among Rossini's works, next to *The Barber* and *William Tell.* But in the past fifty years or so it has seldom been given. I am not sure why—maybe because it takes singers who can sing even faster and more accurately than are required in *The Barber,* especially a coloratura contralto for the role of Cinderella. There aren't many of those around.

ACT I

Scene 1 Any good contralto, however, could sing the quaint little ditty (*Una volta c'era un re*—"Once upon a time there was a king") with which she opens the opera as she cooks coffee for her two spoiled stepsisters, Clorinda and Thisbe. It is, appropriately enough, about a king who chose a poor little good girl for his bride instead of any of the high and mighty ones he might have had. Soon they have a visitor. He is Alidoro, the Prince's guide, philosopher, and friend, come in disguise as a beggar. When Cinderella treats him kindly and the sisters the opposite, he knows at least one piece of advice he can give his master.

Instead of a stepmother, as in the familiar story, Rossini supplies Cinderella with a stepfather. He is a pompous old fool; and though he is already rich, he would like to be still richer. Don Magnifico is his name; and immediately on his entrance he tells his daughters of a silly dream he had. He dreamed he was an ass, and a very wealthy ass, too. The aria (*Miei rampolli femminini*—"My feminine offspring") is much in the style of the *Largo al factotum* from *The Barber of Seville.*

When everyone finally leaves Cinderella alone to do the cleaning up, in comes the Prince. He is in disguise, and he is looking for a bride who will love him only for himself, not because he is a prince. Of course, he at once observes the attractive Cinderella working like a servant around the house. She, for her part, is so much startled at seeing a handsome young man that she lets a tray of dishes drop. At once they fall in love! Neither tells the other, of course, for that would end the story right there. Instead, they sing a charming duet together. It is interrupted at the end, for Cinderella's two unpleasant stepsisters call to her to serve them. But Prince Ramiro's heart has been captured—he does not know the girl's real name.

And when Cinderella has gone off to serve her sisters, enter still one other man in disguise. This is Dandini, the Prince's valet, who has changed clothes with his master. As he tries to pose as a prince (by misquoting Latin texts), Cinderella begs her stepfather to be allowed to go to the ball every girl is invited to. Naturally, her family unite in refusing the permission; but the act closes with Alidoro returning to promise our heroine help—just as the fairy godmother does in the fairy tale. All this gives Rossini a chance to write a wonderful concerted number to close the scene, complete with members of the Prince's court who come in for no better dramatic reason than to swell out the sound and make a mighty effective finale.

Scene 2 takes place in the palace, where everyone is urging Dandini (still disguised as the Prince) to choose his bride. And who should come in but Clorinda and Thisbe, Cinderella's very homely stepsisters? Both of them try to find favor with Dandini, for, of course, they think he is the Prince. He

flees from them to another room, where he reports to his
master. In a very quick and funny duet he tells him what he
thinks of these two girls. They are *just terrible*, he says. But
the relentless girls come running after Dandini, and, to get
rid of them, he explains that he can marry only one. The other
he says, must marry his valet. That, of course, they cannot
think of. The two men are laughing at the girls, when a mysterious lady is announced by Alidoro. The wise old philosopher has dressed up Cinderella beautifully and brought her
to the palace. No one recognizes her, because she is masked;
but everyone sees how beautiful she is, and all the court
knows at once that this is the girl the Prince ought to marry.
As they all sing about how they feel, the act closes with a
wonderful chorus.

ACT II

Scene 1   Only the two fatuous sisters do not share the
sentiments of the final chorus in the first act. They think the
stranger looks so much like Cinderella that the Prince could
not possibly be in love with her. Rather, each thinks she herself is going to win the marital sweepstakes—and, accordingly,
they quarrel. Meanwhile, Dandini himself has fallen in love
with Cinderella. Still disguised as the Prince, he proposes to
her; but she tells him she has fallen in love with his valet. The
Prince overhears this admission and (still disguised, of course,
as Dandini) comes forward to propose marriage. She admits
that she loves him, as she said; but first he must find out who
she is. She gives him a bracelet that matches one she is wearing, as a clue—a sort of counterpart to the slipper business in
the familiar story. As for Don Magnifico, he is certain that
one of his daughters, either Clorinda or Thisbe, will marry the
Prince. The silly old fellow is beside himself with happiness.
He imagines how powerful he will be, how everyone will be
begging favors of him, and how he will kick them all out. All
this he tells us in the aria *Sia qualunque delle figlie*—"Which-
ever of my daughters." But the old fool is in for a quick disappointment. He, like everyone else, thought that Dandini,

the valet, was really the Prince, just because he was wearing princely clothes. Now Dandini comes in and tells the old baron who he really is. Don Magnifico is outraged—angry—hurt. But Dandini, having given up Cinderella, is only amused.

Scene 2 takes us back to the Don's house. Cinderella repeats her little ballad about the king who chose a wife for her goodness only. For she still does not know that it is the Prince, disguised as his own servant, who has fallen in love with her. A storm rages outside. (Rossini liked to write storm music, and this is an excellent example.) During it the Prince and Dandini, now each in his own costume, seek shelter; and Cinderella, trying to hide her face, lets the Prince see the bracelet on her arm. He steps forward, and at last Cinderella learns that the man she loves is not a servant at all, but really Prince Ramiro. Ramiro takes her by the hand and says that she, and only she, shall be his bride. Her relatives—Don Magnifico, Clorinda, and Thisbe—are all shocked and horrified, and they will not speak to her. But finally Don Magnifico decides to ask Ramiro for forgiveness. The Prince wants to have nothing to do with him, but the good, kind Cinderella, in the brilliant rondo *Nacqui all'affanno*—"Born to sorrow" pleads for the relatives who had treated her so shabbily. The Prince gives in to his radiant bride, and the opera ends with everyone rejoicing—and everyone, I presume, living happily ever after.

THE CONSUL

Opera in three acts by Gian-Carlo Menotti with
libretto in English by the composer

JOHN SOREL	Baritone
MAGDA SOREL, *his wife*	Soprano
HIS MOTHER	Contralto
SECRET-POLICE AGENT	Bass
THE SECRETARY	Mezzo-soprano
MR. KOFNER	Bass-baritone
THE FOREIGN WOMAN	Soprano
ANNA GOMEZ	Soprano
VERA BORONEL	Contralto
NIKA MAGADOFF, *a magician*	Tenor
ASSAN, *friend of John Sorel's*	Baritone
VOICE ON THE RECORD	Soprano

applicants in the Consul's office (bracketing THE FOREIGN WOMAN, ANNA GOMEZ, VERA BORONEL, NIKA MAGADOFF)

Time: after World War II
Place: somewhere in Europe
First performance at Philadelphia, March 1, 1950

Gian-Carlo Menotti's first full-length opera was greeted,
during its first year, with a three-gun salute by prize-giving
groups. It received the Pulitzer Prize for 1950 as the most
distinguished musical composition of the year, the New York
Drama Critics Circle citation as the best musical play of the
season, and the Donaldson Award as the best musical play of
1950. It enjoyed a good run on Broadway, and during 1951
it was produced in London, Hamburg, Zurich, Milan, and
Vienna.

How long it may survive on the stage is a difficult question.
It struck many hearers like a blow between the eyes, for it

deals with a peculiarly moving problem that occupied a great deal of space in the newspapers, magazines, and editorial comments of the early 1950's. And though its problem is by no means finally settled as these words are written in the year 1956, the handling of it already suffers from changes in the world picture which make the libretto read a little like last year's newspapers. Perhaps in another five years or more the sin of topicality may be removed and the libretto read like history. Let us devoutly hope so. And at such a time the merits of the score and the personal tragedy of Magda, John, and their family may stand out all the more sharply poignant.

ACT I

Scene 1 John Sorel does some unidentified work for some unidentified underground group in some unidentified country of Europe. The curtain rises on an empty room in his poor home early one morning as a neighboring phonograph plays a French jazz song, *"Tu reviendras"* ("You Will Return"). John staggers into the room; Magda runs in to bandage the leg where he has been shot; and he explains to her and his mother that the police had nicked him while he was escaping from a meeting that had been broken up. Through the window Magda sees police coming, and John just manages to get out of the window and climb up to a ledge before they enter.

The mother sings a bitter lullaby to the child in the cradle as the Police Agent begins to ask questions. The interrogation is all the more ominous because it is carried on with decent politeness, though with scarcely veiled threats. Magda, however, succeeds in giving them no information worth having, and when they have left, John briefly returns. He knows now that he must get away; but when there is a message from him, the window will be broken, he says, and they must send for the glass cutter, Assan. The scene closes with a desolate farewell.

Scene 2 In the antechamber at an unidentified consulate various pathetic figures are waiting, hoping to get visas to leave the country. Each of them runs up against the pitiless red tape represented by a businesslike secretary. One must get photographs of a different size; one must fill in forms and wait two months (though that may be too late); and Magda is not allowed to see the Consul. Nobody may see him. (In fact, nobody does—not even the audience, who are vouchsafed just a shadow of him at the end of the second act.) As Magda fills out blanks, Magadoff, the conjuror, does a few simple tricks to try to impress the secretary. That doesn't help either, and the scene ends with a quintet in which all the applicants express their sense of frustration.

ACT II

Scene 1 A month later, in that dreary room of Magda's, the same song, *Tu reviendras*, sounds through the window. The mother and Magda discuss the chances of securing a visa; and when Magda has left, the mother tries to cheer the ominously quiet child with another lullaby. Magda returns weary; she falls asleep in a chair; and she has a frightful dream in which John introduces the Secretary as his sister, and a dead child is somehow mixed up in it.

Suddenly a stone hurtles through the window, and Magda immediately telephones for Assan. Once more the Police Agent comes for an interview: if only Magda will give him the names of some of John's friends, she may be able to join him. Magda becomes hysterical and threatens to kill the Police Agent if he comes back again.

Before the Agent has left, Assan is in the room repairing the window. He informs Magda that John is waiting for her, hiding in the mountains, and that he refuses to leave the country till he knows that she has a visa and can join him. They agree that John had better be told that the visa has been secured, even though it has not, so that he will leave and save his own life at least.

It is only after Assan has left that Magda sees her child has died in its grandmother's arms. She is too much stunned to cry as yet, but the mother weeps softly for John.

Scene 2 A few days later we are again in the waiting room of the consulate. Again the Secretary is frustrating everyone with her red tape. Again Magadoff tries his conjuring tricks; only, this time he hypnotizes them all so that they engage in a blissful dance. The Secretary makes him bring them out of it, and then Magda demands, once more, to see the Consul. Once again she is refused, whereupon she has her great scene, a tragic satire on official forms: Name? My name is woman . . . Color of eyes? The color of tears . . . Occupation? Waiting . . . and so forth. Even the Secretary is moved. With a petulant "You're being very unreasonable, Mrs. Sorel," she promises to see what can be done and a moment later reports that the Consul will see her. But just then his shadow is seen on the glazed glass door panel, shaking hands with another man. And when this other man emerges, he turns out to be the Police Agent. Magda faints at the sight.

ACT III

Scene 1   Once more at the waiting room, Magda is hoping to see the Consul even though the Secretary tells her that the office will close in ten minutes. One of the other applicants comes in, and this time there is good news for her: her application has been approved. As she and the Secretary sing a happy duet, Assan comes in with bad news for Magda. John has heard that his baby and his mother are now dead, and he is planning to return over the frontier to get his wife. Hurriedly she writes a note for Assan to take to him. She does not say what is in it, though we can deduce its contents from the happenings in the final scene.

When the Secretary is finally alone and preparing to leave, she has a little aria to show that underneath her cold, businesslike exterior she is really moved by the plight of the unfortunates she must deal with. Suddenly John rushes in, looking for Magda. He is followed almost at once by the police; his gun is knocked out of his hand; and the Secretary is politely told that he will come along quietly. The moment they leave she begins to dial the telephone.

Scene 2   The Secretary's call is sounding in Magda's home,

but it stops before she comes in. Drearily she turns on the gas
stove, pulls up a chair to it, covers her head with a shawl, and
leans over. The walls dissolve and show all the people in the
consulate, who, with John and his mother (in a wedding
dress), perform a strange ballet. Magda tries to talk to them,
but they do not answer. Slowly they disappear, and we hear
Magda's deep breathing as she inhales the gas. The telephone
begins its ringing once more, and Magda instinctively begins
to reach for it. It is too late. She falls over in the chair. The
ringing continues.

LE COQ D'OR

(Zolotoy Pyetushok—The Golden Cockerel)

Opera in three acts by Nikolai Andreevich
Rimsky-Korsakoff with libretto in Russian by
Vladimir Ivanovich Byelsky, based on a fairy
tale by Alexandre Sergevich Pushkin, which he,
in turn, had heard from his nurse

KING DODON	*Bass*
PRINCE GUIDON ⎫ *his sons*	*Tenor*
PRINCE AFRON ⎭	*Baritone*
GENERAL POLKAN	*Bass*
AMELFA, *the royal housekeeper*	*Contralto*
THE ASTROLOGER	*Tenor*
THE QUEEN OF SHEMAKHA	*Soprano*
THE GOLDEN COCKEREL	*Soprano*

Time: unspecified
Place: a mythical kingdom
First performance at Moscow, October 7, 1909

Two days before he died, in 1908, Rimsky-Korsakoff
wrote to his publisher, B. P. Jürgenson, as follows: "As regards
Le coq d'or, there is trouble ahead. The Governor-General of
Moscow is opposed to the production of this opera and has
informed the censor about it. I think that they will be against
it in St. Petersburg for the same reason."

The composer was right. Even though Jürgenson had already published part of the score without molestation, it was
sixteen months before the opera finally reached the stage, and
then only after certain changes had been made. The composer,
therefore, never saw it.

Le coq d'or

It has sometimes been thought that objections were raised because a phenomenally silly king has a leading part, and the Czar's employees were still nervous on account of the 1905 revolutionary crisis. Perhaps a better guess is that it was a way of hobbling Rimsky himself, who had been effectively active at the time in wresting some of the control of the St. Petersburg Conservatory away from the bureaucrats and the police. For the tale, coming from the pen of the nationally honored poet Pushkin, could scarcely have been taken exception to. Nor, for that matter, is there anything—revolutionary or otherwise—that can be read into the engaging but utterly obscure symbolism of the libretto.

Ideally, the opera should be performed by a cast that can move bodies and limbs with the same grace and virtuosity as it can sing. Diaghilev, in Paris, put on a production with the singers sitting still, in boxes by the side of the stage, while a ballet troupe mimed the action. The idea was exported, with success, to both England and the United States. More recently it has been given generally with a single cast; and when that cast included such enticing figures as those of Lily Pons and Ezio Pinza, it was certainly worth going to see as well as to hear.

PROLOGUE

The most famous tune from the opera is, of course, the *Hymn to the Sun*, which the Queen of Shemakha sings in Act II. The introduction to the hymn, following immediately upon a muted trumpet call, is almost the first music heard. Then, before the curtain, comes the Astrologer. In a high, thin voice, almost like the xylophone that accompanies him, he tells the audience that he will conjure up a fairy tale with an edifying moral.

ACT I

King Dodon sits on his throne in the magnificent council room of some mythical kingdom in fairy-tale land. He is getting old, he says; the army isn't much good (the guards, as a matter of fact, can be seen sleeping at their posts); and he doesn't like making war. What can he do about all those enemies who are making nuisances of themselves? Just keep everyone at home and not think about it, says his elder son, Guidon. Disband the army, says the younger son, Afron, and have them re-form behind the enemy for an attack. Old General Polkan points out that both these plans are pretty idiotic, but he has nothing more practicable to offer.

The Astrologer happens by conveniently at this moment, and he offers the only solution that could be regarded as sensible in a fairy tale. He gives the King a golden cockerel which will be quiet when there is no danger but will warn everyone by crowing when there is. The delighted Dodon offers anything he wants in exchange for the cockerel, and the Astrologer says he will decide later on what that may be. Thus everyone can go to sleep again for the time being; and the King retires, attended by his housekeeper Amelfa, to sweet dreams graphically described in the orchestra.

The first warning from the cockerel causes the King to be awakened and order off his sons and an army to meet the enemy and come home as soon as possible. Once more everyone else goes to sleep. The cockerel's second summons, however, is more emphatic. General Polkan advises the King that this time he must be off to the wars himself. Grumbling about the inconvenience and the deplorable state of his armor, Dodon gets ready for battle and is cheered off to the wars by his court.

ACT II

Early in the morning, in a narrow mountain pass, it is evident that Dodon's forces have met disaster. There lie the bodies of many soldiers, including his two sons; and when he comes upon them, accompanied by General Polkan, he utters a sad and deeply Slavic lamentation.

As the mists on the scene begin to disperse, a tent comes

into view, frightening the King. He orders up some ineffective artillery, but before the soldiers can make the cannon go off, there emerges from the tent a ravishingly beautiful young woman. This is the Queen of Shemakha, and her rendition of the *Hymn to the Sun* rivets the favorable attention of Dodon, Polkan, and the entire surviving army. At its close she identifies herself, saying that she has come to conquer Dodon's kingdom, not by force, but by her beauty. Dodon orders away the soldiery (who *exeunt,* bearing bodies); the Queen's slaves bring out some cushions for her visitors; and a very unusual exercise in international diplomacy ensues.

Polkan represents his country in the initial questioning period, but his gambits are so undiplomatic and personal that the Queen asks Dodon to dismiss him. (Polkan suggests, for example, that a mysterious voice heard by the Queen during the night was a man under her bed.) With the General in forced retirement behind the tent, whence he occasionally takes a surreptitious peek, the Queen goes to work in earnest on the foolish old King. She sidles up to him; she sings him a frankly voluptuous song about her own beauties when she is completely unclothed; she invites him into her tent (an invitation he does not feel up to accepting); and she asks him to entertain her with a song. When Dodon has obliged with a foolish little ditty, she goes on to describe her own homeland, and to say how much she needs a masterful man in her life.

Overcome by her beauty and her not very subtle suggestions, Dodon is enticed into making a complete fool of himself by dancing for her, and his conquest is completed when she orders out her slave girls to do a slow, suggestive dance for him in return. He offers her his hand, his heart, his kingdom, and the head of the offending General Polkan. With complete cynicism the Queen accepts. Her golden chariot is ordered out, and the two start out on a triumphal march home while her slaves sing a satirical chorus in praise of the king who walks like a camel and has the face of an ape.

ACT III

At home the weather is bad, and the crowd gathered outside King Dodon's palace considers this ominous. Amelfa, however, assures them that Dodon has won a great victory (albeit he has lost his two sons), he has saved a beautiful princess from a dragon, and he is bringing her home to reign by his side.

A great procession arrives, at its close the golden chariot carrying the King and Queen. Everyone greets them with devotion and fervor, but the Queen continues to act disdainfully.

But now the Astrologer comes back and demands his reward. He wants nothing less than the Queen herself. First the King offers almost anything as a substitute, even half his kingdom; but when the Astrologer sticks to his price, the King, in a rage, kills him with his sword. The Queen is cynically interested and not much moved, but the King is afraid that this may be a bad omen for his wedding, especially as a clap of thunder punctuated his fatal blow.

He does not have long to wait before his fears are realized. As the two descend from the chariot, the golden cockerel suddenly leaves his perch, where he has been beneficently quiet all during the act, hovers for a moment over Dodon's head, and then darts down to peck him dead. A crash of thunder; sudden darkness; an evil laugh out of the dark from the Queen; and when the lights go on again, she and the Astrologer have disappeared. The crowd is bewildered and feels lost. It sings a despairing lament.

EPILOGUE

Once more the Astrologer appears before the curtain. Don't let the tragic ending bother you too much, he tells us. After all, only the Queen and he were real people; the others were figures in a fairy tale.

COSÌ FAN TUTTE

Opera in two acts by Wolfgang Amadeus Mozart with libretto in Italian by Lorenzo Da Ponte, possibly inspired by a court incident

FIORDILIGI ⎱ *two wealthy sisters*   *Soprano*
DORABELLA ⎰   *Soprano or Mezzo-soprano*
DESPINA, *their maid*   *Soprano*
FERRANDO, *engaged to Dorabella* ⎱ *two*   *Tenor*
GUGLIELMO, *engaged to Fiordiligi* ⎰ *officers Baritone or Bass*
DON ALFONSO, *man-about-town*   *Bass or Baritone*

Time: about 1790
Place: Naples
First performance at Vienna, January 26, 1790

Mozart's score for *Così fan tutte* has been sung under more names than any other opera in history. For example, the Metropolitan Opera has called it *Women Are Like That*. In England it was once called *Tit for Tat*. In Germany it has had a dozen different names, including such unlikely ones as *Who Won the Bet?*, *The Girls' Revenge*, and even *The Guerrillas*. In Denmark it appeared as *Flight from the Convent*, and in France—believe it or not—as *The Chinese Laborer* and, fifty years later, *Love's Labour's Lost*. This last version was produced by the firm of Barbier et Carré, libretto manufacturers who specialized in transforming the literary works of the great into musical shows. They discarded the original libretto completely and adapted Mozart's music to their own mutation of Shakespeare's early comedy.

There was reason for so much tampering. *Così fan tutte* has

never been so popular as *Figaro* and *Don Giovanni,* yet its
music, most critics agree, is just as fine. Therefore, it was
thought, the trouble must be with the libretto. It was alternately criticized as too immoral, too slight, too artificial.
Maybe so, maybe so. The fact is that none of the alterations
has ever been more popular than the original. So let us be
satisfied with that. I, personally, think it a very fine libretto.
As for its meaning, we can take a hint from the original subtitle, which was *The School for Lovers.*

The story goes that the plot is modeled on something that
had recently happened among the courtiers of the Emperor
Joseph II. Be that as it may, the commission did come from
the Emperor to Da Ponte and Mozart to write a comedy, possibly because a revival of *The Marriage of Figaro* had proved
highly successful. *Così fan tutte* was the delightful fulfillment
of the commission.

OVERTURE

The overture is short and unpretentious, and it is specifically related to the story only in so far as it quotes the tune to
which the three male principals, in Act II, Scene 3, announce
that *così fan tutte* ("all women act like that").

ACT I

Scene 1   The comedy itself begins at a Neapolitan café at
the end of the eighteenth century. Two young officers are arguing with a cynical old man of the world named Don Alfonso.
He says that their fiancées will never prove faithful—no
women ever do. They insist the idea is unthinkable. Finally
Don Alfonso offers to prove his point for a bet of one hundred
sequins. (That comes to about $225—as much as a young offi-
cer would earn in a year.) The terms are simply these: for
twenty-four hours the young men must faithfully act out whatever Don Alfonso tells them to do. And the scene ends in the
third of three trios, as the officers decide what they will do
with their money when they win it (*if* they do!).

Scene 2 introduces us to the two young heroines—Fiordiligi and Dorabella. The two sisters are in a garden overlooking the Bay of Naples, and together they sing about the beauty of their fiancés, the officers Guglielmo and Ferrando. They are expecting the young men, but instead old Alfonso arrives to tell them dreadful news. Their fiancés, says he, have suddenly been ordered away, to active duty. A moment later these gentlemen enter, already in traveling clothes. Naturally, a fine quintet develops out of this, the four affianced youngsters expressing their sorrow over parting, while Don Alfonso assures the boys that it's too early in the game to collect their bets. Scarcely is the quintet over when soldiers and townfolk arrive to sing the joys of a soldier's life. For now it is *really* time for the young men to go—though not so fast that they cannot take part in one final quintet of farewell. A repetition of the soldiers' chorus, and off they do go, leaving their girls with Alfonso to wish them *bon voyage* in a tuneful little trio. The scene closes with some cynical remarks delivered to the audience by Don Alfonso. You may as well, he says in effect, plow the sea or sow the sand as put your faith in women.

Scene 3 brings on at once the sixth and most engaging member of the cast. She is the maid Despina, a coloratura soprano. In a recitative she complains about how bad it is to have to be a maid, and, while complaining, she tastes her mistresses' chocolate. The sisters now enter their drawing room, and Dorabella has a tremendous mock-heroic aria, *Smanie implacabili*. She cannot bear, she says, having fresh air. Shut the windows! She cannot live through her grief! When Despina learns what all the grief is about—that is, the girls' lovers have gone to war—she gives some real Don Alfonso advice: have a good time while they are gone, for *they* won't prove faithful. Soldiers never do. Indignantly the girls storm from the room.

Enter now Don Alfonso. With a half-dollar bribe he persuades the maid to help in his plan, which is to get the girls to look with favor on two new suitors. Ferrando and Guglielmo appear almost at once, disguised in beards and dressed like Albanians. When the girls return, Alfonso makes believe that the Albanians are old friends, and the two young men

Così fan tutte

try making love to their own fiancées. But the girls will have none of it. In an aria (*Come scoglio*) Fiordiligi violently declares her eternal faithfulness. Maybe, like the lady in Hamlet, she protests too much. At any rate, her aria has the most astounding range and huge skips—peculiar, exaggerated difficulties especially composed by Mozart for Da Ponte's talented mistress, who was the first to sing it. Guglielmo tries to plead his suit with a fine tune—but again without any luck. The girls walk out on him—much to the delight of their fiancés. These (in the ensuing trio) try to get Don Alfonso to settle up, but he says it's still too early. Ferrando, the tenor of the team, then sings of his happiness in his love, and the scene ends with Don Alfonso and Despina making further plans to win the girls over.

Scene 4 takes us back to the garden. The two girls have another sweet duet about how sad they are, when there is noise off-stage. Their two lovers, still disguised as Albanians, totter in with Don Alfonso. It seems that they have taken arsenic because of their hopeless passion. (Of course, they have really done no such thing.) Don Alfonso and Despina assure the sisters that the men will die without help—and off they rush for a doctor. While they are gone, the two girls are in delightful confusion, taking their men's pulses and giving other pointless first aid. Then Despina returns, disguised with huge spectacles as a doctor and speaking the most extraordinary jargon. Finally (and this is a bit of satire on Mesmer's theory of animal magnetism), she brings out a huge magnet; she applies it to the prostrate bodies; and—miracle of miracles! —they begin to come to. Their first words are words of love; and though (in the final sextet) the girls continue to protest, it is clear that Don Alfonso's scheme is beginning to work.

ACT II

Scene 1 Despina, the maid, offers some very worldly advice to her mistresses at the beginning of this act. In a typical soubrette aria, she says that by fifteen any girl should be a champion flirt. She must encourage *every* man, lie expertly—

and she will rule the world. Talking it over, Fiordiligi and Dorabella decide that this makes some sense: no harm in a little flirtation. They thereupon proceed to divide up, between themselves, the two love-struck Albanians. Dorabella chooses the dark one (who is really Guglielmo, engaged to Fiordiligi); and Fiordiligi will take the blond (that is, Ferrando, engaged to Dorabella). And the scene ends as Don Alfonso invites them down into the garden to see something really worth seeing.

Scene 2 begins with a duet sung by the two lovers to their mistresses. They are in a boat near the seaside garden, and they have a band of professional serenaders to help them. When the men land, all four lovers are very shy, and Don Alfonso speaks for the "Albanians," while Despina takes up the office for the girls. Fiordiligi and Ferrando wander off among the flowers, and Dorabella and Guglielmo are left to carry on the flirtation. It quickly develops into a melodious duet, and before things have got very far, Dorabella gives Guglielmo a miniature of her fiancé, Ferrando. Then they walk off among the flowers, and Fiordiligi returns, alone. Apparently Ferrando has also been making improper advances, but he has been repulsed, as the soprano tells us in the virtuoso aria *Per pietà*. Still, she does not seem to be confident about how long she will hold out. And so, when the three men meet to compare notes, Guglielmo is triumphant, Ferrando is despondent, and Alfonso promises further developments. Just wait till tomorrow, he says.

Scene 3 develops some difference in character and temperament between the two sisters. Dorabella has already succumbed to Guglielmo's advances, and Despina congratulates her; but Fiordiligi, though she admits she loves the other supposed Albanian, still resists her feelings. She now decides that they ought to dress in the uniforms of their lovers and join them at the front. But scarcely is she decked out in this warlike garb when Ferrando rushes in. He begs her to kill him with the sword rather than deny her love, and he offers marriage—anything she wants. Fiordiligi, already weakened, finally succumbs, and they rush off. But her fiancé, Guglielmo, has

Così fan tutte

been watching with Don Alfonso. It is now the second lover's turn to be in despair, and he curses out the girl thoroughly in her absence. Nor is he more pleased when his self-satisfied friend, having deposited Fiordiligi somewhere, returns. But Don Alfonso soothes them both. In a short speech he advises them to marry their fiancées after all, for, as he says, *Così fan tutte*—"All women act like that!" Together they repeat this solemn generalization: *Così fan tutte*; and the scene ends as Despina announces that the ladies are ready to marry the Albanians.

Scene 4 Despina and Don Alfonso are directing the servants in preparing a large room for the wedding, and then they depart. The happy lovers (the men still in disguise) are congratulated by the chorus, and they themselves sing a self-gratulatory quartet. It concludes with a three-part canon, for only Guglielmo stands aside and mutters his dissatisfaction.

Now Don Alfonso introduces the necessary notary, who is, of course, Despina in disguise, and who brings along the marriage contract. The marriage ceremony is just beginning when, off-stage, the soldiers' chorus is again heard. Can it be the returning lovers? The girls hide their supposedly new fiancés in the next room, and a few moments later the men reappear in their military uniforms. Almost at once Guglielmo deposits his knapsack in the next room, and finds Despina, still garbed as a notary. She quickly explains this away (says she had been to a fancy-dress ball); but when Alfonso carefully drops the marriage contract before Ferrando, the jig is up for the girls. They ask to die for their guilt. But then the two men make a quick costume switch once more; Guglielmo returns Ferrando's portrait to Dorabella; and Don Alfonso finally explains everything. The lovers are properly united and all six principals join in appending a moral: happy is the man who can take the good with the bad—a typical sentiment from the Age of Reason.

DIDO AND AENEAS

Opera in three acts by Henry Purcell with libretto in English by Nahum Tate based on Book IV of Virgil's *Aeneid*

DIDO, *Queen of Carthage*	*Contralto*
AENEAS, *leader of the Trojans*	*Baritone*
BELINDA, *a lady-in-waiting*	*Soprano*
SECOND WOMAN, *another lady-in-waiting*	*Mezzo-soprano*
A SPIRIT, *disguised as Mercury*	*Soprano*
A SORCERESS	*Contralto*

Time: after the fall of Troy
Place: Carthage
First performance at Chelsea (London), 1689

Dido and Aeneas is the first truly great opera ever composed by an Englishman, and there are those unkind enough to call it the last as well. It was composed, in 1689, by young Henry Purcell, the glory of English music, and it was composed *for*—of all places—a girls' school. This school was run by a dancing master named Josias Priest, who seems to have had some influential friends. For not only did England's leading composer write the score, but the libretto was written by England's poet laureate, Nahum Tate. Perhaps he was not a very great poet, but he did write a nice, proper libretto for a girls' school on a classical tale of passion and death. The source is the fourth book of Virgil's *Aeneid*. Perhaps the girls were studying it in school at the time.

ACT I

Scene 1 After a classically tragic overture, Belinda persuades Queen Dido of Carthage, her mistress, that she could fall in love with Aeneas. Aeneas is, of course, the Trojan hero who has been cast up on the shores of Carthage after the fall of Troy. Dido is already more than half in love with the man, and when, toward the end of the scene, he pleads his own case, it is clear that he will win it. The chorus (which seems to be always present at the most intimate domestic conferences in some classical operas) is all in favor of the romance.

Scene 2 In the second scene we meet the villains. These include a sorceress, a pair of head witches, and a whole chorus of assistant witches. They are really more like the witches in *Macbeth* than anything that Virgil ever dreamed of. In their cave they are busy planning to stir up a storm, to separate Dido and Aeneas, and to make the hero desert the heroine. They do it in high spirits, and Purcell provided two delightful passages of laughter, and another (at the end) with an echo to indicate a "deep-vaulted cell."

ACT II

The very short second act concerns the famous hunt that Queen Dido has arranged for the entertainment of her distinguished guest. The chorus, Belinda, and later on a "Second Woman" describe the grove, and Aeneas boasts about the boar he has slain. When Dido and the ladies are driven off by the storm, Aeneas is kept from joining them by a mysterious spirit. This character, who is dressed like the messenger Mercury, tells Aeneas that he must leave Dido that very night, for he is destined to found the great city of Rome. Aeneas laments the necessity of deserting his beloved Queen, but he knows that he must go. The act closes with the witches rejoicing that their plans are going on in great shape.

ACT III

The last act begins with a chorus of Trojan sailors delight-edly preparing to leave the hospitable shores of Carthage. Then come the Sorceress and her chorus of witches, who are even more delighted. My favorite couplet in this joyous passage goes:

> *Our plot has took,*
> *The Queen's forsook.*

That, of course, is strictly seventeenth-century English syntax.

Then the tragic Dido comes on, with her followers. She is completely resigned to her fate, and even when Aeneas offers to defy the commands of Jove and to remain with her, she adamantly insists upon being deserted by her lover. The music becomes more powerfully tragic here as she sings the great aria *When I am laid in earth*. The calm dignity of this farewell has few equals, I believe, in all music. The opera closes with a brief and touching chorus.

DON CARLOS

Opera in five acts by Giuseppe Verdi with libretto in French by François Joseph Méry and Camille du Locle based on the play by Johann Christoph Friedrich von Schiller. Usually sung in the revised Italian four-act version by Antonio Ghislanzoni

PHILIP II, *King of Spain*	*Bass*
ELIZABETH OF VALOIS, *Queen of Spain*	*Soprano*
PRINCESS EBOLI, *her lady-in-waiting*	*Mezzo-soprano*
DON CARLOS, *heir to the Spanish throne*	*Tenor*
RODRIGO, *Marquis of Posa*	*Baritone*
THE GRAND INQUISITOR	*Bass*
TEBALDO, *Elizabeth's page*	*Soprano*
A MONK	*Bass*
THE ROYAL HERALD	*Tenor*
A HEAVENLY VOICE	*Soprano*

Time: 1559
Place: Madrid
First performance at Paris, March 11, 1867

Don Carlos is a fine, mature work, but it is seldom given. One reason is that it demands so large a cast of many fine singers. It requires not only the customary leading soprano, contralto, tenor, baritone, and bass, but an *extra* equally fine basso, and an extra coloratura soprano—no less—in a comparatively minor role. The first performance, in Paris in 1867, was (perhaps for this reason) a comparative failure. Fifteen years later Verdi shortened and revised the whole opera, omit-

ting one whole act. He modeled it, then, more closely on
Schiller's play of *Don Carlos*, and in this form it has had at
least a *succès d'estime* in many opera houses. The following
description is based on the revised version.

Scene 1 The story takes place in sixteenth-century Madrid. In the monastery of San Giusto a mysterious monk, accompanied by other monks, prays for the peace of soul of
Charles V, once the proud Emperor of the Holy Roman Empire. His grandson, Don Carlos, enters a moment later, and
imagines he hears the voice of Charles still haunting the convent. In an aria he speaks of his love for the beautiful Elizabeth of Valois. Elizabeth, whom he had met in France, was
forced, for political reasons, to marry Carlos's father, Philip
II of Spain. As Carlos pours out his heart, his great friend
Rodrigo enters. He advises Carlos to ask for the governorship
of Flanders: there the people are suffering and there he may
forget Elizabeth. The two men, in a fine duet, swear eternal
friendship (*Dio, che nell'alma infondere amor*—"God, who
has filled our hearts with love"). As the scene closes, they see
Philip and his queen going to prayers in the monastery, and
they renew their vows of friendship.

Scene 2 takes place in a garden and begins with a Moorish
love song sung by the Queen's ladies-in-waiting, led by the
Princess Eboli. We shall be hearing more of this Princess, for
she is in love with Don Carlos, just as the Queen is. Following
the love song, Rodrigo has an interview with Queen Elizabeth.
He begs her to persuade Philip to send Carlos to Flanders as
Governor. When Rodrigo retires in the company of Princess
Eboli, there is a scene between Elizabeth and Carlos. At first
he restrains himself, but soon he is passionately declaring his
love, and Elizabeth summons the strength to deny him. King
Philip enters a moment after Carlos has departed, and he is
furious when he finds his Queen unattended. Yet he softens
somewhat in his interview with Rodrigo, for he honors and
trusts this nobleman. He explains to Rodrigo (but does not

convince him) that Flanders must continue to suffer for the good of Spain, and he more than hints that the Church, in the person of the Grand Inquisitor, is the real power to beware.

ACT II

Scene 1 takes place at night in the Queen's garden. Carlos, who has received an unsigned letter, is expecting to meet Elizabeth, and when a veiled lady comes, he begins to make love to her. But it is the Princess Eboli, in love with Carlos, who has written the letter and kept the tryst. When Carlos, greatly confused, discovers his mistake, he reveals that he really loves the Queen. Well—hell hath no fury like a woman scorned; and even the interference of Rodrigo, who threatens to murder the Princess, cannot restrain the Princess from promising herself vengeance. Nevertheless, the scene ends without bloodshed as Carlos turns over some incriminating papers to Rodrigo for safekeeping, and the two again swear eternal friendship.

Scene 2 shows the Spanish Inquisition at work. A group of heretics is about to be burned alive. When King Philip enters, many plead to him for mercy, but he and the monks stand fast. Then Don Carlos, the King's son, requests that he may be sent to Flanders to give that suffering country a kindlier government. The King refuses; Carlos draws his sword, swearing to avenge Flanders; and the King demands that he be disarmed. Only Rodrigo dares to do this for his King, and he is rewarded by being made a duke.

The scene then ends with the fires being lighted to burn the victims of the Inquisition, and strangely (or so it seems to me) everyone joins in a chorus of rejoicing. At the very close a voice from heaven pardons the dying men and women.

ACT III

Scene 1 opens with King Philip's great soliloquy, *Ella giammai m'amò.* Elizabeth, he says, has never loved him; he must always be alone. There follows an uncomfortable dialogue with the Grand Inquisitor, a stern, forbidding, blind old man. Philip offers to have his own son executed for rebellion. The Grand Inquisitor not only approves; he also demands the death of Rodrigo, who, he says, is far more dangerous. The interview ends with distrust on both sides, and then Elizabeth comes in to the King, demanding that her stolen jewel casket be found. Philip has it there. He opens it and he discovers a picture of Carlos. She denies his accusations of infidelity, and when Rodrigo and the Princess Eboli enter, he realizes that Elizabeth was faithful. A great quartet develops, and then the two women are left alone. Repentant, Princess Eboli admits she had stolen the casket and given it to the King. She had done it out of love for Carlos and jealousy when he repulsed her. Elizabeth demands that her former friend choose between exile and the convent, and the scene ends with the Princess Eboli's famous aria *O don fatale*, wherein she laments the beauty that has led her to this ruin.

In *Scene 2* Don Carlos is already in his prison cell. Rodrigo comes to him and tells him that the incriminating papers have been found on him. Carlos must now be the man to save Flanders, for Rodrigo is marked for death. Even as he speaks, a man sneaks into the cell and shoots Rodrigo dead. With his dying breath Rodrigo tells his friend that Elizabeth knows everything, and that she awaits him at the convent of San Giusto.

ACT IV

The brief last act begins with an aria by Queen Elizabeth (*Tu che la vanità*). Awaiting her lover at the convent, she resigns herself to her fate; and when Don Carlos joins her, they sing a sad duet of farewell, for Carlos, to honor his dead friend Rodrigo, must lead the Flemish people to liberty. But as they breathe their last farewells, the King and the Grand Inquisitor find them together. The King demands the death of both, and the Grand Inquisitor agrees. But the mysterious priest appears from the tomb of Charles V. Everyone believes it to be the ghost of the old Emperor himself, and the opera closes as Don Carlos is dragged by the priest into the tomb, to the profound amazement of everyone.

Postscript for the historically curious: Chief among the comparatively few historically reliable underpinnings of this drama is the fact that Don Carlos was affianced to Elizabeth of Valois in 1559 (when he was only fourteen) and that his father married her a few months later. Don Carlos later on aspired to be sent to govern Flanders, but the notorious Duke of Alva was sent in his stead, very likely because the Don, always a willful and difficult young man, was rapidly going insane. At the age of 23, Carlos was imprisoned on the orders of Philip, and he died some months later, possibly assassinated. Elizabeth died very soon after.

No one knows exactly what happened—or at least how or why. But the father-wife-son triangle situation inspired not only the German Schiller to produce a tragedy on the subject but also the Englishman Otway, the Italian Alfieri, the Frenchman Chénier (brother of the hero of the opera), and many others.

DON GIOVANNI

(Don Juan)

Opera in two acts by Wolfgang Amadeus
Mozart with libretto in Italian by Lorenzo Da
Ponte based partially on *The Stone Guest*, an
opera by Giuseppe Gazzaniga with libretto by
Giovanni Bertati. There were also a number of
other earlier plays about Don Giovanni.

DON GIOVANNI, *a young nobleman*	Baritone
LEPORELLO, *his servant*	Bass
THE COMMENDATORE SEVILLE	Bass
DONNA ANNA, *his daughter*	Soprano
DON OTTAVIO, *her fiancé*	Tenor
DONNA ELVIRA, *a lady of Burgos*	Soprano
ZERLINA, *a country girl*	Soprano
MASETTO, *her fiancé*	Baritone

Time: 17th century
Place: in and about Seville
First performance at Prague, October 29, 1787

Don Giovanni is the greatest opera ever composed.
Words to this effect, at least, were written by three men with
peculiarly sound equipment to pass judgment—Gioacchino
Rossini, Charles Gounod, and Richard Wagner. Beethoven
preferred *The Magic Flute*, for he thought the subject of the
Don too immoral.

The intentions of author and composer were, at least on the
surface, completely moral; for *Don Giovanni* was originally
only the subtitle, the real title being *Il dissoluto punito*, or
The Rake Punished. Be that as it may, Mozart and Da Ponte

both classed the work as a *dramma giocoso,* that is, a "jolly play;" and two famous anecdotes concerning the preparation of the opera would seem to indicate that it was undertaken in a spirit of levity rather than with the ponderous metaphysical significance in mind that Teutonic critics have pretended to find.

The first of the anecdotes is told in the entertaining memoirs of the librettist Da Ponte (no mean rake himself). Describing the few weeks it took him to turn out this libretto, along with two others, he wrote:

"I sat down at my writing table and stayed there for twelve hours on end, with a little bottle of Tokay on my right hand, an inkstand in the middle, and a box of Seville tobacco on the left. A beautiful maiden of sixteen was living in my house with her mother, who looked after the household. (I should have wished to love her only as a daughter—but—) She came into my room whenever I rang the bell, which in truth was fairly often, and particularly when my inspiration seemed to cool. She brought me now a biscuit, now a cup of coffee, or again nothing but her own lovely face, always gay, always smiling, and made precisely to inspire poetic fancy and brilliant ideas."

The other anecdote concerns the composer's behavior at one of the rehearsals. Mozart was dissatisfied with the scream given by Zerlina when, at the ball, the Don is supposed to be making improper advances to her. He thereupon undertook to make the improper advances himself by slipping behind her and, at the precisely right moment, administering a sharp pinch. He expressed himself as quite satisfied with the more realistic scream.

OVERTURE

The overture (said to have been orchestrated the night before the premiere) begins solemnly with the music that accompanies the fateful appearance of the stone guest in the last scene of the opera. These thirty measures are in a minor key; but once they are over, the overture breaks into a sunny major and chatters along as briskly as the overture to any *dramma giocoso* should. It leads directly, without a break, into the opening scene.

ACT I

Scene 1 Leporello, Don Giovanni's low-comedy servant, is waiting for his master outside the home of a Sevillian beauty named Donna Anna, as Giovanni is courting her. Leporello complains comically about his job, but pretty soon out comes the Don followed by a maddened Donna Anna. Apparently he had disguised himself as Anna's fiancé, Don Ottavio. Donna Anna runs for help, and her father, the Commendatore of Seville, comes out to challenge Giovanni to fight. The Don has no wish to take advantage of his youthfulness, but he is forced to draw his sword, and quickly disposes of the old gentleman. The Don and his servant run off and Donna Anna returns with Don Ottavio. Over the body of the Commandant the two solemnly swear vengeance.

Scene 2 On a lonely road near Seville the Don runs across an old flame named Donna Elvira, whom he had deserted. He manages to escape from this lady's upbraidings but leaves behind his servant, Leporello, to explain matters. It is a very weird sort of comfort this fellow has to offer: he lists his master's conquests in many lands—something over two thousand in number. This is the famous aria known as *Il catalogo* —"The Catalogue."

Scene 3 In the next scene the Don embarks on what turns out to be the last of his would-be conquests. He and Leporello run across a party of villagers celebrating the engagement of pretty young Zerlina to a stout fellow named Masetto. The Don is smitten with the pretty girl and invites her to his castle in a very charming duet (*Là ci darem la mano*). But he is interrupted by the entrance of Donna Elvira, who takes Zerlina temporarily under her wing, as well as Donna Anna and Don Ottavio. These last two know Don Giovanni only slightly and do not yet suspect that he is the murderer of Donna

Anna's father. But his voice sounds strangely familiar to Anna, and she tells Ottavio that this may be the man they are looking for. He then sings the lovely aria (*Dalla sua pace*) in which Ottavio swears to devote himself to achieving peace of mind for his beloved Anna. To close the scene (though this ending is sometimes performed as a separate scene by itself), Leporello first repeats his complaints about his service, threatening to leave his master, but cheers up when the Don congratulates him on the report of progress he gives. It seems that Leporello has managed to placate the jealous Masetto, to get most of the peasants eating and drinking, and even to get rid of Donna Elvira, who had been warning her new protégé, Zerlina, against the Don. The Don is so much pleased that he breaks into one of the bubbliest of all arias—the so-called *Champagne Aria*—in which he looks forward to more conquests at his party that evening.

Scene 4 Outside the Don's palace Zerlina and her fiancé are having a quarrel about the Don's attentions, but it ends with a most charming apology, Zerlina's little aria *Batti, batti*. This does not prevent the villain, Giovanni, from trying to pursue the girl, but temporarily, at least, Masetto stops him. Soon we hear the strains of the famous *Minuet* from inside the palace. Leporello, standing on the balcony, sees some masked figures approaching, and he hospitably invites them to the party. But before they go in, they sing a solemn and exceptionally beautiful trio (*Protegga, il giusto cielo*). For these three maskers are Don Ottavio and the Ladies Anna and Elvira, calling on heaven to aid them in bringing Don Giovanni to justice.

Scene 5 At the party itself things are going along joyously, with three sets of dancers dancing to three different orchestras playing simultaneously in three different rhythms! While Leporello distracts Masetto by insisting on having him as partner in the dance, Don Giovanni manages to get Zerlina off into an inside room. She screams for help, runs out, and suddenly the Don is threatened by all his enemies at once. Yet the Don is no coward. He draws his sword, and in the exciting finale he makes good his escape.

ACT II

Scene 1 In the opening scene of Act II, the Don is up to his old tricks. He persuades the reluctant Leporello to change cloaks and hats with him so that he may woo Donna Elvira's maid. But it is Elvira herself who appears on the balcony to be serenaded; and when she comes down, it is Leporello who, in his master's clothes, makes love to her and takes her off. Now, wearing his servant's clothes, the Don sings his serenade, *Deh! vieni alla finestra*, as he accompanies himself on the mandolin. However, he is interrupted by Masetto and a group of his friends searching for the Don to beat him up. In the dark they take the disguised man for Leporello, and the Don manages to send off all of Masetto's helpers on a wild-goose chase, while he beats up the poor fellow himself. The scene closes with Zerlina finding her aching swain on the ground, and she sings him the sweet and comforting aria *Vedrai carino*. Her loving heart, she says, will cure his wounds.

Scene 2 Into the garden where the Commendatore lived stray Leporello and Donna Elvira, she still thinking him to be Giovanni. Donna Anna and Don Ottavio also stray into that garden, as do Zerlina and Masetto. Leporello, to save himself from all his master's enemies, gives up his disguise and manages to make his escape. Now Ottavio feels certain that it must have been the Don who murdered the Commendatore (though his reasoning is none too clear), and he resolves to consult the local police. First, he delivers himself of one of the finest—and most difficult—tenor arias ever written, *Il mio tesoro*.

(A low-comedy scene, almost always omitted in modern productions, follows, in which Zerlina catches up with Leporello, drags him around the stage, ties him up in a chair, and even threatens him with a razor. But again Leporello manages an escape. This is followed by Donna Elvira's fine aria *Mi tradì quel alma ingrata*—"All my love on him I lavished," which does get sung in modern productions, usually before a drop curtain.)

Scene 3 At two o'clock in the morning, Don Giovanni and Leporello meet in a churchyard before an equestrian statue of the Commendatore. There is some banter about the possibility of the Don's having made love to his servant's wife, when the two are interrupted by a ghostly voice saying, "Before dawn your joking will end." It is the statue speaking; and Leporello, trembling, reads the inscription on its base: "Here I await vengeance on the impious man who killed me." Braving it out, Don Giovanni instructs his servant to invite the statue to dinner. Twice the stone figure accepts, once by nodding its head and once by uttering the word *Sì*—"Yes." Assuming indifference, the Don merely remarks that it is all very bizarre.

Scene 4 is a very short one. Don Ottavio tries to persuade Donna Anna that, as Giovanni will soon be brought to justice, she should agree to marry him. Her reply is the aria *Non mi dir*. With great tenderness she tells him that she does love him but that while her sorrow for her father is still so fresh she cannot think of marriage.

Scene 5 The last, frightening scene opens in a quite jolly way. The Don is feasting by himself and, amid jests with Leporello, recognizes the various tunes his private dinner orchestra plays for him. One of them is the *Non più andrai*, from *The Marriage of Figaro*. This tune was high on Prague's hit parade for 1787.

Donna Elvira brings in the first serious note when she begs Giovanni to change his way of life, but she is gaily disregarded. Suddenly there is a solemn knock at the door. Donna Elvira goes to the door and then rushes back badly frightened. Despite his master's order Leporello refuses to open it; and when the Don does so himself, he finds the stone statue standing there, come to dinner. The statue grasps the hand of Don Giovanni; and when the Don refuses to repent his way of life, the Don and all his palace disappear in supernatural flames.

But the opera closes on a sweeter note. The Don is dead and, presumably, in hell; but all the other characters have learned a lesson from him, and they tell us of their future plans in a very tuneful finale. Anna promises to marry Ottavio at the end of the year; the nuptials of Zerlina and Masetto are to take place much earlier; Elvira will enter a convent; and as for Leporello—he will seek a better master. Solemn Teutonic opera intendants, still assuming that *Don Giovanni* is a profoundly serious philosophical treatise, often omit the finale as too light to be appropriate. Rather an arrogant criticism of the very stage-wise Mozart!

DON PASQUALE

Opera in three acts by Gaetano Donizetti with
libretto in Italian, prepared, probably in collaboration, by the composer and "Michele Ac-
cursi" (pseudonym for Giacomo Ruffini) on
the basis of Angelo Anelli's libretto for *Ser
Marc' Antonio,* a once popular work by Stefano
Pavesi

DON PASQUALE, *an old bachelor*	*Bass*
DR. MALATESTA, *his friend*	*Baritone*
ERNESTO, *nephew of Don Pasquale*	*Tenor*
NORINA, *a young widow*	*Soprano*
A NOTARY	*Tenor or Baritone*

Time: early 19th century
Place: Rome
First performance at Paris, January 3, 1843

All the histories of opera I have ever read disagree about
how many operas Donizetti wrote. They also disagree about
which number belongs to *Don Pasquale.* Some say it was his
sixty-fourth, some say his sixty-fifth, some say his sixty-seventh.
(I don't know why they skip the number 66.) They disagree,
too, about how long the composition took him. Some say
eleven days, some say two weeks, some say three weeks. Anyway, they all agree it was very fast.

They also agree on something more important. They all say
it is his very finest work—better even than the more famous
Lucia di Lammermoor or *The Elixir of Love* or *The Daughter
of the Regiment.* It contains no world-famous passages like
the sextet from *Lucia,* the tenor aria *Una furtiva lagrima* from

Don Pasquale

The Elixir or the *Salut à la France* from *The Daughter*, but it has throughout an irrepressible bubbling, a masterly wit, an absence of affectation that makes of it, in a worthy performance, a more solidly satisfying work of art than any of the master's earlier, more uneven operas. Unfortunately, one hardly ever hears a performance with artists equally matched on a high level. Masters and mistresses of *bel canto* are hard to come by; and when it is revived for a *basso buffo* with the other roles indifferently filled in, the result is disaster.

OVERTURE

Query to conductors of symphony orchestras: why don't you ever list this piece on either serious or "pops" programs? It contains some of the opera's very best tunes, and it has a pretty, if conventional, shape. Most audiences would love it.

ACT I

Scene 1 The scene is Rome; the time is the early nineteenth century; and the central character is a standard figure in old comedy—the aged, wealthy bachelor who wants to get married. He is fair game for anyone, and his name, this time, is Don Pasquale. This Don has a nephew, his only heir, whose name is Ernesto. When the opera opens, Pasquale, pacing up and down in his living room, is planning a nasty surprise for the youngster. Presently the Don's old friend, Dr. Malatesta, joins him. Malatesta has found what Pasquale wants—a beautiful young girl to be his bride, and he proceeds to describe her in the aria *Bella siccome un angelo*—"Just as beautiful as an angel." Who is she? Why, she is Malatesta's sister. Pasquale is so delighted that he ignores Malatesta's warnings about hurrying into marriage. Instead, he pushes his friend from the house and demands that this paragon be brought to him at once. Then he has a foolish soliloquy in which he already imagines himself the father of six!

Now enter the juvenile lead, young Ernesto. In their discussion it comes out that the old man has found a beautiful

and wealthy lady for Ernesto to marry. But Ernesto has refused—and he refuses again. For (like any good light tenor in
an Italian opera) he is deeply in love and faithful to the one
and only—his Norina. This angers the old fellow all over again.
He threatens to turn Ernesto out of his house, and finally he
tells him that he is about to get married himself. This, of
course, is terrible news for Ernesto. Now he will be disinherited, and he will be unable to marry his Norina. In a duet
made up of contrasts, Ernesto bewails this sad state of affairs
while Pasquale gloats over it. But before he leaves, Ernesto
offers one word of advice: "Do not get married without consulting someone else—say, Dr. Malatesta." Gleefully Pasquale
allows that he has already done so, and that he intends to
marry the doctor's own sister. Poor Ernesto now feels that he
has been betrayed by Malatesta, the one man he has always
trusted.

Scene 2 finds Norina in her room reading a romantic novel
and singing sweetly on matters of love. She congratulates herself that, like the heroine in her book, she also is well versed
in the arts of *amour*. An especially tender love scene in the
novel, which she reads aloud to herself, inspires her to sing
the charming aria *Quel guardo, il cavaliere.* Following this,
a letter is brought, which Norina knows in a moment to be
from Ernesto. Just as she finishes reading it, Dr. Malatesta
rushes in to tell her his plan will be successful. But Norina
hands him the letter from Ernesto. Malatesta reads it aloud
and learns that the young man is brokenhearted. He calls
Malatesta a villain, claims that he will be disinherited because of Pasquale's marriage to Norina, and threatens to leave
Rome and Europe as soon as possible.

Malatesta quickly exonerates himself. He promises that
Ernesto will be only too happy to remain when he hears his
new plan. What is this plan? Why, simply to pass off Norina
(whom Pasquale has not yet seen) as his sister Sofronia, who
is really in a convent. Pasquale, he is sure, will happily consent to the marriage, and Malatesta's cousin, Carlotto, will
act as notary and perform a mock marriage. Norina will then

make life so miserable for Pasquale that he will be desperate
to get away.

Malatesta and Norina then sing an amusing duet in which
he coaches her in her new role. She must learn to act like a
shy country girl one minute, but like a real shrew the next.
The scene ends with these two reveling in the thought of revenge on selfish old Pasquale.

ACT II

Back in Don Pasquale's house a very sad and downhearted
Ernesto delivers himself of the dramatic aria *Cercherò lontana
terra.* Believing that he is disinherited and that he has lost his
Norina forever, he resolves to go far away, to end his days in
sorrow and remorse. He will be happy only in the thought
that Norina is happy: this will make his sorrow bearable. And
off he goes (but not very far).

Now, Pasquale enters. Dismissing his servant, he struts
about admiring his "fine figure." "Not bad for someone aged
seventy," he murmurs to himself—but he carefully makes sure
that no one is around to hear his age!

Then Malatesta arrives to present timid and veiled Norina.
The two old men sing a charming trio with the girl, she pretending to be frightened and on the verge of fainting, Malatesta consoling her and telling her to be brave, and Pasquale
expressing delight, but wondering whether the face under the
veil will prove to be as lovely as the rest.

Norina plays expertly her part of a shy young girl fresh from
a convent. All of her naïve answers to the old Don's questions delight him, and she is finally persuaded to lift her
veil. Needless to say, Pasquale is overwhelmed. He proposes;
she accepts; Malatesta goes off to fetch the notary; and the
marriage contract is drawn up. It is, of course, a counterfeit
contract.

But it seems that a witness is necessary. And who should
that witness be? Why, Ernesto, who just happens to be in
the other room. And a very angry Ernesto he is, for he has
not yet been told Malatesta's plan, and, to add insult to in-

jury, he has been almost thrown out of the house by the servants when all he wanted to do was say good-by. Malatesta, however, draws Ernesto aside and tells him of the fake contract. Somewhat calmed by the news, he consents to go through with the farce. The document is signed, and the notary leaves. Naturally, at this point there is a perfect opportunity for a quartet. The emotions expressed go something like this: Norina is worried lest Ernesto lose his temper and give the plot away; Ernesto thinks he will go mad from confusion; Malatesta begs him to believe in him; and Don Pasquale smugly observes that he *may* deal more gently with his nephew. Finally the ceremony is completed and the papers are signed.

Now the fireworks really begin. Suddenly, according to plan, Norina becomes a shrew. She pushes Pasquale away when he tries to embrace her and tells him he is too old even to take her walking. Ernesto, she says, will do that! Next, she proceeds to try to ruin Pasquale. She orders the present servants' salaries to be doubled and tells the major-domo to hire at least twenty-four more immediately. Furthermore, they must all be young and handsome. Nor does she stop here, but then and there orders a new carriage and new furniture. Meanwhile Pasquale moans and groans that he will be ruined. Norina ignores him and keeps right on, saying that the thousand other items can be taken care of next day. The delighted Ernesto and Malatesta congratulate each other; Pasquale bemoans his fate; and the quartet comes to a grand climax as the curtain falls.

ACT III

Scene 1 finds Don Pasquale virtually tearing out his hair. Norina, his supposed new wife, has ordered all sorts of finery, and poor Pasquale is going over the bills. As he does this, the servants keep on delivering more and more things. Norina grandly enters and, without a glance at Pasquale, blithely announces that she is going to the opera. Pasquale tries to block her way and is rudely rebuffed. "Old men should go to bed early," says the vindictive Norina. She shoves him away, flings one last insult at him, and merrily goes off, accidentally on purpose dropping a letter, which he picks up and reads. It is a love letter to "Dearest Sofronia" and specifies a time and a place in the garden for an assignation. Furious, Pasquale sends a note to Malatesta to tell him that he is sick, and then he staggers out of the room.

Now the servants take over. They are delirious with happiness, they say; for while there is not a moment's peace, what does that matter when there is so much money to be got? They finish up by warning each other to be careful. That way they will be able to keep on working in this fine house.

When the servants leave, Malatesta and Ernesto appear. They are discussing Ernesto's forthcoming rendezvous, for it was Ernesto, of course, who wrote the love letter. It is agreed that Ernesto is to disappear the moment Malatesta arrives with Pasquale. As Ernesto rushes off, Pasquale enters complaining bitterly. He wishes Ernesto had married Norina, he says. His "wife" has squandered his fortune, and now she is planning a rendezvous with a lover. *And* in his own garden! Malatesta, reading the letter, pretends to be appalled, and Pasquale swears revenge. In a very amusing duet Malatesta proposes his own plan. "Surprise them in the garden," he says. "Threaten to expose them. And," he adds, "faced with public disgrace, they are sure to give each other up." Pasquale is sure this treatment is too lenient. He agrees, however, to send his wife away if she is guilty, while Malatesta ironically promises that he will make sure she is properly handled after that.

Scene 2 takes place in the garden, on a perfect spring night. Our hero is heard singing one of the most beautiful arias in the opera (*Com' è gentil*), and the chorus joins in occasionally, answering Ernesto as he sings of his passion. (Incidentally, at the first dress rehearsal of this opera, everyone thought it might fail. Donizetti went home; he found this serenade in a drawer; he gave it to the leading tenor; and on opening night it was the hit of the show.) When it is over, Norina joins Ernesto, and now only one thing is possible—a glorious duet (*Tornami a dir che m'ami*). As their song of longing and loving ends, Pasquale and Malatesta are seen coming toward them, and Ernesto escapes into the house according to the agreement. Norina pretends to be horrified as Pasquale demands to know where her lover is and starts searching with pretended help from Malatesta.

Foiled in finding her lover, Pasquale tells Norina to leave his house, but she pertly reminds him that it is *her* house. Malatesta interrupts them and reminds Pasquale of his promise to let him handle things. He takes Norina aside and quietly instructs her on just how to behave. Aloud he announces that another bride is to enter the house on the morrow. She is to be Ernesto's wife, the widow Norina. Now Pasquale's pretended wife pretends real anger. She swears she will never live under the same roof with this Norina and even demands proof that the new marriage is to be a real one. Ernesto is called and is told that his uncle has approved of his marriage to Norina. For appearance's sake Norina objects, and this, naturally, makes old Pasquale demand the marriage even more strongly. He asks to see the proposed bride. "She is already here," says Malatesta, and leads Norina to him. The plot is then made clear to Pasquale by Malatesta. The poor Don, confused and angry, denounces them all. However, there is good in everyone, even in a selfish old rogue, and he finally gives in to Norina and Ernesto, who are on their knees to him. He puts his arms around them, and Malatesta's words *Bravo, bravo, Don Pasquale* introduce one last quartet in which they all moralize on the foolishness of an old man who marries a young girl, for it can only bring trouble.

ELEKTRA

Opera in one act by Richard Strauss with libretto in German by Hugo von Hofmannsthal, based on Sophocles' *Elektra*

CLYTEMNESTRA, *widow of Agamemnon*	*Contralto*
AEGISTHUS, *her lover*	*Tenor*
ORESTES, *her son*	*Baritone*
ELEKTRA CHRYSOTHEMIS } *her daughters*	*Sopranos*
TUTOR OF ORESTES	*Bass*

Time: after the fall of Troy
Place: Mycenae
First performance at Dresden, January 25, 1909

Elektra is not only a thriller; it is a shocker, too. In fact, when it was first performed in Germany in 1909, some critics thought that the last word (or shall we say note?) had been written in unashamed frankness and passion. What, then, caused all the furor? It was just the familiar Greek legend first outlined by Homer and later immortalized by Sophocles. But the librettist had retold the story more or less in terms of modern psychology, while Strauss had composed a score as explicit and as exciting as only a modern master could make it.

You may recall, from Homer or Sophocles or Bulfinch, that while King Agamemnon of Mycenae was at the Trojan War, his wife Clytemnestra had taken a lover—one Aegisthus. When Agamemnon returned, he was promptly murdered; and since then Aegisthus and Clytemnestra had ruled in his place. Two of Agamemnon's children—Elektra and Chrysothemis—were kept around the palace almost as slaves. A son—Orestes—had escaped, and the two sisters prayed for the return of their brother to avenge the father. Elektra grew up a strange, brooding, savage woman.

The opera opens in a court of the palace as a number of the women servants discuss her odd behavior. Only one of these women has any sympathy for Elektra, for she feels her moral strength and regal grandeur. Soon Elektra herself enters and invokes the spirit of her dead father, Agamemnon. A few moments later she has an interview with her younger sister, Chrysothemis, in which the older girl tries to pour some of her own strong spirit into the younger and weaker one. When Clytemnestra appears, asking what sacrifices she should make on account of her guilty dreams, Elektra offers no comfort. Instead, she predicts the violent end that will overtake her own evil mother.

Now the false news is spread that Orestes lives no longer. Chrysothemis herself brings it to Elektra, who tries to persuade the younger girl to join her in committing the act of vengeance demanded by the gods, now that the brother is gone.

But the fact is that the false news has been brought by two strangers, and one of these is Orestes himself. There is a scene in which brother and sister recognize each other. Orestes, though he is less savagely vengeful than Elektra, knows what he must do, and he grimly enters the palace with his aged companion. A moment later are heard the two despairing cries of Clytemnestra that indicate her murder, and Elektra savagely shouts for joy that the deed has been done. Now Aegisthus enters. He has heard of the news of Orestes' death, and Elektra, with grim mockery, assures him that it is certainly true. She leads him into the palace—and there he meets the same fate as Clytemnestra.

Elektra is deliriously delighted with this solution of the domestic affairs of the Agamemnon family. She dances a brief dance of victory, and then, as the opera closes, faints away in ecstasy.

THE ELIXIR OF LOVE

(*L'Elisir d'amore*)

Opera in two acts by Gaetano Donizetti with
libretto in Italian by Felice Romani

ADINA, *a wealthy girl*	*Soprano*
NEMORINO, *a young peasant*	*Tenor*
BELCORE, *a sergeant*	*Baritone*
DULCAMARA, *a quack doctor*	*Bass*
GIANETTA, *a peasant girl*	*Soprano*

Time: 19th century
Place: Italy
First performance at Milan, May 12, 1832

Donizetti, literally, turned out operas by the dozen. According to the latest count, made by Gianandrea Gavazzeni in his new Italian biography, there were seventy altogether, and *The Elixir of Love* was number forty. The composer was only thirty-four when he wrote it, and a letter quoted by Gavazzeni shows how quickly the composer had to work. Addressing his librettist, Felice Romani, he said: "I am obliged to write an opera in fourteen days. I give you a week to do your share. . . . But I warn you, we have a German prima donna, a tenor who stutters, a buffo with a voice like a goat, and a worthless French basso. Still, we must cover ourselves with glory."

Well, they did cover themselves with glory, and the tenor part was written for a hero who stutters!

ACT I

Scene 1 The action takes place in an Italian village just about the time the opera was written—that is in the thirties of the last century. The heroine, Adina, is a wealthy young woman who owns several estates. On one of them there is a chorus of her friends when the scene opens. They sing a charming number, led by Adina's intimate, Gianetta. Meantime, Adina's hapless peasant lover, Nemorino, sings of his love in a sweet aria (*Quanto è bella*—"How beautiful she is").

Adina herself reads to the assemblage a version of the story of Tristan and Isolda. It tells how they were made to love each other through a magical elixir, and Nemorino, in an aside, wishes he had some of that magical drink.

Now—enter the military. Sergeant Belcore, head of the little garrison stationed in the village, blusteringly asks Adina to marry him. The girl lightly but flirtatiously puts him off; and when everyone else has left, poor, stammering Nemorino presents his suit. In a long duet Adina puts him off, too, for she is quite bored by Nemorino's pathetic love-making.

Scene 2 takes us to the village square. Here the assembled villagers are excited by the arrival of a magnificent coach bearing one Dr. Dulcamara, who introduces himself with a celebrated comic aria (*Udite, udite*). He is a medical quack—the Italian equivalent of the Wild West's snake-oil salesman. And what has he to sell? Why, a magical elixir. Drink it, and you become invincible in love! Almost everyone becomes a customer at a very reasonable price, but the cunning Nemorino stays on and privately asks for Isolda's love potion. At a much higher price—Nemorino's last gold piece, in fact—he gets it. It is, of course, just like all the other bottles—that is, ordinary Bordeaux wine. But Nemorino takes a mighty dose of it, becomes slightly tipsy, and so, quite sure of himself now, acts in a very offhand manner with Adina. This new attitude piques the girl, and she immediately promises to marry Nemorino's rival, Sergeant Belcore.

Poor Nemorino! Dulcamara had told him the elixir takes

twenty-four hours to work, but Adina has promised to marry Belcore that very night, for the Sergeant is ordered away for the next day. As everyone is invited to the wedding, and Nemorino begs—in vain—to have it put off for a day, Act I comes to a close on a concerted number.

ACT II

Scene 1 begins just a few hours after Act I ends. All the villagers are gathered at Adina's house to help prepare for her wedding to Sergeant Belcore. Dr. Dulcamara takes a leading part: together with Adina, he reads off a brand new barcarolle —a very pretty duet beginning *Io son ricco e tu sei bella*—"I am rich and you are pretty." When the arrival of the notary is announced, the distracted lover Nemorino consults Dr. Dulcamara about his predicament. Naturally, the quack recommends another bottle of his elixir—one that will work in half an hour. Unfortunately Nemorino has no more money, and so, when the doctor leaves him, he consults his rival, Sergeant Belcore. Belcore advises enlistment in the Army, for there is a bonus of twenty scudi paid to all recruits. In an amusing duet the agreement is made, and Nemorino gets his bonus.

Scene 2 As everything should in the happy world of musical comedy, things turn out well in the final scene, which takes place the same evening. We learn, in the opening chatter-chorus for girls alone, that Nemorino has just inherited a fortune from an uncle. Nemorino himself does not know about it yet; and when he comes in—now more self-confident than ever through drinking the second dose of elixir—all the girls make love to him. He acts as though completely unimpressed by the attentions, even of his beloved Adina; and she, for her part, is quite upset by this turn of events. Dr. Dulcamara, seeing a chance for a new customer, offers Adina some of his elixir. In a delightful duet, she explains that she herself possesses a better elixir than his—to wit, a compound of various feminine wiles.

It is at this point that Nemorino, finding himself alone, sings the most famous aria in the opera (*Una furtiva lagrima*

—"Down her soft cheek a pearly tear"). He has noticed Adina's unhappiness, and he insists, in the aria, that he would gladly die to be permitted to comfort her. Nevertheless, when Adina approaches him, he maintains his attitude of indifference. Even when she tells him that she has bought his enlistment papers back from Belcore, he does not soften. Finally she breaks down and confesses that she loves him. The duet ends in impassioned happiness, of course; and now the opera draws quickly to a close. Belcore receives the news philosophically: there are plenty of other conquests available for a handsome soldier, he says. The news of Nemorino's new-found wealth is shared with everyone, and good old Dr. Dulcamara takes credit for the happy outcome by claiming that the lovers were brought together through his chemical researches. As the opera closes, everyone is buying one more bottle of his celebrated Elixir of Love.

ERNANI

Opera in four acts by Giuseppe Verdi with libretto in Italian by Francesco Maria Piave, based on Victor Hugo's tragedy *Hernani*

DON CARLOS, *King of Castile*	*Baritone*
DON RUY GOMEZ DI SILVA, *grandee of Spain*	*Bass*
ERNANI, or JOHN OF ARAGON, *a bandit chief*	*Tenor*
ELVIRA, *ward of Silva*	*Soprano*

Time: 1520
Place: Spain and France
First performance at Venice, March 9, 1844

Ernani was Verdi's fifth opera. With his third and fourth, *Nabucco* and *I Lombardi,* he had established himself in Italy as one of the foremost working opera composers, second perhaps only to Donizetti, for Bellini had died almost ten years before and Rossini had stopped composing operas even earlier. With *Ernani,* Verdi's fame crossed the Alps; and though many northern connoisseurs found the score shocking—"brutal" was a favorite word—its sheer emotional power swept all before it.

Furthermore, it represented another victory for the romantic movement on the stage. Victor Hugo, on whose play the libretto is based, was one of the great leaders in this movement, along with Schiller and Dumas. Hugo and Schiller furnished forth the materials for many a successful opera; only Donizetti ever had any luck with a Dumas play, and this one effort (*Gemma di Vergy,* based on *Charles VII*) is now completely forgotten.

Today Hugo's *Hernani* is still read in French schools, but it seems absurdly artificial and incredible anywhere else. The libretto for the opera is, of course, even worse in these respects. Hugo himself objected strongly to the liberties taken with his play. Yet the power of a few of the arias and concerted pieces (*Ernani! involami, Infelice, O sommo Carlo,* and a few others) kept the work in the standard repertoire for over a century; it is still often given in Italy; it is periodically revived in other lands; and individual numbers from it are sung wherever opera stars do congregate.

ACT I

Scene 1 Ernani, the hero of the opera, is really John of Aragon, son of the Duke of Segovia, who has been slain by order of the former King of Castile. That is why John has changed his name to Ernani and taken up the semi-respectable operatic trade of bandit chief. In his mountain camp, not far from the castle of Don Ruy Gomez di Silva, his followers open the opera with a drinking chorus. Their leader then obliges with a song in praise of his beloved Elvira (*Come rugiada al cespite*); his followers assure him that they will collaborate in his plans to carry off the lady; and they all depart in force toward the castle.

Scene 2 Now, this lovely Elvira is a relative of the owner of the castle, and also his ward. A gray-haired basso, he is in love with the young girl, and plans are already afoot for the wedding. Elvira herself, however, is in love with Ernani, and she compares him with her guardian Silva as she sits alone in her room and sings the most famous aria in the opera (*Ernani! involami*—Ernani! fly with me). When a chorus of maidens arrives to congratulate her on the approaching nuptials, she responds graciously, though in an aside she reminds us that it is Ernani she really loves.

Poor Elvira has the misfortune to be loved, not merely by her unwanted fiancé, but also by the present King of Castile himself, known as Don Carlos. As soon as the girls have left, he makes his appearance in the chamber, having got into the place by a complicated ruse I shall not bother here to go into. Elvira protests against this unwarranted invasion of her privacy, and the ensuing duet has scarcely ended when Ernani appears through a secret panel. Elvira manages to avert bloodshed by snatching a dagger from Carlos, when Silva (entering reasonably enough through a door) embarrasses everyone by joining the party. He expresses his own sentiments in a particularly fine aria (*Infelice! e tu credevi*—"All unhappy, I believed you"). Then, when the group is further joined by a large number of members of the household, Carlos tells Silva who he really is; Silva acknowledges his liege lord; and in the final ensemble Ernani is permitted to depart unscathed.

ACT II

In the grand hall of the castle Elvira is preparing for her marriage to Silva, and the chorus of maidens again sings a congratulatory strain. Elvira believes that Ernani has been captured and killed by the King's forces; but the real fact is that he has escaped, disguised himself as a monk, and come to Silva's castle for refuge. It is only when Elvira enters in her bridal gown that he realizes what prospective ceremony he has accidentally come upon. He immediately tears off his disguise and offers Silva a wedding gift—his own life. Let him, he suggests, be turned over to Carlos for execution. But Silva is a Spanish grandee, bound by the laws of hospitality, and he nobly refuses to endanger the life of any guest of his. Fearing that his other rival, the King, may be planning a forced entry, he decides to defend his castle, leaving the two lovers alone for a sad, impassioned duet (*Ah, morir potessi adesso*—"Ah, to die would be a blessing"). When Silva returns to find the lovers making love, his anger is interrupted by the news that the King's men are at the gates. He orders them to be admitted, but, still true to the laws of hospitality, he hides his own worst enemy from the pursuers. Even when the King himself demands that Silva give up Ernani, the old gentleman stoutly refuses. Carlos demands Silva's sword and threatens him with execution, but the lovely Elvira interposes, and the King compromises by taking her as a sort of hostage to ensure Silva's loyalty.

With the rest gone, Silva releases Ernani from his hiding

place, offers him a sword, and suggests a duel. But Ernani is also a noble Renaissance Spaniard. He refuses to turn on the host who saved his life and instead suggests that they combine forces to get Elvira away from the untrustworthy Carlos. Then, after they have succeeded, all Silva need do to get his revenge on Ernani is to blow the horn that he hands him and, no matter where he may be or what he may be doing, Ernani binds himself to take his own life. Silva agrees to this fantastic bargain (in his innocence he had not even suspected that the King might have fell designs on his ward and fiancée), and he orders his men to ride.

In an opera replete with incredible meetings the most incredible of all turns out to be the most dramatic as well. The conspirators against the King have decided to hold their meeting in the vault of the cathedral at Aix la Chapelle, which contains the tomb of Charlemagne, Don Carlos's most famous ancestor. Carlos, however, has got wind of this meeting, and he opens the act with a solemn soliloquy that only partially prepares us for his subsequent complete change of character (*Oh, de' verd' anni miei*—"Oh, of my youthful years"). He thereupon steps into the tomb itself to overhear what goes on.

The conspirators gather, sing an exciting male chorus (*Si ridesti*), and decide that the King must be murdered. They then choose, by lot, who shall commit the murder, and Ernani's name comes up. But outside there is the booming of cannon. The King steps solemnly forth from the tomb (suggesting to the conspirators that it is Charlemagne himself who has been eavesdropping) and strikes three times with his dagger upon the bronze doors of the vault. That booming of cannon meant that Carlos had been elected Emperor of the Holy Roman Empire; and so, to the music of trumpets, the electors enter in procession, followed by soldiers and pages bearing the imperial insignia, torches, the imperial banners, and all the other objects of glory that the opera company can afford. Elvira, of course, is also an invited guest.

Everyone pays homage to the newly elected Emperor Charles V, and he begins his reign by disposing of the conspiracy he has overheard: the noble leaders are to be beheaded, the common herd is to be imprisoned. Ernani, never one to forgo a chance to die conspicuously, steps forward and claims his right, as John of Aragon, to die with the best of them. Elvira, however, once again assumes her role of angerallayer, and pleads so eloquently for Ernani that Emperor Charles is persuaded to begin his reign with an act of genuine clemency. Not only does he pardon all the conspirators; he restores Ernani to his titles and lands and blesses his union with Elvira. The utterly preposterous scene ends with a truly magnificent concerted number—*O sommo Carlo!*

ACT IV

And now the happy couple have been wedded and they are enjoying the briefest of marriages in a duet on the terrace of Ernani's castle in Aragon. But Silva has not forgotten his agreement. He sounds the dread horn, and Ernani, waiting for only one more tenor aria, accepts his fate. Silva offers him a choice of poison or dagger; Ernani chooses the dagger; he stabs himself; and at the close of a most effective trio Elvira falls on her husband's body.

Postscript for the historically curious: There seems to be some historical basis for the strange and sudden change in the character of Don Carlos in the third act. As a young man he was described as weak and vain; later in life he developed real strength of character, generosity, even idealism. He was a grandson of Ferdinand and Isabella of Spain and a nephew of Henry VIII's first wife, Catherine. His election and coronation at Aix la Chapelle, which form the background of Act III, occurred in 1520. At the time he was barely twenty years old—rather young for a robust baritone but quite old enough for a Renaissance Spanish lover and soldier. His son, Philip II, and his grandson, who was named after him, are principal figures in Verdi's *Don Carlos* (see p. 119).

EUGEN ONEGIN

(Yevgeny Onyegin)

Opera in three acts by Peter Ilyitch Tchaikovsky with libretto in Russian largely by the composer based on the narrative poem of the same name by Alexandre Sergevich Pushkin

MADAME LARINA	*Mezzo-soprano*
TATIANA } *her daughters*	*Soprano*
OLGA	*Mezzo-soprano*
FILIPIEVNA, *Tatiana's nurse*	*Mezzo-soprano*
VLADIMIR LENSKI, *Olga's fiancé, a poet*	*Tenor*
EUGEN ONEGIN, *his friend*	*Baritone*
MONSIEUR TRIQUET, *a French tutor*	*Tenor*
ZARETSKI, *a friend of Lenski's*	*Bass*
PRINCE GREMIN, *a retired general*	*Bass*

Time: early 19th century
Place: Russia
First performance at Moscow, March 29, 1879

In May of 1877, a singer named Elizaveta Lavrovskaya suggested to Tchaikovsky the subject of Pushkin's poem *Eugen Onegin* as the subject for an opera. During the same month he received a letter from one Antonina Milyukova, a twenty-eight-year-old conservatory student whom he could scarcely remember having ever met. It said that she had long been in love with him.

In *Eugen Onegin* the heroine, Tatiana, writes Eugen a letter saying that she has long been in love with him. Eugen tells her that he cannot love her in return. The result is disaster.

Tchaikovsky, more than half in love with the heroine Tatiana, thought Eugen a cad. But he was not in love with his real-life correspondent, so he tried to do as Eugen had done and put Antonina off. He wrote a polite, cool answer; he received a warm one in reply; he went to see her; he became convinced that she would never survive his loss; he proposed; he was accepted; he was married. Disaster.

The parallel between the story of the opera Tchaikovsky was working on and the tragedy he was working out in real life can, of course, be pushed too far. There are some striking differences. Tatiana was beautiful, wealthy, intelligent, sensitive; Antonina was plain-looking, poor, bird-brained, insensitive. (When Nikolai Rubinstein, acting for Tchaikovsky, came to ask her to consent to a divorce, she seemed to be more impressed with having so distinguished a guest for tea than with the important message he carried.) Onegin was an independent, blandly brutal, philandering man of the world; Tchaikovsky was a dependent, neurotically sensitive, impractical homosexual. Yet he quixotically tried to act as nobly as he believed Onegin should have acted, and the fearful emotional upheaval that followed, including a serious but ineffectual attempt at suicide, must in some way have been reflected in the opera that he began with his odd courtship and that he completed not very long after the marriage had broken up.

It is a strongly melodic, nervous score, and of all his ten operas only *Onegin* and *The Queen of Spades* remain a permanent part of Russia's repertoire and have made their way all around the world.

ACT I

Scene 1   Madame Larina is a well-to-do upper-middle-class woman who rejoices in her two daughters and large estate. In her garden she and her servant Filipievna, with whom she appears to be on pretty intimate terms, are preparing jam, while inside the house, her two daughters, Tatiana and Olga, are practicing a duet. The duet becomes a female quartet when Madame Larina confides in her servant how romantic she was as a young girl. Deeply affected, she says, by the novels of Richardson, especially *Sir Charles Grandison,* she made a loveless marriage which nevertheless turned out pretty well. A chorus of peasants approaches the domestic scene, and then dances and sings folk music (or at least folk-like music) for the ladies. Tatiana is made rather romantically pensive by the performance; Olga, on the other hand, is made to feel gay; and she gives voice to her pleasantly extrovert philosophy of life in a little aria.

When Filipievna has led the peasants off to reward them with wine, Tatiana is warned by her mother not to be too moody, not to take those romantic novels she has been reading so seriously. There are no real heroes in everyday life, as she herself has learned.

At that moment Tatiana's hero-to-be enters the story. He is Eugen Onegin, a wealthy young fellow who has been so much a man about town that he is, at the moment, weary of it all. He comes for a polite call with his friend Lenski, a neighboring poet engaged to Olga. The mother of the two girls leaves them to entertain the two young men, and in the ensuing quartet it becomes evident that Lenski is in earnest puppyish love with his Olga (he hasn't seen her for a whole day!), while Onegin is rather casually attracted to Tatiana. Tatiana, for her part, is at once attracted to Onegin, and she wanders off to the lake with him, leaving the happy fiancés to moon sweetly to each other.

Supper is ready in the house, and Filipievna summons the two wanderers. When they reappear, Onegin continues his conquest of Tatiana by simply relating a bit of family history. The wise old Filipievna knows exactly what is happening, even if Tatiana does not realize it as yet.

Scene 2 Past ordinary bedtime, and already undressed, Tatiana finds sleep impossible and begs Filipievna to tell her a story. The servant obliges with a recital of her own loveless marriage, thus inspiring Tatiana to confide that she herself is dreadfully in love. She begs Filipievna not to tell anyone, asks for her writing desk, and wishes her a good night.

Now begins the famous *Letter Scene,* which Tchaikovsky

composed even before he prepared the libretto for the rest of the opera. It was the passage in Pushkin's narrative which most strongly attracted him at the time, and this fact lends color to the idea that the poem was at least in part the inspiration for his own unwise behavior in relation to Antonina Milyukova.

The scene begins as she summons up courage to compose a letter to Onegin; she then writes portions of it, reads it aloud, and finally completes it. The letter tells Onegin that she is completely committed to him and asks only for pity in return. Tatiana is inspired by the idea that she has been predestined to love Onegin and Onegin only; and though the letter admits that if she had not met him she might have loved another, yet she herself is convinced that she has been reserved for him by fate.

By the time the letter is signed and sealed, it is dawn, and Filipievna coming to wake her mistress, is surprised to find her already out of bed. Tatiana begs her to ask her son to deliver the letter, and tries to avoid naming Onegin by saying it is for "a neighbor." Filipievna mischievously pretends to be deaf and forces the girl to repeat the name of her lover. She had known all along, of course; and when Tatiana is left alone once more, she wonders what the result of her bold advance may be.

Scene 3 In "another part of the garden" peasants are singing, with dramatic appositeness, about the danger to girls if they choose a wrong lover. Tatiana, very much upset, rushes in. She has seen Onegin approaching and is already regretting her rash impulse.

When they are alone, Onegin tells her, in his aria, almost exactly what Tchaikovsky had tried to tell Antonina in his letter. He is entirely respectful, even friendly, but he makes it clear that marriage is not for the likes of him, and that what might begin as love would surely grow cold. Tatiana is utterly devastated; and off-stage the chorus repeats its folk wisdom about girls who choose wrongly.

Eugen Onegin

ACT II

Scene 1 It is Tatiana's birthday, and Madame Larina has arranged a dance to celebrate the occasion. All the gentry within calling distance have been invited, and to the tune of the waltz that is sometimes played as a concert piece, the older guests comment on the goings-on. The most interesting thing to note is that Onegin is dancing with Tatiana, and the wise-acres predict a possible wedding, even though the groom has a somewhat unsavory reputation. Onegin is annoyed, and, besides, he is angry at his friend Lenski for having brought him to so dull a provincial assembly. By way of retaliation he dances off with Lenski's fiancée, Olga, at the first opportunity; and when that dance is over, Lenski accuses the girl of flirting. Onegin pursues his tormenting tactics by reminding Olga that she has promised him the next cotillion, and, to punish her jealous swain, she walks off with Onegin.

The tension is temporarily relieved when the elderly Monsieur Triquet entertains the company with a formal, gallant song he has composed for the occasion in praise of the birthday child, Tatiana. The verses, being quite neatly turned and in French (the language of all nineteenth-century Russian snobs), pleases everyone but Tatiana, who is plainly embarrassed.

Now the old-fashioned cotillion begins, and when the first turn is over, Onegin taunts Lenski with the observation that he looks as severe as Childe Harolde himself. Lenski becomes more and more outraged and, with the guests crowding around, he finally challenges his friend to a duel. A great ensemble develops, in which each of the characters –as well as the chorus—expresses appropriate sentiments, that of Onegin being regret over having carried his teasing of his friend too far. There is now, however, no help for it, and he accepts the challenge for a duel to take place the next morning. Tatiana weeps and Olga faints.

Scene 2 Beside a mill, beside a stream, early in the morning Lenski and his second, Zaretski, are awaiting Onegin, who

153

is late. The second goes off to talk to the miller, and Lenski sings what is known as *Lenski's Air*, the second-best-known tenor aria in Russian opera. (The most familiar of all is the *Song of India* from *Sadko*.) It is his passionate farewell to Olga, to love, to youth.

Finally Onegin appears with his second, Gillot, a servant who is frightened by the prospect of a duel and hides behind a tree when the shooting begins. First, however, the two principals sing a duet in canon form—that is, one begins the tune, which the other takes up a moment later. Each shows how he would prefer to resume the old friendship; each decides that the formalities must nevertheless be observed. The duet ends with a dramatic "No!" from both of them. Zaretski then gives the formal instructions; each of the principals steps forward three paces; Onegin fires first; and Lenski is killed. Anguish overwhelms Onegin.

ACT III

Scene 1 In the St. Petersburg home of a wealthy and middle-aged retired general, Prince Gremin, a fashionable ball is in progress, and the music to which the ballet dances is the *Polonaise*, often heard at orchestral concerts. It is three or more years since the duel, and Onegin has been spending them wandering in many places and trying to forget. He is now only twenty-six but feels much older, and he has turned up at the home of his distant kinsman in one more effort to overcome his remorse.

Tatiana is now the Princess Gremin, and, not recognizing her distinguished-looking young guest, she asks who he is and is much moved when she hears the name. Meantime, on the other side of the stage, Onegin is asking Gremin the analogous question about Tatiana. In an impressive aria Prince Gremin sings the praises of his wife, telling Onegin how her love has stood out for him as the one truly ennobling thing in all the wicked world he has known. But when Tatiana and her old lover are formally introduced, she pleads tiredness as an excuse to leave the festivities.

Now Onegin is at last in love himself. He wonders that he ever could have given condescending advice about love to so wonderful a creature; he recalls that he still has the letter she sent him; and in the climax of the aria, he sings the very theme (though in a baritone key) that Tatiana had sung in her *Letter Scene,* when she decided to dedicate herself to her love for Onegin.

Scene 2 It has now been Onegin's turn to write a letter. Tatiana, in a room in her husband's house, is awaiting his visit and, holding the letter in her hand, indicates clearly that the next few minutes are going to be trying.

When Onegin rushes to her and goes down on his knees, she attempts to be cold. She suggests that he may be only attracted by the glamour of having a love affair with the wife of a distinguished ornament of society. Onegin's passion, however, is obviously far more genuine than this. He acknowledges that his former behavior had been sheer madness; he begs for pity; he asks her to run away with him. Tatiana, who has been trying to conquer her real emotions by the earlier show of coldness, now melts and finally sinks into his arms. Yet even during the passionate phrases that follow she knows what she owes to her husband. Summoning all her moral strength, she dismisses Onegin and rushes from the room. Again Onegin is overwhelmed with anguish.

FALSTAFF

Opera in three acts by Giuseppe Verdi with
libretto by Arrigo Boito based on Shakespeare's
The Merry Wives of Windsor and bits of
Henry IV

SIR JOHN FALSTAFF, *the fat knight*	*Baritone*
BARDOLPH ⎱ *Falstaff's hangers-on*	*Tenor*
PISTOL ⎰	*Bass*
FORD, *a wealthy burgher*	*Baritone*
ALICE FORD, *his wife*	*Soprano*
ANN (NANETTA) FORD, *their daughter*	*Soprano*
FENTON, *Ann's suitor*	*Tenor*
DR. CAIUS, *another suitor*	*Tenor*
MISTRESS PAGE, *a neighbor of the Fords*	*Mezzo-soprano*
DAME QUICKLY, *servant of Dr. Caius*	*Contralto*

Time: early 15th century
Place: Windsor
First performance at Milan, February 9, 1893

Verdi's *Falstaff* is, as everyone knows, based on Shakespeare's *The Merry Wives of Windsor*. It is, thus, a great
opera by a great composer; and it is based on the work of a
great dramatist who happened, for once, to write a pretty poor
play. Maybe it is not polite to say that anything by Shakespeare is not very good. Anyway, this play was so really second-
rate that many Shakespearean scholars doubt that Shakespeare
wrote much of it.

Be that as it may, Verdi's librettist, Arrigo Boito, took out
some of the unnecessary stuffing, added bits and pieces from

better Shakespeare plays, and gave his friend Verdi an excellent concoction, filled with the champagne of high spirits. And Verdi, though in his eightieth year when the opera was produced, wrote a sparkling score. There is none of the long, passionate melodies here of the youthful *Traviata* and *Trovatore*, but wit, skill, and high spirits in almost every bar.

ACT I

Scene 1   The time is the fifteenth century; the place is Windsor, not far from London; and the scene is inside the Garter Inn. That fat old rascal, Sir John Falstaff, is being upbraided by the foolish old Dr. Caius. Apparently, the night before, Caius has had a drinking bout with Falstaff and his disreputable hangers-on, Bardolph and Pistol, and Caius's pocket has been picked. He gets exactly nowhere with the three: they are merely contemptuous.

When Caius has left, Falstaff is given a bill by the host of the inn. He cannot pay, and so he devises a plot to get money. He tells Bardolph and Pistol how two jolly wives of Windsor —Mistress Ford and Mistress Page—have been attracted to him. Both, he says, control their husbands' purse strings. He means to make love to them and to get money from them. For this purpose he has written each a letter, and Bardolph and Pistol are to constitute themselves the postal department. But, surprisingly, these good-for-nothings refuse: they say they stand on their honor and will have nothing to do with this business. "Honor!" cries Falstaff—and he delivers them a terrific lecture on the meaninglessness of that word. (It is a pretty magnificent lecture, taken largely from Shakespeare's *Henry IV, Part 2*.) Honor cannot fill an empty stomach or set straight a broken limb, and is nothing but a word that floats away. As for Bardolph and Pistol, they are nothing but thieves; and he closes the act by chasing them, with a broom, right out of the inn!

Scene 2   In spite of Bardolph and Pistol, Falstaff has had his letters delivered by a page to Mistress Ford and Mistress Page. And in the second scene of this act, we turn from the purely masculine company of the Garter Inn to meet the ladies in Ford's house. There is Meg Page, and there is Alice Ford (those are the two "merry wives"), there is Alice's pretty daughter Ann, and there is the gossipy old neighbor Dame Quickly, who happens also to be the servant of Dr. Caius. The two merry wives soon discover that they have received identical letters from Sir John Falstaff, and they are convulsed with glee.

Meantime, those rapscallions, Bardolph and Pistol, have told Ford that the fat knight is planning to seduce his wife. The Ford household is a pretty busy place that morning, for Dr. Caius has also come over to complain of the way he has been treated. And, to make the stage quite full, there is also young Fenton, a suitor for the hand of Ann Ford. What with the women plotting against Falstaff on one side of the stage, the men plotting against him on the other, and everyone talking at the same time, Verdi had a fine chance for chattery nine-part writing. He made splendid use of it. And, by way of contrast, he also wrote some light love music for Ann and Fenton. Fenton's suit is not approved by Ford, who wants Ann to marry Dr. Caius. Therefore, the young folks have only brief words with each other on the sly. No full-blown love duets here—just flirtations. The whole scene, in fact, is light and airy as a feather.

ACT II

Scene 1 The plots against Sir John Falstaff now begin to take shape. Back at the Garter Inn, Bardolph and Pistol, the hypocrites, ask to be taken back into Falstaff's good graces. Soon they usher in Dame Quickly. She tells the knight that the two ladies—Mistress Page and Mistress Ford—are both in love with him. Ford, she says, is always away from home between two and three. Won't Sir John pay a call? And Page— why, he's away from home most of the time, so . . . Vastly flattered, Falstaff promises to come; and when Dame Quickly leaves, he expresses his self-satisfaction in the monologue *Va*, *vecchio John.* "Get along with you, old John," he says in effect; "there's life in the old boy yet."

But now Bardolph announces another visitor, one Maestro Fontana, who wishes to meet him, and who brings along a demijohn of wine for breakfast. This Fontana is none other than Ford in disguise. He enlists Falstaff's aid, with the promise of money, in seducing the wife of a certain burgher of Windsor—Mistress Ford, to be exact. Falstaff falls into the trap completely, promising success based on his own attraction for the lady in question. But when he goes off to array himself properly for the conquest, Ford sings a terrific monologue (*È sogno? o realtà?*—"Is it a dream? or is it real?") on the chances he stands of being made a cuckold. He swears a terrible revenge on both Falstaff and his own wife; but the scene ends again in comedy as he and Falstaff, now splendidly attired, bow each other out of the doorway with ludicrous ceremony.

Scene 2 Back in Ford's house things begin to come to a boil. The ladies are together, and Dame Quickly reports her success with Sir John Falstaff. He will come wooing Mistress Ford today, from two to three. Meantime, pretty little Ann tells her mother that Ford wants her to marry old Dr. Caius —a dreadful thought to both of them!

Unfortunately, it is time for Falstaff to come a-wooing. The stage is set for him: Mistress Ford takes up a lute; the others hide behind a screen. The fat old gentleman wastes no time in his ludicrous love-making. Within two minutes he is proposing: he tells Alice how beautiful she is and how handsome he once was, and he does his best to take her into the cushioned circumference of his arms. Alice, of course, resists coquettishly, but they are soon interrupted. Ford is on his way home! And there is a fine how-de-do as the ladies hide His Fatness behind the screen.

Ford breaks in furiously, with a whole retinue of followers. They look everywhere—even in a large laundry basket—but not, fortunately, behind the screen. When the men are off searching other rooms, the fat knight is stuffed into that laundry basket. He is covered with dirty clothes; and when the men return, he occasionally sticks out his head to complain that he's roasting to death. It's a perfectly mad scene, everyone singing at once, or in pairs, or in quartets. Even the two young lovers—Ann and Fenton—have a chance to exchange some tender words behind the screen. Finally, with the men off again searching in another room, the laundry basket, complete with Falstaff, is heaved out of the window and—splash—into the river outside. Huge laughter and merriment close the broadly farcical scene.

ACT III

Scene 1 Poor Jack Falstaff! Honest Jack Falstaff! Rogue Jack Falstaff! He has been thoroughly defeated—thrown, in a laundry basket, into the river, while Ford and his wife have become quite reconciled. But they are not through yet with the fat knight; otherwise there would have been no Act III. There he sits, before the Garter Inn, commiserating with himself. He has been terribly treated, vilely treated. But he gets a big beaker of hot wine, and then we hear the famous trill in the orchestra to show what it does to him. It starts way down (like the effect of wine), and it grows and grows, till the whole orchestra—like Jack's whole body—is one big trill and thrill!

Now Dame Quickly comes. With little difficulty she persuades Falstaff that it was not Alice's fault. She still loves him—and he reads her letter, which Dame Quickly has brought. It is an assignation to meet at midnight, in disguise, at the royal park. The other plotters have been listening to this exchange; and when Falstaff and Dame Quickly enter the inn, the eavesdroppers occupy the entire stage and develop their various plots. And while they are in a conspiratorial mood, Dr. Caius and Ford plot, by means of disguises, to marry the old physician to young Ann that same night.

Scene 2 And now, last scene of all: midnight in Windsor Park. There all sorts of things may happen—especially under Herne's Oak. Herne was a legendary huntsman, and the very opening notes of the scene suggest the hunting horn's echoing in ghostly fashion. There the lovers—Fenton and Ann—meet to sing a brief duet. It cannot go on long, for they must don their costumes for the fun, and to carry out their own plot.

Then, cold on the stroke of midnight, enter Sir John, disguised as the hunter Herne. One . . . two . . . three . . . up to twelve he counts the strokes, when his beloved Alice greets him. Sir John's love-making makes a sharp contrast with young Fenton's; but he too is interrupted. A whole troop of fairies arrives, with Ann, disguised as their Queen, at their head. It is all done to charming, fairylike music, but Sir John hides, frightened to death, before the oak. In his superstitious mind it is death to look on fairies. With everyone assembled—the men, too, in their supernatural disguises—the fun begins. They torture poor Sir John—they stick him, prick him, pinch him, roll him, and tumble him, till the old man can take no more. At length he arises and shakes them off, only to be reviled— and finally forgiven. Never again will he go a-courting the merry wives of Windsor!

But what of the young lovers? Ford, who has plotted to betroth Dr. Caius to his daughter Ann, does so. Only it turns out that the redheaded rascal Bardolph has taken over Ann's disguise as the Queen of the Fairies, and Caius finds himself with a pretty bride indeed! At the same time Ford has blessed another couple in masks, and these turn out to be Ann herself and her true-love Fenton.

In the magic of the night and the wooded scene everyone is reconciled. Falstaff proposes a grand finale, and Verdi ends his long and glorious operatic career with a magnificent fugue in nine parts.

FAUST

Opera in four acts by Charles Gounod with
libretto in French by Jules Barbier and Michel
Carré based on Part I of Goethe's *Faust*

FAUST, *a doctor of philosophy*	*Tenor*
MEPHISTOPHELES, *the Tempter*	*Bass*
VALENTINE, *a soldier*	*Baritone*
MARGUERITE, *his sister*	*Soprano*
SIEBEL, *a boy in love with Marguerite*	*Mezzo-soprano or soprano*
MARTHE, *a mature neighbor of Marguerite*	*Mezzo-soprano*
WAGNER, *a student*	*Baritone*

Time: 16th century
Places: Wittenberg, Leipzig, and the Harz Mountains
First performance at Paris, March 19, 1859

The legend of Dr. Faustus seems to be the perfect story
to attract both dramatists and composers. Marlowe and
Goethe wrote great plays on the subject—not to mention some
thirty lesser dramatists who wrote lesser plays. Beethoven once
toyed with the idea of doing an opera on the subject. Wagner
composed a *Faust Overture*. Liszt did a cantata. And Berlioz,
Boito, and Gounod all wrote very find Faust operas. Spohr
and Busoni wrote less successful ones; and there is even a
Faust opera by that *rara avis*, a female opera composer—
Louise Bertin. Gounod's setting is easily the most popular of
all of them—and in many ways the best. It is based, more
closely than most critics have been willing to admit, on Part I
of Goethe's drama; and its theme is, of course, that of the

old German scientist-philosopher who sells his soul in return
for youth.

PRELUDE

The orchestral prelude begins with slow, soft music in a
minor key and a contrapuntal style skillfully suggestive of the
gloomy medieval scholar's cell on which the curtain will
shortly rise. Then, in a completely different style, the melody
of Valentine's aria *Even Bravest Heart May Swell* is played,
and the prelude closes with a few measures of *religioso* music.

ACT I

Scene 1 deals with the contract Faust makes with the Devil—
Mephistopheles. After the prelude, the old scholar, seated in
his study in the medieval town of Wittenberg, complains that
all his learning has brought him nothing. He is about to poison
himself, when he hears youthful voices outside his study praising the Lord. In desperation Faust calls on the Devil for aid,
and, much to his surprise, Mephistopheles appears, clothed
like a sixteenth-century gentleman. At first Faust turns from
him; but when Mephisto offers whatever he wants, Faust cries
out that he desires—youth!

Nothing could be simpler for Mephisto. He shows the old
man a vision of the lovely young girl, Marguerite, and almost
at once the philosopher is ready to sign the contract. On
earth, Mephisto will serve him in everything. But below, the
Devil will be master. A quick signature, a quick magic potion,
and Faust is changed to a young man in elegant costume. The
scene ends with a spirited duet, as the two go off in search of
adventure—and love.

Scene 2 takes us to a village fair in sixteenth-century Leipzig. Soldiers, students, villagers are milling around and singing
the praises of light wines and beer. Valentine, who is Marguerite's brother, is in a more serious frame of mind. He is
worried about who will guard over his sister while he is at the
wars, and he sings the familiar aria *Even Bravest Heart May*

Swell. (Gounod, by the way, wrote this aria originally using the English words. The French translation begins: *Avant de quitter ces lieux.*) Now a student, Wagner, begins a song about a rat, but he is interrupted by Mephistopheles, who claims he knows a better song. This is the *Calf of Gold*, which is so rhythmic that everyone joins in the chorus, for as yet they do not recognize this genial basso as the Devil. Mephisto then produces, by magic, some excellent wine (much better, he says, than the local stuff), and he proposes a toast to Marguerite. Valentine is angered by having his sister's name thus bandied about, and challenges the stranger. But just as he is about to attack, Mephisto points at him, and Valentine's sword breaks in half. Now the villagers know whom they have to deal with. Led by Valentine, they reverse their swords, thus making the sign of the cross; and as they sing the Chorale of the Swords, Mephisto grovels on the ground.

When they have left him alone, Faust appears on the stage, demanding to meet Marguerite, and the Devil is himself again. The famous waltz from *Faust* begins, and in the midst of the dancing Marguerite comes on the stage. Faust offers her his arm; she very politely declines; and the waltz resumes as the badly smitten Faust voices his newborn love. In a swirl of madder and madder waltz rhythms the scene ends.

ACT II

Act II is the justly famous *Garden Scene*. It takes place the same evening in Marguerite's garden, and the familiar melodies that come from that garden may justly be called a sweet bouquet of great arias and concerted numbers. A list of them will make the action clear. First of all, there is Siebel's *Flower Song*. Siebel is the young man who is in love with Marguerite; and as he sings, he gathers flowers and finally places them where Marguerite cannot fail to see them. The next great aria is Faust's *Salut demeure*—"All hail thou dwelling pure and lowly." In it he expresses his enchantment with the beautiful and simple surroundings wherein the lovely Marguerite grew up. Immediately after it Mephistopheles

comes in and leaves a casket of jewels beside Siebel's bouquet
—a bit of unfair competition, I always thought. And, when
the two gentlemen have retired, in comes Marguerite and, as
she sits beside her spinning wheel, she sings the simple ballad
The King of Thule. Every once in a while she interrupts herself as she moons a little about the handsome young stranger
who had greeted her at the dance. Immediately after this she
discovers first Siebel's flowers, and then the casket of jewels.
This is the signal for the brilliant *Jewel Song,* during which
she decks herself out in the finery she finds.

Marguerite now is joined by her gossipy old neighbor,
Marthe, and then both are joined by Faust and Mephisto.
And while Mephisto makes mock love to Marthe, Faust and
Marguerite get to know each other better. A very fine quartet
is the natural musical outcome. Twilight comes on, and
Mephistopheles solemnly intones his *Invocation to Night.* He
hopes it may lead to trouble for poor Marguerite, and Faust
and Marguerite are then left alone for their great *Love Duet.*
As she superstitiously plucks a daisy for the old he-loves-me-
he-loves-me-not test, as she protests that it is growing too late,
as she says she loves him so much that she would die for him,
Gounod paints a picture of dawning love that few composers
have ever equaled. Faust, who retains some compunctions
about seducing an innocent maiden, finally consents to leave
and return the next day. But the Devil knows his business
only too well. Just as Faust is leaving the garden, he stops him
and points to Marguerite's window. There she is, leaning out
of it, and singing to the stars about her new love. It is one
of the most enchanting bits in the whole scene. Faust rushes
to embrace her passionately; and Mephistopheles, his end
achieved, laughs a hearty, wicked laugh as the orchestra swells
and then fades away, picturing the love of Faust and Marguerite.

ACT III

Scene 1, though based on a famous bit in Goethe's play,
is almost always omitted in modern performances, possibly

because its theme—that of the deserted woman—is the same as the theme of the more dramatically powerful scene which follows immediately.

Marguerite is alone in her room, horrified by the laughing taunts of her girlish ex-playmates, who may be heard outside giggling over her departed gallant. She sits at her spinning wheel, sadly bemoaning the lover who will return no more, in the aria *Il ne revient pas*. Young Siebel calls and gallantly offers to avenge her, but Marguerite admits she loves the man still. Thereupon Siebel sings the consoling aria *Si le bonheur* ("When All Was Young"), which remained a popular drawing-room ballad long after the better judgment of impresarios had banished the entire scene from the stage.

Scene 2 is equally brief. It shows Marguerite praying in the church despite her belief that her sin will never be pardoned. Her prayer is interrupted by the Devil, who, from behind a pillar, mockingly reminds her of the days of her innocence. A chorus of demons punctuates Mephisto's remarks with cries of "*Marguerite! Marguerite!*" Meantime, a holy service is going on in another part of the church; and as the choir intones the solemn *Dies Irae*, Marguerite's voice soars above it, wildly begging for pardon. But when Mephisto cries, "*Marguerite! Sois maudite! A toi l'enfer!*" (that is, "Marguerite, be cursed to hell"), she cries out piteously, and faints away. The quiet, religious tones of the organ close the scene—as it began it.

Scene 3 takes us to the street outside Marguerite's home. Into the square pour the soldiers, home from the wars. They sing, of course, the famous *Soldiers' Chorus* from *Faust*. Among the veterans is Marguerite's brother, Valentine. He invites Siebel into his house, but Siebel, in great confusion, declines. Suspiciously Valentine goes inside, and presently he hears a mocking serenade. It is sung by Mephistopheles, who has brought Faust back with him. The three octaves of *Ha-ha-ha's* that close this serenade bring out a very angry Valentine. He now knows what has happened while he was away, and he immediately challenges Faust to a duel. As the two men prepare, a stirring trio is sung. Then comes the duel, indicated by strong, suspenseful music in the orchestra. Surreptitiously

Faust

the Devil directs the sword of Faust—and it finds the heart of Valentine. As the villagers (who have heard the disturbance) gather, Mephisto takes Faust from the scene.

Now Valentine has his powerful death scene. Painfully he lifts himself to his knees, and he bitterly curses his sister with his dying breath. The villagers are shocked and horrified; and when the soldier dies at their feet, there is a moment of utter silence. They barely whisper a short prayer—and the clarinet sings a mournful tune as the act ends.

ACT IV

Scene 1 is omitted by opera companies that do not wish to expose the inadequacy of their ballet wings and proudly mounted by those with terpsichorean pretensions. It is the *Walpurgis Night* scene and gets its name from the German superstition that on the eve of May 1 (the day of St. Walpurgis, an eighth-century proselytizing nun from England) the Devil holds a festival on the Brocken in the Harz Mountains. Mephistopheles brings his protégé to this festival, conjuring up for him such classical beauties as the Sicilian Lais and the Egyptian Cleopatra. Supernatural females of dubious morality dance for the enchanted philosopher to the strains of the so-called *Ballet Music from Faust*, which still forms a staple part of the repertoire of concert bands. Presently Mephisto calls for drinks, and Faust is joining in the revelry when the orchestra suddenly plays, *pianissimo*, a theme from the *Love Duet*. A vision of Marguerite appears in the background, a red line about her neck, which Faust, horrified and filled with remorse, describes as looking like the cut of an ax. Peremptorily he demands that Mephisto take him to her, and the scene ends with what a movie-pianist friend of mine used to call "hurry-up music."

Scene 2 In the final scene we find Marguerite in a prison cell. She is to be executed that very morning for the murder of her child. Under the terrible strain, her mind is giving way. Mephistopheles and Faust break into the prison; and while Mephisto goes off to fetch horses for their escape, Faust

Faust

awakens the sleeping Marguerite. They sing of their love for each other, but Marguerite's mind begins to wander. She thinks she is again at the fair, where she met Faust, and in the garden, where they made love. We hear music from these earlier scenes. Suddenly Mephistopheles reappears. The horses are ready, he says, and they must hurry. But Marguerite recognizes the Devil at last. "*Le démon, le démon!*" she cries, and sinks to her knees in eloquent prayer. The exciting final trio is then sung, as Mephisto and Faust urge Marguerite to leave and she steadfastly repeats her prayer—each time in a higher key. At the end she sinks, exhausted and dying, to the ground. Mephisto pronounces her damned. But a choir of angels brings the final sound of her salvation—and her soul goes to Heaven as the opera ends.

LA FAVOLA D'ORFEO

(*The Fable of Orpheus*)

Opera in prologue and five acts by Claudio
Monteverdi with libretto in Italian by Alessandro Striggio

ORPHEUS, *singer*	*Tenor**
EURIDYCE, *his wife*	*Soprano*
APOLLO, *god of music*	*Tenor**
PLUTO, *god of the underworld*	*Bass*
PROSERPINE, *his wife*	*Mezzo-soprano*
CHARON, *ferryman of the Styx*	*Bass*
SYLVIA, *a messenger*	*Mezzo-soprano*
MUSIC	*Mezzo-soprano*
HOPE	*Mezzo-soprano*
FIRST SHEPHERD	*High tenor*
SECOND SHEPHERD	*Tenor**
A NYMPH	*Soprano*
FIRST SPIRIT, *in the underworld*	*High tenor*
SECOND SPIRIT, *in the underworld*	*Tenor**
ECHO	*Tenor**

Time: mythological
Places: Thrace and the underworld
First performance at Mantua, February 1607

In Dr. Alfred Loewenberg's monumental *Annals of
Opera* you may find the vital statistics, in chronological order,
of every opera of any consequence (and some of none whatsoever) produced between the years 1597 and 1940. *La favola*

* The tenor parts are often sung in modern performances by baritones and some of the mezzo-soprano parts by sopranos.

d'Orfeo is the sixth one listed, and in many histories of opera you may read that it really deserves first place. The reason given is that the earlier operas (two of which, by the way, also told the story of Orpheus) were not operas in a modern sense at all. They were imitation classical plays in which the idea was to present dramas similar to Greek tragedies in a way that the Italian litterateurs of the day fancied they were presented in ancient Athens. That is, the lines were to be recited in a musical fashion and set to unobtrusive musical accompaniment. The verses were the important thing, not the music.

Now, a casual modern listener to Monteverdi's *Orfeo* who does not know the history of opera or the Italian language may soon come to the same conclusion about that great work. Most of its length of two hours or so is devoted to long, poetic laments set to a kind of melody (mostly in a minor key) that will strike the uninstructed ear as a somewhat elaborate chant. The accompaniment, varied as it is in instrumentation from number to number, remains very discreetly in the background; and the only tunes with an easily recognizable shape to them occur in the choruses (which sound like accompanied madrigals because that is virtually what they are) and in the orchestral introductions and interludes between vocal passages (called *ritornelli*).

If, however, the listener either knows Italian or will take the trouble to follow a performance with a translation and the original in hand, he will undergo a thoroughly rewarding musical experience. For he will discover that the somewhat unfamiliar musical language is an extraordinarily eloquent one, that the melodic line is intimately wedded to both the meaning and the rhythms of the poetry, that the harmonies which at first may seem monotonously simple are in reality strangely modern-sounding, especially in their dissonances, and that the whole effect is at once deeply serious and passionately tragic. Even the unprepared listener will find considerable variety by virtue of the frequent choral comments, the introduction of occasional duets (the first time these were used in an opera), and the variety in the scoring for the orchestra.

This orchestration is an extraordinary thing. It calls for two harpsichords, one double harp, two large lutes, two bass zithers (which might be described roughly as still-larger lutes), three bass gambas (ancestors of our bass fiddles), two organs with wood pipes and one with reeds, two small violins (smaller than modern ones), twelve viols of different sizes, four trombones, two cornets, two high recorders, one high trumpet (called a *clarino*), and three muted trumpets. It would be difficult indeed to get a collection like this together today, let alone a group of forty musicians to handle them adequately. Modern performances of the work, of which there have been many, transcribe the score for mostly modern instruments. Similarly, modern vocal techniques are so different that the vocal lines also call for editing. For instance, the part of Orfeo is sometimes sung by a baritone (though seventeenth-century music had no exact analogue for a modern operatic baritone), sometimes by a tenor, and once, at least (at the Florence Festival of 1949), by the distinguished contralto Fedora Barbieri.

In short, we cannot today reproduce a performance that would sound very much like the ones heard by the composer, and I am not at all sure that we would like it if we could. Tastes, especially musical tastes, change enormously and quickly. No matter. So long as the performers are competent, so long as an understanding spirit is in it, so long as the audience will take the trouble to listen with understanding minds and hearts, the greatness of this work will be apparent.

PROLOGUE

After an overture characterized by what Monteverdi's contemporaries, the Elizabethans, would have called "a tucket of trumpets," a soprano or mezzo steps before the curtain and, in the character of Music, sings a prologue of six stanzas separated by brief *ritornelli*. She avows that she, Music, will tell the tale of Orpheus, and she commands silence even from nature while the beautiful sounds go on.

ACT I

Nymphs and shepherds, in solo song and in chorus, sing with a solemn happiness of their pleasure over the nuptials of Orpheus and Eurydice, to be celebrated this very day. The bride and groom also sing of their happiness, and the act ends with a fine, joyous contrapuntal chorus.

ACT II

In the absence of his bride, Orpheus sings of his happiness, likening her to the sun who turns his nights into days. The shepherds, singly, in duet, and in chorus, delight to hear of his pleasure and ask him to sing to them as he accompanies himself on his lute. This he does, in an aria of four stanzas, contrasting his former sorrow with his present wedded bliss.

The joy is all destroyed by a messenger, an attendant of Eurydice's named Sylvia. In a long and pathetic narrative she slowly breaks the dreadful news: Eurydice has been bitten in the foot by a poisonous snake and has just died in Sylvia's arms. Orpheus is at first struck speechless, and the shepherds sing of their horror. Then Orpheus speaks with tragic determination. He will take his songs to the King of Shadows and bring Eurydice back to see the stars once more. The brief aria ends on an exceptionally eloquent line that slowly rises and then falls: "Farewell to earth; farewell to sky and sun; farewell!"

The rest of the act is given over to the lamentations of the shepherds and the self-reproaches of the messenger for having brought the fearful news. She does not appear again in the opera, but her two passages in this act are enough to project a distinctively lovable and pathetic portrait of a minor character.

ACT III

Hope has brought Orpheus to the borders of Pluto's realm, where he must cross the river Styx. He asks his guide for further help, but she replies that he must go on alone; for there stands the solemn inscription: "Abandon Hope, All Ye Who Enter Here." Then she departs.

The grim ferryman Charon demands to know what Orpheus is doing there. These realms are forbidden to all living men, and he suspects the musician of having designs on Pluto's fierce dog, Cerberus. Alternately playing and singing (a solo violin part is used most effectively), Orpheus pleads his case. Charon admits that he finds this music pleasing and consoling, but as there is no pity in his breast, it will do him no good. Orpheus thereupon becomes even more eloquent, ending his plea with the repeated line, "Return to me my well beloved, O gods of Tartarus!" And though there is no pity in his breast, yet the sweetness of the music puts Charon to sleep. Repeating his eloquent line, Orpheus springs into the boat and rows himself across. A final chorus describes his trip over the stormy waters in his fragile bark.

ACT IV

In Hades, Proserpine pleads with her husband, Pluto, to return Eurydice to the unhappy man who wanders through the broad lands of death crying out her name. Pluto, moved by his beloved wife's tears, agrees to grant her wish. However, if on the way back Orpheus should once look back, he shall lose her forever. He sends messengers to announce this decision to both Orpheus and Eurydice, and his court, consisting of a chorus of spirits, praises him for his generosity.

In a long scene, with considerable variety in the music, Orpheus leads Eurydice on the way, at first very happy, then growing depressed over being unable to see her. He fears that Pluto has forbidden him to look out of pure envy; and when he hears a threatening sound, he is sure that it must be the Furies come to snatch his wife from him. He turns around to look, and at once Eurydice begins to weaken. With a soft reproach, full of love, she dies, and a spirit comes to take her back again. Orpheus resolves to follow after her, but a mysterious force moves him in the other direction, toward the land of the living. The act closes with a chorus of spirits, which moralizes on the fact that, though great Orpheus could vanquish Hell, yet he could not conquer himself.

ACT V

Wandering in the fields of Thrace, Orpheus sings a long lament; and twice his lines are repeated off-stage by Echo, a striking effect. Apollo, god of music, appears to him, addressing him as his son, and offers to take him to the skies, where he may trace the beauty of Eurydice in the sun and stars. Together they ascend to heaven, singing an elaborately figured duet.

A happy shepherds' chorus ends the opera, its nature suggested by its label in the score, which is *moresca*—that is a Moorish dance or (in its British form) a morris dance. Classical tragedies were always expected to end on a note of relief; and that, presumably, is why Monteverdi did not set music to the final scene in the original libretto. In this Orpheus was torn to pieces by Thracian women for lamenting his Eurydice too long. That is the ending to the story of Orpheus as you will find it in all the books on mythology.

FIDELIO

(Fidelio)

Opera in two acts by Ludwig van Beethoven
with libretto in German by Josef Sonnleithner,
based on a French libretto by Jean Nicolas
Bouilly. Sonnleithner's libretto was revised by
Stefan von Breuning in 1806 and by Georg
Friedrich Treitschke in 1814

FLORESTAN, *a Spanish Nobleman*	*Tenor*
LEONORA, *his wife, in male attire known as "Fidelio"*	*Soprano*
DON FERNANDO, *the Prime Minister*	*Bass*
DON PIZARRO, *Governor of the prison*	*Bass*
ROCCO, *chief jailer*	*Bass*
MARCELLINA, *his daughter*	*Soprano*
JACQUINO, *his assistant*	*Tenor*

Time: 18th century
Place: Seville
First performance at Vienna, November 20, 1805

On October 30, 1805, Napoleon's armies crossed the
border into Austria, and Marshal Bernadotte (later to become
Charles XIV, King of Sweden and Norway) occupied Salzburg. Having no panzer divisions, the armies took weeks to
reach an undefended Vienna; but after they got there, Napoleon himself occupied the imperial palace at Schönbrunn and
instructed his soldiery to treat the citizens with a "correctness"
like that exhibited in the following century in Paris by the
occupation troops of Hitler. Included in this early-nineteenth-
century version of correctness was polite attendance by a scat-
tering of officers at the premiere of Beethoven's *Fidelio* on

November 20. Napoleon himself very likely knew nothing of this important event; in any case, his taste was for lighter music.

The house was half full, the performance a failure. After two repetitions it was temporarily dropped from the repertoire. In March of the following year, after Beethoven had with difficulty been induced to make some cuts and other changes, it was tried again. Once more it failed. Still it was tried once more in the following season, but it attracted—like most of Beethoven's so-called "difficult" music in those days —only the *cognoscenti* (i.e., those who could afford the best seats). The composer angrily withdrew the score, tinkered with it on and off, and completely revised it in 1814. Then, with the great Schroeder-Devrient in the title role, it was at last acclaimed.

Thirteen years later, near death, Beethoven presented the manuscript of his only opera to his close friend and biographer, Anton Schindler. "Of all my children," said the dying man, "this is the one that cost me the worst birth-pangs and brought me the most sorrow; and for that reason it is the one most dear to me."

It is an opera most dear, also, to many a music-lover, and it has had an honored place in the repertoire of most great opera houses. Nowadays, however, it is revived only sporadically, for it is seldom a great success at the box-office. Perhaps the reason lies in an odd inconsistency in style: the first scene is largely *Singspiel*, almost light opera, especially when given with the intended spoken dialogue instead of the recitatives usually supplied outside of Germany and Austria. Perhaps the reason lies in the naïveté of the plot and its contrast with the fierce idealism of the emotional music. But one thing is certainly true: few opera composers, if any, have ever written such powerfully expressive music as the *Prisoners' Chorus*, the big arias of Leonora and of Florestan, or the overture known as *Leonora No. 3*.

Fidelio

OVERTURE

There are four overtures available to the producer. The one composed first, and played at the premiere in 1805, is now known as *Leonora No. 2*. *Leonora No. 3* was composed for the March 1806 revision. This one was somewhat simplified for a projected but unrealized performance in Prague the same year; the manuscript was lost until 1832; and when it was found, it was assumed to be the first one Beethoven wrote for the opera. It is therefore called, or miscalled, *Leonora No. 1*. The fourth overture, written for the 1814 performance, is called the *Fidelio Overture*. It is the one usually used nowadays before Act I and introduces the pleasant opening scene far more appropriately than any of the *Leonora* overtures would.

Leonora No. 3 is often played between the two scenes of Act II. To many critics its anticipation of the musical and dramatic effects in the following scene makes this practice abhorrently inartistic. I must say that I agree with them. This overture is so strong, so dramatic, so effective with its off-stage trumpet call (repeated, of course, in the opera) that it needs no stage action to convey, in essence, the musical message of the entire opera. Perhaps that is why Beethoven, having learned from experience in the intervening years, wrote the more modest *Fidelio Overture* for the final revision; and perhaps that is why this great orchestral poem should be reserved exclusively for the concert hall.

ACT I

Sometimes this act is divided into two scenes; sometimes, as in the score, it remains undivided. In either case, the action takes place in the home of Rocco, jailer of the prison at Seville. (In the divided productions it begins inside the house and ends in the courtyard; in the undivided ones, it all takes place in the courtyard).

There is a one-sided romance going on between Rocco's

daughter Marcellina and Rocco's assistant, Jacquino. The young man proposes insistently without any encouragement whatsoever from the girl, and also under considerable difficulties. Not only does Marcellina stick to her ironing, but the poor fellow is repeatedly interrupted at his wooing by summonses to open the door he is supposed to be attending. When he has finally left, Marcellina utters a sigh of relief and a very pleasant little aria (*O wär ich schon mit dir vereint*—"Oh, were we only married now"). Quite frankly she tells us that the man she would like to be married to is Fidelio. What she does not know is that Fidelio is a woman in disguise. She is Leonora, the wife of Florestan, a political prisoner of Pizarro's, the tyrannical Governor of the fortress of Seville. No one knows just where Florestan has been put; but Leonora, suspecting it may be right here, has disguised herself as a man, taken the name of Fidelio, and secured herself a job as first assistant to Rocco. She has been on this job for six months now without finding Florestan, but has won the devoted admiration of both her master and his daughter.

Rocco, accompanied by Jacquino, comes in and says that he is expecting Fidelio back from the city with some new chains; and when Fidelio shows up with a particularly sturdy set, he is congratulated. An enchanting quartet is sung, in the form of a canon or round, in which Marcellina shows that she thinks Fidelio likes her, Fidelio notes Marcellina's affections but cannot approve of them, Rocco thinks they would make a fine couple, and Jacquino fears he may be frozen out. And in simple song Rocco gives some worldly advice to the couple he believes to be virtually engaged: "He who hasn't laid up gold cannot expect a happy life."

In the ensuing dialogue Leonora learns of a prisoner kept so secret that no one but the jailer is allowed to visit him. She is overjoyed when Rocco tells her that, on account of the way work is getting a bit too heavy for him, she may be permitted to help. A trio follows.

It is at this point that many productions change from the inside to the outside of Rocco's house, and a martial tune in the orchestra gives time for the change of scene. Pizarro enters with a troop of guards and gets his mail from Rocco. One of the letters (as he obligingly informs us by reading it aloud) is a secret warning of a surprise visitation from Don Fernando, the Prime Minister of Spain, who has heard that Pizarro has been misusing his powers at the expense of others. He summons Rocco and orders the secret prisoner murdered forthwith but secretly, and he offers the gold-loving jailer a bribe. Rocco, accepting it, soothes his conscience by remarking that death is probably better anyway than the slow starvation the poor fellow has been suffering on orders from Pizarro.

Leonora has been eavesdropping on the latter part of this scheming, and she now sings her great aria *Abscheulicher! wo eilst du hin!* ("O! thou monstrous fiend!") and follows it with another one in which she expresses her hope and her faith that God and her love will yet see them through.

After a brief scene in which Marcellina makes it clear to Jacquino that she is not going to marry him, but Fidelio, Rocco is persuaded, in the Governor's absence, to give the prisoners some fresh air—a luxury they are very seldom accorded. The wretched men, fearful of the guard on the wall, yet ecstatically happy to breathe the air of heaven, file in slowly and sing the *Prisoners' Chorus*, a deeply moving projection of the emotions of bewildered sufferers given a temporary taste of freedom.

Rocco returns from his interview with Pizarro and tells Fidelio that he has permission for him to marry Marcellina, but that now they must prepare to dig the grave of the secret prisoner. Leonora is aghast at this news and asks whether he is already dead or whether Rocco is supposed to murder him. Neither, says Rocco: Pizarro will do his own murdering; all they need do is to dig the grave. He offers to let her off this rather dismal assignment, but Leonora insists on helping the old man even though, in her heart, she feels it must be intended for her husband, Florestan.

Pizarro, having heard of the unauthorized liberty accorded the prisoners, returns to denounce the jailer; but Rocco succeeds in mollifying him through a reference to the man who is about to die. The prisoners are then herded back into their cells; the doors are locked and bolted; and the act ends with soft and ominous sounds in the kettledrums.

ACT II

Scene 1 In his gloomy dungeon Florestan, chained to a stone, comments, even after two years of uninterrupted tenancy, on the dismal aspect of his apartment. Behind him is a long flight of steps leading to the door that gives entry to that part of the prison. He then sings his moving aria *In des Lebens Frühlingstagen* ("In the springtime days of life"), in which he mourns his lost and courageous youth, resigns himself to a death that cannot be far off, and imagines he sees an angel, in the shape of Leonora, leading him up to heaven. Then he sleeps.

Rocco and Fidelio come in, prepared to dig the grave in a cistern by the side of the cell. The scene is composed in what is technically and literally "melodrama": that is, spoken dialogue is carried on, and the orchestra plays snatches of music. As they work, Leonora tries to catch a glimpse of the prisoner's features, but she cannot be sure that it is her husband, even when Rocco speaks with him and offers him a drink of wine. A few moments later, however, she is sure; and when she offers him a crust of bread, she can barely stand it that even her beloved Florestan does not recognize her. Pitifully, in a sweet melody, he thanks the assistant jailer for the deed of mercy.

Now Rocco gives a whistle, the agreed-upon signal to Pizarro, and Florestan, having at last learned who has sent him to this place, suspects that his life is threatened. Pizarro descends the stairs, throws back his cloak, and gloats for a moment over Florestan, who prepares for his own death with consummate dignity and courage. But just as Pizarro, dagger drawn, is about to hurl himself at Florestan, Leonora throws herself between them, crying, "First kill his wife!" Everyone is astonished; and when Pizarro prepares to do a double murder, Leonora pulls a pistol from her doublet and covers him.

At that moment, off-stage, is heard the trumpet call which

everyone remembers from the frequent performances of the *Leonora No. 3* overture. A moment of silence, another snatch from the overture music, and the trumpet call rings out again, nearer this time. Jacquino rushes down to bring the news that the Prime Minister is at the gates. There is a short quartet; Pizarro and Rocco leave; and the scene usually closes with the joyful duet in which husband and wife are reunited.

In the score and the libretto there is a short spoken scene after the duet in which Rocco returns and tells of the list of prisoners submitted to the Prime Minister, which does not contain Florestan's name, showing that he was a victim of the private vengeance of Pizarro. As this scene is not strictly necessary for the drama, and as the spoken dialogue makes a much tamer scene ending, the curtain customarily is lowered after the Leonora-Florestan duet.

Scene 2 In the brief final scene, the Prime Minister, Don Fernando, addresses the assembled prisoners and townspeople on the mercy of the King, recognizes Florestan and Leonora as old friends, and orders Pizarro led away in chains. The opera closes with a general chorus in praise of Leonora and of conjugal love, which is the theme of the whole work.

DIE FLEDERMAUS

(The Bat)

Operetta in three acts by Johann Strauss with libretto in German by Carl Haffner and Richard Genée, based on a French comedy, *Le réveillon* by Henri Meilhac and Ludovic Halévy

GABRIEL VON EISENSTEIN, *a wealthy Austrian*	*Tenor*
ROSALINDA, *his wife*	*Soprano*
ADELE, *her maid*	*Soprano*
ALFRED, *a tenor*	*Tenor*
DR. FALKE, *a friend of Eisenstein's*	*Baritone*
DR. BLIND, *Eisenstein's attorney*	*Tenor*
PRINCE ORLOFSKY, *a rich Russian*	*Mezzo-soprano*
FRANK, *governor of the prison*	*Baritone*
FROSCH, *the jailer*	*Speaking part*
IDA, *Adele's sister*	*Speaking part*

Time: about 1870
Place: probably Vienna
First performance at Vienna, April 5, 1874

Usually Johann Strauss did not seem to care much whether his libretto was a good one or a bad one. He was renowned as the Waltz King, and he wrote fine waltzes—and other good tunes—almost equally well for stupid books and for good ones. *Die Fledermaus* happens to be a good one. That means—for an operetta—that it has brightness throughout, it has characters who are quickly recognized as types and yet are strongly individualized, and it has a story at once amusing and yet so preposterous that no one can feel bad when anyone gets into trouble.

Die Fledermaus

The story was over twenty years old when Strauss got it. It had first been a German play by Roderich Benedix entitled *The Prison*. Then it became a French play by Meilhac and Halévy (the librettists of *Carmen*). Finally, it came back into the German language when Carl Haffner and Richard Genée made an operetta libretto of it expressly for Strauss. Genée, incidentally, was himself a composer, but he wrote a number of excellent librettos for Strauss. In this sense he was to Strauss just what Boito was to Verdi.

It is the most successful and widely loved of all of the Strauss operettas. And its music is so good—and offers so many opportunities to fine singers—that it is often (as with our own Metropolitan) the only operetta in the repertoire of a great opera house.

OVERTURE

The overture—the most famous one Strauss composed—is made up of several tunes from the operetta itself. Most of these come from the last act, which takes place in the prison. But the one tune that predominates—the one everyone remembers—is the great waltz, which is heard in the extremely festive Act II.

ACT I

The scene is an empty room in the home of the well-to-do Gabriel von Eisenstein, and the first sounds heard are the dulcet, off-stage notes of a tenor serenading one Rosalinda. Adele, the maid, enters on a cadenza. She reads a letter from her sister, a ballet girl, telling her that the entire ballet company has been invited to a fine party that night. Can Adele get an evening dress and come? Adele sadly wishes she could, but she fears she will not be allowed to. She is right. Her mistress, Rosalinda, will not hear of it, even though Adele tearfully pleads the excuse of a sick aunt. The trouble is that Rosalinda's husband must begin a five-day sentence in prison that very night. Rosalinda is duly distracted, but she shows considerable interest when that tenor is heard again, singing his serenade. He enters a moment later and turns out to be Alfred, who once had loved Rosalinda and now, soon after her marriage, has returned, hoping for better luck this time. He promises to leave only if Rosalinda will see him when her husband is safely in jail. Unable to resist the thrill of his high C's, the young lady consents.

Her husband, the master of the house, now storms in with his lawyer, Dr. Blind. Blind has made a mess of things at court with the result that Eisenstein will now have to serve eight days instead of only five. A trio develops in which the Eisensteins blame the lawyer, and the lawyer tries to excuse himself.

While Rosalinda is off finding some old clothes for her husband to wear in prison, enter one Dr. Falke. He is an old friend of Eisenstein's, but he bears him a grudge. Once—as a practical joke—Eisenstein had forced Falke to walk through town, in broad daylight, in a carnival costume. He had been dressed as a bat—which is the reason for the title of the operetta. Falke now invites Eisenstein to go to a big party that night, with lots of girls. He can give himself up at the prison in the morning—and Rosalinda will never know. Eisenstein is delighted. He asks for evening clothes to go to prison in, explaining, lamely, that it is a most distinguished prison. As for Rosalinda, she is too much concerned about her old lover's coming back to query this change of costume. In fact, she has given Adele the night off after all for the same reason. And so there is a fetching trio of farewell between Rosalinda, Eisenstein, and Adele.

With all the others gone Alfred returns for his rendezvous. He is just a bit tipsy, but highly melodious. They are interrupted by Frank, the new governor of the prison, who has become impatient for his new prisoner and so is calling for him personally. Frank is a gay fellow. In fact, he, too, is planning to attend that party. But for appearance's sake Rosalinda fobs Alfred off on him as her husband, and so it is Alfred who must go to jail. The tenor's only recompense is a warm farewell kiss—but what can he do? And so the act ends with another gay trio.

ACT II

Act II takes us to that party we heard so much about during Act I. It is given by a gay, dissolute, and extremely wealthy young Russian named Prince Orlofsky. The part is written for a mezzo-soprano but is sometimes sung by a tenor. (Incidentally, this character, it is speculated, was based on either one of two young Russian roués who operated in Napoleon III's Paris—either Prince Paul Demidov or Prince Narashkine.) The party is a very gay one, indeed. Dr. Falke has arranged a good deal of it, and he introduces the maid Adele as an actress and Eisenstein as the Marquis Renard. Presently the Prince sings his famous number, *Chacun à son goût*—that is, everyone must have a good time according to his own taste. The gaudily refurbished Adele and Eisenstein run into each other, but the maid laughs off her master's recognition with a highly fetching song. She says her speech and costume show her to be anything *but* a maid. Frank, the prison governor, is also introduced as a nobleman (the Chevalier Chagrin), and finally Rosalinda herself comes on, wearing a mask and disguised as a Hungarian countess. She offers convincing proof of her nationality by singing an extremely Hungarian czardas.

She is there, of course, by arrangement with Falke, and she proceeds to flirt so successfully with her own husband that she manages to take his watch from him as a souvenir. In the general merriment that follows, everyone becomes great friends —especially Eisenstein and Frank, who (though they don't know it) will soon meet at the prison in their real-life roles. Eisenstein leads the whole crowd in a song praising the champagne that flows so freely. (At this point a ballet is frequently introduced.) The Prince then demands that everyone dance, and to the tune of the familiar waltz the party goes on till six in the morning. It is only then that Eisenstein and Frank —prisoner and jailer—remember they have business to attend to. With great merriment the party breaks up.

ACT III

The final act takes place in the front office of the jail, but it is a very cheerful type of jail, as the brisk little orchestral prelude suggests. Temporarily it is presided over by Frank's assistant, Frosch, the jailer. Apparently he has been drinking slivovitz all night, and he is in high and frothy spirits as he jabbers about it. Off-stage, from Cell No. 12, comes the tenor voice of Alfred, who has been, perforce, spending the night there under the name of Eisenstein. Pretty soon the governor of the prison comes in, still in evening clothes, still a bit high. Frosch reports that the prisoner in No. 12 has called for a lawyer, and so Dr. Blind has been sent for. But the first visitors to show up are Adele and her sister Ida, both fresh from the party. Adele admits she is only a chambermaid, but in a fine and witty aria she shows off her talents as an actress—ingénue, *grande dame*, leading lady, anything. Next, enter Eisenstein, who is delighted to learn that his new friend the Chevalier Chagrin is only the new prison governor. However, he can *not* believe that Eisenstein is already in jail!

But when both Dr. Blind and Rosalinda have arrived, things become really complicated. Eisenstein manages to disguise himself in the lawyer's professional garb and proceeds to examine both Rosalinda and Alfred. He gets the story of their rendezvous out of them, doffs his disguise, and accuses them in great anger. Rosalinda, however, has his watch to prove that extracurricular flirting is really a pastime shared by both. Furthermore, it is explained to Eisenstein that this flirtation was only a part of the great hoax engineered by Falke in revenge for the practical joke of the Bat. At the end everyone from the party arrives, including Prince Orlofsky. *Chacun à son goût*, he cries once more—and he agrees to take Adele under his wing to see that she becomes a real actress.

How should such an operetta end? Why, with a joyful chorus, of course—in praise of champagne. And so it does.

THE FLYING DUTCHMAN

(Der Fliegende Holländer)

Opera in three acts by Richard Wagner with libretto in German by the composer, based on an old legend as set forth in Heinrich Heine's *Memoirs of Herr von Schnabelewopski*

THE FLYING DUTCHMAN	*Baritone*
DALAND, *a Norwegian sea captain*	*Bass*
SENTA, *his daughter*	*Soprano*
MARY, *her nurse*	*Contralto*
ERIC, *a huntsman*	*Tenor*
DALAND'S STEERSMAN	*Tenor*

Time: 18th century
Place: a Norwegian fishing village
First performance at Dresden, January 2, 1843

There were many variants of the legend of the Flying Dutchman before Wagner crystallized it in his opera. Sir Walter Scott, in his role of antiquarian researcher, claimed that it was based on fact: a murder was committed aboard a vessel with a cargo of gold; the plague broke out; and all ports were closed to the ship. From this—and from the sailors' superstition that the ship is still sighted at times near the Cape of Good Hope, always bringing bad luck with it—there naturally developed further embellishments: that the captain must perpetually play at dice against the devil with the captain's soul as the stakes; that once in seven years the captain may land and remain ashore so long as he can find a woman who will be faithful to him; and a number of others. Captain Marryat made a once-popular novel of it, *The Phantom Ship*, and

Heine retold the tale in his *Memoirs of Herr von Schnabele-wopski*, characteristically putting a two-edged satirical point to it: men—don't put your trust in women; women—don't marry a rolling stone.

Wagner, equally characteristically, found more cosmic matter in the tale. He equated the Flying Dutchman with both Odysseus and the Wandering Jew; he equated the devil with flood and storm; and he equated (most characteristically of all) the release of finding a faithful woman with the release of death. Fortified with Wagner's musical genius, his version has eclipsed all others.

The determination to use the theme for an opera came to him, apparently, during a particularly stormy sea voyage between East Prussia and England. What was normally a week-long trip took over three weeks, and the sailors superstitiously thought that the presence of Wagner and his wife was responsible for the bad weather. At one point they put in for safety at the Norwegian fishing village of Sandwike. This became the scene of the opera, and the sailors' call in the opera is supposed to have been suggested to him there, with its echoing from cliff to cliff by the fjord.

Some weeks later in Paris, desperate for money, he sold a scenario for the work to the director of the Paris Opera. They would never put on the music of an unknown German composer, explained *Monsieur le directeur,* so there was no use in composing it. So Wagner accepted five hundred francs for the scenario and went home to compose the opera anyway. The Frenchman turned over the story to the composer-conductor Pierre Dietsch, whose *Le vaisseau-fantôme* beat Wagner's opera to production by three months. It was a failure. But so was the first Paris production of *Tannhäuser,* when Dietsch conducted for Wagner nineteen years later. Wagner's *Dutchman* was not very successful either when it opened at Dresden. After four performances it was shelved, in that city, for twenty years. Today, however, it is standard fare all over Germany and many other places as well.

ACT I

The first act opens with a chorus of Norwegian sailors who have been driven into the harbor of a fjord by a terrible storm. Their captain, Daland, explains this in a monologue and concludes by telling the steersman to keep watch while the rest of the crew gets a well-earned rest. The youthful steersman tries to keep himself awake by singing a sailor's love song, but sleep soon overtakes him, and a strange ship anchors alongside the Norwegian. A stern gentleman, dressed in black, appears on land from this ship. This is the Dutchman, and he sings at some length about his fate. Every seven years he is allowed to land in search of a woman who will be faithful to him unto death. Only such a woman can release him from his curse. Failing to find her, he must spend the rest of eternity on his ship, shunned by everyone, even pirates. When Daland meets this noble-looking stranger, he asks who he is, and learns that the Dutchman is seeking a safe place for himself, and is willing to offer a good share of his treasure for it. The Dutchman also asks whether Daland has a daughter, and when the answer is yes, he forthwith proposes to marry her, offering Daland untold wealth in exchange. He shows Daland a chest full of riches, and the greedy Norwegian accepts at once. He invites the Dutchman to follow him to his home, which is not far distant, and the act ends as the sailors sing again, preparing to take their ship into their own harbor.

ACT II

The second act opens with the familiar *Spinning Chorus*, which is sung by a group of Norwegian girls including Senta and her nurse, Mary, as they sit spinning, and expecting the return of their fathers, brothers, and sweethearts on Daland's ship. The act takes place in Daland's home, and the scene is dominated by a large portrait of the Flying Dutchman, who, up to this point, is only a legend. But the legend has completely captured the imagination of Senta, Daland's daughter, and after the *Spinning Chorus* she sings a ballad that relates the Dutchman's story. She vows that she herself shall be the woman faithful unto death.

A young hunter, Eric, now arrives with the news that Daland's ship is in the harbor. Everyone goes out to greet it, excepting Eric, who detains Senta a while. He is in love with her and expects to marry her, but he is deeply disturbed over her queer fascination for the legend of the Flying Dutchman. Desperately he tries to persuade her to come to her senses and promise to marry him, but she gives only vague, equivocal answers. Their conversation is ended by the arrival of the father, who brings along the Dutchman himself. He looks so much like the picture that there can be no doubt who he is. And when the father tells of his plans to marry Senta to his guest, she agrees at once, as in a trance.

There is then a long, strange love duet between the two who have just met, and the act ends as Daland gives them his blessing.

ACT III

The last act takes us again to the fjord. Both ships—the Dutchman's and the Norwegian's—are in the harbor, and the Norwegian sailors and their girls are trying to get the crew of the mysterious Dutch ship to join them in some fun. For a long time their jolly invitations go unheeded, but then the crew of the Dutch ship answers—briefly, mysteriously, derisively. The Norwegians are mystified, sing their chorus once more, and then depart.

Once more Eric pleads with Senta to give up her infatuation with the Flying Dutchman and to return to her old love. The Dutchman, overhearing this very eloquent love-making, decides that Senta, like all other women, is unfaithful to him. Despite her pleas, he orders his men to get ready to sail once more, and he boards the ship. In desperation Senta climbs high up on a hill. "I shall be faithful unto death," she cries, and she flings herself into the fjord. The Dutchman's ship sinks, and the horrified Norwegians on land see Senta and the Dutchman united at last—under the waters. He has found his typically Wagnerian redemption.

LA FORZA DEL DESTINO

(*The Force of Destiny*)

Opera in four acts by Giuseppe Verdi with libretto in Italian by Francesco Piave, based on a play by Ángel Pérez de Saavedra, Duke of Rivas

MARCHESE DI CALATRAVA	*Bass*
DON CARLO DI VARGAS, *his son*	*Baritone*
DONNA LEONORA DI VARGAS, *his daughter*	*Soprano*
DON ALVARO, *her lover*	*Tenor*
CURRA, *her maid*	*Mezzo-soprano*
PADRE GUARDIANO, *the father superior*	*Bass*
FRA MELITONE, *a Franciscan monk*	*Bass*
PREZIOSILLA, *a gypsy*	*Mezzo-soprano*
THE MAYOR OF HORNACHUELOS	*Bass*
TRABUCCO, *a muleteer*	*Tenor*
A SURGEON	*Tenor*

Time: 18th century
Places: Spain and Italy
First performance at St. Petersburg, November 10, 1862

Verdi's *La forza del destino*, or *The Force of Destiny*, shows us the composer in his fine maturity, that is, at a time when he had already composed the great successes *Rigoletto*, *Il trovatore*, and *La traviata*. He was a famous man, a senator in his native Italy, and known throughout Europe. *La forza* was, in fact, composed for Russia, and it had its world premiere in 1862 at St. Petersburg. It was based on a drama by a romantic Spanish nobleman, the Duke of Rivas, and from its very beginning one senses the romantic and dramatic quality of that play.

La forza del destino

OVERTURE

The overture—perhaps Verdi's very best overture—is thoroughly dramatic and makes use of parts of several arias from the later acts as well as an aggressive little tune sometimes called the "destiny" motive.

ACT I

The story begins in eighteenth-century Seville. Leonora di Vargas, the aristocratic heroine, is in love with one Don Alvaro, who is part Inca Indian. No one of that sort is, of course, considered worthy of marrying a Spanish noblewoman. The proud Marquis of Calatrava, Leonora's father, bids her forget all about Alvaro, but it is this very night that Leonora has already planned to elope with her lover. When the Marquis has left, she confides in her maid, Curra. Her father's kindness, she says, has almost made her give up her plan for elopement; and so, when Alvaro bursts in through the window, he at first thinks she no longer loves him. But in an impassioned duet they swear eternal faith, and they are about ready to fly when the Marquis re-enters, sword in hand. He believes the worst at once, but Alvaro swears that Leonora is innocent. He offers to die to prove it, and he throws away the pistol he has drawn. Unfortunately, as it falls to the ground, it goes off, and the Marquis is killed by the bullet. With his dying breath the old gentleman sets in motion "the force of destiny" by uttering a terrible curse on his daughter—and Alvaro leads his beloved away as the act closes.

ACT II

Scene 1   Much has happened between Acts I and II. Don Carlo, arrived home, has heard that his sister Leonora has fled with her lover, Don Alvaro, Alvaro having first murdered their father, the Marquis. Naturally, as a good eighteenth-century Spaniard of high birth, he has sworn to murder both his sister and her lover. Meantime, the two lovers have become separated, and Leonora, disguised as a young man and guarded by a faithful old muleteer named Trabucco, is in flight.

The force of destiny is at work, as the act opens, for Leonora and her brother Carlo are lodged under the same roof—the inn at Hornachuelos. Fortunately, Carlo has not seen his sister, who does not join the merry crowd but hides from him. The Mayor of the town announces dinner, and this gives Carlo an opportunity to question Trabucco, with whom he gets nowhere.

Preziosilla, a gypsy fortuneteller, now whips up things with a martial tune, urging all the fellows to join up with the Italian Army to fight the Germans. No recruiting sergeant could have done better. Then she tells some fortunes—including Carlo's, which is not very encouraging.

A group of pilgrims is heard passing outside, and a fine, impressive prayer is sung, in which Leonora's soaring soprano is heard above the others. This over, Carlo again tries to question Trabucco, and again he is unsuccessful. And so, at the request of the Mayor, he tells his own story. His name, says Don Carlo, is Pereda, and he is an honor student at the university. And then he goes on to give a thinly disguised version of the murder of his father by his sister's lover. It is a fine baritone aria with chorus, beginning *Son Pereda, son ricco d'onore,* and at its close the gypsy fortuneteller lets Carlo know she has seen through his disguise.

But now it is late. The Mayor tells everyone it is time for bed, and a good-night chorus ends the scene.

Scene 2 Leonora has been badly frightened by so nearly meeting her vengeful brother at the inn, and, still disguised as a young man, she has fled to the mountains nearby. Here she finds a church and convent, and she sinks before the cross outside to sing her touching prayer, *Madre, pietosa Vergine.* The gruff, half-comic Friar Melitone answers her knock but refuses her entry and calls up the head of the convent, Father Guardiano. In a long and eloquent duet, she identifies herself, finally securing his permission to lead the life of a complete hermit in a nearby cave. No human being may ever see her again—which is precisely the fate that this tragic heroine believes she desires, now that she thinks she has lost her lover, Don Alvaro, forever.

The act ends in what is perhaps the most impressive ensemble in an opera especially rich in big concerted numbers (*La Vergine degli angeli*—"The Virgin of the angels"). Guardiano summons the entire convent; he tells them of Leonora's determination; and he calls a solemn curse down on anyone who shall disturb her.

ACT III

Scene 1 The first two acts took place in Spain. The force of destiny now takes many of the principal characters to Italy, to Velletri, to be exact, not very far from Rome. The Italians are fighting invading Germans (a not infrequent occurrence in the history of Italy), and there are many Spaniards fighting on the Italian side. Among them are our friends Don Carlo and Don Alvaro. There is some gambling going on in the Italian camp when the act opens. In the pitiful and melodious aria *O tu che in seno agli angeli* ("Oh thou, among the angels") Don Alvaro bemoans his fate and especially the loss of Donna Leonora, whom he imagines as an angel in heaven. The gamblers start quarreling, and Alvaro saves the life of another man from an attack by fellow-gamblers. This man turns out to be Don Carlo, who has sworn to slay Alvaro. But as they have never before met, and as both give false names, they do not recognize each other, and they swear eternal friendship.

Now, off-stage, a battle commences, and the excited comments tell us that the Germans are beaten off. But Don Alvaro, seriously wounded and believing himself near death, begs his friend, Don Carlo, to do him one last favor. He is to take a packet of letters from his trunk and, without reading a single one, burn them. This Don Carlo swears to do in *Solenne in quest'ora* ("Swear in this hour"), a duet made famous through a very old recording by Caruso and Scotti. Alvaro is now carried off by the surgeon for a quick operation,

La forza del destino

and Carlo is left alone with Alvaro's trunk. A passing reaction of Don Alvaro's has made Carlo suspect his real identity, and he is tempted to examine those letters to confirm that suspicion. However, there is no need to break his oath, for he finds enough other evidence in that trunk to convince him that his new-found friend is in truth Don Alvaro—the slayer of his father and supposed betrayer of his sister.

Just then the surgeon returns to tell Carlo that Alvaro will live after all. In a great burst of excitement Carlo sings his revenge aria, *Egli è salvo!* ("He is to live!"). Now, he exults, he may carry out his revenge not only on Alvaro but on his sister Leonora as well!

Scene 2 takes us to the camp of the common soldiers. Here we meet some of our old friends from the previous act. Preziosilla plies her trade as a fortuneteller; Trabucco, the muleteer, has become a peddler, selling things like scissors, pins, and soap to the soldiers and camp followers; and Friar Melitone (who treated Leonora so shabbily at the convent) preaches a ridiculous sermon till the soldiers can't stand any more of it and run him out of camp. It is a jolly scene, and it ends with one of the jolliest pieces Verdi ever composed. This is the *Rataplan*, in which Preziosilla, carrying a drum, urges the men on to deeds of derring-do. With practically only a drum for accompaniment, this number is a real technical challenge for the chorus of any opera company.

ACT IV

Scene 1 Although the last act is essentially both sad and dramatic, it begins with one of Verdi's few genuinely comic scenes. Back in Spain in the courtyard of the convent near Hornachuelos, the crusty old Friar Melitone is dishing out soup to the beggars. He is so unpleasant about the business that they wish they might again see a certain "Father Raphael" handling the ladle. This so angers Melitone that he kicks over the caldron of soup, and the beggars depart.

The good old Abbot Guardiano reproves Melitone for his bad temper, and they briefly discuss the character of Father

La forza del destino

Raphael. He, of course, is none other than Don Alvaro in disguise, and Melitone tells how he had driven the quiet man almost mad by referring to him as a wild Indian.

Now Don Carlo enters and asks for Father Raphael—the one with the dark skin. While Alvaro—as we may as well call him—is summoned, Carlo gloats over his prospective revenge. Alvaro, dressed as a monk, comes in, and a long duet follows. First Alvaro refuses to fight, for he is now a monk, and he has already slain one member of Carlo's family, even though accidentally. Don Carlo, however, piles insult on insult; and when he finally attacks Alvaro's proud race—the Incas—the monk seizes the second sword that Carlo has thoughtfully provided, and the two rush off to duel.

Scene 2 takes place outside the hut where Leonora has taken up her life as a hermit. She sings her great aria, *Pace, pace,* begging for the peace of the grave. But as she finishes the aria, a cry is heard off-stage. It is Don Carlo, mortally wounded in the duel. A moment later Alvaro rushes on to get help for Carlo. Thus, after many years, the lovers meet unexpectedly and tragically. Leonora goes to help the dying man, but Carlo, with his last strength, carries out his oath: he stabs his sister as she bends to help him.

And so, when the Abbot Guardiano comes to see what has happened, the opera closes in a moving trio, Alvaro cursing his fate, and Leonora assuring him of forgiveness in heaven.

FOUR SAINTS IN THREE ACTS

Opera in four acts by Virgil Thomson with libretto in English by Gertrude Stein

ST. TERESA I	*Soprano*
ST. TERESA II	*Contralto*
ST. IGNATIUS LOYOLA	*Baritone*
ST. CHAVEZ	*Tenor*
ST. SETTLEMENT	*Soprano*
COMPÈRE	*Bass*
COMMÈRE	*Mezzo-soprano*

Time: no particular time
Place: Spain, most likely
First performance at Hartford, February 8, 1934 by the Society
of Friends and Enemies of Modern Music

The music of *Four Saints in Three Acts* is by a now reformed music critic, Virgil Thomson, and its libretto is by a
never reformed modernist, the late Gertrude Stein. It was
written over thirty years ago—in 1928—and it makes absolutely
no sense. It isn't supposed to, really. Mr. Thomson himself
told us how best to understand the libretto when he said:
"You know, Miss Stein's words make perfectly good sense—if
you take them one at a time."

I cannot tell you the story of the opera, for there isn't any.
Miss Stein wrote the libretto and gave it to Mr. Thomson. He
liked it so much that he set all of it to music—even the stage
directions. Then when that was done, a friend of his named
Maurice Grosser tried to give it a scenario, a shape of some
sort. The result is that *Four Saints in Three Acts* has many
more than four saints—and *one* more than three acts.

The opera is clearly about saints, and it probably takes place in Spain. Some of the saints are Spanish ones—for example, St. Teresa (there are two St. Teresas, a soprano and a contralto) and St. Ignatius Loyola. Other saints are ones no one ever heard of before—like St. Settlement and St. Plot. And there are two characters—named Commère and Compère—who are supposed to explain things, somewhat like a Greek chorus. Of course, they explain nothing.

Clearly—all this is something that could have been produced only in the mad 1920's. As for the music—that reflects Mr. Thomson's early life. He was brought up in Missouri, where he was a church organist, and much of the music reflects the tunes and harmonies of Southern Baptist hymns. It is all charming, innocent, and wilfully naïve.

The prelude—in heavy waltz time—has a chorus that begins with these words:

> *To know to know to love her so*
> *Four saints prepare for Saints,*
> *Four saints make it well fish.*

Act I, which follows immediately, is called "St. Teresa half indoors and half out of doors." It seems to have to do with seven aspects of St. Teresa's life, but it is inadvisable to try to follow them too carefully.

Act II is called "Might it be mountains if it were not Barcelona." Toward its close, the two Sts. Teresa look through a telescope and see a heavenly mansion, and the chorus asks: "How many doors how many floors and how many windows are there in it?" The ladies do not answer.

Act III is called "St. Ignatius and one of two literally." It contains the one famous aria in the opera. That occurs when St. Ignatius describes his vision of the Holy Ghost. It goes: "Pigeons on the grass alas, and a magpie in the sky." And then the chorus sings, "Let Lucy Lily Lily Lucy Lucy let Lucy Lucy Lily Lily Lily Lily Lily Lily," etc. That's genuine Gertrude Stein, and it is followed soon after by a charming dance in Spanish style, which is genuine Virgil Thomson.

Act IV is called "The sisters and saints reassembled and

re-enacting why they went away to stay." It is quite short, and it closes with the only two lines I completely understand. Compère (one of the Greek-chorus characters) announces: "Last Act." And the chorus answers loudly: "Which is a fact."

DER FREISCHÜTZ

(*The Free-Shooter*)

Opera in three acts by Carl Maria von Weber
with libretto in German by Johann Friedrich
Kind based on a story by Johann August Apel

MAX, *a forester*	*Tenor*
CASPAR, *another*	*Bass*
KILIAN, *a rich peasant*	*Tenor*
CUNO, *the head forester*	*Bass*
AGATHE, *his daughter*	*Soprano*
AENNCHEN, *her cousin*	*Soprano*
PRINCE OTTOKAR	*Baritone*
A HERMIT	*Bass*
SAMIEL, *the wild huntsman*	*Speaking part*

Time: middle of the 17th century
Place: Bohemia
First performance at Berlin, June 18, 1821

It is a little hard today to imagine the storm created by the first performance, some 140 years ago, of Weber's romantic opera, *Der Freischütz*. For it meant—in Germany, at least —the end of the predominance of Italian opera. The leading lights of Germany—Heine, Mendelssohn, Hoffmann, and others—seemed to understand this, and the reign of Spontini and classical tragedy was soon over. The way was really paved for all the later German romantics, and above all for Richard Wagner. For *Der Freischütz* (which means "The Free-Shooter") is a story of romantic love between commoners, of supernatural evil, with a devil for one of the characters, and a scene in the mysterious Wolf's Glen.

OVERTURE

The music, too, is highly romantic, and its essence is contained in the familiar overture, the only portion of the work with which most modern music-lovers can be counted on to be familiar. It is full of drama, of sweeping melodies, and wonderful effects with tremolo strings and a clarinet solo. It is also just about the first operatic overture to make use of whole tunes from the vocal score—especially of the great joyous outcry made by the heroine when her lover comes to her in Act II.

ACT I

The action of *Der Freischütz* is carried on almost entirely in spoken dialogue punctuated by set musical numbers to paint the emotional situation at the moment. Thus, the first sounds heard after the curtain goes up are a shot and a shout. A shooting contest, held in an open space before a tavern, has just been won by a peasant named Kilian. A male chorus is sung in his praise, while the professional forester, Max (who is the hero of the tale) sits by disconsolately, for he has been defeated. When a rustic march is played in honor of Kilian, Max can stand it no longer and attacks the man who defeated him.

Cuno, the head forester, comes in and stops the brawl; and it soon becomes clear why Max is so much out of sorts. It seems that there is to be a shoot the next day before the Prince Ottokar. If Max wins (as had been fully expected, for he is a famous shot), he will also win his beloved Agathe, who is Cuno's daughter, and the assured succession to the old man's job. Now, the fact is that the reason Max has shot badly is that his rival for Agathe's hand, Caspar (the villain of the piece), had invoked the supernatural help of a devil named Samiel. When Caspar, an unpopular brute, suggests that Max may need some magical assistance the next day, Cuno quickly shuts him up. He then proceeds to relate the history of the shooting match. It began with his own great-great-grandfather, who had saved a man's life with so remarkable a shot at one time that he had been accused of using a "free," or magic, bullet. A free bullet was one supplied by the devil, and it could not miss. Since then the Prince's foresters have had to prove their competence in contests run without supernatural aid. Kilian adds the important detail that the devil, when he grants a man free shots, gives him seven of them. The first six hit whatever the mortal aims at, but the seventh goes wherever the devil directs.

After a short ensemble number, in which everyone comments on the situation, Kilian makes it up with Max, and our hero is left alone to sing his melodious aria, *Durch die Wälder, durch die Auen* ("Through the forests, through the meadows"), in which he bewails the loss of his once-carefree life.

It is now pretty dark, and Caspar joins Max, inviting him to several drinks. He sings a rough drinking song (and twice Samiel makes a discreet appearance in the foliage, frightening both Caspar and the audience). Finally, Caspar thrusts his gun into Max's hand and asks him to shoot at a distant eagle. Miraculously the bird falls to the ground. Caspar explains that this has been a "free" bullet, and he knows where to get more. Tomorrow night Max must meet him at the mysterious Wolf's Glen. Max knows that this may be a disastrous thing to do; but he is desperate by this time, and a little affected by drink, and he agrees. When he has left, Caspar closes the act with a triumphant aria of revenge, full of long and difficult scales that modern basses find pretty hard to negotiate.

ACT II

Scene 1 All the soloists in the first act were men. Weber made up for this in the beginning of the second act, which is populated exclusively by two sopranos. One of them is Agathe, daughter of the head forester and the betrothed of Max. At the moment, Agathe is not too happy about the probable outcome of the shooting match, and her state of mind has not been helped by the framed picture that has mysteriously tumbled off the wall and onto her head. Her cousin, Aennchen, is of a much more cheerful disposition. When the act starts, in Cuno's hunting lodge, she is tacking back the picture on the wall, and Agathe presently joins her in a pretty duet. Briefly, in spoken dialogue, they discuss the absence of Max (who is expected shortly), and then Aennchen sings another cheerful ditty on the ever-engrossing subject of boy-meets-girl.

Now Agathe, left alone, has what used to be one of the most famous of soprano arias, *Leise, leise, fromme Weise*, a prayer for her beloved. At its end she sees Max himself approaching, and she sings a brilliant closing to the aria, expressing her joy.

In the spoken dialogue that follows Max mentions his approaching visit to the Wolf's Glen, and the scene ends as Aennchen joins the two lovers in a trio: the two women try in vain to dissuade Max from visiting so evil a place, while he, for his part, insists upon going.

Scene 2 is the famous scene in the Wolf's Glen. It was originally designed, I believe, to scare the living daylights out of its nineteenth-century German audience, for it is filled with such scary things as a skull with a dagger thrust through it, an eerie off-stage chorus of fiends, weird moonlight playing over a scene of desolate rocks and trees, and a devil who appears and disappears mysteriously and threatens in a high, menacing voice. To a modern audience much of this *looks* like child's play, yet Weber's score makes it *sound* remarkably effective.

The scene opens with the villain, Caspar, going through an interesting rigmarole designed to summon the devil, Samiel. Caspar has sold himself to the devil completely, and now he begs for three more years of freedom in exchange for delivering Max to him. Musically it is a strange scene. Caspar sings, and the devil speaks; and the bargain they strike is this: Max is to have seven magical bullets, six to go unerringly to whatever mark Max aims at, but the seventh Samiel may direct to Agathe's heart. The devil coldly agrees; but should Caspar fail in seducing Max into the bargain, his own soul will be the forfeit.

Now Max appears on the scene. First he sees a vision of his mother, then one of Agathe, and he is so badly upset by these visions that he readily agrees to do whatever Caspar demands. Caspar thereupon brews a wicked brew. It begins to boil and hiss; huge birds fly about; a boar crashes through the underbrush; a storm rages; shadowy figures utter a strange chant— and eventually the bullets are molded. Together the two men call upon Samiel; and as the Demon appears, Caspar falls over in a dead faint, while Max finds, to his terror, that he has grasped the Devil's own hand in the shape of a dead branch! And if all this sounds faintly improbable, please remember that this is a romantic fairy tale. Anything can happen in a fairy tale.

ACT III

Scene 1 of the last act is given over exclusively to attempts to cheer up our lugubrious heroine, Agathe. She is being dressed for her wedding to Max, but she has various misgivings of a superstitious nature. One of these misgivings—as we shall see in the final scene—is well justified by events. She says she dreamed she was a white dove, that Max fired at her, and that she fell to the ground in her natural form as a maiden. In the first aria of the scene Agathe prays to heaven for protection, and in the second she relates her dream. It takes two arias by her cheerful cousin, Aennchen, as well as a chorus of bridesmaids, to give Agathe the courage to complete her nuptial preparations.

Scene 2 is introduced by a jolly hunting prelude, followed by a chorus. It is the big day, and Max is to demonstrate to his prince, Ottokar, and to his prospective father-in-law, Cuno, that he is a good enough shot to be worthy of marrying Agathe. The Prince points to a white dove and tells Max to shoot, but just as he takes aim, Agathe appears and calls for him not to shoot, for she herself is the white dove! But it is too late. Max fires; Agathe falls, and everyone thinks he has slain his bride. But at the same time the villain Caspar falls. With his dying breath he curses the Demon Samiel—and his soul is consigned to perdition.

Now Agathe revives, and Max explains how he went astray

in dealings with Caspar and Samiel. Everyone pleads that he should be forgiven, but the Prince sternly decides to banish the young forester. Fortunately, a wise old hermit appears and the Prince leaves the final decision up to him. In a long and solemn aria the hermit gives his advice, which is to let Max be given a year's probation. If at the end of that time he is again his old virtuous self, let him marry the lovely Agathe. And henceforth, let there be an end to such shooting contests as these.

Everyone agrees that this is a fine idea, and the opera ends on a chorus of jubilation, using one of the most familiar tunes from the famous overture.

GIANNI SCHICCHI

Opera in one act by Giacomo Puccini with
libretto in Italian by Giovacchino Forzano

GIANNI SCHICCHI	*Baritone*
LAURETTA, *his daughter*	*Soprano*
Relations of Buoso Donati:	
ZITA, *his cousin*	*Contralto*
RINUCCIO, *her nephew*	*Tenor*
GHERARDO, *nephew of Buoso*	*Tenor*
NELLA, *his wife*	*Soprano*
GHERARDINO, *their son*	*Contralto*
BETTO DI SIGNA, *brother-in-law of Buoso*	*Baritone or Bass*
SIMONE, *Buoso's cousin*	*Bass*
MARCO, *his son*	*Baritone*
LA CIESCA, *his wife*	*Mezzo-soprano*
SPINELLOCCIO, *a doctor*	*Bass*
AMANTIO DI NICOLAO, *a lawyer*	*Baritone or Bass*

Time: 1299
Place: Florence
First performance at New York, December 14, 1918

Gianni Schicchi is the last and most successful of the
three one-act operas that make up Puccini's Triptych, the
other two being *Il tabarro* and *Suor Angelica*. It is based on
an incident that is actually supposed to have happened in
Florence, in the year 1299, pretty much as given in the libretto.
Dante, who may well have known the jolly swindler Schicchi
personally, put him, in the thirtieth canto of the *Inferno*,
into the eighth circle of Hell among thieves, panders, and
other such. His perpetual companion there is the incestuous

Princess of Cyprus, who loved her father. But Puccini was probably not thinking of this literary detail when he composed the aria, *O mio babbino caro* ("Oh, My Beloved Daddy").

When the opera opens, the wealthy Buoso Donati has just died, and a gang of his relatives is hanging vulturously about his bed. For their names and the relationships they bear to the corpse let me refer you to the cast of characters above. Ostensibly they are there to mourn; but their avariciousness soon gets the better of their manners, and they start to search for the will. It is Rinuccio who finds it and Zita who first reads it. Their worst fears are realized: Buoso has left everything to the monks of a monastery.

Now it happens that young Rinuccio is in love with Lauretta, the daughter of Gianni Schicchi, and Gianni is a shrewd peasant of infinite resourcefulness. Secretly Rinuccio has sent for Gianni Schicchi, and the artful young fellow urges his relatives to consult his prospective father-in-law. He ends his argument with an eloquent paean in praise of Florence (*Firenze è come un albero fiorito*), but they protest right up to the arrival of Schicchi himself.

Lauretta, whom her father loves very much, urges him to find a solution to the troubles of the Donati so that she may marry Rinuccio (*O mio babbino caro*), and, thus inspired, Schicchi contrives a plot. He has the body of old Buoso removed and he himself takes its place in the bed. He fools the doctor when he comes by imitating Buoso's voice and saying he is better. Then he listens to what each relative wishes to have of Buoso's riches, and he promises to dictate a new will accordingly.

A notary is summoned, and Schicchi dictates the new will. However, in this will he leaves everything—to himself! The relatives are wild when the notary leaves, but there is nothing they can do. For Schicchi has pointed out to them that whoever helps falsify a will must, according to the laws of Florence, lose one hand and be forever banished. The maddened flock steal whatever they can, and Schicchi chases them out of the house. Only the lovers remain to sing a happy duet; and when

Schicchi returns, he presents them with the stolen articles he has managed to recapture.

Then, as the opera closes, Schicchi addresses the audience in spoken words: he asks whether Buoso's money could serve a better purpose and suggests that though Dante consigned him to Hell, perhaps the amusement he has afforded the audience will make them reach a verdict of Extenuating Circumstances. And he starts the applause himself.

LA GIOCONDA

(*The Ballad Singer*)

Opera in four acts by Amilcare Ponchielli with libretto in Italian by "Tobio Gorria" (anagram for Arrigo Boito) based on a play by Victor Hugo entitled *Angelo, tyran de Padoue*

LA GIOCONDA, *a ballad singer*	Soprano
LA CIECA, *her blind mother*	Contralto
DUKE ALVISE, *one of the heads of the State Inquisition*	Bass
LAURA, *his wife*	Mezzo-soprano
ENZO GRIMALDO, *a Genoese noble*	Tenor
BARNABA, *a spy of the Inquisition*	Baritone
ZUÀNE, *a boatman*	Bass
ISÈPO, *a public letter-writer*	Tenor

Time: 17th century
Place: Venice
First performance at Milan, April 8, 1876

La Gioconda is well over three quarters of a century old, and it is still one of the most popular operas ever composed. Its story, based on a play by Victor Hugo, has been set by other composers, before and since Ponchielli. In fact, the Russian composer, César Cui, produced one version, entitled *Angelo*, in 1876 just two months before the Italian. Only Ponchielli's still holds the stage. The reason is doubtless the overwhelming passion of the music and its wonderful melodies. These include the *Cielo e mar*, the *Suicidio*, and the ever-popular *Dance of the Hours*.

Hugo's original play took place in Padua. Arrigo Boito, Ponchielli's famous librettist, transferred it to Venice of the seventeenth century. He also rechristened Hugo's play, originally called *Angelo, Tyrant of Padua*, with one of the most ironic titles any opera ever had. *La gioconda* means, literally, "the joyous female," but never had an operatic heroine more unbearable miseries than the one who goes by that name. And there is quite a lot of competition for that honor in the annals of the lyric stage.

The prelude, a fairly short one, is based on the contralto aria in the first act, *Voce di donna o d'angelo* ("Voice of woman or of angel"). Each act is supplied with its own title: Act I—"The Lion's Mouth"; Act II—"The Rosary"; Act III—"The House of Gold"; and Act IV—"The Orfano Canal."

ACT I

The opera opens with a jolly chorus, *Feste e pane*—"Feasting and bread." A crowd before the palace of the Doges of Venice is celebrating a holiday. A nasty fellow, Barnaba (the villain of the opera and a spy for the Inquisition), tells them the regatta is about to begin. As they rush off to the shore, he remarks unpleasantly, "They are dancing over their graves."

Now enter the heroine. She is a beautiful street singer known as "La Gioconda" for her joyous disposition. At the moment she is leading in her blind mother, La Cieca, and they sing a brief, affectionate duet. Now, Barnaba is in love with La Gioconda—or at least he has dishonorable designs on her. He approaches her, but La Gioconda will have nothing to do with him. So he plans revenge. As soon as the crowd comes back from the regatta, Barnaba tells the loser—Zuàne—that Gioconda's blind mother is a witch and that she has cast a spell on him. The crowd turns on La Cieca, but she is saved just in time by the hero of the opera, Enzo Grimaldo. Enzo is a slightly mysterious figure with a complex past, present, and future. First of all, he has been outlawed by Venice, and he is there in disguise. Secondly, he is secretly engaged to La Gioconda. And thirdly, he was once engaged to Laura, the wife of the Duke Alvise—and Laura still loves him.

The crowd is growing more threatening, when the Duke

himself and Laura appear at the palace doors, and they save
both La Cieca and Enzo. The blind old woman, in gratitude,
gives Laura a rosary. Here she sings her fine aria *Voce di
donna*.

Meantime, Laura and Enzo exchange loving glances which
do not go unnoticed by Barnaba. This, he decides, is his
chance. When everyone else has left, he approaches Enzo and
tells him he knows who he is—a proscribed nobleman in disguise. And, much to Enzo's surprise, Barnaba promises to
bring Laura that very night to Enzo's ship. Enzo is happy but
suspicious. He has good reason to be. For as soon as he has
left, Barnaba turns to a public scribe and dictates an anonymous letter to the head of the Inquisition's police. In it he
tells of the proposed meeting that night. Gioconda, however,
overhears him. She is heartbroken, and the act ends as she
voices her lamentations above the evening prayers being sung
by the populace.

ACT II

Ponchielli's colorful music at once suggests the marine setting with Enzo Grimaldo's ship on the lagoon. Sailors are singing, and soon Barnaba, the Inquisition spy, appears, disguised
as one of them. He leads a merry ballad (*Pescator, affonda
l'esca*), but his real purpose is to find out the strength of
Enzo's crew. Soon Enzo appears on the deck. He tells the
sailors that he himself will bear watch that night, and when
he is alone, he sings his great aria *Cielo e mar*. He awaits his
beloved there, on the sea and under the sky. But when Laura
does come, she is soon prey to misgivings; and when Enzo
goes below-deck to prepare for flight, Laura begs for protection
in the lovely prayer *Stella del marinar*.

La Gioconda has meanwhile entered, and an angry scene
between the two women follows. Gioconda threatens Laura
with a dagger; but, even worse, she informs Laura that her
husband is about to come. At this news Laura brings out the
rosary La Cieca had given her and starts again to pray. Gioconda recognizes her mother's rosary and recalls the service

that Laura had done her. Her whole attitude toward her rival now changes. Quickly she shoves her into a boat and makes good her escape. And so, when Enzo comes on deck once more, searching for Laura, he is met by the angry Gioconda. At that moment the guns of the Duke's fleet are heard. Enzo realizes he is lost, and in desperation he sets fire to his own ship.

ACT III

Scene 1 takes place in the palace of the Duke Alvise, known as the House of Gold. Here the Duke is planning both festivities and a dramatic revenge on his faithless wife, Laura. He explains this in a dramatic monologue (*Sì! morir ella de'!*—"Yes, to die is her fate"). As nocturnal serenaders are heard melodiously at work out of doors, he summons his wife, draws a curtain to reveal a bier all ready to receive her body, hands her a phial of poison with instructions that it must be drunk before the serenading is over, and leaves her to herself. He had not counted on our heroine, La Gioconda, who, anticipating something of the sort, had hidden herself in the palace prepared with the proper pharmaceuticals. Swiftly she hands a flask to Laura, explaining that this drug will produce only the semblance of death, not the real thing; and when Laura has taken it and laid herself dutifully on the bier, Gioconda pours the real poison into a phial of her own and leaves the empty one on the table. Thus, when the serenade is over and Alvise returns to inspect the situation, he believes everything is ready for titillating his guests with a shocking surprise.

Scene 2 Then comes the big party. Alvise welcomes his guests, and a ballet is danced for their entertainment to the music of the *Dance of the Hours*. At the end of the dance Barnaba drags in the blind old Cieca, who has been found praying for "the woman who has just died." At that moment a funeral toll is heard. For whom is it? asks a guest. It is for Laura, says Barnaba. At this juncture the masked Enzo reveals himself, and Alvise furiously demands his arrest. A great ensemble number develops, everyone expressing his own emotions about the complex situation. Gioconda, who is also there, offers herself to Barnaba if only he will save her beloved Enzo and, naturally, he agrees. Then, when everyone is hushed, Alvise makes a shocking announcement: he will show the company the wife who had betrayed him. The curtains are pulled aside—and Laura is seen lying on her bier. "It was I who killed her!" cries the outraged Duke. Enzo lunges at him with a dagger, but the guards intervene, and Enzo is arrested as the act closes. There is a good deal of dramatic irony in this close. For neither the Duke nor Enzo nor Barnaba knows that Gioconda had once more saved her rival, Laura.

ACT IV

The last act takes place in a dilapidated palace on an island off Venice. Here Gioconda lives and here she has secretly brought her rival, Laura. She has also saved her lover's life, but only that he may elope with this rival, while she must give herself to the hated Barnaba. Finally, to make matters still worse (if that is possible), she has lost her beloved blind mother. In fact, she has not seen her since Alvise's frightful party. It is therefore no wonder that she sings, at the beginning of the act, her great *scena*—the *Suicidio*—in which she plans to commit suicide.

Off-stage are heard two gondoliers. "What's the news?" cries one. "More corpses in the canal," is the cheery answer.

Enzo comes on the weeping girl, demanding to know where Laura is; and when Gioconda says that she has had the body taken from the burial vault, Enzo almost stabs her in his rage. Gioconda would have welcomed the dagger; but at that moment Laura recovers from the effects of the drug and rushes into Enzo's arms. Off-stage is heard the serenade to which Laura had been ordered to commit suicide. This time it serves as the prelude to a dramatic trio. The lovers thank their love-lorn savior and then depart in a small boat that she had arranged to have ready complete with a crew of two.

Now the miserable Gioconda recalls her compact with Barnaba. She is about to flee from the place, when he comes himself demanding his prize. Yes, she says, she will honor the pact; but first she must decorate herself in her finest clothes. As she does so, she takes up her dagger—and stabs herself to the heart. The frustrated Barnaba shouts into her ear, "Yesterday your mother insulted me. I have drowned her!" But Gioconda—lucky for the first time in this opera—is beyond hearing this news, and Barnaba, in a wild rage, rushes out.

THE GIRL OF THE GOLDEN WEST

(*La fanciulla del West*)

Opera in three acts by Giacomo Puccini with libretto in Italian by Carlo Zangarini and Guelfo Civinini based on the melodrama of the same name by David Belasco

MINNIE, *owner of "The Polka"*	*Soprano*
NICK, *its bartender*	*Tenor*
JACK RANCE, *the sheriff*	*Baritone*
RAMERREZ, ALIAS DICK JOHNSON, *a bandit*	*Tenor*
ASHBY, *agent of the Wells-Fargo Transport Co.*	*Bass*
SONORA	*Baritone*
TRIN	*Tenor*
SID	*Baritone*
HANDSOME ⎫ *miners*	*Baritone*
HARRY ⎬	*Tenor*
JOE ⎭	*Tenor*
HAPPY	*Baritone*
LARKENS	*Bass*
BILLY JACKRABBIT, *an Indian*	*Bass*
WOWKLE, *his squaw*	*Mezzo-soprano*
JAKE WALLACE, *a traveling minstrel*	*Baritone*
JOSÉ CASTRO, *a member of Ramerrez's band*	*Bass*

Time: about 1850
Place: California
First performance at New York, December 10, 1910

On his first visit to the United States, in 1905, Puccini saw a performance of David Belasco's horse opera *The Girl of the Golden West* and was fascinated by the old stage wizard's tricks with moving scenery and an elaborate snowstorm. He was also fascinated by the rather simple-minded melodrama of playing poker for the stakes of a man's life and a woman's body. Finally, he was fascinated by the warmth of the reception that America accorded him.

But it was not till he had returned to Italy that he finally decided to make this play the vehicle for his next operatic score. He had his customary trouble hiring and firing librettists till he got just what he wanted, and he also had serious domestic trouble. His wife became hysterically jealous of a maidservant, accused her publicly of being Puccini's mistress (which was not true), and drove the girl to suicide. There was a trial; Mme. Puccini was found guilty; the case was appealed, and then withdrawn by the girl's family. The Puccinis were, however, both severely punished: they were separated for a long time, and the misery they went through left its mark on both of them.

Had not Puccini, years later, composed the scores of *Gianni Schicchi* and *Turandot*, one might conclude that this experience had broken his spirit and ended his career as a first-class opera composer. For *The Girl*, despite the brilliant success of its premiere, is a tired opera. It does have its dramatic moments—particularly during the poker-game scene—but it notably fails in the one virtue the composer claimed for it. "For this drama," he said, "I have composed music that, I feel sure, reflects the spirit of the American people, and particularly the strong, vigorous nature of the West." But it is almost all pure second-rate Italian opera, and when the Wild West dialogue intrudes ("Vells Fargo! Vells Fargo!" shout the cowboys in Act I), it is difficult not to laugh. Yet, it was revived in Chicago in 1956.

ACT I

The barroom of "The Polka" inn is a favorite spot for the roughnecks of the gold rush to whoop it up, and Minnie, its owner and presiding genius, has the practical assistance of a couple of Indians named Billy Jackrabbit and his squaw Wowkle (pronounced *Vuffkleh* in Italian). The opening local color includes a game of faro, in which one of the miners is almost strung up for cheating, and a Western ballad singer named Jake Wallace.

There is also Ashby, an agent of the Wells Fargo Transport Company, who says that he is on the lookout for a gang of robbers led by one Ramerrez. Rance, the sheriff and local big-shot, claims that he is going to marry Minnie; his claim is disputed by the others; there is a free-for-all; and it is Minnie herself who enforces peace at the point of a gun. Now the Wells-Fargo post arrives with a letter for Ashby telling him that Ramerrez will be in the neighborhood shortly. While Rance, with Italian passion but without success, pleads for Minnie's love, a stranger named Dick Johnson comes in and immediately arouses the dislike of Rance. "Stranger, what's your business?" he asks, sweeping Dick's drink to the floor, and it is only Minnie's intervention once more which saves Dick— for he, being the leading tenor, has immediately caught her fancy.

While Dick and Minnie are in the next room dancing, Castro, a captured member of the Ramerrez gang, comes in and promises to lead the boys to the hiding place in return for his own life. A moment later Dick returns, and Castro recognizes him as none other than Ramerrez himself. He manages to tell his boss that he has given away no secrets: the boys are merely waiting for the sheriff to go away before they raid the place.

When they all go off, Dick is left with Minnie, who is guarding all the gold for the miners. In the duet that closes the act Dick not only gives up his villainous project for the love of a good woman, but promises to defend her against any attack. Still not knowing the real identity of her new flame, she invites him to come up later and see her in her cabin.

ACT II

Up in Minnie's room, Wowkle is singing a lullaby to her papoose and discussing with Billy the advisability of making

it all legal. Their domestic discussion is interrupted by the
boss-woman, who is getting ready to entertain Dick Johnson
with a Western supper. The guest arrives; they discuss life;
they decide Dick had better spend the night (in a separate
bed) on account of the terrible snowstorm, when a gang of
the boys interrupts. Dick, hiding behind a curtain, hears them
tell Minnie that they have found out that Dick Johnson is
Ramerrez himself; but she laughs at them and manages to
shoo them out. Now she turns about and upbraids the bandit.
He admits who he is; he pleads his sad history in extenuation
(his father's death left him no alternative in life if he was to
support his dear old mother and the other kids); and he says
that the sight of Minnie made him decide to turn over a new
leaf. Thereupon he rushes out into the night—only to return a
moment later, shot by Rance.

Quickly Minnie hides the wounded man in the loft, and,
when Rance enters, insists that there is no one with her. Rance
cannot find his quarry, but he harshly accuses Minnie of loving
the bandit. As they argue, a drop of blood falls from the
wounded man; he comes down the ladder and collapses; and
Minnie tries one last desperate stratagem. Knowing Rance for
an inveterate gambler, she suggests three hands of poker. If
she wins, Dick goes free; if Rance wins, he can have Dick—
and Minnie too. They play, and each wins one of the first
two hands. Minnie's last one, however, is weak; and while
Rance is obligingly getting her a drink, she substitutes five
cards from her stocking for the deal she got. Thus, when Rance
shows with three kings, Minnie lays down a full house, aces
high. The lovers are left alone.

ACT III

In a clearing among the giant redwoods of California, a
gang of the boys is again hunting for Dick Johnson, who has
been nursed back to health only to have to go on the lam
once more. Twice there are false alarms of his having been
caught; but at last one of the miners, Sonora, brings him in.
A rope is prepared for him; everyone takes a turn at accusing

him of various crimes; and he replies that he has always stopped short of murder. Finally, they allow him a last word, which turns out to be the one well-known aria from the opera, *Ch'ella mi creda libero* ("Let her believe me free"), in which he begs that Minnie should never know of his inglorious fate but be allowed to believe he may someday return to her.

Rance's reply is to strike him in the face and prepare to pull the rope. But just at this moment in rides Minnie on a horse (if the leading lady is up to it) and brandishing her pistol. Hasn't she always done everything for the miners? she pleads. And won't they do one thing for her now: let off the man she loves so that he may begin a new life with her?

They do.

HÄNSEL UND GRETEL

Opera in three acts by Engelbert Humperdinck
with libretto in German by Adelheid Wette,
based on a fairy tale by Jakob and Wilhelm
Grimm

PETER, *a broommaker*	*Baritone*
GERTRUDE, *his wife*	*Mezzo-soprano*
HÄNSEL ⎱ *their children*	*Mezzo-soprano*
GRETEL ⎰	*Soprano*
THE WITCH	*Mezzo-soprano*
THE SANDMAN	*Soprano*
THE DEW MAN	*Soprano*

Time: once upon a
Place: Germany
First performance at Weimar, December 23, 1893

For many years it has been a custom to perform this
opera at Christmas time as a matinee for the kiddies, though
why a tale which obviously must take place in summertime
should be deemed especially appropriate for the winter is not
entirely clear. Nor does its very skillful but heavily Wagnerian
orchestration and harmonic elaboration strike one as well
adapted for little children to love or appreciate. Yet the custom has been so long established, and so many generations of
grownups think that they loved it when they were not grownups, that the tradition is beginning to fade only in the United
States. Here, for better or worse, the moppets express their
opinions more freely than elsewhere, and a Christmas-time
consensus of those opinions (which has never been taken in a

scientific way) would almost certainly give the palm to Mr. Menotti's *Amahl and the Night Visitors.* Its story is more appropriate—and you don't have to sit still so long.

Nevertheless, it is a treasurable score. The use of genuine children's folk songs in Act I, the *Prayer* as it is sung in Act II, the *Witches' Ride*, and several other pages of music have become part of our culture, and deservedly so. One could, however, almost wish that Humperdinck had reined his enthusiasm for writing notes by confining himself to his original intention—that of composing some incidental music for a children's play that his sister, Frau Adelheid Wette, had written for the family.

OVERTURE

A favorite number on pops concerts, the overture begins with the *Prayer* from Act II, continues with contrasting themes from other parts of the score, and develops quite elaborately till the *Prayer* is thundered out as if it were a hymn to victory.

ACT I

In the cottage of a poor broommaker his two children, Hänsel and Gretel, are hungry but nevertheless working, playing, and quarreling in the best of spirits. They sing the old German folk song about Susie and her geese (who have no shoes), and they end up by singing and dancing the familiar "Brother, come and dance with me" (*Brüderchen, komm tanz' mit mir*). Their mother's entrance puts a quick stop to the laughing, and they guiltily try to explain away the broommaking they have abandoned. In her anger the mother knocks over a pitcher of milk, leaving nothing for supper. With threats of a dire beating she sends them into the woods, warning them not to come back before they have picked a full basket of strawberries.

Peter, the father, returns home, jolly and drunk, and mollifies his wife, Gertrude, by exhibiting a basket of sausages, coffee, and bread and butter, which he has bought after an unexpected windfall of business in the village. As she prepares the supper, he misses the children, and Gertrude tells him that she has sent out the brats for strawberries. She doesn't care if they're at a mountain called Ilsenstein. Peter is horrified; and, as Gertrude does not seem to be up on local sociology, he sings her an aria explaining that there is a witch at Ilsenstein who navigates a broom and bakes little children into gingerbread. Gertrude at once rushes out after the children, and Peter follows, armed with his bottle of liquor.

ACT II

As intermission time can be troublesome when an audience includes many children, the management often labels this act "Scene 2" and the orchestra plays the *Hexenritt* ("Witches' Ride"), a lively little tone poem, while the scenery is being changed.

At the foot of the dread Ilsenstein the children are casually gathering—and eating—their strawberries. Gretel sings the charming folk song *Ein Männlein steht im Walde*, likening a mushroom to a man; but as it begins to grow dark, they begin to be frightened. They have lost their way; they think they see mysterious figures and hear mysterious voices (there is a female chorus off-stage to lend some verisimilitude to this); and they fall into each other's arms in fright. But the Little Sandman comforts them, strews the sand of sleepiness over them, and disappears as they sing the lovely *Children's Prayer* about fourteen angels who will guard them in their sleep.

A light shines on them from the mountain, and the fourteen angels descend, gather round them, and perform a quiet and modest ballet.

ACT III

After a short prelude, the curtain rises on the same scene next morning, except that there is now visible in the back a charming old German house decorated all over with life-size figures of children looking like gingerbread. It is, of course, the Witch's house.

The Dew Man, after singing a little self-identifying song, wakes the children, who are delighted to see the attractive dwelling. Hänsel breaks off a piece of gingerbread and begins to eat it; and they decide it is merely the wind when they hear someone inside singing the old game tune "Who's Nibbling at My House?" But it is really the Witch, who tosses a rope around Hänsel's neck (he frees himself), invites the children into the house (they refuse), and only manages to make them prisoners by the use of magic. She waves a juniper bough, utters the words *"Hocus-pocus Hexenschuss"*—and they are paralyzed. She thereupon places Hänsel in a cage, orders Gretel to work about the house, prepares the big stove, and takes a fiendish ride on her broom.

But this Witch is not very competent. When she tests Hänsel to see how good he is to eat, he presents her with a stick instead of his finger, and she is satisfied that he is too bony to cook. When she isn't looking, Gretel gets hold of the magic wand and frees her brother. And when Gretel asks for instructions about looking into the stove, she shows her how and is pushed into the fire for her pains. Delighted with their arson, the children start gathering sweetmeats from all over the house, when the big stove crackles and then explodes. With this turn of events the children whom the Witch had baked into her gingerbread house become partially free of the spell; Hänsel completes the reverse spell with the wand; and they all join in a chorus celebrating the end of the black magic.

Just then Peter and Gertrude find their children, with all their new friends; the Witch, now in the shape of a great gingerbread cake, is dragged from the debris of her oven; Peter finds an appropriate moral (wickedness gets punished); and everyone praises God in a choral variation of the *Prayer*.

L'HEURE ESPAGNOLE

(*The Spanish Hour*)

Opera in one act by Maurice Ravel with libretto in French by "Franc-Nohain" (Maurice Legrand) based on his own play of the same name

TORQUEMADA, *a clockmaker*	Tenor
CONCEPCION, *his wife*	Soprano
GONZALVE, *a poet*	Tenor
RAMIRO, *a muleteer*	Baritone
DON INIGO GOMEZ, *a banker*	Bass

Time: 18th century
Place: Toledo, Spain
First performance at Paris, May 19, 1911

Maurice Ravel was just about as French a composer as any composer who ever lived. Yet he was born in the Pyrenees, his mother apparently was a Basque, and he liked to write about Spain—sometimes even with a Spanish accent in his music. *L'Heure espagnole* is, of course, about Spain. Its title means, quite literally, "The Spanish Hour," but the word "hour" does not really mean a sixty-minute hour. The word is used, perhaps, as Longfellow used it, in the title of his famous poem *The Children's Hour*. That poem says, in effect, "Now is the time to pay some attention to the children." And the title of the opera suggests: "Let's talk about the Spaniards . . . and what they do with time." The libretto—a very French one—comes from a one-act play written by a Frenchman named Maurice Legrand. He further Frenchified it by using a *nom de plume*—Franc-Nohain.

The opera, first produced in 1911, still seems young and modern—partly, perhaps, because it is so very sophisticated—but its story goes back to eighteenth-century Toledo. It concerns a middle-aged clockmaker, Torquemada, and his young, pretty, and very sexy wife, Concepcion. One hears the ticktocks of Torquemada's clocks in the score almost from the beginning. Anyway, Torquemada, working in his shop one morning, gets a new customer—a big, handsome, muscular, good-natured, simple-minded muleteer named Ramiro. Keep your eye on Ramiro. Concepcion gets rid of her husband by reminding him that it is time to go and regulate the town clocks. That's part of his job. Her reason for wanting to be rid of Torquemada is that she has a rendezvous with one Gonzalve, a romantic poet.

The story (which is as complicated as a French bedroom farce) has to do with Concepcion keeping her men separated. She rids herself of Ramiro, the muleteer, by getting him to carry a grandfather's clock up to her bedroom. But that's only temporary. Gonzalve is more interested in singing and reciting his verses than in making love, so Ramiro returns inconveniently. Concepcion then gets him to carry up another clock, and pretty soon she even gets him to carry up one of the clocks with her lover secretly inside it.

Then—further complications. Another lover—Inigo, the fat banker—appears. Between the two lovers hiding in clocks and Ramiro carrying them up and downstairs within those clocks and Concepcion's growing admiration for Ramiro's strength and good nature—well, there's plenty of comedy. Finally, Concepcion invites Ramiro upstairs without *any* clock. While they are away, the poet finds the fat banker stuck inside a clock, unable to get out. In addition, Torquemada returns from his chores. No one is especially upset by all this, and Ramiro, always the good-natured strong man, pulls the poor banker out to safety.

And so they all join in a jolly quintet saying nothing of any importance at all. For in "the Spanish hour," so to speak, nothing seems to matter but a bit of flirtation.

LES HUGUENOTS

Opera in five acts by Giacomo Meyerbeer with
libretto in French by Augustin Eugène Scribe,
revised by Émile Deschamps and the composer

MARGUERITE DE VALOIS, *sister of*		
Charles IX of France		*Soprano*
URBAIN, *her page*		*Mezzo-soprano*
COUNT DE ST. BRIS		*Baritone*
COUNT DE NEVERS	*Catholic noblemen*	*Baritone*
COUNT MAUREVERT		*Bass*
COSSÉ		*Tenor*
MÉRU	*Catholic gentlemen*	*Baritone*
THORÉ		*Baritone*
TAVANNES		*Tenor*
VALENTINE, *daughter of St. Bris*		*Soprano*
RAOUL DE NANGIS, *a Huguenot nobleman*		*Tenor*
MARCEL, *servant to Raoul*		*Bass*
BOIS-ROSÉ, *a Huguenot soldier*		*Tenor*

Time: *August 1572*
Places: *Touraine and Paris*
First performance at Paris, *February 29, 1836*

It was *The Huguenots* that in 1836 made Meyerbeer the
king of the opera not only in Paris but practically everywhere
else. Not that he lacked detractors even in his own time. Richard Wagner described the typical Meyerbeer libretto as "a
monstrous motley, historico-romantic, sacro-frivolous, myste-
rious-brazen, sentimental-humbugging dramatic hodge-podge"
and, after Meyerbeer stopped being an easy touch, continually

attacked and denigrated him. (Yet, in a rare access of honesty, he once admitted that the fourth act of *The Huguenots* had deeply moved him.) It did not occur to Wagner that his descriptions of these librettos were not inapplicable, at least in part, to his own. Nor were Wagner's librettos, however many detractors they too had in their own day, ever taken seriously enough to frighten those interesting weather vanes of political opinion, the official censors. *The Huguenots* can at least claim the distinction of having had its religious conflict disguised in a number of sensitively Catholic cities. In Vienna and St. Petersburg it was performed as *The Guelphs and the Ghibellines,* in Munich and Florence as *The Anglicans and the Puritans,* and in the last city also as *Renato di Croenwald,* whoever that was.

Today it is difficult to take the pseudo-history of Meyerbeer and Scribe seriously, and, more important, the musical effects seem to have lost much of their impact. The opera is still regularly performed in France, less regularly in Germany, and hardly ever in the United States, England, or Italy. Individual numbers are sometimes sung in concert, and recordings of arias by singers of the Golden Age are collectors' items. Some of the music is therefore still current; but it appears unlikely that there will be a gala revival in an important American opera house before a genuine all-star cast can be assembled equal to the ones in the 1890's at the Metropolitan when the price of seats was raised two dollars for the occasion. For such a "night of seven stars," as it was publicized, the program listed Nordica, Melba, the two De Reszkes, Scalchi, Plançon, and Maurel. Even as late as 1905 one might have heard Caruso, Nordica, Sembrich, Scotti, Walker, Journet, and Plançon. But those days are gone forever, and perhaps *Les Huguenots* with them.

PRELUDE

The prelude consists of a series of repetitions ("variations" is too strong a word), with dramatic contrasts in dynamics, pitch, and orchestration, of the great Lutheran chorale *Ein feste Burg* ("A Mighty Fortress"). This wonderful tune is used a number of times later in the opera for dramatic purposes.

ACT I

It was a time, in France, of the bloodiest work of religious fanaticism, and a series of civil wars between the Catholics and the Huguenots came to an uneasy pause when, in 1572, Marguerite of France married Henry of Bourbon, thus uniting the leading Catholic and Protestant families. But the massacre of St. Bartholomew's Eve put an end to the Huguenot hopes for domination. The opera opens not long before St. Bartholomew's Eve, and the massacre closes it.

The Count de Nevers is one of the leading young Catholic noblemen, and in his castle in Touraine he is entertaining some of his boon companions, jolly blades all. Nevers himself is the only one among them who has some character, and he asks them to show a bit of tolerance toward an expected guest even though he is a Huguenot aristocrat. Nevertheless, when the handsome but distinctly provincial Raoul de Nangis is introduced, they utter some ungentlemanly asides about his looking like a Calvinist.

The banquet now begins, and a rousing chorus is sung in praise of good eating and the wines of Touraine. Next, a toast is proposed to everyone's mistress, but Nevers admits that as he is about to be married, he must decline; in fact, he adds, he finds the circumstance rather embarrassing: the ladies seem to be pursuing him even more ardently than before his engagement became known. Raoul then obliges with an account of his own love—an unknown beauty whom he saved one day from a gang of rowdy students. This aria (*Plus blanche que la blanche hermine*—"Whiter than ermine") features the obbligato of an obsolete instrument, the viola d'amore, which makes it especially effective. He has dedicated his heart to this unknown, a romantic gesture that wins only smiles of condescension from his worldly-wise auditors.

Raoul's retainer, Marcel, a redoubtable old soldier, is completely out of sympathy with his master's making such acquaintances and tries to warn him. He boldly huffs out the Lutheran chorale, A *Mighty Fortress*, and proudly admits that it was he who, in battle, had administered the scar to the face of one of the guests, Cossé. Cossé good-naturedly invites the old soldier to drink. Being an unbending Calvinist, Marcel refuses, but he does substitute something better—the *Chanson huguenote*, a vigorous and brutal anti-papist battle song which features a refrain on the syllables *Piff, paff* denoting the damage inflicted on Catholics by Protestant bullets.

The merriment is interrupted when the host is called out to receive a message from a young lady in the garden. Everyone speculates on Nevers' continuing intrigues even after his engagement, and Raoul is deeply shocked when, looking through a window with the others, he recognizes in Nevers' visitor the unknown beauty he had vowed to love. He swears vengeance. But he does not overhear Nevers when, on his return, he says that his visitor was his fiancée, Valentine, a protégé of the Queen's, who has asked to be released from her engagement. Nevers, though deeply chagrined, has acquiesced.

Another messenger from another lady again interrupts the party. This messenger is the page Urbain, so young a chap that his part is taken by a mezzo-soprano, and in a once-admired aria (*Une dame noble et sage*—"A wise and noble lady") he announces that he bears a letter from an important personage. It turns out to be addressed not to Nevers, as everyone supposed, but to Raoul; and it asks that he permit himself to be blindfolded before going to a rendezvous. When Nevers sees the missive, he recognizes the seal as that of Marguerite of Valois, the King's sister. This mark of esteem for the young Huguenot wins him the respect of all the Catholic gentry present, and they convey their politically motivated congratulations in the finale. Marcel, for his part, strikes in with a *Te Deum* and the observation that Samson has overcome the Philistines.

ACT II

In the garden of her castle of Chenonceaux, in Touraine, Marguerite of Valois is awaiting Raoul de Nangis. The ladies-in-waiting sing the praises of the countryside, as does the Queen herself. The Queen, it appears, has sent for Raoul so that he may become engaged to Valentine, the daughter of the Count de St. Bris, one of the leading Catholic noblemen. Such a marriage, rather than one with another Catholic, should help allay the civil strife. Valentine shows only a lady-like hesitation about being made a political pawn in this fashion: it was long the common fate of aristocratic girls.

The page Urbain is also present at the court, having been thrilled by leading the handsome, blindfolded cavalier through the streets. He is a Cherubino-like figure, in love with Valentine, with the Queen, and with the sex in general. But he is as much coarser in conception than Cherubino as Meyerbeer's music was coarser than Mozart's. The fascination women have for him is projected by his acting as a Peeping Tom when the girls of the court go bathing, which they do at the back of the stage within tantalizing half-sight of the audience. They also sing a bathers' chorus.

When Raoul is finally led blindfolded into the presence of the Queen and left alone with her, he is permitted to take off the scarf and finds himself at once overpowered with the beauty of the young woman he sees. He does not know it is the Queen, and he vows gallantly to serve her. The Queen, for her part, assures him that there will be occasion for her to call upon him.

It is only when Urbain returns to announce that the whole court is about to arrive that Raoul learns whom he has been vowing to serve. And when the Queen tells him that this service must be his marrying the daughter of the Count de St. Bris for political reasons, he readily consents, even though he does not know he has ever seen the girl. The courtiers then enter to the tune of a minuet and range themselves on two sides of the stage, Catholic and Huguenots, with Nevers and

St. Bris heading the former. Some letters brought to the
Queen demand, in the name of King Charles IX, the presence
of the Catholics in Paris for some important but undisclosed
project. Before they leave, however, the Queen demands and
receives an oath from both sides pledging them to eternal
peace. It is a most impressive chorus.

But now St. Bris brings in his daughter, Valentine, whom
Raoul is supposed to marry. Recognizing with horror that
this is the lady who called on Nevers during the banquet, he
vigorously protests that he will never marry her. St. Bris and
Nevers are outraged, and bloodshed is avoided only through
the intercession of the Queen and her reminder that the gentlemen must hurry to Paris. In the grand finale, during which
passions are heated rather than cooled, Raoul insists that he
too shall go to Paris, Valentine faints, and Marcel sings *A
Mighty Fortress*.

ACT III

If you visit the Pré aux Clercs region of Paris today, you
will find it a busy, well-built-up portion of the Left Bank with
the Boulevard St. Germain as its principal thoroughfare. In
the sixteenth century, however, there was still a large field,
bordered by a church and some taverns, and it is here that
the third act opens with a jolly chorus of townsmen enjoying
a holiday. A group of Huguenots also renders an effective number, the *Rataplan Chorus*, in which they bid defiance to the
Catholics and praise their distinguished leader, the Admiral
Coligny. A third choral number follows—a chorus of nuns singing an *Ave Maria*, which precedes a premarital procession into
the church. Raoul having refused Valentine, she has once more
been betrothed to Nevers, and they are making arrangements
for the wedding. When the party, which includes the bride,
the groom, and the father of the bride, has passed into the
church, Marcel asks rather disrespectfully for St. Bris, and
violence is avoided only by the distraction of a group of gypsies, who perform for the townsfolk and the Huguenot
soldiery.

The wedding arrangements having been made, the gentlemen of the party emerge, leaving Valentine inside to pray. Marcel takes this opportunity to deliver his message to St. Bris, which turns out be a challenge to a duel from Raoul. A friend of St. Bris's, Maurevert, suggests that there are other ways than dangerous duels to handle such fellows as Raoul, and they retire to the church to discuss plans to ambush him.

When the sounding of the curfew has dispersed the crowd, the plotters leave the church, making final plans for their treachery, and a moment later Valentine, who has overheard everything, runs out distraught. It appears that she loves the man who has spurned her and wishes to warn him, but Marcel tells her it is too late: Raoul must already have left home. After a long duet on this theme, Valentine re-enters the church while Marcel stands guard, vowing to die with his master if necessary.

He does not have long to wait. The principals come, each with two seconds, and in a concerted number vow to abide strictly by the rules of honor in the ensuing duel. But Marcel knows that Maurevert and other Catholics are waiting just outside the field, and he knocks on the tavern door shouting, "Coligny!" Out come the Huguenot soldiers; out come many Catholic students; out come many women on each side to lend their voices to the general scene of confusion and incipient bloodshed.

Fortunately, Marguerite of Valois happens to be riding by at the time and once more puts a stop to all the violence. She denounces both sides for having broken their oaths. Marcel informs her that a veiled lady had told him that treachery was afoot, and when Valentine emerges from the church and St. Bris removes her veil, everyone is amazed—St. Bris that his daughter should have betrayed him, Raoul that this particular girl should have done him such a service. Once again he is in love with her.

But what of the bridegroom, Nevers? His prospective father-in-law, St. Bris, had carefully kept him uninformed of the dastardly plot, and, all smiling and unknowing, he now comes up the river Seine on a gaily decorated barge to claim his bride.

A wedding always brings out the more peaceful sentiments of human beings (or at least of opera choruses), and so the scene ends with general rejoicing among the populace, including those gypsies, who come back for a return engagement. The Huguenot soldiery, it is true, refuses to be caught up in the celebration but contents itself with mutters. The only outspokenly sad characters are the leading soprano and tenor: Valentine is heartbroken over having to marry a man she hates, while Raoul is now furious over losing her to his rival. All these different emotions supply fine material for the finale of the act.

ACT IV

It is now August 24, 1572, the day of the St. Bartholomew massacre. Valentine, in the home of her new husband, bewails her lost love in the aria *Parmi les pleurs* ("Bathed all in tears"), and then is startled to see Raoul himself enter the room. He has come to bid her a final farewell and then to die, if need be; but when she tells him that Nevers and St. Bris are expected any moment, he consents to hide behind a tapestry.

The Catholic noblemen now forgather and learn, from St. Bris, that Catherine de Médici, the Queen Mother, has decreed a general massacre of all Protestants for that very night. It will be made easier by the fact that many of the Huguenot leaders will be gathered together at the Hôtel de Nesle celebrating the marriage of Marguerite of Valois to Henry of Navarre. Nevers, one of the rarely honorable baritones of opera, declines to have anything to do with such infamy and dramatically breaks his sword. St. Bris orders him held in custody as a renegade from the Catholic cause, and a second impressive oath scene ensues, entitled the *Benediction of the Swords*. Toward its close St. Bris distributes white scarves, which have been brought in by three monks, to be worn as identifying arm bands during the holocaust.

Raoul has, of course, overheard all this. He has overheard St. Bris give the detailed instructions about assuming positions at the sound of the first peal from the church of St. Germain and to strike at the sound of the second. He rushes forth from his hiding place as soon as the men have departed, but the door is locked. Valentine emerges from her own room, and there follows the long duet that moved even Richard Wagner. He wishes to warn his fellow-Protestants; she pleads on behalf of her relatives and the holy cause; he replies that it is a fine cause which demands the murder of brothers. But when she tells him of her love, he is moved to ask her to run away with him. It is the tolling of the bell, however, that brings him back to his sense of duty and of horror; and when it tolls for the second time, he drags Valentine to the window, where she may see the fearful acts commencing in the streets. Finally, praying for her protection, he jumps out of the window. Valentine faints.

ACT V

This is a very long opera, and many managements have simply omitted the three remaining scenes. They are needed, however, to wind up the details of the story, and they offer some fascinating moments.

Scene 1 The Huguenot notables are celebrating, with a ballet among other things, the marriage of Marguerite and Henry at the Hôtel de Nesle. Raoul, already wounded, interrupts the merriment with the frightful news of what is going on outside. Protestant churches are in flames; the Admiral Coligny has been murdered. After a rousing chorus the men draw their swords and follow Raoul into the streets to do battle.

Scene 2 In one of the beleaguered Protestant churches Raoul, Valentine, and Marcel are reunited, the last being badly wounded. Raoul wishes to return to the streets to fight, but Valentine urges safety on him. If he will wear a white scarf and go with her to the Louvre, they will have the protection of the Queen. But as this would mean becoming a Catholic, Raoul refuses. Even the report that Nevers has been killed in the fighting and that he may now marry Valentine does not persuade him to save his life at the expense of his principles. Finally Valentine tells him that her love is so great that she will give up her own religion. The lovers kneel before Marcel to have their union blessed, and from within the church comes the sound of the choir singing *A Mighty Fortress*.

The sound is rudely interrupted by the violence of the Catholic forces breaking in on the other side of the church. The three principals kneel in prayer; Marcel eloquently describes the vision of paradise that he sees in his mind's eye; and at the close of the trio their enemies break in. They refuse the alternative of recanting their religious heresies; they bravely sing the chorale; and they are dragged out into the streets by the soldiery.

Scene 3 Somehow, they have managed to escape their captors, and, amid the rushing soldiers, Valentine and Marcel are helping the mortally wounded Raoul along one of the quays of Paris. St. Bris appears at the head of a troop through the darkness and demands to know who they are. Despite Valentine's frantic efforts to keep him quiet, Raoul shouts out, "Huguenots!" and St. Bris orders his men to fire. It is too late when he recognizes that one of the victims is his own daughter, and she dies breathing a prayer for him.

Once again Marguerite of Valois happens to pass by, and she is aghast when she recognizes the three fresh bodies before her. This time her efforts to bring peace to the scene are in vain. The soldiers are still swearing to wipe out all Protestants when the curtain falls.

JULIUS CAESAR

(*Giulio Cesare*)

Opera in three acts by George Frederick Handel with libretto in Italian by Nicola Francesco
Haym

JULIUS CAESAR	*Male contralto*
CURIO, *his aide-de-camp*	*Tenor*
CORNELIA, *widow of Pompey*	*Contralto*
SEXTUS, *her son*	*Tenor*
CLEOPATRA, *Queen of Egypt*	*Soprano*
PTOLEMY, *her brother*	*Bass*
ACHILLAS, *his adviser*	*Bass*
NIRENUS, *Cleopatra's adviser*	*Male contralto*

Time: 48 B.C.
Place: Alexandria
First performance at London, March 2, 1724

"Handel," said Samuel Butler in his *Note-Books*, "is so great and so simple that no one but a professional musician is unable to understand him."

The typically Butlerian gibe is not really quite fair to professional musicians, for it is they who have valiantly and persistently tried to resuscitate Handel's operas. Dr. Oskar Hagen, with Teutonic thoroughness, attempted, during the 1920's, to revive thirty of them and succeeded with nine. Dr. Werner Josten, during the 1930's, revived a few of them during his tenure as head of the Music Department at Smith College. Various concert and operatic societies in New York and elsewhere have mounted *Julius Caesar* as well as other Handelian operas in concert form, sometimes with great critical acclaim. This same opera has had two different more or less complete productions on long-playing records, though they were soon withdrawn from the catalogues for lack of sales. The ventures will doubtless continue just as long as professional musicians continue to recognize the great qualities of these scores—and that should be, roughly guessing, forever.

Nevertheless, one seriously doubts that productions of Handel's operas will ever attract the wide and devoted attendance they once enjoyed in London, where most of them first saw the light of candles. The hurdles for modern audiences are two—the type of leading singers for whom Handel composed and the nature of the librettos. At least one of the leading male roles in each of Handel's operas (in this case, Julius Caesar himself) was written for a castrato, that is for a male singer who, through a barbarous operation followed by long and arduous training, had developed a soprano or alto voice of such exquisite virtuosity and (to judge from contemporary evidence) such thrilling qualities as to be virtually irresistible. Farinelli, who appeared in a number of Handel's operas, through his singing gained such an ascendancy over two successive kings of Spain that he became one of the most important political figures in the land. In modern productions these roles are assigned usually to baritones or tenors or, occasionally, to countertenors. But modern singers have difficulty with them in any register.

As for the librettos, they are based on pseudohistory, classical mythology, or romantic subjects so badly out of tune with our own times that it is impossible to read them without smiles soon suffocated by boredom. They were conceived as vehicles for star singers; they were strait-jacketed by eighteenth-century ideas of classicism; and they seemed so preposterous to intelligent men of even their own day as to elicit one of the most delightful of all of Addison's polite but devastatingly satirical essays. The following summary of the plot of *Julius Caesar*, based on the libretto of the Handel Society, illustrates the nature of these dramas; yet the reader should be reminded that the score of this opera, as well as those of several others by Handel, contains some of the noblest and most moving pages ever composed for the stage.

ACT I

Scene 1   The overture, which consists of a formal introduction and allegro, leads directly into the welcoming chorus of Egyptians, who greet the conqueror, Julius Caesar, as he crosses a bridge. Caesar sings a dignified aria expressing satisfaction with his latest exploit, and his aide-de-camp, Curio, summarizes the situation with a bromidic quotation from his master's collected literary works: "Caesar came, he saw, and he conquered."

It is Pompey, Caesar's erstwhile partner-in-government, who has suffered defeat and capture, and when Pompey's wife and son, Cornelia and Sextus, appear on the scene, Caesar speaks magnanimously to them, proposing a reconciliation. The joyful occasion is utterly ruined, however, when Achillas brings in a gift. Achillas is the military leader and personal adviser to Ptolemy, Cleopatra's somewhat degenerate younger brother, and the gift he has sent in a basket is the head of Pompey. Everyone is deeply shocked by this action excepting Achillas, who, in an aside, indicates that his first sight of Cornelia has utterly fascinated him. Caesar turns on Achillas and denounces him in a vigorous aria; Cornelia's aria expresses her deep sorrow; while that of Sextus warns us that he means to have revenge. A more modern opera would have taken the occasion to develop these passions simultaneously in a finale; but this was a technique not yet developed, and the convention of arias following upon each other, between recitatives, is consistently followed.

Scene 2   In her own room, attended by her handmaidens, Cleopatra receives the horrid news of Pompey's murder by her brother, Ptolemy. As she is his rival for the throne of Egypt, she decides to counter this possibly welcome act by trying her feminine wiles on Caesar. She prepares to meet him, ordering her friend Nirenus to accompany her; but just then Ptolemy enters to resume the argument—apparently an old one—as to which of the two shall occupy the throne. She dismisses him with the epithet *effiminato amante* (effeminate lover) and departs herself after singing an aria in which she trusts sex to lead her to the throne.

Achillas finds Ptolemy still in the room, tells him of Caesar's anger, and suggests that he himself be instructed to murder the man. All he asks for as a reward is Cornelia. Ptolemy considers this a splendid arrangement and sings an aria already gloating over the death of Caesar.

Scene 3   At the tomb of Pompey, Caesar (in a long recitative) solemnly pays his last respects to his late rival. Cleopatra, disguised as one of her own handmaidens named Lydia, approaches Caesar and asks for help against the tyrant Ptolemy, who, she says, has robbed her. Much impressed by the girl's beauty—as Curio is, too—he raises the kneeling suppliant and promises to see that her fortune is restored. He sings an aria likening her to a meadow flower and departs on his mission.

Cleopatra and Nirenus are congratulating themselves on how well the strategy seems to be working, when Cornelia and Sextus come to the same spot. The widow takes a dagger from among the trophies of war that decorate the tomb, swearing vengeance on the murderer. But Sextus seizes the dagger, declaring that the vengeance should be his.

Cleopatra then closes the scene with a brilliant aria apostrophizing the star of her expected good fortune.

Scene 4   At a banquet in Ptolemy's palace, he and Caesar exchange polite greetings barbed with threats. In an aria, sung as an aside, Caesar lets the audience know that he is on his guard.

Cornelia and Sextus then meet Ptolemy and Achillas, and when Sextus challenges Ptolemy to single combat, both the Romans are arrested, Sextus to be sent to prison, Cornelia to Ptolemy's seraglio. There, he tells Achillas, she will be reserved especially for him.

The act ends with a sorrowful duet sung by mother and son.

ACT II

Scene 1 Music comes from the "Palace of the Goddess of Virtue," which stands in a grove of cedars with Mount Parnassus in the background. Caesar, who is standing in the grove, is enchanted. He is even more enchanted when the palace opens up disclosing Virtue served by the nine muses, and Cleopatra sings a long love song. Nirenus, who has been standing by, sees that this aphrodisiacal show is having its effect on Caesar and offers to lead him to where Lydia lies.

Scene 2 In the garden of his harem Ptolemy, despite his promise to Achillas, tries to make improper advances to Cornelia. She repulses him and runs away, whereupon he sings an aria threatening to use force.

Sextus then occupies the stage long enough to sing a very striking aria in which a snakelike melody suggests the reptile that he likens to his revenge.

Scene 3 Caesar is proposing marriage to Cleopatra, still thinking her to be "Lydia," when Curio rushes in to warn him that a mob outside is crying: "Death to Caesar!" Cleopatra, declaring that she will stay by him to the death, finally reveals her true identity, and goes forth to face down the mob.

Caesar: Curio, these strange adventures paralyze my senses.
Curio: I am stupefied.

After this noble repartee Cleopatra returns, having failed, and urges Caesar to run for his life. Caesar, after an aria declaring his determination to take vengeance, takes her advice. Left alone, she gives voice to one of the finest arias of any Handelian opera, a prayer to the gods for pity accompanied by a particularly eloquent figure in the violins.

ACT III

Scene 1 This is devoted primarily to another fine aria for Cleopatra. Caesar has been defeated; for all she knows, he is dead; and she weeps over her probable fate.

Scene 2   But Caesar has not been killed. He had jumped into the sea and dragged himself onto the beach. In an aria he asks the gods for pity on him. Sextus has not been hurt either; he comes to the beach, weapon in hand, still looking for Ptolemy. Achillas, however, has been badly wounded. He drags himself in wearily, followed by Nirenus (unwounded). Considerably cheered by this sight, Caesar takes Nirenus with him on a search for Cleopatra and Cornelia.

Scene 3   Cleopatra is still bewailing the fortunes of war and the way they have turned against her, when Caesar comes in, victorious, followed by soldiers.

Scene 4   At the port of Alexandria there is played a "victory symphony"; Caesar crowns Cleopatra as Queen of Egypt; they sing a love duet; and the chorus sings a paean to happiness.

LAKMÉ

Opera in three acts by Léo Delibes with libretto in French by Edmond Gondinet and Philippe Gille generally said to be based on Pierre Loti's *Le Mariage de Loti* but bearing only a faint resemblance to that novel

NILAKANTHA, *a Brahman priest*	*Bass-baritone*
LAKMÉ, *his daughter*	*Soprano*
MALLIKA, *her slave*	*Mezzo-soprano*
ELLEN ⎫ *English ladies*	*Soprano*
ROSE ⎭	*Soprano*
MISTRESS BENSON, *their governess*	*Mezzo-soprano*
GERALD, *an English officer*	*Tenor*
FREDERICK, *another*	*Baritone*

Time: late 19th century
Place: India
First performance at Paris, April 14, 1883

Few music-lovers today know much of Léo Delibes's music outside of his two charming ballet scores, *Sylvia* and *Coppélia*, and, of course, *Lakmé*—or at least its *Bell Song*. Despite the color and good, old-fashioned drama of its setting, the opera is given today, outside of France, only as an occasional vehicle for a famous and pretty coloratura soprano. In France, however, it remains popular, having received some 1500 performances at the Opéra Comique in Paris, since its premiere in 1883. On that occasion a Brooklyn-born coloratura, Marie van Zandt, sang it with such success that the role, for some time, was identified with her. However, a list of those sopranos

who have essayed the role would include practically every great
coloratura up to almost the present day, including Adelina
Patti, Marcella Sembrich, Luisa Tetrazzini, Amelita Galli-
Curci, and Lily Pons—not to mention quite a few who had no
particular business trying.

ACT I

The story takes place in nineteenth-century India, where—
as everyone knows—the British were riding high, wide, and
handsome. When the opera opens, the priest Nilakantha is
in his sacred garden exhorting his followers to await the day
when the British shall be driven from the land. Off-stage,
comes the voice of his daughter, Lakmé, and gradually her
voice grows stronger, as she comes on stage and leads the men
in their prayer to the god Siva.

When the prayer is over, everyone leaves the garden excepting Lakmé and her slave Mallika, who, together, oblige
with a charming barcarolle in thirds. Because they are planning to bathe, Lakmé removes her jewels and places them on
a bench before shoving off in a boat with Mallika.

Now there are visitors of another sort. They are two British
officers—Gerald and Frederick—their friends from home, Ellen
and Rose, and, as a chaperone, the young ladies' governess,
Mrs. Benson. All five break into the garden, even though they
know they have no business there, to admire the beautiful
white flowers. These flowers—naturalists call them *datura
stramonium*—are poisonous, and on the warnings of Frederick
the party does not touch them. We shall hear more of them
in the last act.

Happening on Lakmé's jewels, Gerald is so enchanted that
he stays on to make a drawing of them when the others leave.
Here he has his charming aria *Prendre le dessin d'un bijou.*

Naturally, as Gerald is the leading tenor, Lakmé returns
and finds him there. And as Lakmé is the leading soprano,
the two must fall in love at first sight. And as they fall in love
at first sight, a love duet must be sung. But this love duet is a
little different, for Lakmé keeps warning Gerald that if he is

Lakmé

found in the garden, he may very well be killed. At first Gerald
cannot take this warning seriously. After all, he is an officer
in the army of Queen Victoria. But finally Lakmé persuades
him to leave, and it is only just in time. For Nilakantha returns with his followers and, outraged by the desecration of
the holy garden, vows that the man who was there must die.
The other Hindus take up the cry of vengeance.

ACT II

It is a feast day for the Hindus, and our various British
friends are at the bustling bazaar to watch and be amused.
Mrs. Benson has her watch stolen; Rose and Ellen are excited
by all the activity; and the two officers are having their last
good time, for tomorrow they are off to the wars. Gerald admits that he has seen the charming young priestess Lakmé,
and the others are quite curious about her, in a superior British
sort of way. There is also a fine ballet, danced by the natives.
Presently the vengeful priest Nilakantha enters, disguised
as a beggar. He seems to have learned that Gerald was in the
garden and that he has fallen in love with Lakmé. He demands
that his daughter sing, and she obliges with the famous *Bell
Song*. It is the legend of a Hindu maiden and how she attracted the great god Vishnu with her bells. Nilakantha hopes
that Lakmé's singing will attract Gerald so that he may murder him. As British soldiers march by, to drums and fifes,
Nilakantha gathers his followers, and they hide to surprise
Gerald.
Sure enough, Gerald appears; and in their second love duet
Lakmé urges him to join her in a hidden spot where she may
guard him. He, however, is all for Queen and duty, and he
declines this tempting invitation. He might just as well have
accepted it, for now the holiest of the processions arrives,
carrying the image of the goddess Dourga, and singing to it.
Under cover of the excitement created by the procession,
Nilakantha sneaks in, stabs Gerald, and quietly makes off.
Lakmé rushes over to the fallen English officer, sees that the

wound is not fatal, and joyfully plans to take him to her hidden grotto to recover.

ACT III

This grotto is a beautiful spot, full of lush flowers, and Gerald lies quietly on his sickbed as Lakmé nurses him and sings to him. When he awakes, he is enchanted with both his surroundings and his affectionate nurse and tells us so in most persuasive musical phrases.

Now, off-stage, there is a chorus of Indian lovers singing as they go to a secret spring whose waters will make them forever faithful. Lakmé, too, goes there, to get some of the magic water for her lover.

But while she is gone, Frederick comes in. He has been looking everywhere for his fellow-officer and is delighted to find him greatly improved. Their regiment, he says, is about to depart, and Gerald reacts as any British officer should: duty first. When Lakmé returns, she suspects that he will not remain faithful. In the distance there is the sound of marching soldiers, and Gerald refuses the magical drink. In despair Lakmé secretly takes some of the poisonous *datura* blossoms and eats them, just before Gerald decides to drink of the magic waters after all. But it is too late. The vengeful Nilakantha rushes in and is about to strike Gerald dead when Lakmé intervenes. If the gods must have a victim, she cries, let it be herself! Only now do they see that she is dying. Gerald is heartbroken, but Nilakantha closes the opera with the ecstatic thought that his daughter will forever live with Brahma.

LOHENGRIN

Opera in three acts by Richard Wagner with libretto in German by the composer based largely on a medieval poem, the *Wartburgkrieg*

HENRY THE FOWLER, *King of Germany*	*Bass*
LOHENGRIN	*Tenor*
ELSA OF BRABANT	*Soprano*
FREDERICK OF TELRAMUND, *Count of Brabant*	*Baritone*
ORTRUD, *his wife*	*Soprano or Mezzo-soprano*
THE KING'S HERALD	*Baritone or Bass*

Time: 933
Place: Antwerp
First performance at Weimar, August 28, 1850

The history of *Lohengrin* furnishes an interesting footnote to the eternal argument over whether an opera should be given in its original language or in the language of the audience listening. Before the composer, who was also conductor at the Dresden Opera, could produce his new work, he had to flee from Germany on account of his revolutionary sentiments. That was in 1849, when revolution was rife in the land. His temporary home was Switzerland, where there was no chance to produce this opera, and so he turned, in hope, to France and England. But despite the fact that Wagner prided himself as much on his poetry as on his music, it never occurred to him to suggest that either of these countries should produce his operas in German. He wrote to his friend Eduard Devrient at this time: "My immediate object is to get my latest opera *Lohengrin* translated into English and performed in London." Nothing came of these efforts and, as a matter of fact, the first London performance of the opera, which took place over twenty years later, was in neither German nor English, but in Italian.

When the premiere of the work did finally take place a year later, it had the benefit of the original German language, for it was given for a German audience. It occurred in Weimar in 1850, while Wagner was still in exile. The orchestra boasted only five first violins and six seconds, with thirty-eight pieces in all, while the chorus numbered under thirty. Despite the best efforts of the conductor, who was Wagner's great champion and father-in-law-to-be, Franz Liszt, the opera was not well received. (How could it have been with such inadequate forces?)

Liszt reported all the details to the absent composer, and the great Richard was very angry. The performance had taken something over four hours, and Wagner decided that Liszt must have played everything too slowly. However, Wagner had never heard the opera even rehearsed with an orchestra, however small; he had only played it for himself on a piano. He therefore did not realize that those long, sustained passages at the beginning of the prelude—as well as many others like them—are best played very, very slowly by an orchestra. On a piano, which cannot sustain a chord evenly for more than a moment, it would have to go faster. Eleven years later, when Wagner heard a full performance for the first time, in Vienna, he agreed that Liszt had been right. A full performance, without cuts and not counting intermissions, takes upwards of three and a half hours. Therefore, many opera houses habitually cut passages here and there which only the genuine *aficionado*—and the inveterate libretto-reader—will notice.

PRELUDE

The well-beloved prelude is based almost entirely upon the theme of the Holy Grail and was romantically and quite accurately described by Wagner himself in these words:

"Out of the clear blue ether of the sky there seems to condense a wonderful yet at first hardly perceptible vision; and out of this there gradually emerges, ever more and more clearly, an angel host bearing in its midst the Holy Grail. As it approaches earth, it pours out exquisite odors, like streams of gold, ravishing the senses of the beholder. The glory of the vision grows and grows until it seems as if the rapture must be shattered and dispersed by the very vehemence of its expansion . . . The flames die away, and the angel host soars up again to the ethereal heights in tender joy. . . ."

ACT I

Henry the Fowler, tenth-century ruler of Germany, arrives at Antwerp beside the river Scheldt. He addresses the assembled nobles of Saxony and Brabant, telling them of renewed war with the Eastern hordes, and they agree to follow him in battle. But, adds Henry, there is trouble locally, and he calls on Frederick, Count Telramund, to recite his complaint. Telramund steps forward and, with growing excitement, tells a strange story. The boy, Godfrey of Brabant, has disappeared. His sister, Elsa, whom Telramund had once intended to marry, had taken him into the woods, and the boy had never returned. There is but one explanation: she must have murdered him. Telramund has therefore married someone else— Ortrud of Friesland; and now, in the name of his wife, he claims to be the rightful ruler of Brabant. Elsa is then called upon and comes in, the picture of innocence, all dressed in white. She sings her famous aria, *Elsa's Dream*, in which she tells of having seen a handsome knight who promised to come to her in time of need. The issue, it is agreed, must be tried in the good medieval tradition of trial by combat. But who will fight for Elsa? The Herald solemnly calls for a candidate once, but no one offers. He calls again. Again, no answer. Then Elsa and her handmaidens pray earnestly, and lo, in the distance, appears a knight in a boat, drawn up the river by a swan. The knight in shining armor lands. In a simple aria he thanks the swan, then turns to greet the King and to offer his services to Elsa. But first she must make two promises: she must agree to marry him, should he prove victorious, and she must agree never to ask his name or where he has come from. To both terms she consents. The fighting ground is measured off by the nobles; the Herald recites the rules of the combat; and the King leads the entire assemblage in an impressive prayer.

The fight itself is very brief. Telramund is struck to the ground; the stranger knight magnanimously spares his life; and the act concludes with general melodious rejoicing—a chorus of praise to the champion with the unknown name. I hardly think I am violating a secret if I say that the name of the unknown knight is Lohengrin.

ACT II

Although Telramund's life has been spared, both he and his wife, Ortrud, are in disgrace. They have spent the night bickering on the steps of the cathedral of Antwerp, where Elsa and her rescuer are to be married in the morning. Before dawn Elsa appears on the balcony over the square, and Ortrud, pretending friendship, is invited in, and is given an honorable place at the wedding.

Dawn begins to break; the knights and others gather in the courtyard; and the Herald makes two important announcements: Elsa and her champion are to be married that very morning, and the expedition against the Hungarians is to begin soon after under the new leader of Brabant—that is, of course, Lohengrin.

Then begins the long and beautiful *Bridal Procession*. All the knights and ladies gather and sing their blessings on the handsome couple. But suddenly Ortrud interrupts, taunting Elsa for not knowing the name or origin of her fiancé. Elsa is frightened, but she is rescued by the appearance of the King and her warrior. Ortrud is ordered away, and the procession begins again, only to be interrupted once more, this time by Telramund. Standing on the cathedral steps, and backed by four followers, he presses his charges even more strongly than

Ortrud did. He demands that the King himself put the questions of name and origin to the stranger. Now the knight himself speaks up. He will answer no one, he says, but Elsa herself. Does she wish to question him? Well—Elsa is only human, and very, very feminine. For a longer time than any heroine really should she wavers. Then (but only after a very fine concerted number) she proceeds with the ceremonial without asking the fateful questions. Telramund manages to whisper to her that he will be standing by at night; but she dismisses him, and the procession moves on, joyously, to the cathedral.

Then, just as they are about to enter, Ortrud appears ominously once more. The music always associated with the fatal questions thunders out of the orchestra, and the act closes on a skillfully mixed note of doubt and joy.

ACT III

Scene 1 The exciting prelude to the third act leads, with a few bars of modulation, right into the celebrated *Bridal Chorus*. The attendants sing this to the happy couple on the night of their wedding, and then they leave them in their bridal chamber. Elsa and her still-unnamed knight—now her husband—sing a lovely duet, but then her doubts again begin to assert themselves. Her husband tries to allay them with an aria that compares her to the sweetest fragrances of nature. Yet the doubts will not down. Sternly he reminds her of the trust she owes him, and he repeats his protestations of love. But the poison that Ortrud and Telramund have poured into Elsa's ear continues to work. She imagines she sees the swan returning to take her husband from her side. A madness seizes upon her, and over the protest of her husband she finally asks the fatal questions: "Tell me thy name . . . Whence dost thou come? . . . Where is thy home?"

Before he can answer (for answer he must), Telramund and four knights burst into the chamber. Swiftly Elsa hands over the sword, swiftly Lohengrin slays Telramund—with one supernatural stroke of his sword. "Now all our happiness is gone," he sadly sighs, and he orders the corpse to be carried before the King and Elsa herself to appear in the royal presence.

Scene 2 With no pause the scene changes to the kingly presence, as it was in Act I. Telramund's body is carried in, and his slayer explains what he has had to do. Then Elsa comes in; and now the knight prepares to answer her questions. Quietly, but tensely, he tells of his home on the wondrous Mont Monsalvat, where a band of knights guards and serves the Holy Grail. Once every year a dove descends from heaven to renew its powers, and all its knights are guarded by it in their fights for innocence and truth. His father, says the knight, is Percival, king of all the knights of the Grail, and his own name is—Lohengrin. But now, he adds, since his secret is known, he must return. And however much he regrets it, he must leave, not only his bride, but King Henry.

Suddenly a cry is heard from those nearest the shore. The swan is seen returning, with the boat. Lohengrin goes to greet it and then turns once more to Elsa. Had she but waited a year, her young brother Godfrey would have been restored to her. Now, should he return, she must give him Lohengrin's sword, horn, and ring; and with a final farewell he turns to the swan. Then a miracle occurs. The swan sinks into the river, and in his place comes the young Duke of Brabant—Godfrey! Bitterly the sorceress Ortrud relates how she had transformed the boy into a swan. Lohengrin, thereupon, falls upon his knees and prays. A dove is seen descending from the sky and, with a chain, carries off the knight in his boat. Elsa cries after him, "My husband, my husband!" and then sinks lifeless into Godfrey's arms as the curtain falls.

Postscript for the historically curious: Although the story of Lohengrin is legendary, the events may be accurately dated. King Henry the Fowler's reign is fairly well documented. In 923 he made a peace treaty with the Hungarians to last ten years. In his opening speech in the opera (often drastically cut) he tells the assembled warriors that the ten years have now elapsed.

LOUISE

Opera in four acts by Gustave Charpentier with
libretto in French by the composer

LOUISE	*Soprano*
JULIEN, *her lover*	*Tenor*
HER FATHER	*Bass*
HER MOTHER	*Contralto*
THE NOCTAMBULIST	*Tenor*

Time: 1900
Place: Paris
First performance at Paris, February 2, 1900

Paris is really the principal character of *Louise*. That is
the city where it was first given over half a century ago—on
February 2, 1900, to be exact. And Paris, although it was surprised and somewhat shocked by the work, took the self-por-
trait to its heart. In April of 1900—two months after the
premiere—the leading soprano fell ill during Act II. A totally
unknown girl—and a foreigner at that—was the only under-
study. Although she had never been on an operatic stage before, she stepped into the role at a few moments' notice and
made her debut, beginning with the principal aria in the
opera, *Depuis le jour*. A huge success at once, she became a
favorite of the French opera public for over thirty years. Her
name was Mary Garden, and she sang *Louise* at the Opéra
Comique over two hundred times.

There were several reasons that the opera was a bit of a
shocker to Paris at the time. First of all, the music was impressionistic. Its effect is somewhat reminiscent of Debussy;

yet *Louise* is two years older than Debussy's impressionistic *Pelléas et Mélisande*. Secondly, there are scarcely any old-fashioned arias. Louise's *Depuis le jour* and the *Lullaby* in the last act are the only passages often sung by themselves. Thirdly, the libretto, by the composer himself, is in prose, not in verse, and this fact made the play seem startlingly realistic for opera. And fourth—and most important of all—the story took place in the time of its audience and deals almost exclusively with the lower classes, with workers. That is, the leading singers looked like, and used the language of, the men and women who worked in the streets and factories of Paris itself. Nothing just like that had ever been seen before on the stage of a Parisian opera house.

ACT I

The first act takes place in the tenement home of a laborer. His daughter, Louise, has fallen in love with a romantic young poet who occupies a neighboring tenement. This fellow, Julien, might almost be a direct descendant of Rodolfo, the poet of *La Bohème*. When the opera opens, he is standing on his balcony making love, through the window, to his Mimi —that is, his Louise. They recall how they met and speak of eloping together if Louise's parents do not give consent. Her mother, who interrupts them, thinks Julien is a good-for-nothing and doesn't hesitate to say so. Then the father returns from work. He is overtired, and his wife and daughter try to persuade him to take a rest for a while, to give up work. But he feels he cannot afford it; and besides, he thinks the finest thing in the world is to work for his family, and to keep that family happy and all together. At supper the father reads a letter Julien has left for him proposing marriage with his daughter. He is not unfavorably disposed, but the mother is furious; and when Louise talks up against a particularly insulting remark about her lover, her face is roundly slapped for her. Father, however, is all for peace. He asks his daughter to sit quietly by him and read the paper aloud. The article she begins on makes mention of springtime in Paris—always a very sentimental subject—and the girl breaks down, weeping.

ACT II

Scene 1 takes place on a street at the foot of Montmartre, right outside the dressmaker's where Louise has a job. The whole first part of this scene simply pictures life in the Paris streets in the early morning. The prelude is supposed to suggest Paris coming to life at dawn; and when the curtain rises, there are such members of the cast as a milk woman, a newspaper girl, a ragpicker, a junkman, and others plying their trades and commenting, with a sort of Gallic cynicism, on life in general. A character listed as the Noctambulist (he is a reveler in full evening clothes returning home) identifies himself as the spirit of the Pleasure of Paris; and when he has left, a ragman complains about the fellow, saying he had run off with his daughter.

Now Julien appears, too, to show a group of his Bohemian friends where Louise works. He tells them of his plan: if he finds that her parents have refused consent, he will simply carry the girl off. The romantic idea is thoroughly applauded, and one of the friends suggests that Louise should be crowned as their Muse.

Now, however, it is time for Louise's mother to bring the girl to the dressmaking establishment, as she does every morning. Julien and his companions go off, still singing a serenade one of them has struck up, while Julien romantically avows that the medley of sounds he hears all about him is the voice of Paris itself, promising success in his amorous ambitions. Finally Louise shows up, and when the mother has left, Julien manages to intercept her. She tells him, at first, that she loves her parents too much to leave them, but she loves him, too. Julien becomes more and more ardent, and finally Louise gives in. She promises to go off with him soon, but as the scene closes, she goes into the building, into the dressmaking shop. In the distance is heard one more voice of the city—the pipe of a goatherd.

Scene 2 moves inside, into the place where girls are sewing dresses. Louise is teased by everyone for being in love. Soon a raucous band is heard outside, and then the voice of Julien, singing a serenade. All the girls admire him for his voice and his good looks, and as they stand at the window admiring, Louise falls once more under the spell of her lover. Quietly she leaves the room—to run off with Julien.

ACT III

After a prelude the third act begins with the opera's most famous aria, *Depuis le jour*. Louise and Julien have eloped to a little cottage on the hill of Montmartre, overlooking the whole of Paris. In the aria she expresses her ecstatic happiness with her new existence and with her lover. The whole first part of the act is really a long love duet, for the two are not only completely in love with each other, but completely in love with Paris.

When the duet is over, a whole chorus of Bohemians enters. They have come to do honor to Julien and Louise and, at the height of the festivities, Louise herself is crowned Queen of Montmartre. The Noctambulist presides at this ceremony as the King of the Fools.

Suddenly the figure of Louise's mother appears at the back of the scene and puts a quick ending to the gaiety. She has come to tell Louise of her father's illness, of how he creeps sometimes at night into her old room even though they had agreed to regard her as dead. Even Julien is moved by the bitter old woman's story, and he permits Louise to go home on the promise that she may return to him whenever she wishes.

ACT IV

As the act opens, the father seems to have regained his health and customary spirits. He is again working; and though he rails against poverty, he does accept it philosophically. The real reason, we may suppose, is that he has his beloved daughter with him again. He tries to be affectionate to her. He takes her into his arms, and he sings a lullaby. But Louise refuses to be comforted. She longs to return to her lover, to her life of freedom on the heights of Montmartre. From the streets outside their tenement come the voices of merrymakers singing in a waltz rhythm, and Louise takes it up as she madly sings of a free life and a free love. Her parents are deeply shocked, and the father becomes more and more angry. Finally he shouts at his daughter, demanding that she leave. If *that* is what she wants, let her go, let her dance, let her laugh! He even begins to attack her, only her mother standing in the way. But Louise takes her father at his word—and she dashes from the room, to return to Julien.

Only then does the old man realize what he has done. "Louise, Louise!" he calls. But she is gone; and as the opera closes, he shakes his fist at the city that has stolen his daughter from him. "Paris!" he moans, full of hate.

THE LOVE FOR THREE ORANGES

(*Lyubov k Trem Apelsinam*)

Opera in prologue and four acts by Sergei
Prokofieff with libretto in Russian by the composer based on a play by Carlo Gozzi which was
in turn based on an old legend

THE KING OF CLUBS	Bass
THE PRINCE, *his son*	Tenor
PRINCESS CLARISSA, *his niece*	Contralto
LEANDRO, *his prime minister*	Baritone
TRUFFALDINO, *the court jester*	Tenor
PANTALOON, *friend and adviser of the King*	Baritone
CELIO, *a magician*	Bass
FATA MORGANA, *a witch*	Soprano
SMERALDINA, *her servant*	Mezzo-soprano
LINETTA, *a princess*	Contralto
NICOLETTA, *another*	Mezzo-soprano
NINETTA, *another*	Soprano
THE COOK	Bass
FARFARELLO, *a devil*	Bass
A HERALL	Bass
A TRUMPETER	Bass trombone

Time: once upon a
Place: Land of the King of Clubs
First performance (in French) at Chicago, December 30, 1921

The opera was commissioned in 1919, when the com-
poser was a visiting *enfant terrible* of music, by Cleofonte
Campanini, musical director and principal conductor of the
Chicago Opera Company. Prokofieff finished the complex

score in six months; the opera was placed in rehearsal; everyone found it extremely difficult to master; Campanini died; and the project was shelved for two years. Then, in 1921, Mary Garden became artistic director of the company (or "directa," as she termed herself), and trotted the work out once more. Prokofieff was invited to conduct it himself; he did; and the result was financial and critical, if not necessarily artistic, disaster. The production survived only three performances—two in Chicago and one in New York. The story that this failure discouraged Prokofieff from making America his permanent home is probably apocryphal.

The opera was given in a number of European centers later on, but America did not hear it again until 1949 when, with a scenario revised by Theodore Komisarjevsky and Vladimir Rosing and in an English translation by Victor Seroff, it scored a great hit with the New York City Opera Company. The production became a big success for several years, both in New York and on the road, for it was played broadly for laughs and was a great attraction for juvenile audiences on Saturday matinees.

There is a certain irony in the fact that the opera's late popularity should depend upon its appeal to children, for it is a work of the highest sophistication. The libretto is based on an eighteenth-century comedy by Carlo Gozzi, who had written it to win a bet showing that he could get a larger audience than his rivals by taking an old wives' tale and dressing it in a fresh style. This style involved a satirical criticism of his competitors, Goldoni and Chiari, who were virtually driven into exile from Venice on account of Gozzi's success. Prokofieff, well aware of this bit of literary history, satirized, with his score, such well-established opera composers as Massenet, Verdi, and Wagner. True, they were all dead by 1919, but their works lost no performances through the satirical musical comments of Prokofieff, for, apparently, no one understood these. At the time the work just seemed willfully obtuse and hence dull. Today Prokofieff's "modernisms" sound familiar enough, and his satire is lost on a juvenile audience. But like

Gulliver's Travels, which has had an analogous history, it is just dandy for children.

Tragedians, Comedians, Lyricists, and Empty Heads quarrel, before the curtain, about what type of play should be performed. They are all chased out by another group, called "Reasonable Spectators," who announce that something quite different from the customary fare is to be performed. Then a "trumpeter" (who performs on a bass trombone) announces the Herald, and he, in turn, announces that the theme of the play is to be the illness of the son of the King of Clubs, who is unable to laugh. In the New York City production, Komisarjevsky substituted a spoken prologue for most of this esoteric quarrel.

ACT I

Scene 1 In a room in the palace of the King of Clubs the monarch is advised by the royal medical staff that his son's symptoms include pains all over, not to mention a cough, bad eyesight, anemia, biliousness, melancholia, and a few others. Diagnosis: hypochondria. Prognosis: incurable. The King's adviser, Pantaloon, tries in vain to comfort him. Who shall inherit the kingdom if his son cannot rule? Will it be that cruel niece of his, Clarissa? The Reasonable Spectators (who, like the other personages from the prologue, occupy stage boxes and occasionally comment) help him to worry. If only the Prince can be made to laugh, there may be some hope yet. Pantaloon thinks that entertainment may turn the trick, and he shouts for Truffaldino, the court jester. Truffaldino is delighted with the assignment; but Leandro, the prime minister, who is also consulted, thinks such a program can only make the boy worse. However, as Leandro is a villain, one must suspect his motives. At least the King does, while Pantaloon calls him a traitor.

Scene 2 The stage darkens; a curtain decorated with cabalistic signs descends; and before it is played a game of cards between the powerful witch Fata Morgana (who appears in a flash of lightning and represents the evil forces of Leandro) and the magician Celio (who represents the good forces of the King of Clubs). Three times Celio is defeated to the accompaniment of a chorus of little devils and the frightened cries of the Reasonable Spectators.

Scene 3 Back at the palace, Leandro, the prime minister, is visited by Clarissa, who has promised to marry him if he succeeds in encompassing the Prince's death so that she may inherit. Leandro does not seem overly eager for this marriage; nevertheless, he feels sure that he will get rid of the heir apparent by boring him to death on a diet of tragic prose and dull verse. They shall be served up to him in his soup and on his bread. (At this point the Tragedians swarm enthusiastically onto the stage, but the Reasonable Spectators chase them off again.)

Now Smeraldina, a dark-faced servant of Fata Morgana's, is discovered behind a huge vase, eavesdropping on the two conspirators. At first they threaten to kill her; but she assures them that her mistress is on their side, and that only the presence of this powerful witch at the coming festivities may prevent the Prince from laughing. They accept her advice and call on Fata Morgana for help.

ACT II

Scene 1 The Prince, bundled up in an outrageous assortment of garments, sits bored as Truffaldino tries out his best antics on him. Nothing will make him laugh. Instead, he coughs, and Truffaldino, holding a basin for him, notes in alarm that dull verses are coming up. He then asks the Prince to attend the festival to be held especially for the purpose of making him laugh. (Here, once again, there is an interruption: the Comedians rush onto the stage and have to be chased off by the Reasonable Spectators.)

The *March* from *The Love for Three Oranges*—the only portion of the score that has won wide popularity—is played as Truffaldino almost forces the hypochondriac Prince to accompany him to the festival. The jester hurls all the boy's medicines out of the window, throws a cape on his back, and literally carries him from the room.

Scene 2 In the courtyard of the palace, Truffaldino stages two comic acts for the Prince—a battle of monsters, and a milling crowd of drunkards and gluttons. He does not find these at all funny. But when Truffaldino finds Fata Morgana in the crowd, tries to throw her out, and accidentally makes her turn a somersault, the Prince suddenly starts laughing. In an exceptionally clever passage Prokofieff develops this laugh, starting gently with the solo tenor and continuing it, *crescendo*, till everyone on the stage is joining in excepting, of course, Fata Morgana, Leandro, and Clarissa.

Fata Morgana thereupon delivers a curse on the Prince. With the vocal assistance of a chorus of devils, she dooms him to being in love with three oranges whom he shall pursue to the very ends of the earth. In vain the King and his court try to dissuade him from this madness: he merely replies that he shall become melancholy all over again if he remains at home. A little devil named Farfarello appears with a pair of bellows to waft the Prince and Truffaldino on their way as the court, led by the King, joins in a mock tragic operatic finale.

ACT III

Scene 1 Farfarello, the devil, has been blowing the Prince and Truffaldino toward the palace of Creonte, the powerful witch who owns the three oranges. When Farfarello was called on an errand to hell, he had temporarily to leave his charges in the desert asleep; and as he returns, Celio stops him and tries to force him to stop all this dangerous fooling. Farfarello reminds the well-intentioned fellow that, since he lost at cards to Fata Morgana, he has no more power. But before the Prince and Truffaldino are wafted once more on their way, Celio has the opportunity to give them some practical advice. He warns them that the oranges are in the immediate possession of a massive cook with a copper ladle strong enough to

kill them both. In order to distract this cook Celio presents
the voyagers with a pretty ribbon. Perhaps, he suggests, they
may steal the oranges while Cook is admiring this offering. He
also warns them that when they secure the oranges, they must
cut them open only in the immediate neighborhood of water.
The Prince pays no attention to all this practical advice but
continues to sing of his love. Truffaldino accepts the ribbon,
and Farfarello reappears to waft off the travelers with his bellows.

Scene 2   Before the castle of Creonte, Truffaldino is fearfully frightened, and even the dauntless Prince hides when the
Cook (sung by a basso) emerges with her huge ladle. When
she finds Truffaldino, she threatens him with sudden death;
but, suddenly espying Celio's ribbon hanging about his neck,
she coyly asks for it. The Prince takes the opportunity to slip
into the kitchen and emerge with three enormous oranges.
With Truffaldino he escapes once more into the desert as the
Cook bounds with delight about the stage, enchanted with the
ribbon, and delivering a coarse aria that is likely to be the hit
of the show.

Scene 3   In the desert the Prince is asleep, while Truffaldino is suffering from thirst. At the back of the stage stand
the three stolen oranges, now grown large enough to contain
human beings. Truffaldino is so desperate with thirst that he
opens up one of them, and out steps a lovely princess named
Linetta, who says she is dying of thirst. The second orange
yields a second princess named Nicoletta, who is equally
thirsty. In fact, they are both so thirsty that they die prettily
right there and frighten Truffaldino into running away.

When the Prince awakens, he is not especially surprised to
see a couple of pretty dead girls lying next to him; and when a
quartet of soldiers conveniently happens to pass by, he orders
an elegant funeral for them. When they have removed the
bodies, he declares himself in love with the remaining orange
and proceeds to cut it open. Out steps a third princess, this
one named Ninetta, who is just as thirsty as her sisters were,
though she does have breath enough to acknowledge her rescuer from thraldom and a keen interest in the Prince's extrava-

gant vows of love. However, she begins to faint away in his arms, whereupon the Reasonable Spectators descend upon the stage with a pail of water so that she may drink and the drama go on.

The Prince then announces their forthcoming nuptials and proposes to take his beloved directly to his father's palace. She, however, refuses to go without a suitable wardrobe and sends him off to secure one. As soon as she is left alone, Fata Morgana, accompanied by Smeraldina, slinks in and stabs the girl in the head with a hatpin, changing her into a rat (or a pigeon, depending upon what production you are seeing). The powerful witch then instructs her black-faced assistant to impersonate the Princess.

The familiar *March* is heard once more; the whole court enters the scene; and Smeraldina announces herself as the Princess. The Prince knows better; he refuses to marry such an ugly girl; and the King, who claims that one must live up to his word, offers her his arm to lead her back to the palace.

ACT IV

Scene 1   In a brief scene before the curtain with cabalistic signs used in Act I, Fata Morgana and Celio argue violently. The Reasonable Spectators take a part in this argument, seize upon Fata Morgana, and shut her up in a box.

Scene 2   Back at the palace, in the throne room, Leandro and an assistant are making preparations for the return of the King; and when he arrives with his entourage, the curtains are drawn from before the throne—and there sits a huge rat (or pigeon, as the case may be). Everyone is shocked; but Celio's magic—strengthened by his recent victory over Fata Morgana —is finally equal to the task of transforming the animal into its original form, that of the Princess Ninetta. While the Prince expresses his joy, Smeraldina is at a loss for explaining her presence satisfactorily. Finally, she is accused of being a conspirator with Leandro and Clarissa. The King decides that they are all traitors and must be hanged, and even the amiable Truffaldino's pleas for mercy are in vain. However,

as they are about to be seized, Fata Morgana appears in their
midst; a trap door opens conveniently; and they disappear
down it, presumably for the nether regions.

The King leads off with the toast: "God save the Prince
and Princess," and the opera closes with a repetition of the
March.

LUCIA DI LAMMERMOOR

(*Lucy of Lammermoor*)

Opera in three acts by Gaetano Donizetti with libretto in Italian by Salvatore Cammarano, based on Sir Walter Scott's novel, *The Bride of Lammermoor*

LORD ENRICO ASHTON OF LAMMERMOOR	Baritone
LUCIA, *his sister*	Soprano
ALISA, *her companion*	Soprano or Mezzo-soprano
EDGARDO, *Master of Ravenswood*	Tenor
LORD ARTURO BUCKLAW	Tenor
RAIMONDO, *chaplain of Lammermoor*	Bass
NORMANNO, *follower of Ashton*	Tenor

Time: 1669
Place: Scotland
First performance at Naples, September 26, 1835

Scott's novel *The Bride of Lammermoor* is seldom read nowadays, for it is not one of his best. It nevertheless attracted opera composers as a promising subject, three of them—Bredal, Carafa, and Mazzucato—having made use of it before Donizetti. None of the earlier versions survives on the boards, and of all of Donizetti's works this is the one most frequently played.

He may have been additionally attracted to the subject because one of his grandfathers, Donald Izett, was a Scot. Nevertheless, for the purposes of opera, the names of Scott's characters were sensibly changed to their more mellifluous Italian equivalents. Thus, Lucy becomes Lucia; Henry, Enrico; Edgar, Edgardo; but place names remain the same, and Ravenswood is Ravenswood still, though pronounced, "Rahvensvood." Other changes were made, too, besides the necessary cutting. For instance, Scott's Edgar meets a highly unoperatic end by wildly riding his horse into a quicksand. No tenor could sing two long arias ending in a high D-flat under such circumstances, and so Donizetti's Edgardo quite conventionally stabs himself. An Italian tenor is sure to sing well given this advantage. The final aria, by the way, one of the best ever written by Donizetti, was tossed off in half an hour while the composer was suffering from a severe headache.

But the opera is a vehicle primarily for a coloratura soprano, not for the tenor, and many great sopranos have chosen it as a debut piece in New York. Among them were Patti, Sembrich, Melba, Barrientos, and Lily Pons. Both Pons and Sembrich also chose the role to celebrate the twenty-fifth anniversaries of their respective debuts at the Metropolitan.

ACT I (*"The Departure"*)

Scene 1 In the garden of Lord Enrico Ashton's castle a group of guards, under their leader Normanno, is searching for a prowler. While they are out beating the bushes, Enrico himself tells Normanno and the family chaplain, Raimondo, about his straitened circumstances. He hopes to improve them by arranging a marriage between his sister Lucia and the wealthy Lord Arturo Bucklaw. Unfortunately, Lucia is unwilling to cooperate. Normanno, having a shrewd suspicion as to the cause of Lucia's unwillingness, tells of the day when a certain stranger saved her from a maddened bull and how the two meet secretly each morning in the park. That stranger is Edgardo of Ravenswood, who happens to be Enrico's chief enemy.

At this opportune moment the guards return. They have caught sight of the trespasser but have been unable to apprehend him. However, they do report unequivocally that he is none other than Edgardo. The scene ends as Enrico energetically expresses his hatred of the man who is an enemy of the family and who threatens to upset his plans for Lucia's marriage of convenience.

Scene 2 is introduced by an extremely pretty harp solo—perhaps suggesting the park where the scene takes place, perhaps the two pretty young women who are deep in earnest consultation beside the fountain. Lucia of Lammermoor tells her attendant, Alisa, a kind of ghost story about that fountain, and Alisa warns her that it would be better to give up the lover she meets at this place. But Lucia insists on her love for Edgardo and sings his praises. The story of the fountain is told in a smoothly flowing melody (*Regnava nel silenzio*) and her love is sung in the cabaletta of the aria (*Quando rapita in estasi*).

When Edgardo comes to meet his love, Alisa tactfully retires. He must, he says, depart for France; but before going, he would like to become reconciled with Enrico and tell him of his love. This idea frightens Lucia, who begs him not to do so. Edgardo bitterly recounts the reasons he has for hating the Ashtons, but the scene ends with a loving farewell duet (*Verranno a te sull' a ure*) in which first Lucia, then Edgardo, then both together sing one of the finest melodies in this ever-melodious opera.

ACT II (*"The Marriage Contract"*)

Scene 1 Through a conversation between Enrico and Normanno that takes place in a hall of the castle of Lammermoor, we hear that all of Edgardo's letters to Lucia have been intercepted. In addition, a letter has been forged to show that Edgardo has been unfaithful to Lucia and is now married to someone else. When Normanno retires, Enrico uses every device possible to persuade his sister to marry Arturo. He breaks her heart by showing her the forged letter, and he adds that it is her duty to the family to marry her wealthy suitor. Poor Lucia never actually consents to the marriage, but she is too distracted to resist.

Scene 2 As a matter of fact, Lord Arturo is already at the castle, and the next scene takes place in the great hall. There is a festal wedding chorus; Arturo pledges his good faith; and when Lucia, still in tears, comes in, the marriage contract is signed.

Just at this point a heavily cloaked stranger enters. It is Edgardo, returned from France; and when he sees the signed marriage contract, he turns on Lucia and all his enemies in wrath, and with drawn sword. It is only the faithful old chaplain, Raimondo, who saves the wedding party from ending in bloodshed and murder. In the ensuing *Sextet from Lucia,* all the principals, not to mention the chorus of wedding guests, express their many conflicting emotions at the same time—and with stunning effect. At its close Edgardo marches angrily from the hall.

ACT III

Scene 1 Immediately following the wedding, Enrico visits Edgardo in his lonely room in the Wolfscrag tower to vilify him and to taunt him with the details of the ceremony. The two men defy each other heroically and, in the final duet, agree to meet at dawn to fight a duel among the moldering tombstones of Ravenswood. The scene is usually omitted in performance.

Scene 2 The assembled wedding guests are still making merry in the great hall when Raimondo, the chaplain, interrupts the gaiety. Lucia, he announces in horrified accents, her mind having deserted her, has murdered Arturo.

A moment later Lucia herself appears. She is still in her nightdress. She looks deathly pale, almost like a ghost, and carries the fatal dagger. Now comes the celebrated *Mad Scene.* Lucia imagines herself with Edgardo; she relives some of their earlier and happier days; she imagines herself married to him. And at the end, knowing that death is near, she promises to wait for him.

Scene 3 takes us outside the castle, where Edgardo is wandering, disconsolate, among the graves of his ancestors. A train of mourners, led by Raimondo, interrupts his sad philosophizing. He asks for whom they are mourning, and learns of the sad events that have just taken place. A death bell tolls. It is for Lucia. Only now does Edgardo realize that she has always been faithful to him. He sings his final farewell (*Tu che a Dio spiegasti l'ali*—"Thou hast spread thy wings to heaven") and then, before Raimondo can stop him, plunges a dagger into his own heart. With the cello taking up the melody, he breathes his last words of farewell.

Postscript for the historically curious: Scott's *The Bride of Lammermoor* was based on a real marriage of convenience resulting in tragedy that took place in Scotland in 1669. Janet Dalrymple (Lucia) attacked her new husband, David Dunbar (Arturo), whom she had been forced to marry by her father, Viscount Stair (Enrico) instead of the man she loved, Lord Rutherford (Edgardo). In real life the unsuccessful suitor was the bridegroom's uncle.

MADAMA BUTTERFLY

(*Madam Butterfly*)

Opera in three (originally two) acts by Giacomo Puccini with libretto in Italian by Giuseppe Giacosa and Luigi Illica, based on David
Belasco's play of the same name, which was in
turn based on a story by John Luther Long

MADAME BUTTERFLY (CIO-CIO-SAN)	*Soprano*
SUZUKI, *her servant*	*Mezzo-soprano*
BENJAMIN FRANKLIN PINKERTON, *Lieutenant U. S. Navy*	*Tenor*
KATE PINKERTON, *his wife*	*Mezzo-soprano*
SHARPLESS, *U. S. Consul at Nagasaki*	*Baritone*
GORO, *a marriage broker*	*Tenor*
PRINCE YAMADORI, *a rich Japanese*	*Baritone*
THE BONZE, *Cio-Cio-San's uncle*	*Bass*
THE IMPERIAL COMMISSIONER	*Bass*
THE OFFICIAL REGISTRAR	*Baritone*
TROUBLE, *Cio-Cio-San's child*	*Mute*

Time: about 1900
Place: Nagasaki
First performance at Milan, February 17, 1904

Three of the most popular Italian operas in the repertoire
—*The Barber of Seville, La traviata,* and *Madama Butterfly*—
were resounding failures on their opening nights, and of those
three failures *Butterfly's* was perhaps the most resounding of
all. Everyone, from the composer and cast down to the orchestra players and the stagehands, had confidently expected
nothing but another triumph for the composer of *Manon
Lescaut, La Bohème,* and *Tosca.* Yet even the glorious entry

music of Butterfly (sung by the great Rosina Storchio) was greeted with silence—and silence from an Italian audience is an ominous thing at best. Later in the first act there were cries of "That's from *Bohème* . . . Give us something new!" Hisses greeted the first-act curtain; and when, near the beginning of the second act, a breeze billowed up Storchio's gown, someone cried out: "Butterfly is pregnant!" From then on it was a long series of catcalls, moos, cock-a-doodle-doos, and obscenities. And the reviews, on the whole, were not much more polite.

Puccini, bewildered and heartbroken, canceled the other scheduled performances at La Scala though it meant the payment of a considerable sum, took back his score, and made a number of revisions, the chief of them being to divide the long second act into what we now hear as Acts II and III. Three and a half months later the revised version was mounted in Brescia under the baton of Arturo Toscanini.

Now the opera was a huge success. In the first act the audience applauded the scenery and demanded an encore for Pinkerton's little aria as well as of the entire love duet. Four more numbers had to be repeated later on, and after each of them, in the quaint Italian fashion, the composer came on the stage to take a bow along with the singers. "Never again," to quote George Marek, Puccini's finest biographer, "did *Butterfly* fail. No other first performance proved short of a triumph."

Why the first failure and then the triumph? It cannot be explained, as with *La traviata*, by an inadequate first cast: *Butterfly's* was absolutely first-class. Maybe, as has been surmised, the violence was inspired by the composer's ill-wishers, as was possibly the case with *The Barber*. I rather think, however, it can best be attributed to the nature of Italian opera audiences, who love nothing better than to express their opinions unmistakably, whether right or wrong.

ACT I

At the turn of the century—about forty-five years before an atom bomb destroyed it—the harbor town of Nagasaki was a very pretty place. On the outskirts of the town, and overlooking the harbor, is a pretty Japanese villa. In the garden, when the opera begins, there are a Japanese busybody and an American naval officer. The busybody is Goro, the marriage broker; the officer is Lieutenant Benjamin Franklin Pinkerton, U.S.N. Goro has arranged a marriage for the Lieutenant, and he shows him over the house that has been rented for 999 years (with, of course, a convenient cancellation clause). The marriage contract, by the way, has the same convenient clause—cancelable at a month's notice.

When the United States Consul, Sharpless, calls, he tries to persuade Pinkerton that there is danger in this arrangement, for Sharpless knows the prospective bride, her name being Cio-Cio-San, or Madam Butterfly, and he fears that the probable result will break her tender heart someday. But Pinkerton cannot be made to take anything seriously, and he even proposes a toast to the day when he will be *really* married—in the United States.

And now it is practically time for the wedding ceremony. Butterfly, accompanied by her relatives, makes her entrance as her voice soars above the close harmony of her female companions. She tells Pinkerton about herself and her family and her age—which is only fifteen—and she shows him various trinkets she carries in her large Japanese sleeve, including a dagger her father had used to commit suicide on the order of the Mikado. The general tone of the meeting, however, is very gay. The Imperial Commissioner performs the brief legal ceremony, and everyone sings a toast to the happy pair when, suddenly, an ominous figure interrupts. He is Butterfly's uncle, the Bonze, a Japanese priest, who has learned that Butterfly has renounced her traditional religion in favor of Christianity and has come to cast her out. All the relatives side with the Bonze, and they turn on the young bride. But Pinkerton orders them all away; and in the long and wonderful love duet that closes the act, Butterfly forgets her troubles. Together, Lieutenant and Madam Pinkerton enter their new home.

ACT II

Three years have passed quietly in Butterfly's house, but Lieutenant Pinkerton has not been heard from. Suzuki, who has been praying to her Japanese gods, tries to tell her mistress that he never will come again. At first Madam Butterfly is angry, but then she sings her famous ecstatic aria *Un bel dì*, describing in detail how one fine day he will sail into the harbor, come up the hill, and again meet his beloved wife.

Soon there is an embarrassed visitor—Sharpless, the American Consul. He has a letter he wishes to read, but Butterfly makes such a hospitable fuss over him that he cannot get going. They are interrupted by the marriage broker, Goro, bringing with him the noble Prince Yamadori, who wishes to marry Butterfly. The lady politely but firmly refuses the Prince, whereupon Sharpless again tries to read the letter. Actually it tells of Pinkerton's marriage to an American girl, but the Consul does not have the heart to break the news—and so only a portion of the letter is read aloud in the *Letter Duet.* Instead, he asks what Butterfly would do if Pinkerton never returned. For a moment she thinks that suicide would be the only answer. Gently Sharpless advises her to accept the Prince. That is impossible, she insists—and she brings in the reason for the impossibility. It is her young son, named Trouble. But, she adds, he will be called Joy when his father returns. Utterly defeated, Sharpless leaves.

And now a cannon is heard from the harbor. An American ship—Pinkerton's ship, the *Abraham Lincoln*—has arrived! With joy Butterfly and Suzuki decorate the house as they sing their lovely *Flower Duet.* Then they prepare to await the arrival of the master. Through holes in the screen, Butterfly, Suzuki, and Trouble prepare to watch the harbor throughout the night. A beautiful melody (used earlier in the *Letter Duet*) is played and hummed by an off-stage chorus, and the act quietly closes.

ACT III

The beginning of the last act finds Suzuki, Butterfly, and Trouble just where they were at the close of the second, excepting that the child and the maid are now sound asleep. It is morning and there are noises from the harbor. Butterfly takes her sleeping little boy into another room, singing him a lullaby. Into the garden comes the Consul Sharpless, accompanied by Lieutenant Pinkerton and Kate Pinkerton, his American wife. Suzuki almost at once realizes who this is. She cannot bear to tell her mistress, and neither can Pinkerton. He sings a passionate farewell to his once-happy home, and leaves. But Butterfly, coming in now, sees Kate and realizes that inevitable tragedy has struck her. With dignity she tells Kate that she may have her boy if Pinkerton will come soon to fetch him.

Left alone with the child, she knows there is only one thing to do. First she blindfolds him; then she goes behind a screen; and with her father's dagger she stabs herself. As she drags herself toward the boy, Pinkerton comes rushing back, crying, "Butterfly! Butterfly!" He is, of course, too late. He falls on his knees by her body as the orchestra thunders forth the fateful Asiatic melody heard before, each time that death has been mentioned.

THE MAGIC FLUTE

(Die Zauberflöte)

Opera in two acts by Wolfgang Amadeus Mozart with libretto in German by Emanuel Schikaneder, possibly with the help of Karl Ludwig Gieseke

TAMINO, *an Egyptian prince*	*Tenor*
PAPAGENO, *a birdcatcher*	*Baritone*
SARASTRO, *High Priest of Isis and Osiris*	*Bass*
THE QUEEN OF THE NIGHT	*Soprano*
PAMINA, *her daughter*	*Soprano*
MONOSTATOS, *chief of the temple slaves*	*Tenor*
PAPAGENA	*Soprano*
THREE LADIES-IN-WAITING TO THE QUEEN OF THE NIGHT	*Two Sopranos and a Mezzo-soprano*
THREE GENII OF THE TEMPLE	*Two Sopranos and a Mezzo-soprano*
THE ORATOR	*Bass*
TWO PRIESTS	*Tenor and Bass*
TWO MEN IN ARMOR	*Tenor and Bass*

Time: unspecified but roughly about the reign of the Pharaoh Ramses I

Place: Egypt

First performance at Vienna, September 30, 1791

The Magic Flute is what the Germans call a *Singspiel* (a "sing play")—that is, a play with a good deal of singing, like an operetta or a musical comedy or a ballad opera or even an *opéra comique*. Well, most operettas and musical comedies present certain absurdities and inconsistencies in their books, and this one is no exception. For instance, the Queen of the Night seems to be a good woman in the first act and a villainess in the second. Again, the story starts out as a romantic fairy tale, pure and simple, and later takes on serious religious significance. In fact, the rites of the Temple of Isis and Osiris are generally regarded as being reflections of the ideals of the Masonic order, while various critics, writing long after the death of the authors, have found political symbolism of the most profound sort in Act II. There may be something in this if for no other reason than that both Mozart and his librettist were Masons, and Masonry was officially frowned on at the time.

Today such questions seem to matter very little. Far more important is the fact that Schikaneder, a swashbuckling, in-and-out actor-singer-writer-impresario commissioned the work from his old friend Mozart in the last year of the composer's life, when he needed such a commission badly. Mozart wrote his glorious score with specific singers in mind—for example, Schikaneder himself, with a very limited baritone, did Papageno, while Josefa Hofer, Mozart's sister-in-law, was the brilliantly pyrotechnical coloratura for whom the Queen of the Night's arias were composed. Gieseke, who may have written parts of the libretto (he later claimed the whole of it), was a gifted man of science and letters and probably served as the model for Goethe's Wilhelm Meister; but he possessed no great talent for the stage and was assigned the role of the first man in armor.

As for the inconsistencies in the plot, they may be accounted for by the fact that, while the libretto was being written, a rival theater put on a successful musical show called *Casper the Bassoonist, or the Magic Zither,* which was based on the very story Schikaneder was working on—*Lulu,* by one Liebeskind. It is conjectured that Schikaneder changed the whole plot in midstream, that is, after the first act and the beginning of the second were completed. This is a tidy theory, but the only evidence for it is circumstantial.

Despite the inconsistencies (and maybe even because of them!) the opera has always had the dream fascination of a

The Magic Flute

fairy tale, and it was a huge success from the beginning. That success did not help Mozart much. He died thirty-seven days after the premiere. As for Schikaneder, he was able, partly with the proceeds from the continued success of the opera, to build himself a brand-new theater seven years later and crown it with a statue of himself dressed in the feathers of Papageno. It was the high point of his career, and fourteen years after that he died as poor as Mozart, and insane.

OVERTURE

The overture begins solemnly, making use of three heavy chords which appear later at some of the most solemn moments connected with the rites of the temple. But, excepting for a later repetition of these chords, as a sort of reminder, the rest of the overture is just as light and gay, in its contrapuntal fashion, as the prelude to a fairy tale ought to be.

ACT I

Scene 1 The fairy tale itself begins—as a fairy tale should —with a handsome young prince lost in a valley. His name is Tamino, and he is being chased by a vicious serpent. He cries for help, sinks unconscious to the ground, and is promptly saved by three lovely ladies. These are ladies-in-waiting to the Queen of the Night—a supernatural personage, of course—and they vastly admire the handsome young man, who has fainted away. When they have gone, the leading comedian comes on the scene. He is Papageno, a birdcatcher by trade, and he introduces himself in a gay, folksy tune (*Der Vogelfänger bin ich ja*—"It's a birdcatcher I am"). He says that he likes catching birds, but he'd rather catch a wife. He also plays a snatch of a tune on his pipes—one we shall hear more of later on.

Papageno informs Tamino that he is in the realm of the Queen of the Night, and he also takes credit for having killed the snake. For this lie the three ladies return and place a lock on the birdcatcher's lips. Then they show Tamino the picture of a beautiful young girl. She is the Queen of the Night's daughter, who has been stolen and whom Tamino is to rescue. Tamino at once falls in love with the picture and sings the so-called *Portrait Aria*. Now the Queen of the Night appears, and in a dramatic and extremely difficult aria she tells Tamino about her daughter and promises him her hand in marriage when he rescues her. The first scene then ends with a quintet, a beautifully sustained lyric-dramatic composition quite in a class with the wonderful finales of *The Marriage of Figaro* though in an appropriately different style. During this finale the three ladies-in-waiting present Tamino with a magical flute that should make everyone who hears it happy, and they give the birdcatcher, Papageno, a set of musical bells. For Papageno is to accompany Tamino on his quest, and the bells will always protect him.

Scene 2 takes us to the palace of Sarastro. He is the head of a secret and powerful Egyptian religious order, and it is he who has Pamina, daughter of the Queen of the Night, in his power. At the moment she is under the care of a blackface comic villain named Monostatos. This Moorish gentleman drags in Pamina, threatening her with death if she refuses to love him. At the critical moment the birdcatcher Papageno wanders in. He and Monostatos are terribly frightened of each other—but it is the sort of fright that is really comic. No child of eight would be taken in by it. Monostatos finally flees, and when Pamina and Papageno find themselves alone together, he assures her that someone who loves her will come to the rescue, while she assures him that he too will find someone to adore. It is a charming duet in praise of tenderness (*Bei Männern welche Liebe fühlen*—"The man who loves possesses a kindly heart").

Scene 3 And then the scene changes once more—this time to a grove outside the Temple of Sarastro. Tamino is led there by three boys, the genii of the temple, who encourage him but will answer no questions. Left alone, he tries to enter three different doors. From two he is warned away by a voice off-stage, but from the third appears a priest. In a rather long (and, I must admit, slightly dull) exchange Tamino learns that Sarastro is not the villain he had thought, and that Pamina is somewhere around and still safe. In his gratitude for this information Tamino plays a fine tune on his magic flute, and then sings the same tune himself (*Wie stark ist nicht dein Zauberton*—"O voice of magic melody"). Suddenly he hears Papageno's little pipes, and he rushes off to find them. If only he had stayed, he should have met both Pamina and Papageno coming in. They are pursued by the comic villain Monostatos, who summons slaves to bind them in chains. At the last moment Papageno thinks of his magic bells. He plays them (they sound like a child's music box), and the delightful magical tune makes the slaves and Monostatos both dance harmlessly away. Pamina and Papageno then have another short and charming duet, when they are interrupted by the arrival of the dread Sarastro and his court in a solemn march. Pamina begs Sarastro's forgiveness for having tried to flee, which is granted with kindly understanding. Prince Tamino is then brought in by Monostatos, who demands a reward from Sarastro. He gets the reward he deserves—a sentence of seventy-seven strokes from the bastinado for his impudence; and as the act ends, Tamino and Pamina are solemnly prepared to undergo the rites of initiation, which may or may not prove them worthy of each other.

ACT II

Scene 1 The second half of the opera has more swift changes of scene than the first. It also has more serious music in it. For example, the very first scene is a meeting of the priests of Isis and Osiris in a palm grove. Sarastro informs the priests that Tamino has been chosen to marry the captive Pamina, but first the couple must prove itself worthy of entering the Temple of Light. He then intones his magnificent invocation *O Isis und Osiris*. Of this grand, simple, and dignified aria with male chorus George Bernard Shaw said: "It is the only music which might be put into the mouth of God without blasphemy."

Scene 2 Outside the temple Tamino and Papageno undergo some elementary religious instruction. Two priests (who

sing in octaves—possibly to make their instructions quite
clear) warn the Prince and the birdcatcher to be on guard
against women, the root of most of man's troubles. Sure
enough, right on their heels come the three ladies from the
Queen of the Night. These, in turn, warn the men against
priests. Papageno is inclined to discuss the matter with the
ladies, but the high-minded Tamino will have nothing to do
with such temptations. A lucky thing, too. For a moment later
an off-stage chorus of priests sends the girls right back where
they came from—the kingdom of the nether regions!

Scene 3 Once more the scene changes, this time to a garden. Monostatos rather horridly gloats over the lovely Pamina
as she lies asleep, practically at his mercy. Just in time, her
mother, the Queen of the Night, interferes. In her terrific
Revenge Aria she demands that her daughter murder Sarastro. She hurls a dagger to Pamina for the purpose and swears
that, should she fail, her daughter shall be disowned. This
Revenge Aria, with its two high F's, has defeated dozens of
otherwise quite able coloratura sopranos.

Immediately after her departure Monostatos returns,
threatens to reveal the plot, and demands the love of Pamina
as the price for silence. But she is again saved, this time by
the entrance of Sarastro. When Pamina begs forgiveness for
her mother, he explains that within the sacred halls of this
temple there is no such thing as revenge and that only love
binds man to man. It is an aria of extraordinary beauty and
dignity (*In diesen heil'gen Hallen*—"Within these sacred
halls").

Scene 4 In some productions there is an intermission at
this point, and the next scene is given as the first of Act III.
In most printed scores, however, it is simply the next scene
in Act II—a hall, and a pretty bare one. Two priests continue
their instruction of Tamino and Papageno, enforcing on them
the oath of silence and threatening punishment with lightning and thunder if the oath is broken. Tamino is a very good
boy about this, but the birdcatcher cannot hold his tongue,
particularly when a sprightly old crone appears and tells him
two startling bits of gossip—one, that she is just eighteen years

and two minutes old, and, two, that she has a sweetheart a little bit older named Papageno. But just when she is about to tell her own name, that thunder and lightning come, and off she goes as fast as she can. Immediately after, the three boys enter once more and, in a charming trio, present Tamino and Papageno, not only with food and drink, but also with the magic flute and the bells that had been taken from them. As the birdcatcher solaces himself with the comestibles and the Prince with his flute, Pamina comes in and runs confidently up to her lover. She does not know about his oath of silence and, misinterpreting his actions, sings a mournful aria (*Ach, ich fühl's, es ist verschwunden*—"Ah, I feel it all is vanished"). At its close the trombones sound out, calling the men to the test.

Scene 5   In the following scene, outside the temple gates, Pamina is fearfully afraid that she will never again see her beloved Prince Tamino. Sarastro, in his most comforting tones, assures her that all will be well, but in the trio that follows, with Tamino, she is far from reassured. As Tamino is led off, the two lovers utter a prayer that they may meet again.

Scene 6   And now—as a sort of change of pace from the serious goings-on—we switch again to the birdcatcher Papageno. He is told that he may have one wish granted, and after drinking a glass of wine he sings a delightful little aria that makes a single request: Please, he says, let me have a sweetheart or, at any rate, a wife! Promptly the little old woman reappears, demands a vow of faithfulness, and then reveals herself as a young and feathery counterpart of Papageno. Her name—Papagena! But before they can do much about it, she is dragged off by the Orator.

Scene 7   The next scene takes place in a garden, where the three boys of Sarastro's temple are looking forward to the triumph of goodness. But poor, distracted Pamina wanders in, dagger in hand. She is convinced that she will never see Tamino again, and she prepares to kill herself. Just in time, the boys stop her and promise to take her to Tamino.

Scene 8   The boys are as good as their word. For in the next scene Tamino is about to endure the tests of the four elements—fire, water, earth, and air—and is brought in by the priests and the two men in armor, who again give instructions in octaves. Just before he enters the dread gates, Pamina rushes in. She wishes only to share the Prince's fate, and the two men in armor give their permission gladly. Tamino takes up his magic flute; he plays upon it; the two lovers stroll unharmed through the tests of the elements; and a joyous chorus welcomes them as they come through.

Scene 9 But what of our friend Papageno? Why, he is still looking for his sweetheart, his Papagena. He calls and calls throughout the garden, and finding no one, he decides, like Pamina, to commit suicide. With great reluctance he throws a rope over the bough of a tree, ready to hang himself. But those three boys who saved Pamina save him too. They advise him to play his magic bells, and he does. The sweet little bird-girl appears, and in a delightfully comic stuttering duet, *Pa-pa-pa-pa-pa-pa-Papageno,* they decide to raise a simply huge family.

Scene 10 And finally—still one more change of scene. Monostatos is now in league with the Queen of the Night, who has promised him Pamina. They invade Sarastro's temple, together with the three ladies-in-waiting. But the power of Sarastro is too great for them. There is thunder and lightning, and the villainous quintet disappears into the bowels of the earth. The Temple of Isis and Osiris appears, and a chorus of triumph of the forces of good ends this fairy opera.

MANON

Opera in five acts by Jules Massenet with libretto in French by Henri Meilhac and Philippe Gille, based on Antoine François Prévost's novel *Les aventures du Chevalier des Grieux et de Manon Lescaut*

MANON LESCAUT	*Soprano*
LESCAUT, *of the Royal Guard, her cousin*	*Baritone*
COUNT DES GRIEUX	*Bass*
CHEVALIER DES GRIEUX, *his son*	*Tenor*
GUILLOT DE MORFONTAINE, *an old roué*	*Tenor*
DE BRÉTIGNY, *a nobleman*	*Baritone*
POUSETTE	
JAVOTTE *actresses*	*Sopranos*
ROSETTE	

Time: 18*th century*
Places: Amiens, Paris, and Le Havre
First performance at Paris, January 19, 1884

The Abbé Antoine François Prévost's semi-autobiographical novel *Les aventures du Chevalier des Grieux et de Manon Lescaut* supplied the inspiration for stage works by a number of distinguished composers. Before Massenet, Auber had made an opera of it and Halévy a ballet. And after the present work, Puccini wrote an opera on the subject described in this book, and still later Massenet himself came back to the same theme in *Le portrait de Manon*—a one-act sequel that has never been very popular.

There is no question, however, about the popularity of

Manon (a title which Massenet claimed he had copyrighted: the other operas are called *Manon Lescaut*). After *Faust* and *Carmen* it is the most popular French opera there is, both in and outside of France. It is also Massenet's most durable work, and one for which he felt a particular affection. Perhaps one reason is the lively personal attraction he seemed to feel for the character of the attractive and unfortunate heroine.

In his memoirs the composer tells two stories that seem to be to the point. The first has to do with the time when he was composing the score. On a walk, one day, he saw a florist's assistant with sparkling eyes who, he imagined, was yearning for rich pleasures beyond her station. "There she is," he said to himself. "That is Manon." And he goes on to tell how he kept the image of that girl in his mind during the entire composition of the score, even though he had never seen her before and never saw her again.

The other story has to do with casting the production. His first thought was of Mme. Miolan-Carvalho, the wife of his impresario and a fine artist. (She was the original Marguerite in Gounod's *Faust*.) However in 1884 she was fifty-six, too old to undertake the role of a fifteen-year-old girl. The gallant Massenet, intent on getting her into the picture somehow, dedicated the score to her.

Next he thought of a young soprano named Vaillant, to whom he showed parts of the score. Unfortunately, when the time came, she was appearing in an operetta, and her manager would not release her. But even while he was talking to the manager in the lobby of the theater, a familiar figure kept passing by, newly arrayed in a gorgeous hat (a gray one, with lots of roses on it).

"Heilbronn!" I cried (so go the memoirs).

"Herself."

"You still sing?" I asked her.

"No, I am rich; and yet, shall I admit it to you? I miss the theatre. It haunts me. Ah, if I found a good part—l"

"I have one: Manon."

"Manon Lescaut?"

"No, just Manon. That tells the entire story."

"Can I hear the music?"

"Whenever you like."

That very night Massenet played and sang the score for her, finishing at half-past four in the morning. At its close the widely experienced but still youthful soprano was moved to very real tears. "It is my life," she said. "But it is my life— that!"

That is how Marie Heilbronn happened to be engaged to create the role. Her performance, like the opera itself, was an enormous success, but the soprano died after appearing in it some eighty times. Massenet was deeply grieved. "I preferred," he wrote, "to stop the performance rather than to see Manon sung by another."

The stoppage at the Opéra Comique was of considerable duration, for the theater burned down shortly afterward and did not revive *Manon* till ten years later. Meanwhile, it became a hit pretty much all over the world, and when the Opéra Comique did finally get back to it, it did so with a will. It has now had some two thousand performances at that theater alone and is still a staple of the repertoire.

ACT I

The first act takes place in a busy inn-yard in Amiens, France. A rich old fellow named Guillot and his younger companion, De Brétigny, are having themselves a fine time with three young women who are, clearly, no better than they should be. Among the crowd there is also a swaggering soldier named Lescaut, awaiting his teen-age cousin, Manon. The coach arrives, amid a great deal of bustle, and out steps pretty Manon. She is on her way to a convent, and Lescaut, who is seeing her for the first time in his life, is delighted with her sweet appearance and her pretty confusion, for she is making her first trip out into the world. While Lescaut sees to Manon's luggage, old Guillot tries to flirt with her. Though she laughs at him, he offers her the use of his private carriage. Lescaut interrupts this interview and tells Manon that she must guard the honor of the Lescaut family. As Lescaut goes off to gamble with some military buddies, she is left alone and sings a little aria (*Voyons, Manon, plus de chimères*) telling us how much she would prefer learning more of the world to being immured in a convent.

Now, enter the hero—the handsome young Chevalier des Grieux. He sees Manon; she sees him; and they fall in love with a precipitancy that one finds only in the first acts of operas. At any rate, their love duet leaves no room in your mind as to how they feel about each other. She sees Guillot's coach, and it is but the work of a minute for both of them to hop in and ride off, on the way to love—and to Paris. The act ends with the general confusion of everyone else when it is discovered that Manon and Des Grieux have eloped.

ACT II

Manon and Des Grieux have now been living for some time in a small apartment in Paris. The second act opens as together they read a letter that the young man has just written to his father, the Count des Grieux. In it he describes the charms of Manon's personality and character, and he begs for permission to marry her. Before he can mail the letter, two officers force their way in. One is Manon's blustering cousin, Lescaut, who fiercely demands to know whether Des Grieux intends to marry Manon. To prove his good intentions, the young lover shows Lescaut the letter he has just written his father. But while Lescaut reads, Lescaut's companion (who is De Brétigny in disguise) takes Manon aside. Apparently he knows her quite well by this time and is more than half in love. He tells her that, on the Count des Grieux's orders, her young lover is to be kidnaped this very evening. But she should not fear, for she will be taken care of very well—by himself. The scene—with Manon and De Brétigny on one side, and Lescaut and Des Grieux talking about the letter on the other side—results in a remarkable quartet.

When the two officers have left and Des Grieux has gone to mail the letter, Manon sings a sad little farewell to the table (*Adieu, notre petite table*), which has seen so much of her happy times with Des Grieux. And when the young man returns, he sings to her his dream—a quiet, intense, loving description of how they will live when they are married. Even this show of devotion does not inspire Manon to warn her lover of the plot to kidnap him.

And so, when there is a knock at the door, and Des Grieux is dragged out, her feeble cries of "No! No!" come too late. Thus the little home is broken up.

ACT III

Scene 1   The action now shifts to a busy square in the city of Paris, the Cours la Reine. Old Guillot is busily flirting and so is Lescaut as he sings a sentimental ditty (*Ma Rosalinde*). De Brétigny makes fun of Guillot, warning him not to try to steal Manon from him—which is exactly what the old fool resolves to do. Manon arrives on the scene and charms everyone with the famous *Gavotte from Manon*.

Soon the Count des Grieux enters, and Manon discovers from him that her former lover, the young Des Grieux, has entered the seminary of St. Sulpice, resolved to devote his life to the priesthood. Then Guillot comes back bringing with him the entire ballet company from the Opéra in an attempt to win Manon from De Brétigny. But she has no heart for the entertainment. As the curtain falls, she departs for the church of St. Sulpice—and Des Grieux.

Scene 2   The strains of the organ quietly transport us to a reception room in the church of St. Sulpice. Our hero, now the Abbé des Grieux, has just delivered his first sermon, and everyone is praising him. The old Count des Grieux comes on a visit to his son to try to persuade him to leave the church, marry some respectable young lady, and settle down. But the young *abbé* resolutely refuses, for he has resolved to forget Manon in the religious life, and the worldly old Count leaves his son with an ironical farewell. Des Grieux, however, finds it extremely difficult to forget Manon. He sings of this difficulty in the aria *Ah! fuyez, douce image*, in which he bids the memory of the beloved girl to leave him in peace.

Manon

Now a religious service begins. Manon slips into the room and, as off-stage sound the noble strains of a *Magnificat*, she prays earnestly for pardon and for reunion with Des Grieux. The second part of this prayer, at least, is successful. For when Des Grieux sees Manon, he at first tries to resist her. Her charms, her pleadings, and the memory of their past love are, finally, too much for his resolution. As the act closes, the two young people flee from the church.

ACT IV

In a luxurious—and notorious—Paris gambling hall known as the Hôtel de Transylvanie, the guests include Lescaut (who is winning for a change), old Guillot, and his three charmers. Manon brings in her idealistic lover, Des Grieux, who is rather unhappy over being in such a disreputable resort. But she urges him to try his luck, and he does so, accepting the challenge of Guillot. Beginner's luck is with Des Grieux, and he keeps winning large sums, much to Manon's delight. The old rascal thereupon accuses Des Grieux of cheating, and there is almost a fight. Guillot, however, departs, muttering a threat and soon returns with police officers. He points out Des Grieux and Manon as the guilty ones, and they are at once placed under arrest. At the crucial moment Count des Grieux enters, and a general ensemble follows, in which the son begs for mercy for himself and for his beloved Manon. The father tells his son that he will arrange to have him freed later. But Manon, who knows the fate of women such as herself when they get into trouble, murmurs: "*Ah! c'en est fait! je meurs.*" It is the end for her—and she is ready to die.

ACT V

Manon has been sentenced to deportation to Louisiana, and Des Grieux, together with Lescaut, is waiting on the road to Le Havre to try to free her from the guards who are to take her to the ship. They overhear the guards singing in the distance. Then two of the soldiers come on, discussing one of

288

their prisoners, who appears to be dying. It is Manon they are talking about. Lescaut manages to bribe these guards, and so Des Grieux and Manon are left discreetly alone to sing their final duet. Let them go together to a new country, says Des Grieux, and live a new and happy life. But Manon, who is half out of her mind with illness and repentance, can think only of the happy days they once had together. As night descends, Des Grieux urges her to flee with him, but it is too late. Slowly she becomes weaker and weaker.

As she is dying, cradled in her lover's arms, her last words are these: *"Et c'est l'histoire de Manon Lescaut!"* And that is the story of Manon Lescaut.

MANON LESCAUT

Opera in four acts by Giacomo Puccini with libretto in Italian by Ruggiero Leoncavallo, Marco Praga, Domenico Oliva, Giuseppe Giacosa, Giulio Ricordi, and Luigi Illica, based on *Les aventures du Chevalier des Grieux et de Manon Lescaut*, by Abbé Prévost

MANON LESCAUT, *a girl of fifteen*	*Soprano*
LESCAUT, *her brother*	*Baritone*
CHEVALIER DES GRIEUX, *her lover*	*Tenor*
GERONTE DE RAVOIR, *her aging suitor*	*Bass*
EDMONDO, *a student*	*Tenor*
A MUSIC MASTER	*Tenor*
A MUSICIAN	*Mezzo-soprano*
A LAMPLIGHTER	*Tenor*
A NAVAL CAPTAIN	*Bass*
A WIGMAKER	*Mime*
A SERGEANT OF ARCHERS	*Bass*

Time: 18th century
Places: Amiens, Paris, Le Havre, Louisiana
First performance at Turin, February 1, 1893

Both Massenet's *Manon* and Puccini's *Manon Lescaut* are based on the Abbé Antoine François Prévost's popular little novel *Les aventures du Chevalier des Grieux et de Manon Lescaut*, but Massenet's work was already an established success when Puccini produced his version. Such considerations never seemed to bother Puccini very much. His friend Leoncavallo, the composer of *Pagliacci*, had already begun work on a *La Bohème* when Puccini started his masterpiece on the same subject. Leoncavallo's *Bohème* is virtually forgotten, while Puccini's is one of the most frequently performed of all operas. However, both *Manon* treatments are still very much alive in the international repertoire (though Auber's, which preceded both of them, is exclusively a matter of historical record).

But when, in 1890, Puccini decided to undertake a version of *Manon*, both he and Leoncavallo were poor and virtually unknown. True, Puccini had had two operas produced—*Le villi* and *Edgar*—but neither was a real success; and as for Leoncavallo, *Pagliacci* was two years off. It was Leoncavallo who wrote the first draft of a *Manon* libretto for Puccini; but it took two more years and five more men to bring it into final shape. And when the opera was finally performed, Puccini for the first time was acclaimed a great operatic composer. He was thirty-five at the time and was to have, with the exception of *La rondine*, almost nothing but successes thereafter.

ACT I

The scene is the courtyard of an inn in the French town of Amiens, and it's a very busy place. Students are all over it—drinking, gambling, flirting with the girls. Two of the students stand out particularly—one is Edmondo, an exceptionally lighthearted fellow, successful with the ladies, and the other is a more serious-minded young man named Des Grieux, who gets teased, in fact, by the others for his earnestness. Soon a coach arrives, and out of it come three important characters. One is a rich old aristocrat named Geronte, another is an army officer named Lescaut, and the third is Lescaut's pretty sister, Manon, the heroine. Only fifteen, she is on her way to enter a convent. Her brother, a worldly youngster, thinks this is a waste of good looks. So apparently does Geronte, for the old fellow soon plots to abduct her and, in fact, arranges with the innkeeper to have a swift coach brought to the back of the inn for that very purpose.

Meantime, Manon's beauty has made quite an impression

on everyone in the place, especially on Des Grieux, who introduces himself, asks her name and her plans, and demands that she should meet him secretly. In no time at all he is terribly in love and tells us so in a particularly fine aria, *Donna non vidi mai.*

Now, the lighthearted student, Edmondo, has overheard everything that went on. He tells Des Grieux of Geronte's arrangement for the coach, and so it happens that when Manon comes out to keep her engagement with Des Grieux, the young fellow whisks her off before Geronte knows what has happened. Lescaut (who has been playing cards instead of guarding his sister) takes it all in stride. He tells Geronte that Des Grieux will never be able to support the pleasure-loving Manon in Paris, and *that* will be the time to step in and take over. On this very cynical note the first act ends.

ACT II

As Lescaut predicted, Manon does not stay long with Des Grieux. He is too poor, and old Geronte has now got the girl and set her up in luxury, while Des Grieux, under Lescaut's guidance, has been trying to make money by cheating at cards. When the curtain rises, Manon is in her boudoir, making herself beautiful with the assistance of servants. Her brother visits her and learns that she is bored with this luxury: she yearns for Des Grieux. While they talk, a group of singers performs a madrigal which has been especially composed for her by old Geronte. A little later Geronte comes in with friends and with a dancing master for Manon. While she has a lesson, they all express their admiration, and she sings prettily to the tune of the *Minuet.*

At last, they all leave, and a distraught Des Grieux comes in. The lovers exchange reproaches—and also vows of eternal love. But at the height of the scene Geronte returns. He is at first ironically polite. But then Manon makes a mistake: she tells him why she prefers Des Grieux, and shows Geronte his wrinkled face in a mirror. Immediately the old roué departs, uttering veiled threats. The lovers are about to fly, when Lescaut, out of breath, runs in to warn them that Geronte has denounced Manon, that she is about to be arrested, and that they must flee at once. But Manon takes too long gathering up her jewels, and before they can make good their escape, Geronte returns with officers of the law. Deportation is the fate in store for her, and, with Des Grieux crying protests, Manon is dragged off to jail.

ACT III

Before the act opens, there is a short but very eloquent orchestral *Intermezzo*. When the curtain goes up, that busy conniver, Lescaut, is telling Des Grieux that through bribery he has arranged an interview with Manon, and that soon he will have her free. The scene is at the harbor of Le Havre, where the ship waits to deport Manon and other girls like her. Manon appears at her prison window, and there is a brief, passionate love scene. But Lescaut's plans—as usual—miscarry. He has brought some men to carry Manon off from the guards, but a noise off-stage tells us that they have been routed. Now the Sergeant calls the roll of the girls to be deported, and they come onto the ship, one by one, as the crowd comments on them. Manon is among them, and in desperation Des Grieux appeals to the Captain of the ship to let him come along—as a servant or any other way—so long as he may be with his beloved. The Captain is touched by the aristocratic young fellow and gives his permission. Des Grieux rushes up the gangplank into the arms of his Manon, and the act closes.

ACT IV

Puccini's librettists placed the last act in a rather startling location. They wrote it like this: "*Una landa sterminata sui confini del territorio della Nuova Orleans.*" In brief—a desert in New Orleans. But if we remember that the story takes place before the Louisiana Purchase of 1803, and that the territory included, roughly, all the land between the Mississippi and the Rockies, it is not quite so startling. Anyway—

the geography of this act is rough and rugged. Manon and Des Grieux have arrived in America, and they have become lost in some desolate spot. Manon is clearly too ill to go much farther, and she tells Des Grieux so. She urges him to leave her and find help, which he does, and she sings her despairing aria *Tutto dunque è finito*—"All is now over."

When Des Grieux returns without help, he finds a dying Manon. Tenderly he takes her into his arms, and tenderly they sing of their love. But Manon only grows weaker, and with a last effort she bids him farewell and dies.

THE MARRIAGE OF FIGARO

(*Le nozze di Figaro*)

Opera in four acts by Wolfgang Amadeus
Mozart with libretto in Italian by Lorenzo Da
Ponte, based on the French comedy of the
same name by Pierre Augustin Caron de
Beaumarchais

COUNT ALMAVIVA	*Baritone*
FIGARO, *his valet*	*Baritone*
COUNTESS ALMAVIVA	*Soprano*
SUSANNA, *her maid and Figaro's fiancée*	*Soprano*
DR. BARTOLO	*Bass*
MARCELLINA, *his housekeeper*	*Soprano*
CHERUBINO, *a page*	*Soprano*
DON BASILIO, *a music master*	*Tenor*
ANTONIO, *a gardener*	*Bass*
BARBARINA, *his daughter*	*Soprano*
DON CURZIO, *counselor-at-law*	*Tenor*

Time: 18th century
Place: near Seville
First performance at Vienna, May 1, 1786

If Mozart's *Don Giovanni* is the greatest of operas, as
many musicians have testified, *The Marriage of Figaro* is
surely the best-beloved of musicians. And not only of musicians, either, for it has the distinction of being the oldest
opera in the permanent repertoire of virtually every lyric stage
in the Western world (Gluck's masterpieces being given more
intermittently) and it has won the affections of countless thousands who do not greatly admire the standard fare of *Faust*,

Aïda, La Bohème but make an exception for *Figaro.* Who, indeed, could fail to love Cherubino and Susanna or to relish a Figaro so much more elegant though no whit less vital than Rossini's bumptious barber?

It is a little difficult, then, to remember that this adorable work was thoroughly revolutionary. The portrait of a group of servants mocking their aristocratic master, lightheartedly overthrowing his cherished *droit du seigneur* (the right to sleep with a nubile servant before turning her over to her servant husband), and making him beg for mercy at the end was something to frighten rulers at a time when the French Revolution was brewing. Beaumarchais's play was in print a long time before it was permitted on the Paris stage, and Emperor Joseph sanctioned the operatic version only after the librettist, Da Ponte, had assured him that the more scandalously revolutionary lines had been deleted.

But the opera is no less revolutionary musically than it is politically. The famous finale of Act II (not to mention the one of Act IV) is the first example in operatic history of a long, complex development in plot and character entirely set to expressive music throughout. No recitatives, no set arias, no stalling with the action and character while some prima donna exhibits her wares or some tenor titillates with *tessitura.* It is all straight musical storytelling, such as Wagner strove after and sometimes managed to achieve, such as is still the ideal of virtually every modern opera composer. And what music!

But it is completely unnecessary to understand how revolutionary the work once was in order to love it. It was a smash hit from the beginning with audiences who doubtless did not appreciate its revolutionary characteristics either. Michael Kelly, Mozart's Irish friend who created both tenor roles (singing under the Italian-looking name of Ochelli), reports its instantaneous hit in his *Memoirs:* every single number was encored, and a ruling had to be made in subsequent performances that only arias, not concerted numbers, could be repeated. When Mozart visited Prague the following year, he wrote to his father that he heard *Figaro* tunes wherever he went; they were the top numbers on the hit parade. And so it has been ever since.

Originally, Mozart had considered an overture for this opera in the conventional Italian form, that is, a slow section sandwiched between two fast ones. But he discarded the slow section—even a slow introduction—and presented a swiftly moving, scampering little masterpiece just as tuneful as the opera itself and consistently high-spirited. It is a perfect piece of mood-setting.

ACT I

The opera begins with a duet between Figaro and Susanna. These are the two who are going to be married—according to the title of the opera. Both servants in the household of the Count Almaviva, they are preparing the room they are to occupy after the wedding. Figaro, it seems, is delighted with the room. But Susanna points out to him that the Count has shown her some interesting attentions—and that the room is very close to his. Thus challenged, the witty Figaro sings his aria *Se vuol ballare, Signor Contino*, that is, "If you wish to go dancing, my little Count, go right to it; but *I'll* play the tune."

Now a new pair of characters comes on—Dr. Bartolo and his housekeeper Marcellina. The doctor does not like Figaro on account of some past disfavors received; Marcellina, on the other hand, wants to marry the young man even though she is old enough to be his mother. In fact, she has lent him money and received in exchange a guarantee that he will marry her if it is not repaid. The dialogue between them ends with an aria by Dr. Bartolo (*La vendetta*) in which the old fellow swears to get even with Figaro. But before Marcellina leaves, she meets her rival, Susanna, and gets roundly trounced in a polite exchange of unpleasantries.

When the defeated Marcellina retires, we are introduced to one of the most charming characters in any opera. This is the young page Cherubino, who is perpetually in love with one girl or another—and it has got him into quite a mess, the Count having threatened him with dismissal for overzealous flirtation. He confides in Susanna and then sings his quick little aria *Non so più cosa son*. This expresses perfectly the breathless delights and bewilderments of half-baked crushes, his latest being on the Countess herself.

But now the Count comes on, and Cherubino must hide himself. The Count's advances to Susanna are, in turn, interrupted by Don Basilio, the music master, and the Count also hides. Basilio is little better than a common gossip, and what the Count overhears makes him step forward from his hiding place, for Basilio has been saying that Cherubino is too attentive to the Countess. As the Count relates Cherubino's recent adventures with Barbarina, the gardener's daughter, he discovers the young flirt himself—and a fine concerted number follows.

Presently Figaro re-enters with a group of peasants, singing a song in praise of the Count. The Count, of course, must receive them graciously, and peace is at least temporarily restored. Then, when the peasants have left, the Count gives Cherubino a commission in his regiment. This, he hopes, is a way to get rid of the young nuisance. And the act closes as Figaro, in the mock military aria, *Non più andrai*, ironically congratulates Cherubino on his impending military career.

ACT II

In her room the Countess Almaviva is singing unhappily of the lost love of her husband, the Count. The aria is the lovely *Porgi amor*. This is followed by a sort of conference between the Countess, Susanna, and Figaro, all of whom wish to make the Count behave better—that is, to leave Susanna in peace and to pay more attention to his wife. Susanna, they decide, is to write a note to the Count inviting him to meet her alone at night in the garden. But the page boy Cherubino, disguised as a woman, is to keep the appointment. Then the Countess is to surprise them, and thus they hope to embarrass the Count into behaving more to their liking. Cherubino himself comes in (for he has not yet joined his regiment) and sings an utterly charming song he himself has written. It is *Voi che sapete*—a love song, of course—and Susanna accompanies him on the guitar.

Susanna starts to dress Cherubino up as a woman, but she has difficulties because the young jackanapes tries continually to make love to the Countess.

Suddenly they hear the Count approaching, and Cherubino is hidden in the next room and the door locked. Unfortunately, he stumbles over something; the Count hears the noise; and he demands to know who is in there. When the Countess refuses to open the door, he goes for some tools to break it down, but Susanna saves the day by taking the place of Cherubino, who has jumped out of the window. Thus, when the Count and Countess return, they are dumfounded to find the servant girl behind the door, especially as the Countess has already admitted that Cherubino was there. A moment later Figaro enters to invite the Count to the wedding festivities but is temporarily nonplussed by the Count's asking him who wrote the anonymous letter. With some dexterous help he manages to extricate himself, but things grow more complicated when the gardener, Antonio, arrives to complain about someone who jumped into his garden from the window of the Countess. The quick-thinking Figaro again almost manages to explain everything with a series of complicated fibs, but the Count is still suspicious.

Finally, to cap the complexities, in come Dr. Bartolo, Don Basilio, and Marcellina. The old woman insists that Figaro must marry her, not Susanna, and the Count announces that he himself will decide this matter later on. The act closes with a remarkable ensemble in which everyone comments at the same time on this very complicated situation.

ACT III

Scene 1 finds the Count badly confused by everything that has happened. But Susanna soon comes in and, in an exquisite duet (*Crudel, perchè finora*), assures him that she will do exactly as he wishes. (Of course, she does not really mean this, but the Count does not know it—yet.) Then there follows a sort of comic trial scene. Don Curzio, a local man of the law, has decided that Figaro must marry Marcellina on account of the promise he made in writing at the time he borrowed money from her. Figaro, of course, protests, saying that he needs the consent of his unknown parents. In the course of the argument he mentions a birthmark on his right arm. And the trial ends in a triumph of comedy, for that birthmark proves who the parents of Figaro really are. His mother is none other than—Marcellina herself! And the father? Marcellina's co-conspirator, Dr. Bartolo! In the midst of the family reunion, Susanna enters to find her fiancé, Figaro, in the arms of her supposed rival. At first she is furious; but when she is told that Marcellina is no longer a rival, but her own future mother-in-law, there is a delightful sextet to end the scene.

Scene 2 begins with a brief and jolly discussion, in which it is decided that Marcellina and Dr. Bartolo shall be wedded the same day as Figaro and Susanna.

The whole tone of the music changes as the Countess Almaviva sings her second sad soliloquy, the beautiful *Dove sono*, in which she again laments the lost days of her love. But when her maid Susanna enters, she brightens up and dictates a letter for Susanna to write. This confirms the maid's assignation in the park with the Count which the disguised Cherubino is to keep instead of Susanna. This *Letter Duet*, with the two feminine voices first echoing each other, and then joining together, is of a sweetness that with any lesser composer must have descended into saccharinity.

Now everyone comes on the stage—including the chorus— to prepare for the marriage festivities of the evening. A group of peasant girls offers flowers to the Countess, and in the group is the page boy Cherubino, disguised as a girl. The irate gardener, Antonio, spots him and pulls off his wig. He is about to be punished, when the peasant girl Barbarina steps forward. She reminds the Count that he promised her anything she wished—and she now wishes to be married to Cherubino. Now there is dancing to some stately Spanish ballet music, and in the middle of it the Count receives and opens Susanna's letter. Figaro, who does not know about this part of the plot, notices this and becomes suspicious too. But the whole scene ends with rejoicing by everyone as the happy couples are about to be married.

ACT IV

A great many things happen rather quickly in the last act, and the musical numbers fairly trip over each other's heels. It takes place at night in the garden of the Count's estate, and the first music heard is Barbarina's worried little aria about losing a pin that Susanna is sending to the Count. Figaro discovers her secret—and his suspicions about his bride and his master are confirmed. Then the music master, Don Basilio, makes some ironical comments to Dr. Bartolo on the subject, and these are followed by Figaro's great aria, *Aprite un po' quegl' occhi*, in which he warns all men against the machinations of women. Finally, there is sung another great aria, *Deh vieni, non tardar*, in which Susanna ecstatically sings about her approaching love. Figaro overhears this and it makes him still more jealous.

Now Susanna and the Countess exchange costumes, and the action speeds up swiftly and furiously. The page boy Cherubino starts to make love to the Countess (thinking her at first to be Susanna). The Count, coming to his own rendezvous with Susanna, sends the boy packing—and starts to make love too. (He is, of course, wooing his own wife, but he does not know it.) And Figaro starts to make love to Susanna (his own wife, disguised as the Countess), much to her chagrin. He has, however, really penetrated the disguise, and after he has enjoyed her anger, they have a fine time making things up.

At the end the Count is shown up as having made a fool of himself. In a noble melody he begs pardon of his wronged and neglected lady, and the opera ends on a wholesome note of rejoicing by everyone.

MARTHA

(*Marta*)

Opera in four acts by Friedrich von Flotow
with libretto in German by W. Friedrich (pen
name for Friedrich Wilhelm Riese) based on
Lady Henriette, a ballet-pantomime with scenario by Vernoy de Saint-Georges and some of
the music by Von Flotow

LADY HARRIET DURHAM, *Maid of Honor*	
to Queen Anne	*Soprano*
LORD TRISTRAM MICKLEFORD, *her cousin*	*Bass*
NANCY, *her waiting-maid*	*Mezzo-soprano*
PLUNKETT, *a young farmer*	*Baritone*
LIONEL, *his foster brother*	*Tenor*
SHERIFF	*Bass*

Time: early 18th century
Place: in and about Richmond, England
First performance at Vienna, November 25, 1847

Although the composer and the language of this opera
were originally German, its origin, character, and appeal are
all pretty international. First of all, it was composed in Paris,
where Flotow spent most of his musical life. Secondly, its
libretto, by Friedrich Riese, is based on a French ballet libretto. Thirdly, the story takes place in eighteenth-century
England and is quite, quite British. And fourthly, it used to
be sung at the great multilingual opera houses mostly in Italian. In fact, it afforded one of Caruso's best roles. And the
two most familiar arias are known to us, not by their German
names, but by their Italian and English names. They are, of
course, *M'appari* and *The Last Rose of Summer*.

The overture, a familiar number in pops concerts, is made up chiefly of music for the Richmond Fair scene in Act I and the broad melody from the finale of Act III.

ACT I

Scene 1 Lady Harriet Durham, our heroine, is an aristocratic lady-in-waiting to Queen Anne of England. That places the story in the beginning of the eighteenth century, and the opening scene takes place in milady's boudoir. She is such an aristocratic lady-in-waiting that she has her own staff of ladies-in-waiting to wait on *her*. And she is bored. Oh, terribly bored. She is even bored by the charming little chorus they sing for her, and so she dismisses them. That is, all except one—her special favorite, Nancy. Nancy suggests, in an aria, that maybe Harriet is in the dumps on account of love. No, says Harriet, it's nothing like that. Just plain, horrid old boredom. (As a matter of fact—from all I've read about it—Queen Anne's court really was a pretty stuffy sort of place.) Anyway, the two girls liven things up a bit with a pyrotechnical coloratura duet on the subject of *ennuie*. And then, in comes one of the causes of the boredom—Sir Tristram Mickleford. This middle-aged dandy imagines that Harriet is in love with him. Nothing could be further from the truth, wherefore the two girls amuse themselves by making fun of him.

Just then a troupe of girls is heard going past the window, singing. It turns out that they are on their way to the Richmond Fair, where they intend, according to the custom of the day, to offer their services as maids to those farmers who ask for them. "Fine idea," thinks the bored Harriet, and she immediately suggests that she and Nancy should disguise themselves and join these girls. Sir Tristram is to join them, himself disguised as a country squire. The old fool objects strenuously, but the girls cajole and bully him into it; and as the scene ends, they are rehearsing a country dance and leading the old gentleman out to catch up with the others.

Scene 2 takes us to the famous Richmond Fair. It's fine, sunny, British sort of weather, and all the girls and farmers are out, melodiously explaining the business of the day in the jolly opening chorus. That is, a girl makes a bargain with a farmer to serve him for a wage they agree on, and once the agreement is made, it is binding for a whole year.

Now enter the two heroes—Lionel and Plunkett. They are there to get servants for their farm, and it appears that they are foster brothers. Through a very melodious duet we learn the following important facts: Lionel's father had appeared with the little boy at the farm of Plunkett's parents, and soon after he had died, without ever revealing his name. But he had left a ring for the little boy—a ring which, if shown to the Queen in time of need, would get help from her. The two boys had been brought up together as brothers, and now they are jointly running the prosperous farm that Plunkett's parents had left them.

This important piece of exposition being tunefully disposed of, the Fair begins. Maids offer themselves, reciting their accomplishments; farmers make bargains with them. Meanwhile, the disguised Lady Harriet, Nancy, and Sir Tristram look on, amused. Plunkett and Lionel are attracted by the girls and come over to inquire about their services. Sir Tristram tries to get the girls away, but they are attracted by these two handsome fellows, and by the joke as well. In a fine quartet a bargain is struck. The girls will serve these farmers for one year. Wages: fifty crowns per annum, porter to drink on Sundays, and plum pudding on New Year's. Lightheartedly they agree, and they even accept the initial binding fee. But then, when they think that ends it and wish to go home with Sir Tristram, the men insist on their bargain. All the farmers—and the Sheriff as well—join in on the side of sound business. The act ends as the two men take off the two girls in their farm wagon. Sir Tristram tries desperately to intervene, but the whole chorus holds him back.

ACT II

Lionel and Plunkett have brought home their newly acquired servant girls, knowing them only as Martha and Julia. It does not take long to realize that there are going to be some labor troubles in this household, for the two girls not only seem unable to perform any tasks, they actually refuse to do them. Two fine quartets develop out of this comic situation. The first expresses the farmers' original amazement and may roughly be translated as "Well, what do you know about that?" The second is known as the *Spinning Quartet*, in which the employers try to show the girls how to work a spinning wheel. The result is complete futility so far as work is concerned and complete delight for the audience with its musical expression. Plunkett gets really angry and chases the supposed Julia out of the room. But Lionel has been smitten with his "Martha," and he speaks very gently to her. In a duet he promises never to ask her to do anything she does not want to do; all he asks is that she sing him a folk song. Touched by the handsome young man, she obliges. It is the Irish song *The Last Rose of Summer* that she sings. He is so much moved by it that he impulsively asks her to marry him, but she only laughs. Then, seeing his seriousness, she is once more touched. Just at that moment Plunkett returns, dragging in Nancy. Then the clock tolls twelve, and there is a sudden change in the charged atmosphere. Everyone grows quiet, and they sing the lovely *Good Night Quartet*.

The two men then lock up and go to their rooms. No sooner are they gone than Harriet's silly old lover, Sir Tristram, comes in by the window. He has a carriage awaiting the two girls outside to escape in, and after a brief trio they scamper out.

ACT III

The act begins with a fine drinking song delivered by Plunkett as he downs a mug of good old English porter with his farmer friends at an inn at Richmond Park. Then they go off to try to catch a glimpse of good Queen Anne, who is hunting in the park that day with her ladies-in-waiting. Sure enough—the ladies-in-waiting, dressed in hunting garb, come right up to the inn a moment later and, naturally enough, they sing a hunting song. But Plunkett, coming out of the inn, finds Nancy there—the girl he had hired as a servant for a year under the name of Julia. Immediately he tries to get her back, but of course she refuses, and her companions drive the rude fellow off with their spears.

When they are gone, Plunkett's foster brother, Lionel, wanders in disconsolately. He is still in love with *his* hired girl, the Lady Harriet, whose name he believes to be Martha, and he sings the famous aria known in English as *How So Fair*, in Italian as *M'appari*, and in German as *Ach, so fromm*. As he finishes, the Lady Harriet herself also wanders in, dressed like a huntress. He begs her to return; she refuses; an angry duet develops; and finally Sir Tristram is called for. Everyone else also comes in (except, that is, the Queen), and the farmers are put quite in the wrong. Now the great ensemble number, heard first in the overture, develops. It is led by Lionel, who begs heaven's forgiveness—not for himself, but for the girl who, he believes, has wronged him. A fanfare is heard off-stage. The Queen is approaching; and Lionel, suddenly remembering his ring, gives it to his friend Plunkett to deliver to the sovereign. For Lionel is now under arrest, and he knows that the ring, when presented to the Queen, may save him. He is led off under guard as the act closes.

ACT IV

Scene 1 Lionel, through the good graces of his ring and Queen Anne, has been released, and Lady Harriet visits him, for she loves him after all. She explains all this to Nancy, and then she sings, once more, *The Last Rose of Summer*. But Lionel, who has been put into jail on her account, will have none of her now, for he does not believe her to be sincere. Now Harriet tries to win him over by telling him a great secret. She herself had brought the ring to Queen Anne, and it turns out that Lionel (unbeknownst to himself) is not a farmer at all, but none other than the Earl of Derby! Even this startling piece of court gossip does not change the mood of the angry young man, and the duet ends with his leaving her rudely.

But a high-spirited English lassie is not so easily defeated, and she enlists the aid of Nancy and Plunkett in a plan she has up her sleeve. These two, for their part, engage in a very flirtatious duet, and it is clear, long before it is over, that as soon as the tenor and soprano can be got into each other's arms, the mezzo and the baritone will imitate the higher aristocracy.

Scene 2   And in the final scene the plan is carried out. A replica of the Richmond Fair has been constructed. Everyone looks, dresses, acts, and—to some extent—sings, just as he did at the Fair early in the opera. Lady Harriet (looking once more like Martha) says that she can do pretty well, not as a servant girl perhaps, but as a woman and a wife, and Nancy allows as how she's pretty good at spinning after all. Lionel is thus completely won over; Nancy is not surprised to find herself in Plunkett's arms; and everyone ends with a final reprise on *The Last Rose of Summer*. How else *should* a musical comedy end?

A MASKED BALL

(*Un ballo in maschera*)

Opera in three acts by Giuseppe Verdi with libretto in Italian by Antonio Somma based on Augustin Eugène Scribe's text for Daniel Auber's *Gustave III ou Le bal masqué*

RICCARDO, *Count of Warwick and Governor of Boston* Tenor
RENATO, *his friend and secretary* Baritone
AMELIA, *Renato's wife* Soprano
ULRICA, *a fortuneteller* Contralto
OSCAR, *a page* Soprano
SAMUELE ⎫ *conspirators* Bass
TOMMASO ⎭ Bass
SILVANO, *a sailor* Baritone

Time: 18th century
Place: Boston
First performance at Rome, February 17, 1859
Note—Sometimes the scene of the opera is shifted to Naples, sometimes to Stockholm; sometimes the names of the characters are changed accordingly, sometimes not. The music remains the same.

A *Masked Ball* is the only one of Verdi's opera stories to take place in what is today the United States. Even so, it was transplanted only by accident—or rather, by censor. It is based on a play by the French dramatist Scribe, and its story originally had to do with the murder of King Gustavus III of Sweden. But in 1858, when the opera was about to be mounted, an attempt on the life of Napoleon III had just been made. The authorities in Naples were frightened: they thought that an opera about a murdered king might give the Neapolitans some unhealthy inspiration. Therefore the story had to be changed. The censors (who are always very wise and subtle folk) agreed that no one could get excited if the murdered man were to be no king at all, but merely the Governor of colonial Boston. Perhaps they knew (though I doubt it) that colonial Boston had no governor, rather Massachusetts had one. Who cared, anyway? And so the opera came finally to be performed the following year, not at Naples after all, but in Rome. And sure enough—there was no riot at all, and not a single king was murdered because of this opera.

When the Metropolitan Opera revived it in the 1940's and again in the 1950's, they put the scene back into Sweden, where it originally belonged. But that made for certain absurdities too. For instance, they had to keep the names of the characters as the singers had learned them. And so the hero was still Riccardo—that is Richard, Earl of Warwick, who might have been a perfectly splendid Governor of Massachusetts, but certainly was never a King of Sweden. And the two villains, Sam and Tom, who are sometimes played as Negroes or as Indians, were suddenly transformed into Samuele and Tommaso, a couple of elegantly dressed Swedish noblemen!

Well, to avoid all this complicated nonsense, let us stick to the simpler nonsense of the story as it was first told on the stage of the Apollo Theater at Rome on the evening of February 17, 1859. It's really quite a good operatic story.

ACT I

Scene 1 After a prelude, which includes some of the principal themes from the opera, the stage business begins with a chorus in praise of Riccardo, that is, the Governor of colonial Boston. His court is assembled, and the page boy, Oscar, announces the Governor's entrance. Riccardo examines a number of state papers, among them a list of guests to be invited to a masked ball. He sees the name of Amelia on the list and rhapsodizes about her in the aria *La rivedrò nell èstasi*. However melodious, this tune is an aside; that is, it is heard by no one present except the audience in the auditorium. A good thing, too. For the beloved Amelia is the wife of Renato, and Renato is Riccardo's secretary and closest confidant. Meantime, a group of conspirators in Riccardo's court keeps muttering about their discontent.

Now Renato enters, and the rest of the court departs. The secretary warns his master about plots on his life that he has heard about, and in the aria *Alla vita che t'arride* tells him how valuable that life is. But Riccardo is not impressed with his danger at all, and a moment later some judges enter with an order for Riccardo to sign. It is to banish the soothsayer Ulrica. Oscar returns to plead on the old woman's behalf—and to show off his virtuoso vocal technique in the aria *Volta la terrea*, for his part is assigned to a coloratura soprano.

The good-natured Riccardo sees a chance for fun in this. Despite Renato's warnings, he invites the whole court to join him in a visit to the fortuneteller's hut. For himself he plans to assume the disguise of a sailor. In the closing ensemble everyone is looking forward to this lark. Even the two conspirators, Samuele and Tommaso, see in it a good chance to help along their wicked designs.

Scene 2 takes us to the hut of Ulrica, the fortuneteller. Before a large crowd, she is mixing her witch's brew, and she intones an incantation to the words *Re dell' abisso affrettati*. A sailor named Silvano now has a question to ask her. Will he ever get the money or the promotion he thinks he deserves? Ulrica predicts that he will. And Riccardo (who has slipped in, in his disguise) secretly puts a promotion and some money into Silvano's pocket. Naturally, everyone is surprised and delighted when Silvano, a moment later, finds them there.

Next, a messenger from Amelia comes to ask private audience with Ulrica, and when everyone has left (excepting Riccardo, who hides himself in the hut), the lady enters. She tells of her love for Riccardo and asks how she may forget him. Ulrica says there is but one way: she must gather, this very night, some herbs that grow beneath the gallows outside the city gates. Furthermore, she must go unattended. But in the trio that follows this advice, Riccardo lets the audience know that Amelia shall not be unguarded.

Now all the rest of the crowd returns, including the courtiers. Riccardo (still disguised as a sailor) sings a delightful barcarole (*Di' tu se fidele*) and demands to know his future. Ulrica recognizes his hand as belonging to a nobleman and a warrior, but her prediction is a very sour one: Riccardo is to be murdered! And by whom? By the next man to shake his hand. Riccardo takes this as a huge joke and, laughingly, he demands that someone shake his hand at once. Everyone refuses; but just then, enter Renato, his friend and the husband of Amelia. He has come to protect his beloved master, and, all unwittingly, he takes his hand in his. Now Riccardo reveals his true identity to the witch. He also tells her that her prophecies are patently nonsensical, and therefore she may safely remain in the country. The act ends with another chorus in praise of the genial Riccardo, son of England.

ACT II

It is late at night when the second act begins. Amelia slinks in, before the snow-covered gallows, and is about to commence her fearful task. Bitterly she laments the fact that she must extinguish forever the love she bears Riccardo, but she is resolute nonetheless. At the close of her aria (*Ma dall' arido*) she sees a figure approaching in the darkness. At first she is frightened, but it turns out to be Riccardo himself. In the long duet that follows, he begs for her love; but she points out its dishonor, for her husband, Renato, is Riccardo's most devoted friend. Nobly he agrees; and as their tragic emotions come to a musical climax, they see another figure approaching. This time it is—Renato! Quickly Amelia hides her face in her cloak. Renato has come to warn Riccardo once more, for the conspirators are even now on his trail. Riccardo asks Renato to escort the lady with him back to the city, and he must do so without once speaking to her or trying to find out who she is. Renato readily consents, and Riccardo quickly leaves.

A *Masked Ball*

It is just in time. For now the two villains enter—Samuele and Tommaso—ready to kill the Count. When, in their disappointment, they find only Renato and not Riccardo, they start to taunt the veiled beauty with him. Renato angrily draws his sword, the conspirators draw theirs, and Amelia steps in to save her husband. As she does so, her veil drops—and Renato discovers who she is. A dramatic quartet follows, punctuated by the villainous ha-ha-ha's of the two conspirators. As the act closes, Renato invites these men to his house. Now he is on their side, and against his former friend and master, Riccardo, the noble Governor of Boston.

ACT III

Scene 1 begins with the drama of Renato's return home with his wife, Amelia. She has apparently betrayed him with his best friend, and, in the tradition of French drama and Italian opera, there is only one thing the baritone can demand—the death of his wife. Eagerly she tries to explain, but to no purpose. And then, in the aria *Morrò, ma prima in grazia*, with cello obbligato, she makes a last pitiful request—that she may once more see their little son. When she is gone, Renato sings the one aria from *A Masked Ball* that everyone knows, *Eri tu che macchiavi*. It is addressed to a portrait of Riccardo that hangs on the wall—Riccardo, the former friend who has ruined all Renato's happiness.

Now enter, once more, the villains, Samuele and Tommaso. Renato tells them he knows of their plot to take the Count's life and, much to their surprise, he demands a part in that plot. Each of the three wishing to strike the deathblow, they decide to draw lots for this rather revolting privilege. At that moment Amelia returns and, in a fine, sardonic mood, Renato requires her to do the drawing of the name. To the accompaniment of sinister chords in the orchestra, she draws out the slip of paper, and the name on it is—Renato! The scene comes to a climax with a quartet in which each character voices his own emotions. But a fresh voice and tone is added to the ensemble as Oscar, the page, brings in the invitation to the masked ball. As the scene closes, Oscar describes the splendor of the approaching festivities; Amelia tragically voices her despair; and the three men look forward to the consummation of their wicked plot. It is an especially brilliant piece of part-writing, this final quintet.

Scene 2 takes place on the evening of the ball itself. Count Riccardo is alone: he has resolved to send Renato and Amelia back to England. Thus, through self-sacrifice, he may achieve peace of mind for himself and happiness for his friend and his beloved Amelia. At the end of the aria he receives an anonymous note advising him not to attend his own ball. But Riccardo is fearless, and he resolves to go.

Scene 3 And now, without an intermission, the scene shifts and the ball is in progress. Everyone is, of course, disguised; but by questioning and threatening young Oscar, Renato manages to find out the disguise of Riccardo. Presently, during the dance, Amelia, masked like everyone else, meets Riccardo. Trying to disguise her voice, she gives him one more warning of the plot against his life, for, of course, it was Amelia who had sent the warning letter. But Riccardo recognizes his beloved. He tells her of his plan to return her and Renato to England, and their voices join in one final love duet. Renato, overhearing them, steals up behind Riccardo—and, with an exultant cry, deals him a deathblow. Immediately Renato is seized; but with his last words Riccardo forgives him and hands over the order, already signed, for his return to England with Amelia. With everyone sorrowing over the loss of so noble a ruler as Riccardo, the opera closes on a rich but somber concerted number.

Postscript for the historically curious: On the night of March 16, 1792, the liberal-minded monarch Gustavus III of Sweden was shot at a masked ball by a leader of the aristocratic party, Jakob Johan Anckarström. Gustavus lingered on for thirteen days before he died; and Anckarström was arrested, tried, and sentenced to be flogged, to have his offending hand hacked off, and then to be beheaded. However, the sentence was to be remitted if he would name the other members of the rather widespread conspiracy. This he refused to do. The sentence was carried out, and the others involved, against whom there was no conclusive evidence, fled the country.

IL MATRIMONIO SEGRETO

(The Clandestine Marriage)

Opera buffa in two acts by Domenico Cimarosa
with libretto in Italian by Giovanni Bertati
based on the English comedy The Clandestine
Marriage by George Colman the elder and
David Garrick

GERONIMO, *a merchant*	Bass
ELISETTA ⎫	*Soprano*
CAROLINA ⎭ *his daughters*	*Soprano*
FIDALMA, *his sister*	*Mezzo-soprano*
PAOLINO, *his assistant*	*Tenor*
COUNT ROBINSON, *an Englishman*	Bass

Time: 18th century
Place: Bologna
First performance at Vienna, February 7, 1792

The Secret Marriage is what the opera is usually called
in English; but I have chosen to translate it as The Clandestine Marriage, for that is the name of the comedy by George
Colman the elder and David Garrick on which Giovanni
Bertati based his libretto. True, Bertati made extensive alterations. He made all the original English characters but one
Italians, he eliminated one of the most important members
of the cast (the father of the noble suitor), he shortened and
simplified as librettists must, and he transposed the scene
from London to Bologna. But the plot and the motivations
remain essentially the same, and it would seem worth while
to retain the title of a minor classic of the English stage which
was a huge success a quarter of a century before Bertati dis-

covered it, and it has remained a part of our literature ever since.

As an opera, it was also a huge success from the beginning and has remained the only one of Cimarosa's sixty-five operas to be heard in our century. It was his forty-ninth attempt, his biggest but by no means his only success. The wandering Italian composer had recently come from a period as court composer to Catherine of Russia to take up an analogous post in Vienna—the post that Mozart had so much wanted to have. He composed *Il matrimonio* for the court of the Holy Roman Emperor Leopold II. The opera so delighted that monarch (so the story goes, at least) that he invited the cast to dinner and then demanded, as an encore, the entire score. No encore of equal length is recorded in operatic history.

ACT I

Scene 1 After a thoroughly gay overture, sometimes performed as a concert piece, the curtain rises on the eighteenth-century drawing room of Geronimo, a wealthy merchant of Bologna with social ambitions but somewhat deaf. The social ambitions he hopes to realize through the marriage of both his daughters with members of the nobility, but he is not aware that Carolina, the younger of the two, is already married to Paolino, his business assistant. That young couple opens the proceedings with a couple of duets. In the first of these— and the recitative passages between them—we learn the state of things. Carolina urges her husband to reveal the clandestine marriage to Geronimo. After all, she says, despite his gruff exterior he is basically a kind man and is sure to forgive them after a day or two. Paolino, however, is for waiting a bit longer. He has arranged a visit from Count Robinson, an English milord, who, for a dowry of 100,000 scudi, is ready to marry the elder sister, Elisetta. If that comes to pass, Geronimo should be so grateful to Paolino that he will forgive him. He shows her a letter from Robinson announcing his imminent arrival, and Carolina agrees that it might be better to wait.

The second duet is a lighthearted leave-taking between the lovers.

When Geronimo blusters onto the stage, he finds Paolino alone and receives the letter from Robinson. He is beside himself with joy to learn that a count is coming to make a countess of his elder daughter; and when, a moment later, the two daughters enter with their aunt Fidalma, who runs the house for her brother, he announces the good news in a typical eighteenth-century basso-buffo aria (*Un matrimonio nobile*). Carolina comes in for some scolding because she shows envy of her sister's good luck.

The three ladies of the cast then have an amusing trio in which Carolina pretends jealousy of her sister's prospective elevation, kneeling to her in mock subservience, Elisetta complains of Carolina's bad behavior, and Fidalma tries to placate them both. At its close Carolina exits in a huff and Fidalma confides to Elisetta that she too hopes to be married soon. She won't tell the girl to whom, but she lets the audience know, in an aside, that she is in love with Paolino.

In a brief scene Geronimo tells his younger daughter, to her consternation and mystification, that he is arranging a noble wedding for her as well as for Elisetta. He does not have time to give her any details before Count Robinson arrives. This gentleman turns out to be a fatuous fool, full of meaningless compliments to everyone; and he proceeds to assume first that Carolina is to be his bride, then Fidalma, and only lastly Elisetta. And when he finds out that it is Elisetta, he is patently upset, for Carolina's bright eyes have already captured his fancy. The scene ends in a quartet sung by Robinson and the three women in which they are in full agreement on only one thing: the situation is not developing the way it had been planned and no one knows what will happen next.

Scene 2 Paolino visits Robinson in Geronimo's study, hoping to get his help in breaking the news of his own marriage to the old man. Robinson, however, forestalls him with the announcement that he does not like Elisetta and that he proposes instead to marry Carolina. In fact, he is willing to take only 50,000 scudi as dowry if the exchange is made; and he sends Paolino off to make the proposal to Geronimo. He could not have chosen a more unwilling agent.

Carolina now wanders into the study, and the Count takes the opportunity to propose. At first Carolina pretends to be outraged by his lack of honor and then, in one of the best arias in the opera (*Questa cosa accordar*), tells him how unsuited she is to marry into the nobility. She is too humble, she says, she lacks poise, she is too small, she doesn't know how to behave, and she has no command of French, English, or German. In short, she's nothing but a silly little girl—and she runs off with an utterly unconvinced Count in pursuit.

The other four members of the cast then come into the room, Elisetta tearfully complaining about the Count's lack of attention to her and Geronimo trying to excuse the man. Paolino speaks up—but not to deliver the Count's message. He merely tells them that everything's been got ready in the banquet hall for a celebration, and they all leave to inspect the festive board.

This leaves the room free for the Count to resume his pursuit of Carolina, and she is still trying to fend him off when Elisetta discovers them together. She immediately sets up a great cry about her sister's trying to ensnare her man. Everyone else hurries in; and in the grand finale to the act, both sisters try to explain their positions at once, Paolino and Fidalma say they are greatly mystified by what's going on, and the Count and Geronimo are fairly reduced to singing gibberish, so inadequate are they to dealing with the women.

ACT II

Scene 1 The second act, like the first, begins with a pair of duets, but not between the same two principals. The Count finds his prospective father-in-law in his study and attempts, in the first duet, to tell him that he refuses to marry Elisetta as she does not please him. Between his own addlepatedness and Geronimo's deafness, he has some difficulty in getting over the idea; and when he succeeds, it is met with indignation and a determination on Geronimo's part to keep him to his

Il matrimonio segreto

bargain. But in the second duet the Count proposes to marry Carolina instead, taking 50,000 scudi less in settlement. This proposal appeals to the old merchant much better, and he accepts on condition that Elisetta agrees.

Geronimo's study must be in a magically central location in his house; for as soon as he has left it, Paolino conveniently passes through, and Robinson tells him of the new agreement, suggesting that he himself bear the glad tidings to the lucky Carolina. The young fellow, left in despair, resolves to consult Fidalma about what he should do. As she conveniently happens by at this moment, he begins hesitantly to explain; but she, misinterpreting his emotions, tells him not to worry, and she promises to marry him out of hand. This is too much for him, and he faints dead away. Now it is Carolina's turn to happen by conveniently, and she, too, misinterprets the situation. When Fidalma goes and then quickly returns with smelling salts, Paolino fails to convince Carolina of his innocence; but when Fidalma finally leaves them alone, Paolino, in one of the few genuinely serious arias in the opera (Ah! No, che tu così morir), persuades his wife of his fidelity and proposes that they elope together.

Elisetta and Fidalma are now both the sworn enemies of Carolina and, in a short duet, decide that she had better be packed off to a convent. And when Geronimo comes on the scene, prepared to persuade Elisetta to give up the Count, both women turn on him and get him, in a swiftly paced trio, to agree to the plan. Therefore, when Carolina comes to her father intending to tell him finally of her clandestine marriage, he brutally announces that she must go to a convent the next morning and then leaves her. She expresses her sorrow and confusion in the aria E possono mai nascere; and when the Count presses his suit once more by swearing that he will do anything for her in his power, she is about to take him literally at his word. However, they are interrupted by the other members of the family; and in the ensuing quintet her elders all insist that Carolina must go to a convent, Carolina tries in vain to tell them that she has not been encouraging

319

her noble suitor, and the Count resolves to run out on the whole mess.

Scene 2 That night Paolino and Carolina are about to elope when they hear someone moving and they quickly retire to her room. It is Elisetta who has heard their whispering and who immediately decides that her sister is entertaining the Count in her room. She summons first her aunt and then her father, and the three of them demand loudly, outside Carolina's room, that the Count open the door. This he does—but it is his own door he opens, on the other side of the stage, where he has been awakened by all the noise. (Apparently he has decided not to leave after all.) Thereupon everyone shouts for Carolina to come forth and explain. The door opens, and Paolino and his wife throw themselves on their knees before Geronimo, admit that they have been married for two months, and beg for forgiveness. The old blusterer does not want to give in; but in the final sextet everyone else—even Fidalma and Elisetta—is so eloquently inspired by the romance of a clandestine marriage, that Geronimo finally gives in. The most improbable plea of all comes from Count Robinson. He says that he is a man of the world and must be listened to. He is so much in love with Carolina, he says, that she ought to be forgiven, and to promote that end, he will marry Elisetta. If one gives the matter any thought at all (as one shouldn't), it is hard to foresee a jolly future for the Count and Countess Robinson, but his generous offer gives the occasion for a suitably joyous finale to the opera.

THE MEDIUM

Opera in two acts by Gian-Carlo Menotti with
libretto in English by the composer

MADAME FLORA (BABA), *a medium*	*Contralto*
MRS. GOBINEAU ⎫	*Soprano*
MR. GOBINEAU ⎬ *her clients*	*Baritone*
MRS. NOLAN ⎭	*Mezzo-soprano*
MONICA, *her daughter*	*Soprano*
TOBY, *a mute*	*Dancer*

Time: the present
*Place: Italy, or the U.S.A., or practically anywhere in Western
civilization*
First performance at New York, May 8, 1946

Long before he wrote *The Medium*, Mr. Menotti had
already had two one-act operas produced at the Metropolitan
Opera House—*Amelia Goes to the Ball* and *The Island God*.
Neither of them lasted very long in the repertoire (the standard fate for American operas in that institution); and *The
Old Maid and the Thief*, written for radio production, has
not lasted too well either. *The Medium*, however, despite
poor attendance during its first few weeks in a Broadway
theater, slowly gathered momentum and developed into a big
hit. With *The Telephone* as a curtain-raiser (for it is too short
to be a full evening's entertainment), its success convinced
many American composers that they should write operas not
for the big repertory houses but for less ambitious productions
which could be made to pay off by running night after night.
Subsequently *The Medium* showed another possible outlet

for the wares of opera composers: it was the first American opera to be shown commercially in movie houses.

Mr. Menotti himself has recorded how he came to think of writing *The Medium*:

"Although the opera was not composed until 1945, the idea of *The Medium* first occurred to me in 1936 in the little Austrian town of St. Wolfgang near Salzburg. I had been invited by my neighbors to attend a séance in their house. I readily accepted their invitation but, I must confess, with my tongue in my cheek. However, as the séance unfolded, I began to be somewhat troubled. Although I was unaware of anything unusual, it gradually became clear to me that my hosts, in their pathetic desire to believe, actually saw and heard their dead daughter Doodly (a name, incidentally, which I have retained in the opera). It was I, not they, who felt cheated. The creative power of their faith and conviction made me examine my own cynicism and led me to wonder at the multiple texture of reality."

ACT I

The entire action takes place in the parlor of a spiritualist medium known either as Madame Flora or simply as Baba. It is a lower-middle-class, stuffily furnished room, with a lamp that may be raised and lowered for séances and a puppet theater with a large curtain in one corner. Through this theater Madame Flora produces the crude supernatural phenomena with which she deludes her happily gullible customers.

Baba's two assistants, her daughter Monica and a graceful waif named Toby, who is a mute, both teen-agers, are happily playing with some of Baba's property costumes when they hear her slam the door and coming upstairs. She is angry with them because they are fooling around when they should have been getting things ready for an imminent séance. As they hurriedly prepare, Monica (who in some ways seems to be more mature than her middle-aged mother) soothes Baba into a better humor.

Presently the three clients wander in—Mr. and Mrs. Gobi-

neau and Mrs. Nolan, who is there for the first time. The
Gobineaus, in their shabby-genteel way, tell Mrs. Nolan how
good are the ministrations of Madame Flora, and presently, in
a semi-darkened room, the séance begins. As they sit about
the table, hands touching, Baba begins to moan, Monica appears in the puppet theater in a faint blue light, and her
voice is heard singing, "Mother, mother, are you there?" Mrs.
Nolan, who has lost her daughter Doodly, asks various simple
questions; but when she begins to ask specifically about a
gold locket (which Monica cannot answer confidently) the
blue light disappears. Mrs. Nolan rises to run toward the
theater, and the séance is interrupted.

The Gobineaus long ago lost a child, who had been drowned
in the fountain of their garden in France. When the séance
is resumed, Monica, from behind the curtain, imitates the
laughing of a little child, which is the comfort for which the
bereaved parents come regularly to this place and pay their
fees. But suddenly Madame Flora cries out hysterically: someone, she thinks, has touched her. She turns up the lights and
will not be appeased even when the three clients sing a perfectly reasonable question: "Why be afraid of our dead?" She
shoos them out as fast as she can get rid of them, turns on
Toby, and accuses him of having played some tricks.

Obviously, Baba is much more put out than she would be
by some innocent diversion of Toby's. Monica has to comfort
her with a long, soothing lullaby that develops into a duet,
as Toby accompanies the melody on a tambourine ("O black
swan, where oh where is my lover gone?"). Even at its close
Baba is still nervous. She thinks she hears voices; she sends
Toby downstairs to look; and when he reports, in sign language, that no one is there, Baba falls on her knees and prays.

ACT II

It is a few days later when **Act II**, like Act I, begins with
Toby and Monica playing together. This time, however, the
play is more extended and ends as the mute does a dance for
the attractive girl. He is obviously in love with her.

When Madame Flora drags her tired body upstairs, Monica goes to her own room and the medium begins to question the boy about what happened the other day. Did he touch her on the throat? Repeatedly he denies it, and finally she picks up a whip and lashes him unmercifully.

But the Gobineaus and Mrs. Nolan arrive once more: it is the regular evening for a séance. Thoroughly unnerved, Baba tries to tell them that the séances were all faked. She shows them the props, she has Monica imitate the voices; but the believers will not be convinced and even refuse to have their money returned. Driven to fury, Baba virtually chases them downstairs and, despite Monica's pleadings, sends Toby after them into permanent banishment.

She then locks Monica into her room, takes a bottle of whiskey from the cupboard, and sits soddenly by the table. She thinks she hears the voices once more; she thinks of all the dreadful experiences she has had during a hard life; she is overcome by nameless fears; she tries to allay them by singing the lullaby; she prays; and finally, emotionally and physically exhausted, she falls asleep. It is a powerful scene.

Toby steals upstairs, tries to get into the locked room, and hides behind the sofa when the sleeping Baba knocks over the bottle. Coming out once more, he looks for something in the prop trunk and wakes Baba by accidentally dropping the lid. Quickly he hides behind the curtain of the puppet theater and, naturally, cannot answer Baba's shout of "Who's there?" She takes a revolver from the drawer and shoots directly at the curtain. Blood begins to stain it, and it is torn down with the falling body of Toby.

As Monica frantically pounds on the door, Baba mutters, "I've killed the ghost."

MEFISTOFELE

(Mephistopheles)

Opera in prologue, four acts, and epilogue by
Arrigo Boito with libretto in Italian by the
composer, based on the drama by Johann Wolfgang von Goethe

MEPHISTOPHELES, *the Devil*	Bass
FAUST, *a philosopher*	Tenor
WAGNER, *his favorite student*	Tenor
MARGHERITE, *a peasant girl*	Soprano
MARTHA, *her mother*	Contralto
HELEN OF TROY	Soprano
PANTALIS, *her companion*	Contralto
NEREO, *an attendant*	Tenor

Time: medieval and ancient
Places: Heaven, Germany, and Greece
First performance at Milan, March 5, 1868

Of making *Fausts* there is no end. Between the time
that Marlowe wrote his great play (itself based on a dubiously
historical account of the medieval philosopher and probably
on some lost stage pieces) and the time that Goethe's masterpiece first saw the stage, some thirty German dramas on the
subject are said to have been written and produced. And once
Goethe's work discouraged other dramatists from trying to
surpass him, the operas began. Besides the three represented
in this book (Boito's, Gounod's, and Berlioz's), there have
been operas on the subject by Spohr, Bertin, Brüggemann,
Busoni, and Lutz. Beethoven considered an opera on the
subject; Schumann composed some of the music for one; Wag-

ner got as far as an overture; Liszt wrote a *Faust Symphony*, some choruses, and a song; and many other composers have written cantatas, individual scenes, songs, and incidental music inspired by Goethe. One composer, Florimond Hervé, even wrote a highly successful French operetta called *Le petit Faust*, which held the stage in France, on and off, for sixty-five years and was exported to many European countries and New York.

Boito, who wrote his own libretto, was the highly literary composer who supplied the first-rate books for Verdi's *Otello* and *Falstaff*, and the less literary but more popularly successful one for Ponchielli's *La Gioconda*. He was one of the few composers to tackle the second as well as the first part of Goethe's huge philosophical drama. As a result, the premiere in 1868 took six hours and was a failure—too much philosophy, not enough action. Boito, always a careful worker, took seven years to shorten and revise it for a new production, and then another year to work it into final shape. The following brief description is based on this final version.

PROLOGUE

As in Goethe, the prologue consists of a dialogue between Mephistopheles, who sticks his head through some stage clouds, and the hosts of Heaven, who don't appear at all. Mephisto, with a kind of sardonic politeness, wagers that he will be able to tempt the renowned philosopher, Dr. Faustus, to sin. The mystic choirs, the cherubim, and others do not seem to be particularly concerned by this boast, but they sing some very impressive choruses.

ACT I

Scene 1 represents a lively Easter Sunday in medieval Frankfort am Main with students, burghers, children all joining in the merriment. The old philosopher, Johann Faustus, observes these goings-on with his favorite pupil, Wagner, and when the crowd disperses, they engage in brief philosophical colloquy. A strange Gray Friar passes, and Faust believes he

sees something supernatural about him. As the philosopher
leaves the stage, the stranger follows him.

Scene 2 Alone in his study, Faust sings his beautiful aria
Dai campi, dai prati in praise of natural goodness; and yet he
is troubled. The mysterious Gray Friar, who has followed him
into his study, suddenly doffs his cloak to reveal himself as
Mephistopheles—the Devil himself. He sings what is aptly
called the *Whistle Aria* and describes his own evil nature.
Faust is not frightened; yet, before the scene is over, he has
signed a contract with Mephisto. On earth Mephisto must
serve Faust and show him some beauty. But below, in Hell,
Mephisto will have the soul of the learned old gentleman.

ACT II

Scene 1 is the famous *Garden Scene.* In the evening, in
Margherite's garden, Faust (now a handsome young man by
grace of the Prince of Darkness) is wooing that innocent young
German girl. To help him out, Mephistopheles is, at the same
time, wooing her mother, Martha. Naturally, the two males
are entirely successful in their nefarious scheme, which is carried on in a highly melodious series of duets and quartets.

Scene 2 is the *Walpurgis Night* scene. Mephisto takes his
protégé to the heights of the Brocken Peak high up in the
Harz Mountains. The Devil leads a fiendish chorus of male
and female witches, and they enact their satanic rites. Suddenly Faust sees a vision of Margherite. She is bound in
chains, and there is a bloody line around her throat. But the
fiendish chorus only goes on, and on.

ACT III

Margherite has poisoned her mother and drowned her illegitimate child. She is now insane and is soon to be taken
from her prison cell to be executed. Pitifully she sings an aria
about it, the expressive *L'altra notte.* Mephistopheles brings
Faust to her, ready to help her escape. But poor, demented
Margherite does not understand. She is comforted in again

seeing her old lover, and they sing a moving duet. But when Mephisto appears, she is frightened. She refuses to leave despite his urgings; she prays to Heaven; and in the last effort she dies. For a moment Mephisto thinks that he has won her soul for Hell, but from on high comes an angelic choir. *È salva*—"She is saved!" it sings; and both Mephisto and the executioner are cheated of their prey.

ACT IV

A complete change comes over the music in the final act. Hitherto we have been in medieval Germany; now we are in ancient Greece. Mephisto has transported Faust here—in time and space—in the philosopher's search for beauty, and they have found the most beautiful woman of all—Helen of Troy. She sings ravishingly with her companion, Pantalis. Mephisto —strictly a medieval character—feels out of place here. He says so, and he retires before a ballet begins. The balance of the act is given over to a love duet between Faust and Helen while a chorus and a male attendant named Nereo comment admiringly on the high-class love affair that is going on before their eyes.

EPILOGUE

Faust, once again an aged philosopher, is seated in his study at night. Mephistopheles is still trying to win his soul, but Faust, repenting his ways, is no longer tempted. Even when the Devil fills the room with visions of sirens, the old philosopher only prays to God. From high above come the voices of the cherubim in answer. In vain Mephisto tries to work his magic. Faust now has a new idea of beauty: it is the vision of the celestial gates. And as, in an ecstasy, his earthly body expires, the cherubim send over it a shower of roses. He is forgiven forever—and the Devil has lost his wager.

DIE MEISTERSINGER VON NÜRNBERG

(The Mastersingers of Nuremberg)

Opera in three acts by Richard Wagner with
libretto in German by the composer

WALTHER VON STOLZING, *a young Franconian knight*	Tenor
EVA, *daughter of Pogner*	Soprano
MAGDALENA, *her nurse*	Mezzo-soprano
DAVID, *apprentice to Hans Sachs*	Tenor
HANS SACHS, *cobbler*	Bass or Baritone
VEIT POGNER, *goldsmith*	Bass
KUNZ VOGELGESANG, *furrier*	Tenor
CONRAD NACHTIGALL, *buckle-maker*	Bass
SIXTUS BECKMESSER, *town clerk*	Bass
FRITZ KOTHNER, *baker* *mastersingers*	Bass
BALTHASAR ZORN, *pewterer*	Tenor
ULRICH EISSLINGER, *grocer*	Tenor
AUGUSTIN MOSER, *tailor*	Tenor
HERMAN ORTEL, *soap boiler*	Bass
HANS SCHWARZ, *stocking weaver*	Bass
HANS FOLTZ, *coppersmith*	Bass
A NIGHT WATCHMAN	Bass

Time: middle of the 16th century
Place: Nuremberg
First performance at Munich, June 21, 1868

Played without any intermission, a complete performance of *Die Meistersinger* would take just about four and a

Die Meistersinger von Nürnberg

half hours. Yet when, prompted by his reading of a history of German literature, Wagner first considered the subject of the mastersingers of Nuremberg, he planned a one-act comedy —a half-hour afterpiece to *Tannhäuser*. It was sixteen years before he again took up the subject and another six before he completed it. By that time the original plan had succumbed to Wagner's penchant for giganticism, and the most endearing of his operas was produced. Paderewski called it "the greatest work of genius ever achieved by any artist in any field of human activity." Very few other musicians would rate it quite that high, and even the most rabid Wagnerians might prefer to give the palm to the *Ring* or to *Tristan*. Yet there is little question that it ranks, along with Verdi's *Falstaff* and Richard Strauss's *Der Rosenkavalier*, as the best of the operatic comedies since Mozart; and in popularity it outranks the two later works.

PRELUDE

Wagner seems unwontedly modest in calling his introductory thoughts merely *Vorspiel*, or *Prelude*, equating it with, say, one of Chopin's one-page poems. The very opening theme is that of the mastersingers, the sixteenth-century guild of vocalists, Nuremberg chapter. It is followed by each of the other principal themes of the opera—*Longing, Prize Song, Love Confessed, The Art of Brotherhood, Ridicule*, and others, which have been so labeled by leitmotiv detectives. In the development, two, three, and one time even four of these are juggled together with consummate skill. A tremendous climax is achieved with the reiteration of the opening theme; and (excepting in Wagner's own concert arrangement) the *Prelude* leads directly into

ACT I

In the church of St. Catherine, in Nuremberg, services are going on, the chorale to St. John being sturdily intoned. A handsome young knight of Franconia, Walther von Stolzing, stands by a pillar ogling Eva, daughter of the wealthy gold-smith Pogner; and between the stately lines sung by the choir she and the orchestra register a happy amorous confusion. At its close, as the congregation leaves, Walther, who has never met the girl, manages to learn from her attending nurse, Magdalena, that Eva is *not* betrothed. She is, however, to be bestowed the next day on the winner of a song contest. Wasting little time on the oddity of this circumstance, he resolves to enter the contest himself.

With the church emptied, a bustling group of apprentices prepares the place for a hearing of would-be members of the guild of mastersingers. David, who is affianced to Magdalena, is the leader of the group; and as they work, he gives a confused and confusing account to Walther of the guild's technical rules—all about modes and tablatures which neither Walther nor a modern audience manages to understand very well but which, nevertheless, bear some relationship to the actual rules of the time as Wagner had found them in a book.

The apprentices make fun of Walther's pretensions, but they scatter when the august members of the guild enter in their Sunday best. Beckmesser, the town clerk, feels confident of winning the contest, but there is one little thing that bothers him. Pogner has stated that he will bestow his daughter on the winner only if she approves of the choice. With good reason the nasty little clerk feels that this may stand in the way of his getting the girl of his dreams. Pogner, however, refuses to alter the ruling; and in a long *Address*, he moralizes on the charges of commercialism that have been leveled against the burghers of Nuremberg. To show his devotion to art, therefore, he promises not only Eva but his own worldly wealth to the winner; and should Eva refuse the man's hand, she may marry no one else.

Now Hans Sachs, the real hero of the opera, speaks up. He is the local cobbler and very popular with the ordinary people of Nuremberg. Suppose, he suggests, that Eva herself and the people make the judgment. Perhaps he is not wholly disinterested in this proposal, for he, too, is in love with Eva, and, as Beckmesser points out, he has composed some songs that are dangerously popular. At any rate, his proposal, too, is turned down by the members of the guild.

The examination of Walther, as a candidate, then begins. He has learned his art, he says, from the teachings of Walther von der Vogelweide, a real historical character, who, having been dead for more than three centuries, could not be a member of the guild. The more narrow-minded members object to this training, but Sachs's liberality wins the day. Kothner, the baker, thereupon reads out the formal rules; Beckmesser, as "marker," takes his place behind a curtain with a slate and piece of chalk; and Walther starts his trial song—a handsome tune about love and spring, beginning *Am stillen Herd.* Almost at once the scratching of Beckmesser marking down mistakes sounds furiously from behind the screen; and when Walther commits the blunder of rising from his chair as he sings, the outraged masters unanimously decide that he has been "outsung." Unanimously, that is, excepting for Sachs. The cobbler's pleas on behalf of the young man's gifts go unheard. Walther and the others leave the church in various degrees of disgust, and the curtain descends on Sachs alone, who regards the matter with a wry humor.

ACT II

That evening the apprentices are putting up the shutters on the houses in a street where Pogner's showy dwelling stands on one side and Sachs's more humble one on the other. Tomorrow is the festival of St. John, and they are anticipating the fun. They are also making fun of David, who has come into the bad graces of Magdalena on account of Walther's failure to benefit by his instructions. Sachs, however, chases all the boys home, seats himself at his cobbler's bench outside his door, and has a nice long think—the brooding monologue *Wie duftet doch der Flieder.* The summer breezes lead to thoughts of Walther's song, which still haunts him. Even if it broke many rules, yet it was full of magic and beauty. (Sachs, you see, was, in Wagner's mind, one of the rarest of phenomena—a broad-minded music critic.)

Die Meistersinger von Nürnberg

Eva shyly crosses the street, and in the ensuing dialogue it becomes clear that she is in love with Walther but, despairing now of having him, would not find the highly respected, middle-aged Sachs entirely unacceptable. But Sachs, though he has loved the girl since she was so high, is too wise to take advantage of this, and he quietly resumes his work, within the door of his house, when she leaves. A moment later, however, he observes Eva and Walther across the way. They are making plans to elope but are interrupted first by the light from Sachs's window and then by the entrance of Beckmesser carrying a lute. The town clerk makes believe he has come to inquire about a pair of shoes, but his real purpose is to serenade Eva. Sachs agrees to act as "marker" for him, and Beckmesser begins. Meantime, however, Magdalena has appeared at Eva's window, and so it is the maid who receives her mistress's compliments. They are not very lyrical in nature, however, and Sachs unmercifully hammers away at his shoes to mark each of Beckmesser's anti-musical mistakes. The noise arouses many of the neighbors, who appear at their windows; and David, seeing the town clerk serenading his fiancée, rushes out and starts trouncing the intruder unmercifully. This is the signal for a general melee of the men of the town, dressed mostly in nightgowns. Walther and Eva take advantage of the confusion by trying to elope, but Sachs pushes the girl back into her father's house, draws Walther into his own, and kicks David back in as well. By this time the women of the town have put an end to the midsummer madness by pouring water from the windows (though this detail is omitted in many performances). With quiet descended again upon the street, the night watchman appears, sings a quaint old ditty, blows somewhat discordantly on his horn, and wanders off as the curtain falls.

ACT III

Scene 1 Act III has an exceptionally beautiful prelude made up partly from the long soliloquy Sachs sings in the first scene and partly from the magnificent chorale sung in the second.

The action takes place next day—St. John's Day—June 24 —the day of the Song Contest. Sachs is sitting at home, reading, and he barely notices David, his apprentice, when he comes in. David is quite embarrassed on account of his bad behavior the night before. But the good-natured Sachs bears him no ill will and asks him to sing the carol of St. John in honor of the day. Now, the familiar name for John (or Johannes) in German is "Hans," and suddenly David realizes that if this is the day that honors St. John, why, it must honor his master too, whose name is Hans. And—as we shall see in the second scene—Hans Sachs *is* the honored figure on that day.

Left alone, Sachs sings his second monologue, *Wahn, wahn!* All the world is mad, he says, and one thinks (though he does not mention it) that perhaps his sadness may be inspired by his hopeless love for Eva. Suddenly Walther, his overnight guest, comes in. He has just wakened from a wonderful dream, and he proceeds to tell it to Sachs. This is the familiar *Prize Song*, and Sachs, struck with its beauty, writes down the words as Walther sings.

When the two men have left the room, Beckmesser steals in, still limping from his beating of the night before. He finds Walther's song and puts it into his pocket. Then, when Sachs re-enters, he scolds him for wanting to enter the contest himself. Sachs at once sees that Beckmesser takes the song to be his own and, without telling him who the real author is, makes him a present of it. For Sachs knows that Beckmesser is so bad a musician he will never get a good tune for it. Delighted, Beckmesser leaves.

The next visitor at the Sachs house is Eva. She is beautifully dressed, ready for the contest. She says, however, that her shoe pinches. Sachs begins to fuss with her foot, at which point enter Walther, also dressed, like a knight, for the contest. Struck with Eva's beauty, he repeats the last stanza of his *Prize Song*. Eva, now deeply in love with Walther, tries to hide her emotion. Even Sachs is a little perturbed, and, to cover up, he sings a stanza of a sturdy cobbler's song.

Die Meistersinger von Nürnberg

Now David and Magdalena are called in. The apprentice is told his days of service are over: he has been graduated in his trade, and he may now marry Magdalena. The scene ends with the great quintet in which each expresses his own emotions. It is, I think, one of the loveliest passages Wagner ever composed.

Scene 2 On an open meadow, beside the river Pegnitz, the good folk of Nuremberg are gathered. In come all the guilds in procession—the tailors, the shoemakers, the bakers. The apprentices come too, and dance to a delightful little waltz tune. Finally, the mastersingers come in, to the melody that opens the prelude to the opera. At their head is the revered Hans Sachs, and the people honor him with a beautiful chorale, the second melody heard in the prelude to Act III.

The first contestant is the comic villain—Beckmesser. Accompanying himself, he tries to sing the poem he had practically stolen. But his voice is so bad, and his tune is so tuneless, that he is simply laughed at. Enraged, he accuses Sachs of having written the poem. But Sachs says it is really a very good poem, if well sung, and so Walther is allowed to sing it. The people are so much enchanted with his *Prize Song* that they join in in wonder. Of course, Walther is awarded the prize. However, he is angry with the mastersingers because they had not admitted him to the contest in the first act. He at first refuses the prize, and it takes some very eloquent pleading on the part of Sachs to make him change his mind. Even then Sachs might have failed had not Eva been the great stake that was being played—or sung—for. And so the opera ends, with the people proclaiming their love of the art of music—and of Hans Sachs.

MIGNON

Opera in three acts by Ambroise Thomas with libretto in French by Michel Carré and Jules Barbier, based on Goethe's *Wilhelm Meister*

MIGNON, *a girl stolen by the gypsies*	*Mezzo-soprano*
WILHELM MEISTER, *a student*	*Tenor*
PHILINE, *an actress*	*Soprano*
FRÉDÉRIC, *a young nobleman*	*Tenor or Contralto*
LAERTE, *an actor*	*Tenor*
LOTHARIO, *a wandering harper*	*Bass*
JARNO, *leader of the gypsies*	*Bass*

Time: 18th century
Places: Germany and Italy
First performance at Paris, November 17, 1866

Once upon a time there were a couple of literary hacks named Michel Carré and Jules Barbier. In the middle of the nineteenth century they took great works of literature and made French opera librettos out of them. Many of these mutilated works became famous French operas. One was *Romeo and Juliet,* another was *Hamlet,* a third was *Faust,* a fourth was *Wilhelm Meister.* This last was Goethe's novel—very philosophical, very tragic. But when our friends the librettists were through with it, it was very unphilosophical and quite gay. Its name as well as its nature was changed: it was called *Mignon.* It was set to music by Ambroise Thomas, and it became one of the most popular operas France ever produced. Since its premiere in 1866 it has had over 2000 performances at the Opéra Comique alone. That's an even longer run than *South Pacific* had on Broadway.

ACT I

The story takes place in eighteenth-century Germany, and after the popular overture, which features the most familiar tunes in the opera, the action opens gaily in the courtyard of an inn. A troupe of gypsies is there, led by a ruffian named Jarno. He tries to make a mysterious and lovely little gypsy girl dance. This is Mignon, the heroine; and when Jarno threatens to beat her, enter our hero, the tenor, Wilhelm Meister. He saves her from Jarno, and eventually he buys her freedom.

Meantime, there is also a company of traveling actors at the inn. The leading lady is Philine, a gay coloratura soprano who is perpetually either giggling or singing scales and roulades. Her friend and leading man is young Laerte, whose interest in her is strictly platonic. Therefore, he looks on amused as Philine proceeds to snare the interest of that solemn, handsome, and comfortably off young student, Wilhelm Meister. Philine also has an aristocratic young fool hanging about her —one Frédéric, nephew of the Baron Rosenberg. And when, toward the end of the act, Philine receives a letter from Frédéric's uncle inviting the actors' troupe to his castle, everyone accepts. Wilhelm is to go along as the poet of the troupe, and Mignon will be his servant, dressed as a boy. Thus the act ends, with everyone off to the Château Rosenberg. I have, however, deliberately omitted to mention one other important character. He is an old harper named Lothario, and he is a little touched from grief. Apparently he has a special interest in Mignon, and he does his best to protect her. Every time a harp is heard prominently in the orchestra, one also hears Lothario's bass voice singing. At the end of the act he goes off by himself—but more of him later.

Mignon's touching aria *Connais-tu le pays* occurs about the middle of the act. In it she tells Wilhelm of a country she remembers—one where she lived very well indeed. But, like Lothario, she is a bit vague about her past. There is also a very lovely duet between Mignon and Lothario (*Légères hirondeles*) that has some of the same quality.

Scene 1 takes place in the castle of the Baron Rosenberg. The boudoir of the Baroness has been turned over to the actress, Philine, for the occasion. There is to be a performance of *A Midsummer Night's Dream* that evening, and Philine is making herself up as her fellow-actor Laerte makes jokes with her. Mignon, now dressed as a page for Wilhelm Meister, is teased by Philine. Wilhelm defends the little girl again; but it is obvious that he is falling madly in love with Philine, and poor little Mignon is desperately jealous. When she is left alone, she starts to dress herself in some of Philine's finery, and as she does so, she sings a charming little air, a *Styrienne*. But she is interrupted when the Baron's nephew, Fred Rosenberg, quarrels with Wilhelm over Philine. And when Mignon interferes, Frédéric goes off laughing.

Now Wilhelm, seeing Mignon dressed like a woman, believes he can no longer keep her in his service. He sings her a sad aria of farewell (*Adieu, Mignon, ne pleurez pas*). He does not realize how deeply she loves him. Condescendingly he tells her that at her age she will soon forget. But before she leaves, Philine taunts her once more; and now Wilhelm, seeing that Mignon is genuinely jealous, begins to have his eyes open. But it is time to get ready for the play. Laerte summons Philine for the show, and they all go out as the orchestra murmurs the tune of the *Gavotte*. All, that is, but Mignon. She has one last line: *"That Philine: I hate her!"*

Scene 2 takes place outside the castle and by a lake. Poor Mignon has not been invited to the performance of *A Midsummer Night's Dream*, and she thinks of how her beloved Wilhelm seems to have fallen in love with the coquettish actress Philine. She sings her sad aria *Elle est aimée* and then is joined by her old and harmlessly crazy protector, Lothario. He, too, is suffering; and they tell us all about it in the duet *As-tu souffert?* Meantime, applause is heard from within the castle, and Mignon carelessly utters the wish that the place would burn down.

But now the performance is over. Philine has had a triumph, and to everyone's approval she sings *Je suis Titania*. It is one of the gayest—and most popular—showpieces in the repertoire of any coloratura soprano.

Unfortunately, Philine orders Mignon to go back to the castle to fetch a bouquet she had left. It happens to be a bouquet Mignon had picked for Wilhelm, who had lightheartedly handed it over to Philine; but, to be entirely fair, Philine did not know its origin when she sent Mignon to fetch it. Before the young girl can come back, the castle bursts into flames. Who had set fire to it? The half-demented Lothario, of course. The heroic young Wilhelm dashes back into the castle, rescues little Mignon, and comes back carrying her in his arms. In her hands are Philine's withered flowers.

ACT III

The last act transports us from Germany to Italy. It begins with the familiar sound of Lothario's harp as he sings a sweet lullaby for Mignon. He has brought her to this country she once knew—the country she sang of so sweetly in the aria *Connais-tu le pays*. Wilhelm is there too. He now knows that Mignon loves him, and he has decided he loves her, too. But it appears to be too late. Mignon, after her dreadful experiences, has not yet recovered her mind, and Wilhelm sings the aria *C'est en vain que j'attends*—"I wait in vain." And when a pale, suffering Mignon appears, he tries to tell her he loves her, but she cannot believe him. Off-stage, comes the voice of Philine, singing *Je suis Titania*, and her presence is proof enough for poor little Mignon.

But now—wonder of wonders—the crazy old Lothario appears dressed like a noble lord. It turns out that he was a wealthy nobleman all the time, that he had temporarily lost his mind, and that Mignon is his own daughter. Naturally, everyone, including even Mignon, finds this a little difficult to believe. But Lothario shows her a child's scarf she once owned, a coral bracelet, a prayerbook. He utters her old name, Sperata—and finally he shows her a portrait of her mother. Now everything comes back to the girl's shaken mind. It is almost too much joy for her to bear. But Wilhelm takes her in his arms; she recovers quickly; and the opera closes with a trio of rejoicing.

NORMA

Opera in four acts (originally in two, but divided into four scenes) by Vincenzo Bellini with libretto in Italian by Felice Romani, based on a French play of the same name by Louis Alexandre Soumet

NORMA, *High Priestess of the druidical temple*   Soprano
OROVESO, *her father, the Archdruid*   Bass
CLOTILDA, *her confidante*   Soprano
POLLIONE, *Roman Proconsul in Gaul*   Tenor
ADALGISA, *a virgin of the temple*   Soprano or Mezzo-soprano
FLAVIO, *a centurion*   Tenor

Time: about 50 B.C.
Place: Gaul
First performance at Milan, December 26, 1831

Like the rest of the world, Bellini himself regarded *Norma* as his masterpiece. If on a shipwrecked boat, he once said, he had only one of his operas to rescue, that one would be *Norma*.

And though today it strikes most of us as a vehicle for a great soprano, with some very wonderful arias and concerted numbers but with the most unrealistic and formalized plot, it was not always so. "This opera among all the creations of Bellini," wrote one nineteenth-century critic, "is the one which, with the most profound reality, joins to the richest vein of melody the most intimate passion." The critic was Richard Wagner.

Whatever one may think of the way the composer took dramatic advantage of the genuinely dramatic situations offered him by the librettist, his score has always presented a worthy challenge to the greatest singers for more than a century and a quarter. The first Norma was Giuditta Pasta, who saved the first performances in both Milan and London through her magnificent performance. It later became one of her best-loved roles; and when she was too old to sing it, the most-admired Norma became Giulia Grisi, who had sung the role of Adalgisa at the premiere. María Malibran also liked to star in the role—so much so that the memorial statue erected to her by her husband at Laeken presents her in the costume of Norma. Jenny Lind often attempted the role, though one would hardly think that the Swedish nightingale's generally placid stage temperament would suit the passionate Druid priestess; and Lilli Lehmann sang it often but had so much respect for its difficulties that she said it took more out of her than singing all three of the *Ring's* Brünnhildes.

In more recent times revivals of the opera have been especially staged for such outstanding sopranos as Rosa Raisa, Rosa Ponselle, and Zinka Milanov. And in 1956, after years of dickering with Maria Meneghini Callas, the Metropolitan finally secured her signature to a contract to open as Norma. She had a triumph.

OVERTURE

The overture used to occupy a fairly prominent place in the standard repertoire of popular concerts. As the opera deals in conflicts between martial and amatory sentiments, the music of the overture presents a similar contrast, and it also makes use of the opening chorus of the Druid priests.

ACT I

The story takes us back to approximately 50 B.C., when, as you may recall from your high-school Caesar, the Roman legions were busy occupying Gaul. It is nighttime, and the Druids, to martial music, gather in their sacred forest, before the sacred tree of their god, Irminsul. They are led by their high priest, Oroveso, who expects them to rise against the Romans. He tells them that Norma, the High Priestess and his own daughter, will, at the right moment, perform the rite of cutting the sacred mistletoe, and this shall be the signal for the rising.

When the Druids have departed, the Roman proconsul, Pollione, enters with his friend, the centurion Flavio. From their conversation we learn that Pollione is, secretly, the father of Norma's two children, but he is now in love with the vestal virgin Adalgisa. In the aria *Meco all'altar di Venere* he relates how his dream of being with Adalgisa in Rome bothers his conscience. At its close we hear the sacred bronze shield sounding to summon the Druids once more, and the two Romans depart.

The familiar *March* from *Norma* is now played, as the Druids gather once more to listen to their priestess. In a noble recitative, Norma tells them that the time to rise has not yet come, for Rome is to be defeated by its own vices. Then follows the famous aria *Casta Diva*, which Bellini is said to have rewritten eight times before he was satisfied with it. She begins by invoking the moon and calling for peace. Then, as the chorus cries out against the Romans, she sings—for herself alone—of the love she bears the Roman proconsul, Pollione.

When the priests have again departed, Adalgisa, Pollione's new love, is left alone, and she prays for help from the gods. There Pollione finds her; and in the eloquent duet that closes the act (*Va, crudele*) he persuades her to follow him to Rome.

ACT II

Norma has raised the Roman Pollione's two children in a secret home with the aid of her confidante, Clotilda. As the second act opens, she tells Clotilda that she both loves and hates these children, for she fears that Pollione will leave for Rome and desert her. Now the young priestess, Adalgisa, sworn to chastity, enters. She confides in Norma, saying that she is in love. Norma, commiserating, promises to release her from her vows, but Adalgisa mentions that her lover is about to depart for Rome. At once Norma is suspicious. Who can this lover be? "There he is," says Adalgisa as Pollione enters. An exciting trio develops, as Norma curses Pollione for his faithlessness, Pollione, conscience-stricken, begs Norma not to reproach him before Adalgisa, and Adalgisa herself is filled with remorse. The sacred bronze shield is heard once more, as it is struck to summon Norma to her priestly duties, and the act closes.

ACT III

It is nighttime in Norma's secret home, and after a prelude she enters carrying a lamp in one hand and a dagger in the other. To revenge herself on the faithless Pollione, the High Priestess has decided to murder their two children as they sleep. But as she bends over them, she cannot bring herself to do the horrid deed, for they are not only Pollione's children, they are her own as well. Quickly she sends Clotilda for Adalgisa. Norma has decided to die, and she commands Adalgisa to marry Pollione and take the children with her. Moved by Norma's nobility, Adalgisa refuses. In the great duet *Mira, O Norma*, she begs for pity on the two children, and she offers to bring Pollione back to Norma. The act closes as the two priestesses embrace.

ACT IV

The last, dramatic act takes place, like the first, in the sacred forest of the Druids, before the altar of the great god Irminsul. The assembled warriors of Gaul cry for war against the Romans. Oroveso, the High Priest and father of Norma, alone advises patience. They leave; and then, at the altar itself, Norma awaits Pollione's return. But her confidante, Clotilda, brings news that Adalgisa has failed—that Pollione refuses to return to Norma. In great anger Norma now summons the priests and soldiers by striking the sacred shield. She calls for war—*Guerra, guerra!*—and for blood—*Sangue, sangue!*

At this point Clotilda reports that a Roman has been found in the cloister of the Druid virgins. Pollione turns out to be the transgressor, and the Gauls demand his death. But Norma desires first to question him alone. She offers her former lover either death or his life—if he will leave Gaul without Adalgisa. Pollione scorns this offer: he is not afraid to die. But when Norma threatens to take the life of Adalgisa as well, he attempts to seize her sword. Norma thereupon summons the soldiers and priests once more. She tells them that a priestess has violated her vows, and that she must be burned to death. Pollione, believing her to be about to name Adalgisa as the erring priestess, tries to stop her. But with a great gesture Norma announces that she herself is the offending priestess, and that she must die—and she commends the care of her children to her father, Oroveso.

Only then does Pollione understand the greatness of the woman's spirit, and he says that he will die with her. The funeral pyre is prepared, and—united again—the lovers, Norma and Pollione, mount to their death.

Postscript for the historically curious: "About 50 B.C." a distinguished Roman politician and poet, still in his twenties, was appointed by Mark Antony as proconsul for a portion of Gaul. The young man's name was Gaius Asinius Pollio ("Pollione" in French); he survived his term of office among the Druids; he became a consul of Rome ten years later; and he died peacefully in his Italian villa at the age of eighty-one, full of honors, mostly literary.

OBERON

Opera in three acts by Carl Maria von Weber
with libretto in English by James Robinson
Planché based on a medieval French tale entitled *Huon de Bordeaux*

SIR HUON OF BORDEAUX	*Tenor*
SHERASMIN, *his squire*	*Baritone*
OBERON, *King of the Fairies*	*Tenor*
PUCK	*Contralto*
REZIA, *daughter of Haroun el Rashid*	*Soprano*
FATIMA, *her attendant*	*Mezzo-soprano*
CHARLEMAGNE, *Emperor of the Franks*	*Bass*
HAROUN EL RASHID, *Caliph of Bagdad*	*Bass*
BABEKAN, *a Saracen prince, fiancé of Rezia*	*Baritone*
ALMANZOR, *Emir of Tunis*	*Baritone*
ROSHANA, *wife of Almanzor*	
TITANIA, *Oberon's wife*	*Speaking parts*
NAMOUNA, *Fatima's grandmother*	

Time: *9th century, if any*
Places: *Fairyland, Bagdad, Tunis, the court of Charlemagne*
First performance at London, April 12, 1826

James Robinson Planché, who concocted the dreamlike,
romantic semi-drama which forms the libretto of *Oberon,* was
an antiquary of some distinction, a successful playwright, and
an important innovator in the London theater. He was the
first man in the history of the English stage to costume a historical play in something like the clothes the characters might
actually have worn. (The play was Shakespeare's *King John,*

the producer Charles Kemble.) He also developed a form of theatrical entertainment, part music, part dancing, part acting, all romantic, which is now known as "the pantomime," a peculiarly British institution to which English mamas in huge numbers still take their children in still larger numbers every Christmas.

Oberon is very much like a pantomime: most of its characters sing, but others don't; there is opportunity for spectacle and ballet; there is magic; there is a joyful ending. Yet its nature is not so different from that of *Der Freischütz* as to have caused Weber any feeling of oddness when he received the book. Kemble, who had been much impressed by that opera, traveled to Germany to persuade Weber to compose an opera especially for Covent Garden, and the subject of Oberon was one of the two he suggested, the other being Faust. Weber chose Oberon, and Kemble chose Planché to write the book.

Both librettist and composer were highly conscientious men. When Planché had written it in English (he was an Englishman, despite his name), he translated it into French especially for Weber and sent it to him. But Weber had, in the meantime, gone to the trouble of learning English, and wrote his collaborator the following charming acknowledgment: "I thank you obligingly for your goodness of having translated the verses in French; but it was not so necessary, because I am, though yet a weak, however, a diligent student of the English language."

It was this very conscientiousness of Weber's which puts a sad ending to our story. Not yet forty, he was a very sick man when he undertook Kemble's commission. Nevertheless, he wrote the music in six weeks, went to London to supervise every one of the fifteen rehearsals, conducted a round dozen performances of it as well as several concerts, and then quietly died. He knew perfectly well that he stood little chance of surviving, but he forced himself to the effort. The $5355 he earned from his three months in London were a godsend to his impoverished wife and children.

The spectacular nature of the opera and the severe demands it makes on the leading soprano and tenor have given pause to many an imaginative impresario who has thought of reviving it, and many revivals of the past have severely modified the work in one way or another. Even then they have failed as often as not. But in the mid 1950's the Paris Opéra mounted it as a spectacle so grand that the wonderful score was, apparently, the smallest attraction for the huge crowds that went to see it. Maybe there really is no way to rescue the music from the rest of the show, excepting to play the overture and to sing the one great soprano aria at concerts. That is practically all that most of us ever hear of it.

OVERTURE

Experienced concert-goers are so accustomed to the *Oberon Overture* as standard fare that they seldom think of the music as made up out of specific dramatic ingredients. Yet, on looking into the score of the opera itself or hearing it performed in its entirety, one finds that each of the thrice-familiar themes is associated with some dramatically significant part of the tale. Thus, the soft opening horn call is the tune played by the hero's own magical horn; the quickly descending chords in the woodwinds are used to paint the background of the fairy kingdom; the excited upclimbing violins that open the *allegro* are used to accompany the lovers' flight to the ship; the beautiful, prayer-like melody played first by a solo clarinet and then the strings turns out indeed to be the hero's prayer; while the triumphant theme with a kind of gulpy effect, played quietly at first and then with a joyous fortissimo, reappears as the climax of the great soprano aria *Ocean, thou mighty monster.*

ACT I

Scene 1 In the bower of King Oberon of the Fairies, the monarch lies sleeping while a group of his supernatural attendants sings for him. That handy fairy-of-all-work, Puck, tells us that Oberon and his Queen Titania have quarreled, and the King has sworn never to be reconciled till he has found a pair of mortal lovers who will be faithful unto death or the next thing to it.

When Oberon awakens, repentant over this arrangement, Puck tells him about a young knight of legend named Huon of Bordeaux. This hero has, in fair fight, killed a son of Charlemagne's, and that great monarch has sentenced Huon to go to Bagdad, kill whoever is sitting on the Caliph's right-hand side, and marry the Caliph's daughter. Oberon sees this as a opportunity for fulfilling his vow and, with his supernatural powers, magically produces Huon and his squire Sherasmin, both of them sound asleep. In their sleep, Oberon shows them a vision of the Caliph's daughter, Rezia by name, who calls for help. When the vision has disappeared, Huon is awakened, told to rescue the girl, and given a magical horn to help him when there is need. The scene closes as Huon, musically assisted by the chorus, joyfully accepts the assignment. Oberon wafts him off to Bagdad.

Scene 2 In a purely dramatic episode—that is, the lines are spoken and there is no accompanying music—Sir Huon rescues an unknown dark gentleman from a lion. When the danger is over, the stranger turns out to be a Saracen prince named Babekan, who is engaged to marry the lovely Rezia. Babekan, a nasty fellow, attacks Huon, calling on his followers for assistance, but our doughty hero and his squire defeat the unthankful villain.

Scene 3 Huon meets an old crone named Namouna, who is the grandmother of Rezia's pretty attendant, Fatima. Thus Namouna is in a position to know all the court gossip, and she tells him that Rezia and Babekan are to be married the very next day. However, it appears that the bride has seen Huon in a vision and has sworn to belong to no one but him. The scene, like the previous one, has been carried on in spoken dialogue up to this point; but when Huon is left alone, he has a long aria, and a very difficult one, in which he strengthens his resolution to win the girl.

Scene 4 In her chamber in the palace of Haroun el Rashid, Rezia tells her handmaiden Fatima that she will never marry anyone but Sir Huon, and that she will die before being wed to Babekan. Fatima tells her that help is at hand; the two girls sing a duet; a march, sung off-stage, is heard; and Rezia sings joyfully over it.

Scene 1   In the throne room of Haroun el Rashid a chorus is sung in praise of the fabled Caliph. Babekan asks that there be no more delay in his marriage to Rezia, and the fair bride, preceded by dancing girls, comes sorrowfully in. But outside one hears the sound of the rescuers. They fight their way in; Huon finds Babekan sitting at the Caliph's right-hand side and slays him; he blows on his magical horn, thus temporarily paralyzing everyone else; and then he and Sherasmin run off with Rezia and Fatima.

Scene 2   Outside the palace the guards try to hinder the four fugitives, but Huon's horn solves this problem for them too—though, in the confusion, he manages somehow to lose that valuable musical instrument. Fatima and Sherasmin find that they are falling in love, like their master and mistress, and sing a love duet, and there is also a quartet for all four of the lovers. They then board a ship.

Scene 3   To make sure that his chosen sample of lovers-unto-death is the genuine article, Oberon has prepared another severe test. Puck and his fairy band raise a huge storm, causing the ship on which the lovers are fleeing to sink. Huon, however, manages to drag an exhausted Rezia to shore, where she recovers after a touching prayer sung by her lover. He then goes off in search of Sherasmin and Fatima, and Rezia is left alone to sing the most famous aria in the opera (*Ocean, thou mighty monster*), a long, varied, and very dramatic address to the ocean. At its close (which is like the close of the even more famous overture), she sights a ship. This, alas, turns out to be a pirate ship. The pirates land and are bundling up Rezia for an abduction when Huon rushes back and attacks. However, he is outnumbered; and as he has lost his trusty horn, he also loses the battle and is left on the shore for dead as the pirates embark with their captive.

But the act closes on a softer note. Puck returns, bringing the fairies and Oberon with him. The two principals sing a duet; the fairies sing a chorus; everyone on the stage is satisfied with the way the machinations are going; and everyone in the audience is enchanted with the fairylike atmosphere projected by the music.

ACT III

The pirates have sold Rezia into slavery in Tunis, where Fatima and Sherasmin have undergone the same fate. The two junior lovers are, fortunately, working for a good-natured North African named Ibrahim (who never appears on the stage), and their duet indicates that they are not too unhappy in their captivity.

Puck, according to plan, brings Huon in to them. He learns that Rezia is said to be somewhere in the same town, and so they plan to get him into Ibrahim's service so that he may look around. (The whole situation here, as well as some of what follows, is strikingly similar to the happenings in Mozart's *Abduction from the Seraglio*.)

Scene 2 Rezia's new master turns out to be the Emir of Tunis himself, whose name is Almanzor. At his palace Rezia is sorrowfully bemoaning her fate, when Almanzor comes in to tell her that, though he loves her, he will not force his attentions on her.

Scene 3 In a brief scene, back at Ibrahim's, Huon receives a message couched in the flower-language of the East, which Fatima has to interpret for him. It is from Rezia, who summons him to come to her. Ecstatically he goes.

Scene 4 But at the Emir's palace he is met not by Rezia but by Roshana, the Emir's justly jealous wife. Roshana offers him herself and her throne if he will kill Almanzor, but not even the seductive dancing of the Emiress and her female attendants can mislead our faithful hero. He starts to rush from the room, but just then the Emir comes in with his guard and Huon is made captive. When Roshana tries, hereupon, to stab her husband, things look very black. She is led away, and Huon is condemned to be burned alive. Rezia tries desperately to plead for him, but Almanzor, who has now turned stern, only condemns her to the same horrid death.

But somehow and somewhere Sherasmin has found the good old horn still in working order. He arrives on the scene at the critical moment, bringing Fatima with him; he sounds the horn; all the Africans are paralyzed; and the four lovers decide it is time to call upon Oberon for help. (After all, he is to blame for all their discomforts.)

Oberon graciously appears, like the god out of the machine at the end of a Greek tragedy, and immediately transports them to the court of Charlemagne. Huon reports his mission accomplished; he is duly forgiven; and the opera closes with a grand chorus of rejoicing.

Postscript for the historically curious: The only unquestionably historical figures among the *dramatis personnae* are Charlemagne, who flourished in the ninth century, and Haroun, who flourished in the eighth. No early Victorian like Planché could, unaided, have dreamed up anything quite so wildly romantic as the plot of *Oberon*. Most of its main incidents may be found in the thirteenth-century *chanson de geste* of *Huon de Bordeaux*, where our hero is an even more wildly improbable figure than he is here. A summary of the history of this hero of romance may be conveniently found in Bulfinch.

ORPHEUS AND EURYDICE

(*Orfeo ed Euridice*)

Opera in three acts by Christoph Willibald von
Gluck with libretto in Italian by Raniero da
Calzabigi based on Greek mythology

ORPHEUS, *a singer*	*Contralto (or Tenor)*
EURYDICE, *his wife*	*Soprano*
AMOR, *the god of love*	*Soprano*
A HAPPY SHADE	*Soprano*

Time: Mythological antiquity
Places: Greece and Hades
First performance at Vienna, October 5, 1762

Orpheus was the greatest human musician of Greek mythology. In fact, he was so great that a religion—Orphism—was
founded, and Orpheus was worshiped as a god some twenty-
five hundred years ago. Naturally, therefore, his story has always been a logical one for opera composers. In fact, the oldest
operatic score in existence is based on the story—Jacopo Peri's
L'Euridice. It dates from 1600, and several more operas on the
same subject were written soon after. Eighteenth- and nineteenth-century composers continued to deal with it, and so has
the modernist Darius Milhaud.

But the only version often heard nowadays is Gluck's—*Orfeo
ed Euridice*. It is also the oldest opera in the standard repertoire, dating from 1762. On October 5 of that year the composer conducted the world premiere in Vienna. The language
was Italian, and the role of Orpheus was sung by Gaetano
Guadagni, a castrato—that is, a male alto. When, later on, the
opera was given in France, where *castrati* were not accepted on

the stage, Gluck rewrote the part for a tenor. But in modern times, outside of France, the Italian version is usually used, and the role of Orpheus is sung by a contralto—a female contralto, of course.

Gluck and his librettist, Raniero da Calzabigi, omitted many details of the legendary story, and so there is not too much action on the stage. Instead, there is a good deal of choral singing (especially in Act I), and a good deal of ballet. On account of the lack of action the opera is well adapted for concert form and for phonograph records.

ACT I

Orpheus has just lost his beautiful wife Eurydice, and the opera opens, after a rather cheerful overture, in the grotto before her tomb. First with a chorus of nymphs and shepherds, and later on alone, he bitterly mourns her death. Finally, he decides to win her back from the gods of the underworld by invading Hades armed only with tears, courage, and a lyre. But the gods have mercy on him. Amor, the little god of love (that is, Cupid), tells him that he may descend to the Inferno. There he must play his lyre and sing sweetly, and the local officials will be moved to give her up. Only one condition is made: he must on no account look at Eurydice before he has led her safely back to earth. It is a condition that Orpheus knows he may find hard to fulfill; and he prays for help as drums suggest the thunder and lightning that mark the beginning of his dangerous journey.

ACT II

The second act takes us to the underworld—Hades—where Orpheus first wins over the Furies, or Eumenides, and then receives his bride, Eurydice, from the Blessed Spirits. The chorus of the Furies is dramatic and fearsome; but gradually, as Orpheus plays the lyre and sings, the Eumenides relent. It is extraordinarily simple music that paints this dramatic contrast, for the same rhythmical pattern is used throughout. At the close the Furies dance to a ballet that Gluck had composed sometime earlier to describe Don Juan's descent into hell.

Then comes the very familiar *Dance of the Blessed Spirits*, with its eloquent flute solo. After Orpheus has departed with the Furies, Eurydice sings together with the Blessed Spirits of their quiet life in the Elysian fields. Then, when they in turn have departed, Orpheus comes in alone; and as he sings of the beauty of the sky and sun in this place (*Che puro ciel, che chiaro sol!*), the orchestra seems to play a hymn to the delights of nature. Drawn by his singing, the Blessed Spirits return once more, bringing Eurydice with them; and as the act ends, Orpheus leads her off, carefully averting his eyes, as the gods have decreed.

ACT III

The last act begins with Orpheus leading his wife back to earth through gloomy passages, twisted paths, and dangerous, overhanging cliffs. Eurydice does not know that the gods have decreed that he must not once look upon her before they are safely back on earth. She is slowly changing from a Blessed Spirit (which she was in Act II) into a real, living, warm-blooded woman, and she bitterly complains of her husband's treatment. Does he no longer love her? she asks. As Orpheus alternately urges her on and complains to the gods, she becomes more and more urgent. Finally, she tries to send him away: she prefers death to this treatment, and their voices join together at this dramatic moment. At last, Orpheus defies the gods. He turns toward Eurydice; he takes her in his arms; and the moment he touches her, she dies. Now comes the most famous part of the opera—the aria *Che farò senza Euridice*—"I have lost my Eurydice." In desperation Orpheus is about to stab himself; but at the last moment, the little god Love, Amor, appears, brings Eurydice back to life, and restores her to her husband. The gods, he says, have been so much impressed with his constancy they have decided to reward him.

The final scene of the opera, which takes place in the Temple of Amor, is a series of solos, choruses, and dances in praise of Love. It is a far happier ending than the one given us by mythology. In that one Eurydice remains dead, and Orpheus is torn to pieces by a band of Thracian women who cannot bear his constant mellifluous mourning. The eighteenth century, however, liked to have happy endings to its tragic operas.

OTELLO

(Othello)

Opera in four acts by Giuseppe Verdi with libretto in Italian by Arrigo Boito based on Shakespeare's play

OTELLO, *a Moor, general in the Venetian Army*	*Tenor*
DESDEMONA, *his wife*	*Soprano*
IAGO, *his ensign*	*Baritone*
CASSIO, *his lieutenant*	*Tenor*
EMILIA, *Iago's wife*	*Mezzo-soprano*
RODERIGO, *a Venetian gentleman*	*Tenor*
LODOVICO, *Ambassador of Venetian Republic*	*Bass*
MONTANO, *predecessor of Otello in Cyprus*	*Bass*
A HERALD	*Bass*

Time: end of 15th century
Place: Cyprus
First performance at Milan, February 5, 1887

In the history of opera Verdi's *Otello* is really something of a miracle. In 1871, *Aïda* had been produced. Close to sixty then, and full of honors, the composer had apparently retired. Younger men were coming up. Verdi no longer competed. Some even thought him a little old-fashioned. Then—fifteen years later—on February 5, 1887—*Otello* was produced. It was a new opera, in a new style, full of vitality—and the composer was in his seventy-fourth year!

Verdi had, as his collaborator, one of those very composers who once thought him old-fashioned. This was Arrigo Boito, composer of *Mefistofele* (see p. 325). But this time Boito did not compose a note. He was the librettist; that is, he adapted

Shakespeare's great tragedy for Verdi's operatic masterpiece. A fine job he did, too. In most operatic adaptations of Shakespeare very little is left of the great poetry and drama, but Boito managed to maintain most of the dramatic qualities of the original, and Verdi's music is completely worthy of one of the finest tragedies in any language.

ACT I

As it takes longer to sing anything than to say it, Boito had to condense Shakespeare's play. He omitted (excepting for a few references) the entire first act, and so the opera opens on the island of Cyprus. A terrific storm is raging as the population watches Otello's ship battling its way into port. Finally he arrives safely, and he comes on the stage announcing a victory over the storm, and over the Turks, with his great cry, *"Esultate!"* Then, after a pleasant chorus sung as the people build bonfires, the familiar plot develops quickly enough. Iago, the officer who is jealous of his Moorish general, Otello, is, of course, the villain. He has the support of a foolish young man, Roderigo, who hopes to seduce Otello's beautiful bride, Desdemona. Iago is particularly angry because Cassio, another officer, has been promoted above him, and he now proceeds to get Cassio drunk. It is at this point that Iago sings his drinking song, an appropriately cynical passage in which others join in. Iago, furthermore, manages to provoke a quarrel between Cassio and Montano, another officer, and at the height of the racket, when Montano is wounded, Otello returns to the scene. He dismisses the drunken Cassio for such unsoldierly conduct, and he orders Iago to take over and bring quiet to the city.

And then, when all have gone, the act closes with one of the most beautiful love duets in all of opera. Otello is reunited with his young and deeply loved bride, Desdemona. They recall the details of their strange courtship, and the duet ends as the skies have cleared and the stars shine out.

ACT II

Act II of Boito's libretto follows quite closely the plot as it is given in Shakespeare's Act III. Cassio wants his commission back, and as the act opens off a garden in a hall of the palace, Iago pretends friendship to Cassio and offers some good advice. Go to Otello's wife, Desdemona, he says, and ask her to plead for you. Cassio acts on this advice at once, going into the garden to await the lady. At this point the libretto makes its most striking departure from the play. Iago sings his great *Credo*, in which he tells the audience quite frankly that he believes in a god—but it is a cruel god, and Iago acts accordingly.

And now—almost as though in answer to a prayer—Iago has a piece of rare luck. Otello comes by and sees Cassio in the garden, pleading with Desdemona. "Ha—I like not that," says Iago, and he begins to sow the seeds of doubt in Otello's mind. Maybe Cassio is spending a little too much time with Desdemona, he suggests. Oh, he does it ever so reluctantly, ever so politely, and in ever so friendly a fashion. But the poison is surely there. A chorus in praise of the gentle Desdemona is now sung by her ladies, by some sailors, and by some children. It almost persuades Otello that he is foolish to doubt his lovely wife for a moment. Unfortunately, when they meet she immediately pleads for Cassio, and Iago's poison begins to work. Otello becomes angry with his wife, and when she tries to wipe his perspiring brow with her handkerchief, he snatches it from her and throws it to the ground. A fine quartet occurs here, for the scene has been watched by both Iago and his wife Emilia, who is Desdemona's lady-in-waiting.

When the women have left, a powerful duet develops between Otello and his false friend Iago. The villain pretends to soothe the wretched General, but before the scene is over, he has suggested a way in which Desdemona may be tested. He says that he has seen Desdemona's handkerchief in Cassio's possession. (Of course, Iago has it himself at that very moment, for he has recovered it from Emilia, who picked it up.)

If Desdemona cannot produce the handkerchief, suggests Iago subtly, Cassio must have it—and have Desdemona's favor, too. The poor, passionate Otello is now in a fever of doubt and jealousy, and the act closes as their voices join powerfully in a vow of vengeance.

ACT III

Shortly after the curtain rises, Iago promises to let Otello overhear a conversation with Cassio—Cassio, the man whom he thinks to be Desdemona's lover. But even before this eavesdropping can be arranged, Otello gets more food for his jealousy. Desdemona again asks that Cassio be restored in Otello's favor. Enraged, the General asks for his wife's handkerchief, and when she cannot produce it, Otello is more than ever convinced of her guilt. He accuses her boldly, while poor Desdemona, utterly bewildered, pleads her innocence. Finally, he rudely orders her away, and he is badly shaken when Iago returns. The scene is set—says the villain—for the eavesdropping. As Otello hides behind a pillar, Iago engages Cassio in light talk. They are really talking about Bianca, who is Cassio's light-of-love, but Otello, overhearing only snatches of the conversation, thinks they are speaking lightly of his own wife. When, toward the end, Iago produces Desdemona's handkerchief, Otello naturally jumps to the wrong conclusions.

Thus, when an ambassador from Venice is announced, Otello is in a terrible mood. He decides to kill Desdemona that very night. Ironically, at that moment an off-stage chorus hails Otello as the "Lion of St. Mark," and the Ambassador from Venice, Lodovico, enters with the whole populace. There is an order from Venice for Otello to return, and for Cassio to take over the governorship of Cyprus. As Otello reads this order, he keeps a wary eye on his wife. He overhears her commenting on Cassio to Lodovico, and before the whole assembly he strikes her and hurls her to the ground. Everyone is deeply shocked, and a fine, impressive ensemble develops as each expresses his own feelings. Finally, Otello orders them all away.

Left alone with Iago, he rants for blood and vengeance. So

excited does he become that he falls down in a convulsion. Off-stage, the crowd is again hailing the "Lion of St. Mark." But on-stage, Iago triumphs over his fallen General. *Ecco il Leone!*—"Look at the Lion!" he cries with a poisonous arrogance, and the curtain falls.

ACT IV

The brief, touching, violent, and tragic last act is really a combination of two different scenes from Shakespeare's play. It takes place in Desdemona's bedroom, where, with Emilia's help, she is preparing for bed. She sings a sadly appropriate ballad (*The Willow Song*) about Barbara, whose lover went mad. Otello apparently has done the same thing. When Emilia leaves, Desdemona utters her very touching prayer—the *Ave Maria*. She then goes to bed, and a moment or two later (with a sinister passage in the double basses of the orchestra), Otello strides in. He puts out the candle; he kisses her to the melody of the first-act love duet; and then, with a heavy heart, he asks whether she has prayed. Quickly she realizes what is on Otello's mind: he plans to kill her. All her pleas are in vain; everything she gently or fearfully urges is misunderstood; and finally, in a terrible rage, he strangles her.

Silence. Then a knock at the door. It is Emilia, who sees at once what has happened. Yet, Desdemona, with her dying breath, says that she has killed herself. "Liar," cries Otello, "'twas I that killed her!" And when Emilia tries to maintain the innocence of the dead, he threatens her, too. It is only when Lodovico, Cassio, Iago, and all the others are summoned by her cries that Otello finally learns the truth. Aghast and heartbroken, he lays down his sword. He goes to the bed, looks tenderly at the wife he had so dearly loved, and takes out a dagger and stabs himself. "*Un bacio—un altro bacio,*" he sings softly, as he takes a final kiss to the music of the earlier kisses.

PAGLIACCI

Opera in two acts by Ruggiero Leoncavallo
with libretto in Italian by the composer

CANIO, *the heavy lead of the players*	*Tenor*
NEDDA, *his wife and leading lady*	*Soprano*
TONIO, *the clown*	*Baritone*
BEPPE, *the juvenile lead*	*Tenor*
SILVIO, *a villager*	*Baritone*

*Time: the Feast of the Assumption (August 15) in the late
1860's*
*Place: on a crossroad near Montalto, a village in Southern
Italy*
First performance at Milan, May 21, 1892

One usually thinks of *Pagliacci* as beginning with the
famous *Prologue—Il pròlogo*, as Italian baritones denominate
it quite simply. But as a matter of fact, there is a fairly long
introduction to the *Prologue*, and in it are heard all the themes
that will later be developed in the score—the love theme, the
jealousy theme, the players' theme, etc. For the young composer, writing in the 1890's had been bitten by the Wagner
bug and was using the leitmotiv as skillfully as any other fashionable opera man. He was also bitten by the *verismo* bug,
which means that his story would deal with common folks doing ordinary everyday things—like making love to other men's
wives and committing murder.

Pagliacci

Suddenly, in the midst of this orchestral introduction, the character of Tonio, the clown, steps out before the curtain and speaks directly to us. He tells us how the opera was written—from the composer's heart. And in fact, Ruggiero Leoncavallo, who wrote both the libretto and the music, based his story on a criminal case that his own father, a district judge, had tried. Then Tonio goes on to explain that actors have feelings and passions just like everyone else. That is the theme of the entire opera. Finally, Tonio rings up the curtain—at which point there is great applause, for Tonio has finished the *Prologue* and sung a high G.

ACT I

Now the opera itself begins. In a small village in Southern Italy a crowd welcomes a troupe of traveling players. There are shouts as the troupe comes in, and the leader—a powerful tenor much given to hamming—invites everyone to come to the performance that evening. When Tonio, the clown, tries to help the leading lady out of the wagon, the leader kicks him aside. For this leading lady, Nedda, is the wife of the principal, Canio; and Canio warns everyone off his private preserves in the aria *Un tal gioco*. It is not a good idea, he says, to make love to his wife—not anywhere outside of a play, that is. Then he goes off to the village for a drink with friends, and the pretty *Bell Chorus* is sung by those who remain.

Now Nedda, the leading lady, is left alone; and she sings a happy song to the birds, known as the *Ballatella*. It shows her essentially carefree nature. At its close—enter the villain. This is our friend Tonio, the clown, who is an ugly hunchback. He tries desperately to make love to Nedda; but she first laughs at him, and then, when he persists, she sets on him with a whip. Vowing vengeance, he stumps off to the village to join his master.

There follows a long and melodious love duet, for Nedda

has a swain in this village named Silvio. As the duet closes, they make an appointment to meet that night after the performance.

Unfortunately, Tonio has brought back his master just in time to hear those last words. In fearful anger Canio chases after Silvio, but he cannot find him. When he returns, he demands to know the name of Nedda's lover. Steadfastly she refuses to give it, until Canio, fearfully enraged, takes out a wicked-looking knife to threaten her. Nedda's life is saved, however, just in time, by Beppe, another actor in the troupe, the one who plays juvenile leads. He reminds Canio and the others that it is time to prepare for the performance; and as the rest go off, Canio is left alone.

It is then that he has his famous laugh-clown-laugh aria, *Vesti la giubba*. Though his heart is breaking, he knows that the play must go on. Sobbing with anguish, he enters the now-hated theater to dress for his part.

ACT II

Before Act II there is an orchestral intermezzo based on the Prologue. This reminds us of the theme of the opera—that life off the stage is very much like life on it. When the action starts, the villagers are busily assembling for the evening performance outside the temporary stage set up on the roadside. Their hubbub is hushed as the play-within-a-play commences. Nedda, in the role of Columbine, listens to a serenade sung off-stage by Beppe, who plays the role of Columbine's lover, Harlequin. Soon Taddeo—the clown, played by Tonio—comes in to make love to her, just as he did in real life only that afternoon. He is again repulsed, but this time he good-naturedly blesses the lovers. Columbine and Harlequin thereupon sing a pretty duet over their evening meal, when Taddeo, in mock terror, interrupts them. Columbine's husband, Pagliaccio, is coming! Quickly Harlequin exits by the window. But Pagliaccio enters just in time to hear them arrange a rendezvous. This, again, is exactly what had happened that afternoon; in fact, exactly the same words are repeated. Canio tries hard to act the part of Pagliaccio in the play, but the parallel is too terrible for him to bear.

Suddenly he tears off part of his costume and cries: *No, Pagliaccio non son:* "No, I am Pagliaccio no longer." Pitifully, he recalls the early days of his love for Nedda—and the crowd applauds his realistic acting. Now Nedda tries to make him come to his senses by taking up the lines of the play. But Canio becomes more and more furious, demanding to know the name of her lover. Finally he draws out his terrible knife, and before anyone can interfere, he has driven it into her back. With her dying breath Nedda calls for Silvio's help. Silvio rushes up, out of the audience—only to meet the same terrible knife. As Canio realizes that he has committed a double murder, he turns brokenly to the audience. *"La commedia è finita,"* he sobs. "The comedy is finished." And the orchestra blares out the laugh-clown-laugh theme.

Postscript for the historically curious: Leoncavallo, who said he was present, as a small boy, at the trial of "Canio" in his father's court, used to tell the sequel to his tale. The culprit's real name was Alessandro, and he had murdered his wife after the performance, not during it. He was found guilty, sentenced to a term in prison, and then cried: "I do not repent the crime! Quite the contrary: if it had to be done over again, I'd do it!"

After he got out of prison, he did not go back to the stage but became a servant in the ménage of one Baronessa Sproniere.

Catulle Mendès threatened suit for plagiarism against Leoncavallo on the ground of a similarity of situation in his popular drama *La femme de tabarin* (with incidental music by Chabrier). In this play an actor also murders his wife during the course of a play-within-a-play. But there had been a much earlier nineteenth-century work using the same device; and, in fact, the idea goes back at least as far as Thomas Kyd's *Spanish Tragedy.* Eventually Mendès withdrew his charges and offered a handsome apology.

PARSIFAL

Festival stage play in three acts by Richard
Wagner with libretto in German by the composer, based on the poem *Parzifal* by Wolfram
von Eschenbach, on *Perceval, ou le conte
du Grail* by Chrétien de Troyes, and the
Mabinogion

AMFORTAS, *King of Monsalvat*	Baritone
TITUREL, *founder and former King of the Grail*	Bass
GURNEMANZ, *a veteran knight of the Grail*	Bass
KLINGSOR, *a magician*	Baritone
PARSIFAL, *the "pure fool"*	Tenor
KUNDRY, *a sorceress*	Soprano

Time: the Middle Ages
Place: Spain
First performance at Bayreuth, July 26, 1882

Wagner did not call this work an "opera" but a "festival
stage play." Legend has it that he regarded it so much as a
sort of religious ceremony, rather than entertainment, that he
insisted on there being no applause and that it should never
be given in any opera house less consecrated to noble music
than his own Festspielhaus at Bayreuth, where only works by
the master were to be performed.

The fact is, however, that Wagner himself liked to lead the
applause at the end of the second act; and while the prohibition against applause is generally followed today after Act I
(at least by that part of the audience which is aware of the
tradition), everyone voices approval of the Flower Maidens

after Act II, and Act III is also generally clapped, though not at the august Metropolitan Opera House. As for the prohibition against playing *Parsifal* outside of Bayreuth, Wagner did have that idea once, but shortly before his death he seems to have given oral consent to the tenor-impresario Angelo Neumann to take it on the road. The change of heart never evolved into a written contract, and so that first extra-Bayreuth production took place at the Metropolitan on Christmas Eve twenty-one years after the premiere and over the futile legal gestures of Wagner's widow. It was a gala and vulgarly publicized occasion. A special "Parsifal Limited" express was chartered from Chicago; the *Evening Telegram* brought out a "Parsifal" extra; and premium prices were put upon seats.

The religious and philosophical ideas of the libretto are a mixture of Christianity and Buddhism, while the symbolism of the cup and the spear is still older. But as the trappings of the Wolfram poem which inspired the story are essentially Christian, it is most convenient to remember that the beneficent Grail is the cup from which Jesus drank at the Last Supper and in which Joseph of Arimathea is supposed to have caught His blood, while the spear is the one which pierced His side on the cross.

PRELUDE

The prelude, a slow, religious tone poem, is based on the themes sometimes identified as the motives of the *Love Feast*, the *Spear*, the *Grail* (which is the famous *Dresden Amen*), and *Faith*. Wagner himself wrote a close for the prelude to be used in concerts, but when it is played in the opera house, the curtain rises on an unresolved chord.

ACT I

Scene 1 is near the castle of the Holy Grail at Monsalvat, in Spain. Gurnemanz, one of the knights of the Holy Grail, and several followers offer their morning prayers. They are ready to help Amfortas, the King of the Grail, to bathe in the lake nearby, hoping to ease the pain of his wound. Kundry, a weird, ill-kempt woman, interrupts them. She, who serves both the Knights of the Grail and their enemy, Klingsor, has brought balsam from Arabia to help heal Amfortas. The King, who is now carried in on a litter, wishes to thank the woman, though he despairs of all help.

When he has gone, Gurnemanz tells his squires some of the history of the Grail. Old Titurel, the father of Amfortas, had received two holy treasures, the Cup—or Grail—from which Jesus drank at the Last Supper, and the Spear which pierced His side. To guard these, Titurel built the sanctuary of Monsalvat and gathered a brotherhood of knights. Now Titurel has grown too old for his office, and Amfortas is King. But there had been a villain—Klingsor. He had failed, through his bad character, to be made a knight of the Grail, and, as a sorcerer, he had acted the part of enemy to the whole group. With the aid of beautiful women he had enticed Amfortas into his magical garden; he had captured the Spear; and he had inflicted the wound on Amfortas from which he still suffers. Only the recapture of the Spear and the aid of a pure and guileless innocent—or fool—can save the King and the order of knights.

At the end of Gurnemanz's narrative there is a cry from the lake, and a dying swan falls before them. A youth follows quickly; and when Gurnemanz upbraids him for killing the bird, he cries out in his ignorance—for he knows nothing of evil. In fact, this lad, who is Parsifal, does not know even the names of his parents. Kundry, however, seems to know about him, and she tells him that his mother has died. It now seems to Gurnemanz that this boy may, indeed, be the guileless fool to save Amfortas. Solemnly he leads him to the castle, and the eloquent *Transformation Music*, during the change of scene, is heard.

Scene 2 Within the castle, in the great hall of the Holy Grail, the knights are assembled. Old Titurel, as though speaking from a tomb, urges his son to proceed with the ceremony. At first Amfortas demurs: he feels unworthy. But presently the Cup is revealed; the consecration of the bread and wine is carried out; and Amfortas suffers bitterly. But Parsifal only stands foolishly by, takes no part, and seems unimpressed. As the long act closes, Gurnemanz, in anger, turns the boy from the door.

ACT II

Scene 1 finds Klingsor, the evil magician, in his castle. He summons Kundry to help him, and unwillingly she appears, subject to his magical powers. He demands that she change once more into a beautiful seductress, for she must help him in defense against a warrior who is invading him. Even thus had she once helped him when he overcame Amfortas.

Scene 2 The scene now changes to Klingsor's magical garden. On its walls stands the victorious young Parsifal, who has slain some of Klingsor's wicked knights. Klingsor's maidens, who had loved these knights, at first upbraid him. But he seems so innocent that they come to like him and, dressed as flowers, they make love to him.

Presently Kundry, the most beautiful of all, appears. When the others have departed, she tells him of his noble father, Gamuret, and his mother, Herzeleide. She says that it was she herself who gave him his name, which means "guileless fool." She proceeds to make love to him and at last to kiss him. But the kiss awakens him to passion—and to knowledge. Suddenly he seems to know the meaning of the wound of Amfortas—and that *he* may heal it. Vigorously he repels Kundry, and she cries to Klingsor for help. The sorcerer appears and hurls the sacred Spear at Parsifal. But a miracle occurs. The Spear sticks in the air directly over Parsifal's head, and he grasps it and makes the sign of the cross. Klingsor's whole castle falls in ruins; the garden becomes a desert; and Kundry sinks to the ground. Turning to her, Parsifal cries: "You know where only you may see me again!" And he disappears.

ACT III

Scene 1 Years have passed since the dramatic events of Act II. The young hero has been unable to find his way back to the Temple of the Grail, and the brotherhood of knights has suffered as Amfortas, still wounded, remains unable to perform his holy office.

It is a beautiful morning on Good Friday as the aged Gurnemanz issues from his hut. Again, after many years, he finds the repentant Kundry lying on the ground only half conscious. She has at last returned, to resume her service for the knights. Now a knight in black armor, a visor hiding his face, approaches. At the request of Gurnemanz, he removes the warlike clothing in this sacred place, and he kneels in prayer. Both Gurnemanz and Kundry recognize the knight as Parsifal, and he tells them of his many wounds and hardships as he has searched for Monsalvat. And Gurnemanz, in return, tells of the sufferings of the fellowship of knights and of the death of the old King Titurel. Parsifal faints with grief over the recital, blaming himself for all the suffering. But Gurnemanz solemnly baptizes the knight, and Kundry, with a golden phial, bathes his feet. Parsifal, in turn, asks Gurnemanz to anoint his head as well, and so Parsifal becomes the new King of the Grail. As his first act, the new King baptizes Kundry. And now, as the beauty of the natural scene strikes Parsifal, we hear the extraordinary *Good Friday Music*. There is a tolling of bells, and the three depart to attend the final rituals over the body of old Titurel.

Scene 2　Inside the great hall of the Grail, Amfortas is helped to the throne. His suffering still makes it impossible for him to uncover the Grail, and he begs for death. But Parsifal now steps forward and touches the wounds of Amfortas with the sacred Spear. At once they heal; and Parsifal proclaims himself King. He takes the Grail from the shrine, and as he kneels in silent prayer, it sheds a glow that spreads into a shining radiance. The voices of the knights, the squires, and the choir boys rise through marvelous harmonies; Kundry falls lifeless to the ground; and as Parsifal holds the Grail aloft before the sacred brotherhood, the orchestra plays the final, transfigured themes of the *Grail* and of the *Last Supper*.

PELLÉAS ET MÉLISANDE

Opera in five acts by Claude Debussy with
libretto in French by Maurice Maeterlinck

ARKEL, *King of Allemonde*	*Bass*
PELLÉAS	*Tenor*
GOLAUD } *the King's grandsons*	*Baritone*
GENEVIÈVE, *the Princes' mother*	*Mezzo-soprano*
YNIOLD, *Golaud's son*	*Soprano*
MÉLISANDE, *a lost princess*	*Soprano*
PHYSICIAN	*Bass*

Time: the Middle Ages
Place: a fictional kingdom called Allemonde
First performance at Paris, April 30, 1902

When Claude Debussy first met the cast that was to perform his setting of Maeterlinck's poetic play, *Pelléas et Mélisande,* he made a very strange opening remark. He said: "First
of all, ladies and gentlemen, you must forget that you are
singers." What he meant, I am sure, is that the music was only
one element in the effect he wished to produce. Here there
were no set arias, duets, or quartets—not even any high C's to
take! There were few melodies one could whistle on the way
out. All was done for one purpose: to capture and to project
the magical feeling of the sad, highly poetical, almost mystical
air of Maeterlinck's story about a medieval land that never
existed. It was a striking departure from any opera ever staged
in France—or anywhere else, for that matter; and it took many
months of rehearsal for the singers to master their roles. No
wonder, then, that it was misunderstood by most of its first

audience! Even today, fifty years later, many first-time listeners find it strange. But as one listens—even for the first time—one inevitably falls under its magical spell. That spell springs from the other-worldly poetic nature of Maeterlinck's play. It is infinitely enhanced by Debussy's unobtrusive, impressionistic score and marvelously sustained through the quietly eloquent interludes played between the many scenes as the stage sets are changed.

ACT I

Scene 1   After a short prelude, the story begins: Deep in a forest, Prince Golaud has lost his way. Soon he comes on a beautiful girl with long and lovely blond hair, weeping beside a spring of water. Her answers to his questions are vague and mysterious—and childlike, too. She has dropped a golden crown into the spring, but she will not let the prince get it back for her. She seems to be a lost princess, and her name is Mélisande. Golaud sees it is growing dark. He does not touch the frightened girl, but he leads her away to find a place of shelter.

Scene 2   And now there is a lovely orchestral interlude as the scene changes to the castle of King Arkel of Allemonde, who is the grandfather of Golaud. Geneviève, the mother of Golaud, is reading a letter from her son. He has married Mélisande without the King's consent, and he fears to return. The letter is addressed to Pelléas, the half brother of Golaud, and it asks Pelléas to find out how Arkel will feel about this marriage. Arkel is forgiving. He tells Pelléas to place a light at the top of the tower of the castle, toward the sea. This will be the signal for Golaud's return with Mélisande.

Scene 3   Once more there is an orchestral interlude, once more a change of scene. It is a darkling garden by the sea. Mélisande is unhappy about the constant darkness in and about the castle, but Geneviève assures her one gets used to it. Pelléas joins them, and they watch a ship departing. It is the ship that brought Mélisande—and this too makes her sad. And then—at the very end of the scene—Pelléas says that he may leave the next day. Quietly, pathetically, Mélisande murmurs, "Oh, why do you leave?" for she already is half in love with her husband's handsome younger brother.

Scene 1 It is a hot, midsummer day, almost noon, when Mélisande and Pelléas find themselves deep in the woods, beside a deserted fountain. Pelléas speaks of the magical qualities the fountain once had, but Mélisande scarcely listens. She throws herself down beside the fountain and plays with her hands in the water. "Be careful!" begs Pelléas. But Mélisande plays on, and her wedding ring drops into the fountain. They cannot get it back, for the water is too deep. Mélisande is worried, but Pelléas tells her not to be upset. It is time to go back, for it has struck noon. "But what shall we tell Golaud?" asks Mélisande. "The truth, the truth," murmurs her brother-in-law.

Scene 2 And then, after the orchestral interlude, the scene changes to Golaud's room. He is in bed, for just at noon (when Mélisande had dropped her ring into the water), his horse had shied and thrown him. Mélisande is by his side, and he tries to comfort her by telling her his wounds are not serious. Still, she is troubled; she cannot say why, except that it is always so dark. Tenderly he takes his young wife's hands in his—and notices that the ring is gone. Suddenly he is afraid, and angry. She tries to avoid his questions and finally says that she lost it in a grotto by the sea—that she was there with little Yniold, Golaud's son by an earlier marriage. It must be found, insists Golaud; Pelléas will go with her. "Pelléas? Pelléas?" she cries. But Golaud insists; and as Mélisande leaves, she weeps: "Oh, oh! I am not happy!"

Scene 3 Once more an interlude, once more a change of scene. It is dark, and the orchestra seems to describe the mysterious grotto by the sea. That sea does not sound happy tonight, says Pelléas to Mélisande—and suddenly the moon comes from behind a cloud. In the light they see three white-haired beggars sleeping against a rock. Little Mélisande is frightened; she wants to leave quickly. "We shall come back another day," says Pelléas.

ACT III

Scene 1 Mélisande is at her window, combing her long, golden hair, and singing an ancient ditty. Up the path comes Pelléas and stops beneath Mélisande's tower. He tells her he must leave on the morrow, but Mélisande begs him not to. She will not let him kiss her hand unless he says he will not leave. So Pelléas promises to wait. She leans out to reach him her hand, and her long tresses tumble over him. Passionately he kisses them as he cries that he will not let them go. Some frightened doves fly away—and suddenly Golaud comes up the path. Nervously he laughs; he calls them "children"; he says they must not play there in the dark—and he leads away his half brother, Pelléas.

Scene 2 The music of the interlude grows darker, more ominous. Into a subterranean passage of the castle Golaud leads Pelléas. He calls attention to the smell of death there; he points to the dangerous abyss; and Pelléas understands his warning. "I am stifling here," he says miserably as the two brothers leave the unpleasant place.

Scene 3 The music grows lighter again as they come out, and Pelléas is happier. But Golaud warns him more directly. He says he saw what happened beneath Mélisande's window, and from now on Pelléas must avoid his sister-in-law—only, not too obviously. For Mélisande must not be worried; she may soon be a mother.

Scene 4 Golaud is before the castle with little Yniold. He questions the child about Pelléas and Mélisande. "What do they speak about?" he asks. "About me," says the child. "Do they kiss each other?" But Yniold only kisses his father by way of answer. The man becomes tense and the child is frightened. Suddenly there is a light in Mélisande's room above. Golaud makes Yniold climb up and spy for him. He asks questions; but all the child can see is Pelléas and Mélisande standing quietly, looking at each other. Suddenly the frightened child

cries that he is afraid he will scream if he must stay there;
and the frustrated, tormented father leads him away. The final
sounds of the orchestra suggest the harsh torment of the man.

ACT IV

Scene 1   Pelléas is with Mélisande and, in a very restrained
scene, he begs for a rendezvous near the fountain. Now—almost
ironically—there is a long, quiet soliloquy by old King Arkel.
Impressed by the simple beauty of Mélisande, he says how
much he believes that youth and beauty make everything turn
out happily. He could not, of course, be further wrong in this
tragic story.

Soon Golaud appears. His head is wounded, but he refuses
to let Mélisande bandage it for him. And when Arkel remarks
on the innocence in Mélisande's eyes, Golaud works himself
up into a rage. He demands that she bring him his sword;
and when she has fetched it, he seizes her by her long, golden
hair. Violently he drags her along the floor—to the right, to the
left—but Mélisande utters no word of protest. Finally, Arkel
intercedes, and Golaud leaves in anger. Then, only, does Mélisande speak: "He loves me no longer," she says. "I am not
happy." And the scene ends with Arkel's profoundly moving
sentence: "If I were God," he says, "I should take pity on the
hearts of men."

Scene 2   Now there is an especially eloquent interlude. By
the fountain in the park little Yniold is playing, looking for
his lost golden ball. A flock of bleating sheep passes by, and
suddenly they are silent. "Why do they no longer speak?" asks
the little boy. "Because they are not on the right road home,"
answers a shepherd. All this, of course, is a kind of symbolic
commentary on the unhappy situation of Yniold's elders. It is
a poetic scene usually omitted from stage performances, and
ends with Yniold's running off. He sees it is growing dark
and feels he must—as he says—"say something to someone."

Scene 3   Then Pelléas comes to the fountain for his rendezvous with Mélisande. He is determined to run off from his
hopeless, guilty love; but when she joins him, he inevitably

tells her that he loves her. It is the first open declaration he has made, and Mélisande responds simply and truthfully: she, too, has loved him ever since she first saw him. The love scene works softly to a climax. In the distance is heard the closing of the palace gates, and the lovers sense that fate has overtaken them. And now, in the darkness, they feel—and then they hear—the approaching footsteps of Golaud. He has a sword in his hand. Desperately the lovers embrace. Pelléas begs Mélisande to flee with him, but she will not. Quickly, without uttering a word, Golaud strikes Pelléas down. Little Mélisande flees into the dark woods, crying, "Oh, oh! I have no courage!" Golaud runs after her, into the woods.

ACT V

Now Pelléas is dead, slain by his brother Golaud. But Mélisande is hardly aware of it. She has been found; she has given birth to a child; and she lies, dying, in bed. Old King Arkel is with her; so is Golaud; so is the doctor, who gives the old, hopeless, helpless professional encouragement. Golaud is full of remorse—and yet he is still jealous and tortured by uncertainty. He asks to be left alone with his young wife, and he torments her with questions. Did she love Pelléas? Of course, the girl answers simply. Were they guilty? No, says Mélisande. But her answers, her whole speech is so vague—so otherworldly in its quality—that Golaud can never feel sure. And when Arkel and the doctor return, Mélisande once more—as she had done before—complains of the cold, the darkness. They bring her the baby girl, and Mélisande says simply, "She is little . . . She too will weep . . . I pity her." Everyone feels the approach of death as the servants of the house file quietly into the room. Once more Golaud brutally demands the truth, but Arkel intervenes. It is too late to disturb the dying girl, and her soul passes from the earth. Slowly, Arkel leads the sobbing Golaud from the room. "It was not your fault," he says. And finally, turning to the baby, he tells her that she must live to take the place of Mélisande.

PETER GRIMES

Opera in prologue and three acts by Benjamin
Britten with libretto in English by Montagu
Slater based on the narrative poem "The
Borough" by George Crabbe.

PETER GRIMES, *fisherman*	*Tenor*
JOHN, *his apprentice*	*Silent*
MRS. ELLEN ORFORD, *schoolmistress*	*Soprano*
CAPTAIN BALSTRODE, *retired*	*Baritone*
AUNTIE, *landlady of the Boar Tavern*	*Contralto*
HER TWO NIECES	*Sopranos*
ROBERT BOLES, *Methodistical fisherman*	*Tenor*
SWALLOW, *lawyer and Mayor of the Borough*	*Bass*
MRS. SEDLEY, *called "Nabob," wealthy,*	
gossipy widow	*Soprano*
THE RECTOR	*Tenor*
DR. GEORGE CRABBE	*Silent*
HOBSON, *carter*	*Bass*

Time: before 1830
Place: The Borough, a small fishing town on the East Coast
First performance in London, June 7, 1945

Peter Grimes, first produced in 1945, is the second of
Britten's eight operas, the others being *Paul Bunyan* (1941),
The Rape of Lucretia (1946), *Albert Herring* (1947), *Let's
Make an Opera* (1949), *Billy Budd* (1951), *Gloriana* (1953),
and *A Midsummer Night's Dream* (1960). All, with the exception of the first, were received with at least a good measure
of critical acclaim, but none of them, with the possible ex-

ception of the children's *Let's Make an Opera*, seems to stand much chance of frequent revival. *Peter Grimes* is the one that had the widest international acceptance in its first years, being produced all over Europe, and in North and South America.

It was commissioned for Tanglewood by the Koussevitzky Foundation, and it was hailed, by some critics, as the finest English opera since Purcell's *Dido and Aeneas* (see p. 116). Its fine orchestral interludes and preludes are still sometimes played at concerts; yet it has not kept the stage in its entirety. One can only guess at the reason. It is a masterly piece of writing, but it is difficult to take warmly to one's heart. One reason may be its sombre, rather repellent subject matter; another may be the involved, almost tortured language of the libretto, which is based on George Crabbe's thoughtful and compassionate series of poetic letters descriptive of life in his native Aldeburgh, Suffolk. Whatever its faults, it remains one of the most interesting of modern operas in terms of the musico-dramatic problems it seeks to solve.

PROLOGUE

In the moot hall, or local court, of The Borough, a small town on the East Coast during the opening years of the 19th century, an inquest is being held. Lawyer Swallow swears in the principal witness, Peter Grimes, who tells haltingly how his apprentice had died on a fishing trip. They had had a huge catch, but the wind blew them off their course, drinking water ran out, and after three days the boy died. On his return, Peter cried for help; and the people immediately showing enmity, he abused Mrs. Sedley, the town's strait-laced old busybody who is very wealthy and known as "Mrs. Nabob." eventually, the widowed schoolmistress, Mrs. Ellen Orford (who is the nearest thing to a heroine in this opera), helped Peter carry the body home.

Through this brief, swift scene, the dramatic line-up is quickly made clear. Grimes is a peculiar, silent, gruff man thoroughly distrusted by almost the entire village, but pitied and befriended by Ellen and understood only by Balstrode, a retired merchant skipper. Peter is advised not to take on any more boys as assistants—or to get a woman to look after him if he does. A woman is precisely what Peter aspires to have, and Ellen specifically. This becomes clear when the couple are left alone; but it also becomes clear in their duet that until he has cleared his name and reputation, he feels too bitter about the town gossips to tie her to himself.

ACT I

Scene 1 Several days later, there is the usual crowd on the street by the sea, outside the "Boar Tavern," with the moot hall on one side and Ned Keene's apothecary shop on the other. The retired sea captain, Balstrode, sits on the breakwater eyeing a coming storm; fishermen are welcomed into the "Boar" by Auntie; a methodistical fellow, named Bob Boles, refuses to have anything to do with them; Ned Keene joshes Auntie about the two girls who are the main attraction of her pub and whom she refers to as her "nieces"; "Mrs. Nabob" tries secretly to get more laudanum from Keene; and everyone busily comments on the scene and on the worsening weather. Among the crowd is the figure of Dr. Crabbe (the respected physician who wrote fine books which inspired this opera). Amidst all this, Grimes asks for help in hauling up his boat, but only Balstrode and Keene will give him a hand. The latter tells him he has secured a new boy for him from the workhouse, but that he will have to be called for. Hobson, the carter, refuses to do this job, giving the excuse that he cannot supervise the boy and do all his other errands as well; but Ellen saves the day—much to almost everyone's disapproval—by offering to go along and take care of the lad. She even turns on the crowd and in an aria (*Let her among you without fault*) lectures them for their lack of Christianity.

The storm is rising now in earnest, both on the stage and in the orchestra pit, and after a large concerted number on this subject (*Look out for squalls*), the stage is left alone to Grimes and Balstrode. The retired captain advises Peter to leave the village and enlist with a merchantman, but the grim young man is bound to fight his fight against the village, win over its respect by prospering, and then marry Ellen. "She'll have you now," suggests Balstrode. But Grimes will not be married out of pity, and he grows angry at the older man for tendering him good advice. And when Balstrode goes off to help Auntie shutter up her pub, Grimes closes the scene with a passage in which he passionately yearns for the comfort of Ellen's breast.

Scene 2 The interlude depicts the storm growing ever stronger, and it is still raging when the curtain goes up on the inside of the "Boar" at 10.30 that night. "Mrs. Nabob" is there hoping to get her laudanum from Keene; the two "nieces" come in in their night-clothes, afraid of the storm; and the methodistical Boles, now quite drunk, tries to make passes at them. Fortunately, Captain Balstrode is there to keep him under control.

Grimes comes stumbling in out of the storm without the oilskins all the others are wearing, and looking like a thing completely apart. That is how he is treated, and when he sings a strange song about the stars and the storm (*Now the great Bear*), the drunken Boles decides the man has sold his soul to the devil and tries to hit him over the head with a bottle. Balstrode intervenes once more, and peace is temporarily restored as everyone breaks into an elaborate and effective round concerning fishing, three strikingly different tunes being sung simultaneously. But when the strong tenor voice of Peter takes up the round alone with a saturnine variation on the words, the others recoil temporarily in horror, then take it up again. At the climax, Hobson the carter breaks in accompanied by Ellen and the new boy for Grimes; and the scene closes as Grimes insists on taking the boy home directly, despite the storm and despite the fact that it has washed away the cliff outside his house.

Peter Grimes

ACT II

Scene 1 It is several weeks later and a fine, sunny Sunday morning, as the music of the intermezzo (or Act II Prelude) suggests. Ellen is outside the church, whence issue sounds, now and again, of the music of the service and even a portion of the sermon. Ellen sits knitting, sings philosophically about the weather, and speaks comfortingly to little John, Grimes's new apprentice, who stands gloomily by never uttering a sound. Presently she discovers a tear in his coat and a bruise on his neck. Peter, she realizes, has been maltreating the boy despite his promises to reform. The gloomy fisherman comes in to get the boy to go out in his boat and roughly repulses Ellen when she asks that the child be allowed to rest on Sunday at least. No, says Peter, he must solve his problems by "lonely toil," by amassing wealth, and forcing the good opinion of The Borough. In despair, Ellen declares that this plan is not a good one, that they have failed together. Peter cries out in anguish, strikes the woman he thought would save him, and runs off after John.

But Boles, Keene, and Auntie have overheard some of this quarrel, and they come out from their shops and sing a trio —*Grimes is at his exercise.* Gradually the stage fills with the congregation from the church, and a strong feeling against Grimes is again worked up despite Ellen's attempts to explain what had happened. The chorus works up to a pitch where they feel sure that murder is afoot, and a party of men is organized to go to Grimes's place expecting to find him doing something dreadful. Even the respected Balstrode cannot dissuade them, especially after the Rector is persuaded that something must be done. Only Auntie, her "nieces," and Ellen remain behind to sing a quartet about the childishness of men:

> *Shall we smile or shall we weep*
> *Or wait quietly till they sleep?*

Scene 2 Grimes's hut turns out to be only an upturned boat, but it is in ship-shape order. There are two doors—one

381

to the road, the other to the cliff that, as we have heard, has been recently washed away in the storm. Peter shoves the boy into the hut and throws his sea-going clothes towards him. The boy only sniffles, and Peter has a long aria in which he speaks of his ambition to have a good home with Ellen and with children of theirs. But at its close, he seems to be haunted by a vision of the boy who had died in the boat. Just then he hears the posse on its way up. He thinks the boy has been complaining about him, and rudely pushes him out of the hut on the cliff side. Then he climbs out after him—and we hear a terrible scream: the boy has fallen down the cliff that isn't there. But the posse has not heard it; and when they come snooping in, they are only impressed with the neatness and innocent appearance of the hut. Ironically, Swallow is inspired to comment that this should put an end to the anti-Grimes gossip; but Balstrode, looking out of the hut on the cliff side, remains there after the others depart.

ACT III

Scene 1 After a quiet prelude, descriptive of the moonlight, the curtain rises on the street outside the "Boar Tavern." It is an evening several days later, and first a polka, later a waltz, is heard as it is danced at the tavern. Outside, the drunken Swallow makes heavy-handed advances to the "nieces," and when they have escaped him, Mrs. Sedley tries to impress Ned Keene with her suspicions about Grimes and his new apprentice, who have not been seen for two days. Keene only laughs at her. Then, after a group of respectable folk have said goodnight to the Rector and Dr. Crabbe, Ellen and Balstrode come in, much worried. Though Peter has been missing two days, his boat is still on land, and Ellen has found the boy's jersey, all wet. They fear the worst, and go off, rather hopelessly, to try to help him. Mrs. Sedley then seeks out Swallow, insists that Grimes's disappearance without his boat clearly points to murder, and finally manages to work up the people to a point where they are ready to form another posse to go after the outcast.

Scene 2 After a strange intermezzo, suggesting the madness that is finally descending on Peter Grimes, we see him, several hours later, beside his boat. Off-stage, the calling of the posse is heard now and again, as he has a long, weird scene by himself. He sings of the sea, refers to the deaths of his apprentices, imagines he is again with Ellen, curses his persecutors and defies them. Ellen and Balstrode come upon him there; and over Ellen's protest, Balstrode—quietly and in a speaking voice—advises Peter to take his boat out to sea and sink with it. In a kind of trance, and with Balstrode's help, Peter launches his boat.

Dawn comes, and with it the mob enters and disperses. Life in the fishing village starts again; Swallow notes that the coastguard reports a boat sinking at sea; they decide it is just a rumor; and everyone goes about his business.

PORGY AND BESS

Opera in three acts by George Gershwin with
libretto in English by DuBose Heyward and Ira
Gershwin, based on the play *Porgy* by DuBose
and Dorothy Heyward

PORGY, *a cripple*	*Bass-baritone*
CROWN, *a stevedore*	*Baritone*
BESS, *his girl*	*Soprano*
JAKE, *a fisherman*	*Baritone*
CLARA, *his wife*	*Soprano*
ROBBINS, *an inhabitant of Catfish Row*	*Tenor*
SERENA, *his wife*	*Soprano*
SPORTING LIFE, *a dope peddler*	*Tenor*
PETER, *the honeyman*	*Tenor*
UNDERTAKER	*Baritone*

Time: the 1920's
Place: Charleston, South Carolina
First performance at Boston, September 30, 1935

As a play, *Porgy*, by DuBose and Dorothy Heyward, was
a success. But when Mr. Heyward and Ira Gershwin made an
opera libretto of it, with music by Ira's brother George, it was
a smash hit. The general critical opinion was: "Here is the
first completely successful and completely American opera."
That was in 1935. Since its first successful run—first in Boston
and later on Broadway—it has been repeatedly revived, sometimes with spoken dialogue, sometimes with Gershwin's original recitatives. It reached Europe in 1945, when it was given
in Switzerland and Denmark with largely European casts; but

it did not become really popular on that continent till an all-Negro company toured there in 1952–53, when Germany and Austria could not seem to get enough of it, while London provided crowded houses for several months on end. No previous or subsequent American opera—not even Gian Carlo Menotti's great successes—seems to have found so strong a place in the Western world's musical life. And even the East, at least as represented by Soviet Russia, has welcomed it enthusiastically.

ACT I

Scene 1 is a square in Catfish Row, Charleston, South Carolina. Here aristocrats once lived, but now Negro workers are crowded into it. The atmosphere of a hot, southern, summer night is set at once by the lovely lullaby *Summertime*, sung by the contented young wife and mother, Clara. Her husband, Jake, expresses the local male attitude toward the opposite sex in the jolly tune *A Woman Is a Sometime Thing*. Porgy, a cripple well liked in Catfish Row, comes in on his goat cart. The crap game, begun casually enough, develops in earnest, and becomes even more exciting when Crown takes part, for Crown is the local bully. A fight springs up like a flash fire, and Crown kills one of the men. Immediately he has to run off, leaving his girl Bess there. One of the flashier fellows, Sporting Life, tries—and fails—to get Bess to go with him to New York, and the women all shut their doors on her.

This is Porgy's chance. He had always loved Bess, but from a distance because he was a cripple. Now she has no other place to turn, and as the scene ends, she enters Porgy's home.

Scene 2 takes place in the room that used to be occupied by Serena and Robbins; but it is Robbins who has been murdered by Crown, and Serena's neighbors are now gathered to sing over the body and to collect money for the funeral. Porgy, accompanied by Bess, comes in and contributes money and, a natural-born leader, he takes the principal part in the prayers and encouragement. Serena herself sings a deeply moving dirge (*My Man's Gone Now*). A pair of white detectives breaks in on the sorrowing group to warn Serena that the body must be buried the next day. Before they leave, they drag off with them old Peter, a perfectly innocent suspect.

A rather sympathetic undertaker—also white—now comes in; and although not enough money for a funeral has been collected, he accepts Serena's promise to pay up later. The mourners approve of this, and the act ends as Bess leads them in a rousing song beginning: "Oh, the train is at the station."

ACT II

Scene 1   It is now a month later in Catfish Row, and even though the September storms are due, the fisherman Jake is getting ready to sail for the blackfish banks. As for Porgy—he is living with Bess and is completely happy. He sings about it in fetching syncopation: *I Got Plenty o' Nuttin*—and "nuttin's" plenty for him. He even buys a fake divorce for Bess—a divorce from Crown, to whom she never was married—and he gets good news about his friend, old Peter, who is to be let out of jail. This is the occasion for another happy song—the *Buzzard Song*, originally cut out of the score by Gershwin in order to make the opera shorter. Sporting Life now makes one more attempt to get Bess to leave with him, but Porgy, a powerful man even though a cripple, scares the little nuisance almost to death. Left alone at last, Porgy and Bess sing the love duet, *Bess, You Is My Woman Now.*

A military band comes on now, followed by the crowd getting ready for a community picnic to Kittiwah Island. At first Bess wants to stay with Porgy, but when Porgy urges her to have fun, she goes along.

Scene 2 is at the picnic on Kittiwah Island. Sporting Life sings his worldly-wise ditty, *It Ain't Necessarily So,* and this is followed by a brief, dramatic scene between Crown and Bess. Crown—still hiding from the police—emerges from a thicket. He manages to get Bess alone, and she finds it impossible—in spite of her love for Porgy—to resist him.

Scene 3 begins at dawn one week later. There are threats of a storm, as Jake the fisherman prepares to leave Catfish Row. As for Bess, she has been unconscious for a week after her encounter with Crown on Kittiwah Island. Her neighbor Serena, Porgy, and others pray over her, and finally "Dr. Jesus" makes her well. Somehow Porgy knows she has been with Crown, and he tells her so. But he forgives her, and she admits she has promised to return to Crown. She wants to stay with Porgy but fears her own weakness should Crown return. Porgy promises to defend her against him.

Scene 4 takes place in Serena's room. The terrible storm is now at its height, and all the superstitious neighbors are praying, for some of them really believe that Judgment Day is at hand. Suddenly Crown forces his way in. He taunts the crippled Porgy and shocks everyone by claiming God as his friend. But when Clara sees—through the window—that her husband Jake's boat is overturned, it is only Crown who is ready to help. Leaving the baby with Bess, Clara follows Crown out into the raging storm.

ACT III

Scene 1 All three short scenes in this act take place in Catfish Row. The first opens with the women mourning the loss of Jake, Clara, and Crown in the storm. But Sporting Life wanders in and hints that Crown has survived somehow. Offstage, when the square is deserted, one hears Bess singing Clara's lullaby to the little orphan.

Then Crown appears, crawling toward Porgy's door, from which he can hear Bess's voice. As he passes the window, the powerful hands of Porgy shoot out, seize Crown by the throat, and quietly choke him to death. "Bess, you got a man now," he remarks. "You got Porgy."

Scene 2 A few hours later a detective comes to find Crown's murderer, and after some questioning he drags off Porgy to identify the body. This is Sporting Life's chance. Thinking himself rid of both his rivals, he again starts to woo Bess, promising to take her to a great life in *There's a Boat That's Leavin' Soon for New York*, a jazzy description of the joys of Harlem. He also tempts the girl with drugs—"happy dust," he calls it; and Bess, though she talks harshly to her tempter, is obviously weakening.

Scene 3 One week later Porgy returns, for the police have not been able to charge him with the murder. He looks everywhere for his Bess. Finally he learns that she has gone to New York with Sporting Life. He knows nothing about New York —only that it is far north, way "past the custom house." Crippled as he is, he calls for his goat and cart. As the opera ends, he is being sped on his way by all his neighbors, and he leads them in a chorus like a spiritual (*Oh, Lawd, I'm on My Way*).

PRINCE IGOR

(Knyaz Igor)

Opera in prologue and four acts by Alexandre
Porfyrevich Borodin with the help of Nikolai
Andreevich Rimsky-Korsakoff, Alexandre Kon-
stantinovich Glazounov, and Anatol Konstan-
tinovich Liadov, with libretto in Russian by
Vladimir Vasilevich Stassov and the composer,
based on a medieval prose poem of unknown
origin entitled *Song of the Army of Prince Igor*

PRINCE IGOR		*Baritone*
YAROSLAVNA, *his wife*		*Soprano*
VLADIMIR, *his son*		*Tenor*
PRINCE GALITZKY, *her brother*		*Bass*
SKOULA	} *gudok players*	*Bass*
EROSHKA		*Tenor*
KONTCHAK	} *Polovtsian khans*	*Bass*
GZAK		*Bass*
KONTCHAKOVNA, *Kontchak's daughter*		*Mezzo-soprano*
OVLOUR, *a Polovtsian renegade*		*Tenor*
YAROSLAVNA'S NURSE		*Soprano*

Time: 1185
Places: Poutivle and the camp of the Polovtsians
First performance at St. Petersburg, November 4, 1890

Let us start, for once, by giving credit to a critic. Vladimir
Vasilevich Stassov was the monstrously learned archaeologist,
librarian, and music critic who constituted an intimate ad-
junct to the Mighty Five of Russia—Balakirev, Cui, Borodin,
Moussorgsky, and Rimsky-Korsakoff. Among the many services

389

he performed for these composers (including writing biographies of all but Balakirev) was the suggestion to Borodin of Prince Igor as the subject for an opera. Not only did he suggest it, he also wrote out a synopsis for the libretto.

The source of the story is a fourteenth-century prose poem entitled *Song of the Army of Prince Igor*, which deals with a twelfth-century military expedition undertaken against the Tartars. To understand it properly—particularly the prologue and Act I—one should know that Novgorod was, at that time, a cross between a democracy and a constitutional monarchy. That is, the princes were elected, their chief function was to act as military leaders, and they derived their authority and subsidies from their subjects, not from the nobility.

But it was not so much the political aspects of the story that attracted Borodin as it was the chance to write music in contrasting colors—Russian and Tartar. And how well he took advantage of it!

Borodin was a chemist—and a distinguished one—by profession, a composer only by avocation. It may have been for this reason that, while Stassov came up with his notable suggestion as early as 1869, the score was still uncompleted when Borodin died of a heart attack, eighteen years later, during a costume party he was giving in his own home. Rimsky-Korsakoff and Glazounov, with help from Liadov, orchestrated more than half the opera and completed the composition of several of the scenes that remained unfinished. But these composers often worked so closely with each other (they had shared assignments for different parts of the same string quartet, the same ballet) that it is almost impossible to detect where one hand leaves off and the next begins. Stassov left an account of who did what, but so well did they subject their individualities that it is a matter of interest only to the historian.

PROLOGUE

After an overture based on a number of the themes to be heard later, the curtain rises on a square in the city of Poutivle, and the chorus sings in praise of the military leader, Prince

Igor, who has just left the cathedral preparatory to leading an expedition against the Tartars. Suddenly an eclipse of the sun frightens everyone, and the boyars attempt to dissuade Igor from embarking on the expedition: it is a bad portent, they say. Igor, however, refuses to be moved, and orders his army on its way. All the soldiers go, excepting a couple of rascals named Skoula and Eroshka—players on an ancient stringed instrument called the *gudok*—of whom we shall hear more later.

Even Igor's beloved wife, Yaroslavna, cannot persuade him to remain home. He commends her to the care of her brother, Prince Galitzky, who is to rule the city in Igor's absence. Galitzky thanks his brother-in-law; an old priest offers a blessing; Igor and his son Vladimir join the army; and the chorus again chants the praises of their leader.

Scene 1 The true character of Galitzky, which had before been suggested only by the nature of the music assigned him, now comes out clearly. At his court he has won over the mob by giving them various luxuries and entertainment; he freely admits that he loves a life of ease himself; and more secretly he hopes that he may replace Igor on the throne. As for Yaroslavna—let her get herself to a nunnery.

The nature of his administration of justice is revealed when a couple of frightened girls ask his protection against his own men, who have abducted a third girl. Galitzky simply tells them that the girl is better off where she is now. Finally, when he has left the stage for some private carousing, the crowd opens a barrel of wine and thoroughly enjoys itself in a lively chorus. Skoula and Eroshka, who have been prominent in the anti-Igor demonstrating earlier, don't stint themselves with the wine, and they are left behind, drunk.

Scene 2 In her room Yaroslavna bewails the absence of her husband and son; but her spirit is roused when the two girls who have been so badly treated in the previous scene come to her for protection. It seems that Galitzky himself has violated their friend, and when he comes in, Yaroslavna threatens to have him punished on Prince Igor's return. Galitzky only laughs at his sister, but she is more than a match for this bluffer. Before she is through with him, he has promised to bring the girl back to her home. He then bows himself out of the room and the opera—a good loss in terms of the company we are expected to keep, but a bad one in terms of missing a well-drawn character.

Bad news ends the act. A group of boyars reports that the army has been defeated by the dread Khan Gzak and that Igor and Vladimir are prisoners. Despite the fact that destruction is already threatening the city itself, with flames leaping at the windows and alarm bells ringing, they all swear to defend Yaroslavna to the end.

ACT II

Borodin was a great student of Eastern folk music, and the next two acts are strongly colored with that idiom. In the camp of the Khan Kontchak of the Polovtsians, the girls sing and dance, and Kontchakovna, Kontchak's daughter, sings a fine, juicy love song. These are a hospitable people, and the Novgorodian prisoners, though well guarded, are also well treated. Night begins to fall; the prisoners return from work; the girls offer them refreshments; and then everyone retires excepting a patrol, which intones a brief occupational chorus before departing on its duties. Young Vladimir wanders into the night and sings the second love song of the act, one clearly indicating that he has fallen classically in love with the daughter of his enemy; and when Kontchakovna joins him, they sing an unexpectedly contented love duet. For her father, the Khan, has no objections to a wedding; it is only Igor who may be opposed.

Igor is much more discontented with his lot than is his son. In a fine aria he bewails his state, the loss of his army, and the certain loneliness of Yaroslavna. Ovlour, a Polovtsian renegade, secretly approaches him and offers to give him a horse to make good his escape. He points to the approaching dawn and suggests that this is a symbol of Russia's enventual victory. Igor contemptuously refuses this aid: it would be completely dishonorable, he claims.

Good nature and respect for its noble prisoners seem to characterize the Kontchak family. The Khan most graciously offers Igor practically anything he wants in return for a non-aggression pact. He even offers him an alliance. But Igor refuses to acknowledge defeat and frankly tells Kontchak that one day he will return to the attack stronger than ever. This is an attitude the Tartar warrior not only understands but respects, and he invites Igor to be his personal guest at the entertainment to follow.

It follows at once—the series of Polovtsian dances that are the most familiar music in the score because of a splendid ballet made of them by Michel Fokine and because they are often performed separately in the concert hall (though usually without the choral parts).

ACT III

The Tartar army that had been attacking Igor's home town at the end of Act I was not the same as the one that had taken him prisoner and was entertaining him so colorfully at the end of Act II. The former was the army of Khan Gzak; and now, at the beginning of Act III, it returns with booty and prisoners to the tune of a vigorous Oriental march. Khan Kontchak, in a grim aria, welcomes and congratulates his brothers-in-arms, and the men look forward to further rapacious raids on Russian cities like Kiev and Poltava.

The Russian prisoners have meantime been watching the proceedings, and they dread the thought of what has been happening to Poutivle. Vladimir even suggests to his father that he had erred in not taking the opportunity to escape while he had it. The Russians, however, are herded back into their tents by a group of guards, and presently the Polovtsi traitor, Ovlour, brings them brandy. As they sing in praise of their intrepid khans, the guards drink themselves to sleep.

It is now night, and Ovlour repeats his offer to Igor. This time it is welcomed. Before everything can be got ready,

Kontchakovna begs Vladimir either to remain with her or to take her along. Igor sternly forbids her to come; and while the young man is torn between love and duty, Kontchakovna precipitates a decision by sounding an alarm on a sheet of iron that hangs near the tents. Igor escapes; Vladimir is taken prisoner; and Kontchak, over the protests of his fellow khans, decides that Vladimir shall, after all, marry his daughter and remain as a hostage. The drunken guards, however, are ordered hanged. This Kontchak is a most interesting fellow: he can be relentlessly brutal in military matters, yet he shows nothing but respect for his noble adversaries. He even says that in Igor's place he should have done the same thing.

ACT IV

Back in Poutivle, Yaroslavna sings sadly of the absence of her husband, making use of the same melody Igor had sung in Act II lamenting the absence of Yaroslavna. The countryside in the background is a scene of devastation, and a peasant crowd drags itself across the square of the town singing a doleful chorus. But off in the distance Yaroslavna now sees two horsemen approaching, and they turn out to be Igor and Ovlour. Gladly the royal couple embraces, and goes off to the citadel.

Our old friends, Skoula and Eroshka—drunk, as usual—come on the stage, lamenting the disaster that Igor's leadership has brought to the country; but seeing Igor, they quickly change their tune. They know it is now more politically expedient to change sides; and so they sound the bells that summon everyone and thus are the first to announce the return of their great leader. Ovlour tells the crowd the details of the escape; Skoula and Eroshka are rewarded by the boyars: they now insist that they always hated Galitzky anyway; and everyone joins in a fine Russian chorus of thanksgiving. Finally, Igor and Yaroslavna show themselves on the walls of the citadel, and the opera closes with shouts of "Long live Prince Igor!"

I PURITANI

(The Puritans)

Opera in three acts by Vincenzo Bellini with libretto in Italian by Count Carlo Pepoli based on the French drama *Têtes Rondes et Cavaliers* by François Ancelot and Xavier Boniface Saintine, which was based, in a vague way, on Sir Walter Scott's novel *Old Mortality*

LORD GUALTIERO VALTON		Bass
SIR GIORGIO VALTON, *his brother*	Puritans	Bass
ELVIRA VALTON, *his daughter*		Soprano
SIR RICCARDO FORTO, *a suitor*		Baritone
ENRICHETTA, *widow of Charles I*		Soprano
LORD ARTURO TALBO, *engaged*	Cavaliers	
to Elvira		Tenor

Time: 1650's
Place: Plymouth, England
First performance at Paris, January 25, 1835

For a long time I *Puritani* was standard repertoire for every accomplished singer, and it has been heard all over the world—from Paris (where it had its premiere) to Philadelphia, to Rio de Janeiro, to Sydney, Australia. Recently, in England, it was revived for Joan Sutherland, the great young Australian soprano. But few other vocal virtuosi have the courage to tackle it. It is just too difficult, for it has, among other features, baritone coloratura arias and a tenor role that calls for two D's above high C, not to mention one F!

As a matter of fact, the opera was composed with four leading singers in mind—Giulia Grisi, soprano; Giovanni Battista

Rubini, tenor; Antonio Tamburini, baritone; and Luigi Lablache, bass. After they sang together in this work, they toured as a team for many years billed as the "*Puritani* Quartet."

Today the opera is seldom put on outside of Italy, partly, one suspects, on account of its somewhat ridiculous libretto. Count Carlo Pepoli fashioned it for Bellini out of a French play named *Roundheads and Cavaliers*, but Pepoli called his opera *I Puritani di Scozia*, or *The Puritans of Scotland*. And where do these Scottish Puritans live, love, and have their castles? Why, in Plymouth, England, which, as everyone knows, is hundreds of miles from the Scottish border. But everything about the opera is unabashedly Italian; and so in telling the story I shall use the Italian versions of the English names of the characters, as Bellini did. (Even Cromwell is called "Cromvello" in the libretto.)

ACT I

In the seventeenth-century days of Cromwell the Puritans are fighting the Cavaliers, supporters of the Stuarts. The Puritan Governor General, Lord Gualtiero Valton (that is, Walter Walton) has the widow of Charles I as his prisoner. Enrichetta (Henrietta) is her name, and her presence in the castle complicates our plot. Its principal theme is a sort of *Abie's Irish Rose*, or *Romeo and Juliet*, story: Valton's daughter, Elvira, is in love with a dashing royalist named Lord Arturo Talbo, and in the opening scenes of Act I, Elvira's father is persuaded to let her marry Arturo. Unfortunately, she is already engaged to a Puritan warrior named Riccardo—and Riccardo is a baritone to be reckoned with. Nevertheless, preparations are being made for the wedding, when Valton announces that Enrichetta has been summoned to London. At once Arturo realizes that this means she may meet the fate of Charles, who was beheaded. Despite his pending marriage to Elvira, he resolves to save his Queen, and he gallantly offers her his services when the others have departed. After this duet Elvira enters, accompanied by her beloved uncle Giorgio and others, and sings her happy aria *Son vergin vezzosa*.

When she leaves her bridal veil with Enrichetta, Arturo sees his chance: disguised in the veil, Enrichetta can escape with him. Just as they are about to leave, Riccardo stops them; but when he sees what is happening—his rival for Elvira running away on his wedding day—he helps them to get out. A minute later the escape is discovered, and great excitement ensues as soldiers are sent after them. As for Elvira—she does as any coloratura soprano of the 1830's would do: she goes completely insane. The act ends with her singing about her imagined wedding while everyone else comments musically on how sad it all is and curses the defaulting Arturo.

ACT II

There is little dramatic action in Act II, but some of the finest Bellini music. In the opening scene Giorgio describes the distressing symptoms of Elvira's madness to a sympathetic chorus. Presently they are joined by Riccardo, the man she had deserted for Arturo. And then Elvira herself enters to sing the splendid *Qui la voce sua soave*. "Her face," to quote the stage directions, "her eyes, and every step and gesture reveal her madness." And so, I might add, does the music. It is quite as fine a mad scene as the more celebrated one in Donizetti's *Lucia di Lammermoor*, an opera produced the same year as *I Puritani* and also featuring a Scottish maiden who goes mad. Only, this time there is no flute obbligato. Instead Elvira answers questions of her companions, and she identifies her uncle as her father and Riccardo as Arturo.

The balance of the act is given over to a martial duet between Giorgio and Riccardo (*Suoni la tromba*) in which they swear to fight faithfully on the side of the Puritans against the Cavaliers.

ACT III

The fugitive hero, Arturo, has secretly returned to the home of his beloved in Plymouth. He is being hunted by the Puritan soldiers, who are heard passing by. However, he manages to escape, while off-stage is now heard the voice of the demented heroine singing a plaintive ballad (*A una fonta afflitto*). Arturo decides to answer, and she responds to his serenade by appearing herself. A long and very difficult duet follows. Arturo explains why he had deserted Elvira on their wedding day: it was only to save his Queen. Reassured, Elvira's teetering mind begins to regain its balance. Unfortunately, at that moment they are discovered—and she goes mad once more. Practically everyone demands that Arturo be at once arrested and sentenced to death. Only Giorgio and Riccardo try to defend him, for they know that if Arturo should die, the beloved Elvira will not survive him long. It is, I suppose, not a very realistic or sensible dramatic situation. Yet—as everyone expresses his own emotions simultaneously, an extraordinarily fine ensemble number develops.

Then—just ninety seconds before the opera is over—a message is received: the Stuarts have been defeated. And so Arturo is pardoned, Elvira regains her senses, and everyone lives happily ever after.

THE RAKE'S PROGRESS

Opera in three acts by Igor Stravinsky with libretto in English by Wystan H. Auden and Chester Kallman suggested by William Hogarth's lithographs of the same title

TRULOVE, *a country squire*	*Bass*
ANNE, *his daughter*	*Soprano*
TOM RAKEWELL, *her sweetheart*	*Tenor*
NICK SHADOW	*Baritone*
MOTHER GOOSE, *a brothel-keeper*	*Mezzo-soprano*
BABA THE TURK, *bearded lady in a circus*	*Mezzo-soprano*
SELLEM, *an auctioneer*	*Tenor*

Time: 18th century
Place: England
First performance at Venice, September 11, 1951, in English, the composer conducting

Mr. Igor Stravinsky is one of the most fascinating, most accomplished, and most varied of modern composers. His early works, like *The Firebird, The Rite of Spring,* and *Petrouchka* —all composed before World War I—have become something like popular classics. Since then he has composed in many other styles, none of them quite so popular, and he has half modeled much of his work on earlier music. "Neoclassical," he has been called. *The Rake's Progress* appears to be modeled on late eighteenth- and nineteenth-century opera—anything from Mozart to Rossini, or even Donizetti. Not that you can ever mistake him for these earlier men. It is rather—says one critic—almost as though you were listening to them through one of those crazy Coney Island distorting mirrors. You do have old-fashioned arias, recitatives, concerted numbers—but with what a difference!

The story of the opera is based on Hogarth's famous series of lithographs called *The Rake's Progress*. Perhaps it would be better to say that it was inspired by that series, for it does not follow the narrative very closely. Rather, the mood, the setting, the morals, a few characters, and a few situations are the same. Mr. Stravinsky worked it out—in general—with the fine English-born poet Wystan H. Auden, and Auden, in turn, worked out the details with another writer, Chester Kallman. It was done in English. Yet, even when it is sung in the original by an English-speaking cast, there is some difficulty in getting the words, for Mr. Stravinsky does not believe it is always wise to respect the accents of the language.

ACT I

Scene 1   In an English eighteenth-century garden we find a couple of lovers billing and cooing. Their names—Tom Rakewell and Anne Trulove. Anne's father, on one side of the stage, expresses some doubts as to Tom's making a quite reliable son-in-law. He therefore—after Anne retires into the house—comes forth and offers Tom a good, steady job. The boy refuses; and when he is left alone, he sings a defiant aria, saying that he will rely on fortune. Only, he adds at the end, he wishes he had some money. Immediately, as in *Faust*, Nick Shadow appears (that's the Devil in disguise). He tells him, in the presence of Anne and Mr. Trulove, that a forgotten uncle has left him a fortune. This is the occasion for a quartet. Tom and Anne are, of course, delighted, but the father still has some doubts. It seems that it will be necessary for Tom to go to London to settle the business, and Nick offers himself as a servant. He even refuses to accept a definite wage. At the end of a year and a day, he says, Tom may decide what his services were worth. (Anyone who has read much about the Devil knows what *that* means.) As Tom goes off, Nick turns to the audience and announces: "The Progress of a Rake begins!"

Scene 2 is inspired by the Hogarth picture that takes the hero to a brothel. A bawdy contralto known as "Mother Goose" is the madam of the place, and at the moment a chorus of whores and so-called "roaring boys" (that is, eighteenth-century London no-goods) is hymning the delights of Venus and Mars. Tom Rakewell has been under the tutelage of Nick Shadow for a while now, and Nick gets him to recite a sort of catechism of evil. He successfully defines Beauty and Pleasure; but when he comes to Love, he falters, remembering, perhaps, Anne Trulove. He wishes to leave because it is getting late; but Nick sets the clock back, the general reveling begins again, and the young neophyte is introduced to the gang. Tom now recalls his vows of love in an aria notable especially for the rippling figure in the accompanying clarinet. For a short while Tom's new acquaintances sympathize; but Mother Goose herself takes Tom in hand, and the scene ends gaily as the chorus sings the refrain of the old ballad of *Lanterloo*.

Scene 3 belongs almost entirely to Anne Trulove. She is in her garden, badly missing her Tom, from whom she has not heard, and she delivers a formal recitative and aria on this subject. There is a brief interruption from her father, and then—in old-fashioned Italian-opera style—she has a brilliant cabaletta to the aria. She resolves, in this finale, to follow Tom to London.

ACT II

Scene 1 Tom Rakewell hasn't found much happiness in London, making his rake's progress, and he complains about it as he sits at breakfast in his bachelor's quarters. He does not even dare think of Anne; and at the words "I wish I were happy" Nick Shadow appears. He shows Tom a broadside, advertising a circus that features Baba the Turk, a bearded lady. In his aria Nick advises his master not to be bound by conscience. What, in fact, could be more fun than marrying the bearded lady? Again Tom falls under the spell of degeneracy that Nick Shadow throws about him, and the scene ends with a duet as his evil spirit helps Tom to dress and make ready to woo Baba.

Scene 2 takes place outside Tom's London house. Anne has come to persuade him to return to the country, and she waits (for one aria) for him to come. As servants begin to carry packages into the house, she wonders what it is all about. She does not have to wait long. A sedan chair comes in and disgorges Tom. In the duet that follows, he begs her to return to the country, for he is not worthy of her. But Tom has not been alone in that sedan chair. Baba, the bearded Turk, sticks her head out; Tom admits that he has just married her; and in the ensuing trio Tom and Anne regret how things have turned out, while Baba expresses her dislike of being kept waiting. Finally Anne leaves, and Tom helps his rather spectacular bride out of the chair. As they enter the house, Baba unveils her beard for the benefit of the assembled crowd.

Scene 3 takes us into the not-so-happy home of Tom Rakewell and his bride. The recent benedict sulks at breakfast, while Baba jabbers away, in an aria, about the roomful of junk she has brought into Tom's room—stuffed animals, china, gewgaws of all sorts from everywhere. Tom remains utterly uninterested, and finally she flies into a rage, smashing the worthless stuff. Spang in the middle of her tantrum, Tom covers her face with his wig, silencing her. Quite disillusioned, he goes to sleep, when Nick comes in silently with a strange machine. Into it he puts a loaf of bread and a sliver of china. A moment later Tom awakens to tell him of a dream about a machine that would change stone into bread and bring happiness to man. At once Nick turns the handle of his machine —and out comes the bread. Now, he suggests, Tom can make his fortune. Hadn't he better tell his wife? "My wife?" asks Tom, "I have no wife. I've buried her." And he points to Baba, still silent behind the wig.

ACT III

Scene 1   Things have gone from bad to worse with Tom. It is spring now—several months since the close of the last act. Baba still sits in the room, Tom's wig over her face. But there is a crowd there too, for the contents of the room are about to be auctioned off. Among the crowd is Anne Trulove seeking her former fiancé, but nobody pays much attention to her. Then, enter Sellem, the auctioneer. In a fine, nonsensical patter—set to a silly waltz tune—he puts up an auk, a pike, a palm—even Baba herself, whom he describes simply as "an unknown object." Much to everyone's astonishment, she shoves aside her wig and begins singing in the middle of the phrase that Tom had interrupted months before.

Off-stage, the voices of Tom and Nick are heard singing a ballad. But the splendid bearded lady turns to Anne, says that she knows she loves Tom, and advises her to set him right. As for herself, Baba will return to the stage. Off-stage, Tom and Nick are heard again in their ballad, and Anne excitedly sings, to the assembled folk: "I go, I go, I go, I go to him!" As for Baba, she orders Sellem to get her carriage, shoos the crowd away, and tells them that *next* time they'll have to pay to see her.

Scene 2   In a few bars of weird music for four string instruments Stravinsky sets the stage, which shows a dismal graveyard. Nick Shadow has served Tom for a year and a day. Now he demands his wages: Tom's soul. Still—he offers Tom a chance by playing a game of cards. As Anne Trulove's voice is heard off-stage, Tom wins three games. Sworn love, says Anne, can plunder hell itself of its prey. Nick sinks into the grave he had intended for Tom, but before he disappears, the frustrated Devil strikes his former master insane.

For a few moments the stage is in darkness. When the lights come up again, there sits Tom, on the mound of the grave, truly mad. He is putting grass upon his head, thinking it roses; and as he sings his ballad (the tune heard in the previous scene) he calls himself "Adonis."

Scene 3   Our hero is now in Bedlam, the infamous lunatic asylum of eighteenth-century London. He still sings of himself as Adonis and asks his fellow madmen to prepare for his wedding to Venus. They only scoff; but soon the jailer brings in Anne Trulove. She addresses him as "Adonis"; he calls her "Venus." It is a very odd love duet; and at its close she puts him on his straw pallet and sings him a soft lullaby. Her father comes to lead her home, and they bid the sleeping madman a farewell. When they are gone, Tom awakens and sings wildly of Venus, but his fellow madmen will have none of it; they do not believe she was there at all. Driven to complete hopelessness, the broken man sinks back—dead.

But the opera is still not quite over. Composer and librettist wanted to be sure their opera was a "moral" one, and so there is a little epilogue, a quintet for all the principals—Tom, Nick, Baba, and the two Truloves. And the moral is this:

> *For idle hands*
> *And hearts and minds*
> *The Devil finds*
> *A work to do.*

RIGOLETTO

Opera in three acts (often given in four) by
Giuseppe Verdi with libretto in Italian by
Francesco Maria Piave based on the French
play *Le roi s'amuse* by Victor Hugo

THE DUKE OF MANTUA	*Tenor*
RIGOLETTO, *his jester*	*Baritone*
GILDA, *Rigoletto's daughter*	*Soprano*
GIOVANNA, *her nurse*	*Mezzo-soprano*
SPARAFUCILE, *professional assassin*	*Bass*
MADDALENA, *his sister*	*Contralto*
COUNT MONTERONE	*Bass or Baritone*

Time: 16th century
Place: Mantua
First performance at Venice, March 11, 1851

Everyone today knows the tunes of *Rigoletto* so well—
La donna è mobile, the *Quartet*, and the others—that it is
hard to believe it was once thought dangerous and shocking.
Many an American school child has chirped the sweet little
song "Over the Summer Sea" without knowing that the original words were about the joy of making love to featherbrained
women. Nevertheless, the first readers of the libretto, who
were the censors of Venice, found it so shocking that they
insisted on some important changes. And some years before
that, the play on which the opera is based had to be withdrawn after two performances in Paris. This in spite of the
fact that the author was the great Victor Hugo.
This play was *Le roi s'amuse* ("The King Amuses Him-

self"), and its principal figures were historical ones—King Francis I of France and his jester Triboulet. The story was essentially the same as the one told in the opera, and what bothered the censors both in Paris and in Venice was the unflattering picture it gave of a real French king. That was in 1832, when romanticism and revolution were both easily sniffed in the European air. The censors thought such presentations would give inspiration to subversives. The libretto that the Venetians read had a different title—*La maledizione* ("The Curse")—but the disreputable ruler was still Francis I

Verdi was to meet similar troubles when he submitted the original libretto of *A Masked Ball* to the censors of Naples In the case of *Rigoletto* the changes demanded were comparatively easily met. The locale was moved to Italy; the King was reduced in rank to a duke and his name changed to that of a line which, if not fictitious, was at least extinct; and the name of the jester was changed to the wholly fanciful one of "Rigoletto." This name, which someone suggested would "swallow as easily as, for example, soup and soft bread," was also given to the opera.

In less troublous times Hugo's play regained the stage, and it became very popular as a vehicle for Edwin Booth under the title of *The Fool's Revenge*. He played the part of the jester.

ACT I

Scene 1 The profligate Duke of Mantua is giving a gay ball in his palace. His attitude toward women is shown in his lithe aria *Questa o quella*—"This or that one," and he soon leaves the scene briefly, escorting the wife of one of his courtiers. Presently the general merriment and the dance music are interrupted by a stern voice. It is the old Count Monterone, who has come to denounce the Duke on behalf of his daughter. Now the Duke's professional jester, the hunchback Rigoletto, steps forward and makes cruel fun of the old man Monterone keeps his dignity; and though he is arrested at the order of the Duke, he turns on his tormentor and delivers a powerful curse on his head. It is the curse of a father, and

Rigoletto, who is a father himself and deeply superstitious, turns away in horror.

Scene 2   After Monterone's terrible curse Rigoletto returns home. Just outside his house he is accosted by a tall, evil-looking man. It is Sparafucile, a professional cutthroat, and, as one professional to another, Sparafucile offers the court jester his services on any suitable occasion. As the sinister figure shambles off, muttering his own name—*Sparafucil'*—on a very low note, Rigoletto cries out *Pari siamo!*—"We are the same!"—and he sings his great soliloquy, cursing his own shape, his fate, his character. There follows then a long and beautiful duet with his daughter, the innocent young Gilda. She is all that is good in the jester's life, and he wishes to protect her from the world and its evil ways. His last instructions, as he leaves the house, are to Gilda's nurse, Giovanna, to keep all the doors locked.

His commands are in vain. Even before he has gone, the Duke of Mantua, disguised as a student, slips into the garden, bribes the nurse, and proceeds to make the most melodious love to Gilda. And when he leaves on account of some noises outside, Gilda sings her aria of ecstatic young love (*Caro nome* —"Dearest name").

The noise outside is a group of the courtiers who have come to abduct Gilda, thinking she is Rigoletto's mistress, not his daughter. To make the joke better, they secure Rigoletto's help, blindfolding him and making him hold the ladder. It is only after the men have left with Gilda that Rigoletto tears off the blindfold. He rushes into the house, crying *"Gilda, Gilda!"* and the act ends as he recalls in fear and trembling the father's curse—*La maledizione.*

ACT II

The morning after the girl's abduction the Duke, in the antechamber to his bedroom, sings of his beloved Gilda. His aria, *Parmi veder*, is so sweet that one almost believes him to be truly in love. And when the courtiers tell him, in a jolly chorus, how they abducted the girl and brought her to his palace, he is overjoyed and dashes from his anteroom to greet her.

Now comes one of the most moving and dramatic scenes Verdi ever wrote. Rigoletto, heartbroken, enters, pitifully singing, "*La-ra, la-ra, la-ra, la-ra,*" as a court jester should. He looks everywhere for his daughter; and when a boy enters briefly with a message for the Duke, he realizes, from what is said, that his daughter is with the Duke. With intense fury he turns on the men, crying, *Cortigiani, vil razza!*—"Foul race of courtiers!" He tries to break through them to get to the door; he falls weeping to the floor; he pleads piteously—but all in vain. Only when his daughter appears and throws herself into his arms, are the courtiers shamed into leaving. The tearful duet of father and daughter is interrupted as Monterone is brought through, under guard and on his way to execution. Rigoletto swears that the old man shall be avenged on the Duke, and the act closes powerfully as Rigoletto sternly repeats his oath and his daughter pleads for mercy on her lover.

ACT III

At night, outside a desolate inn on the bank of a river, stands Rigoletto, still swearing vengeance on the Duke while Gilda still pleads for him. The inn is owned by Sparafucile, the assassin, and his guest for the night is none other than the Duke—this time disguised as an officer. Presently he sings the most popular tune in the opera (*La donne è mobile*—"Woman is fickle"), and then he starts to make love to Maddalena, the pretty sister of Sparafucile. Now comes the great *Quartet*. Inside the inn, the Duke gives Maddalena a very smooth line to which she replies coquettishly. At the same time, on the outside, Gilda bewails her lover's falseness, while Rigoletto tries to comfort her.

Then things happen quickly. Gilda is sent off to change into traveling clothes, for her father plans to leave for other parts that same night. He then, for twenty scudi (about nineteen dollars), hires Sparafucile to murder the Duke, and he too departs. After the nobleman retires to bed, Maddalena persuades her brother to spare the handsome stranger and substitute the body of any late visitor who happens along. The night grows stormy, and Gilda, who has overheard these arrangements, knocks on the door of the inn. She has decided to sacrifice herself for her faithless lover. With merciful speed Sparafucile strikes her down and stuffs her into a bag, and when Rigoletto comes back and receives the heavy bundle, he begins to gloat over his victim. Not for long, though. Inside the inn, he hears the familiar voice of the Duke singing, once more, *La donna è mobile*—a most ironic touch. Rigoletto tears open the bag and finds his daughter. With her last breath she sings a farewell, as he begs her not to die. And when she is silent—forever—he shakes his fist at heaven and cries, once more, "*Ah! la maledizione!*" The curse is fulfilled.

DER RING DES NIBELUNGEN

(*The Ring of the Nibelung*)

The Ring of the Nibelung is the greatest work of art ever produced by a single man, or the most colossal bore, or the work of a supreme megalomaniac. It has been called all three repeatedly—and the epithets are by no means mutually exclusive.

Its entire production, words, music, and first stage production, took twenty-eight years, though, to be sure, there was an interval of eight, part way through the work on the score of *Siegfried*, when Wagner took a breather and wrote those two tiny *jeu d'esprit*—*Tristan* and *Die Meistersinger*.

In 1848 he began the libretto for an opera to be called *Siegfrieds Tod* ("The Death of Siegfried"), which ended with Brünnhilde leading Siegfried into Valhalla. But before he set a note of the score to paper, he realized that he ought to preface this work with one detailing the history of the hero, and accordingly he wrote the libretto for another opera to be called *Der junge Siegfried* ("The Young Siegfried"). These two, of course, eventually became *Die Götterdämmerung* and *Siegfried* respectively, the fourth and third work in the tetralogy, *Götterdämmerung* being provided with a far more significant and tragic ending.

Then, having dug back that far into the tale and observed ever greater social and ethical significance in it, he wrote *Die Walküre* as a preface to *Siegfried*, and finally *Das Rheingold* as a general preface to the three larger works.

It was only after the four librettos (or "poems," as he called them) had been written and printed that consistent work on the musical composition began, this time in forward order rather than in reverse. Even some of his good friends, when they read the poem, tried to discourage Wagner from attempting to complete so grandiose a scheme. Undeterred by friends, by enemies, by a series of dramatic marital, financial, even political crises, he persisted not only in completing the great work but in having a theater built especially to produce it—the Festspielhaus at Bayreuth.

Nor does the story end with the triumphant premiere in 1876. That first production was only the beginning of a war of aesthetics. More words were spilled, pro and con, on the subject of the *Ring* than, probably, on any single work of art in the history of man. Despite the vigorous attacks, despite the obvious difficulties and great expense of producing it, it made its way triumphantly through most of the great opera houses of the world, not only in Wagner's original German but in Hungarian, French, Swedish, English, Italian, Flemish, and Polish as well. Nevertheless, the attacks continued; but none, perhaps, was so damaging as Hitler's vigorous espousal of the work. For the generation of World War II this, outside of Germany, was a kiss of death. Of the four operas only *Die Walküre*, always the most popular of them, remained in the repertory of many of the great houses that used to give annual productions of the complete *Ring*. As for the younger critics and musicians, many of them began to look at the work as an interesting historical phenomenon no longer worth the trouble of serious study.

Then in 1953 came the notable revivals at the Festspielhaus itself, with new ideas of staging under the supervision of the composer's grandsons. Immediately the critical battle and the public interest started raging all over again. Opera houses in other countries began to revive the entire series, and the battle of the *Ring* raged still more vigorously. It still rages.

DAS RHEINGOLD

(*The Rhinegold*)

Opera in one act* by Richard Wagner with libretto in German by the composer. (Wagner intended this opera to be regarded as a prologue to the trilogy of three operas to follow; but as the four operas are usually given as a series, they are referred to in the discussion as a "tetralogy.")

WOTAN, *ruler of the gods*		Bass-baritone
FRICKA, *his wife, goddess of marriage*	*brothers and sisters*	Mezzo-soprano
DONNER, *god of thunder*		Bass or Baritone
FROH, *god of sun, rain, and fruits*		Tenor
FREIA, *goddess of youth and beauty*		Soprano
LOGE, *demigod of fire*		Tenor
ALBERICH	*brother Nibelungs*	Baritone
MIME		Tenor
FASOLT	*brother giants*	Bass
FAFNER		Bass
WOGLINDE	*sister Rhinemaidens*	Soprano
WELLGUNDE		Soprano
FLOSSHILDE		Mezzo-soprano
ERDA, *the earth goddess*		Contralto

Time: mythological
Place: in and about the Rhine
First performance at Munich, September 22, 1869

* Some opera houses divide this long work into two acts, granting an intermission between Scenes 2 and 3.

Scene 1 The remarkable prelude consists of nothing more than 136 bars of rising sequences in an undulating 6/8 rhythm based entirely on the E-flat tonic chord, yet presenting two of the most important themes to appear again and again through the four operas. Before it is quite over, the curtain rises to disclose the depths of the river Rhine with Woglinde, one of the three Rhinemaidens, swimming about and singing happily. (These girls are remarkable natators, accomplishing —with the aid of invisible wires—graceful swings across the width of the stage while employing their breath in full-voiced harmonizing.) She is presently joined by her two sisters, and the three of them play girlish games, all the time conscious that they ought really to be guarding the hoard of gold that gives its name to the opera—the Rhinegold.

A hairy and otherwise repulsive gnome named Alberich is attracted by this display of femininity and tries, in crude and awkward fashion, to seize one after another of the maidens. At once repelled by the gnome and attracted by the sport of teasing, they arouse and frustrate his desires to a point where he curses with ungentlemanly gestures.

At that moment a change in the light reflects the beams from the Rhinegold near the top of the stage. The delighted maidens, in neighborly fashion, tell Alberich about it. They have been instructed by their father to guard it; yet who would want to steal it? For while it is true that anyone who can fashion a ring from it may rule the whole world, yet, in order to do so, the ambitious smithy must forswear love forever. Certainly it is safe from this would-be seducer. But they have reckoned wrongly. Alberich climbs up, frightens the girls away, reaches out for the gold, and with a curse on love, wrenches it from the rocks and plunges into the depths.

The whole stage grows dark as the gold disappears. The Rhinemaidens plunge down hopelessly after the mocking Alberich; the waters seem to rise, then change into clouds, and a mist covers everything.

Scene 2 Through that mist we slowly perceive the new scene. Wotan, the ruler of gods, is asleep with his wife, Fricka, on a mountainside; and back of them, across a narrow valley, rises an imposing castle. When Fricka awakens, she sees it and, wakening her husband, points it out. It is the great fortress that has been some time in the building and is to be their new home. Instead of rejoicing, domestic bickering ensues, one of the principal points of irritation being the agreed-upon price tag—nothing less than Fricka's sister Freia, the goddess of youth and beauty, to be paid to Fafner and Fasolt, giant builders. Fricka thinks the price is too high—and this leads to all sorts of recriminations, especially concerning Wotan's frequent extramarital affairs.

The quarrel is interrupted by Freia herself, running from the giants, who now want their bill paid. Wotan, who had entered into this agreement on the advice of Loge, the god of fire, expects this same shifty character to get him out of paying somehow or other. Freia calls on two absent brothers for help—Donner, the god of thunder, and Froh, the god of fruitfulness. The two giants now come in to demand their payment, and Wotan tries to temporize, saying that he had never intended to give up Freia. The giants point out that the contract is written in runes on Wotan's own spear, and that disaster will rule the world if he should go back on a solemn treaty. Froh and Donner arrive just as the giants are about to take Freia forcibly, and Donner, with his huge hammer, stands before her threateningly.

Finally Loge joins the unhappy family gathering, fresh from his travels around the world looking for some substitute for Freia as payment to the giants. He is a thoroughly untrustworthy fellow—especially in the eyes of Fricka—and now that he reports failure in his mission, he is more unpopular than ever. But he does tell them about the Rhinegold—how Alberich had stolen it from the Rhinemaidens, how they had asked him to get Wotan's help in restoring it, and what its potentialities are when fashioned into a ring. This last detail immediately attracts both the giants and Wotan, and even Fricka is attracted to the idea that such a ring might have the power to make a husband faithful.

But when Loge tells them that by this time Alberich has already forged the Ring, they realize that the gods themselves are threatened. As for the giants, they have a private conference and then tell Wotan that if he can deliver the gold to them by nightfall, they will accept it in exchange for Freia. Meantime, they will hold onto her as a pledge, and they drag her, shrieking, off the stage.

Almost at once the gods start growing paler and paler: it is the result of Freia's absence, Loge explains: without the golden apples that she gives them their eternal youth is leaving them. Now desperate, Wotan makes up his mind to go to Nibelheim, where Alberich dwells, and somehow secure the gold. With ironic asides Loge shows him the way, and Wotan follows down the side of the cliff as mist again rises from the depths of the valley to cover the change of scene.

Scene 3 With the power of the Ring, Alberich has made himself absolute dictator of the Nibelungs, a race of dwarfs that lives in the depths of the mountains. In cold, cavernous Nibelheim, Alberich is driving the other gnomes to dig more gold for him and to fashion whatever objects he wants. His brother Mime has just finished a special assignment—the manufacture of a cap of golden network which makes its wearer invisible. It is called the Tarnhelm, and Alberich snatches it from his snarling brother, places it on his head, and disappears at once, a column of steam showing where he had been. From his hiding place he continues to taunt and torture his slaving brethren.

Wotan and Loge descend into this sweatshop and are told ruefully by Mime, an old acquaintance of Loge's, how Alberich's recently won ascendancy has transformed what was once a rather jolly place into its present wretched state. He also tells them about the Tarnhelm, and of how he had hoped to keep it for himself. But Alberich, now in visible shape and wearing the Tarnhelm hanging from his belt, drives a band of workers cruelly before him and chases Mime out with them. He then turns to his distinguished guests and boasts of his power, even threatening that he plans to put an end to the present regime of gods.

Wotan is disgusted, but the wily Loge plays upon the dwarf's vanity. He flatters Alberich with wonder over what he says he is able to perform, and, to show the power of the Tarnhelm, Alberich transforms himself into a writhing reptile, then back again into his own shape in order to boast properly. But, asks Loge, apparently impressed, can he also change himself into something small—say, a toad? At once Alberich obliges; at once the gods seize the little animal; and Loge tears off the Tarnhelm. Together, they bind up the now helpless dwarf and drag him, still struggling, out with them. Clouds and mist once more cover the stage.

Scene 4 It is still misty back on the mountain where the gods had last held conference. Loge and Wotan have Alberich captive and tell him he can have his freedom only at the expense of the entire hoard of gold. Using his Ring for commanding power, the dwarf summons the Nibelungs to bring up the hoard, which they do and at once depart, the curses of their master following them. Wotan, despite Alberich's shrieks of rage, tears the Ring itself from his finger and puts it on his own. At last Alberich is released from his bonds. But before he goes, he utters a terrible curse upon the Ring: it will bring misery to its wearer, murder shall follow in its wake, and its lord shall be its slave unto the time that it is returned to Alberich himself. Before the tetralogy is over, the curse is often and bitterly fulfilled.

The misty stage now becomes somewhat clearer. But it is nearing nightfall, and all the gods reassemble while the giants bring back Freia. Fasolt so dotes on Freia that he would almost rather keep her than get all the gold; but he finally consents to carrying out the bargain if the gold can be piled so high that Freia is completely obscured by it. There is almost gold enough for this, but Fafner says that he still can see Freia's hair, and Loge contributes the Tarnhelm to hide that. Still there remains a crevice through which Freia's eyes can be seen, and Fafner insists on covering it up with the Ring on Wotan's finger. At first the god refuses, but suddenly Erda, the earth goddess, rises through the ground. Solemnly she warns him to give up the Ring: it is the only way to avoid the curse of Alberich. Thus persuaded, Wotan throws the Ring on the pile, and the giants release Freia.

But as Fafner and Fasolt are dividing the spoils, an argument arises about who should have the Ring. Fafner, with a mighty blow, kills his brother, calmly packs up all the gold into a bag, and lumbers off, dragging the body after him. The motive of the curse rises ominously in the orchestra: murder has already accompanied the gold.

Donner now ascends a mountain; his hammer strokes and cries are heard; lightning flashes across the stage; the clouds disappear; and the new castle is seen in all its glory across the valley. A rainbow bridge crosses to the feet of the gods, and as the orchestra plays the piece known to concert-goers as *The Entry of the Gods into Valhalla,* the family of gods crosses the bridge to take up its new residence.

Only Loge remains behind. He has no illusions about Valhalla's affording much security and decides to return to the ordinary world in his normal form, which is that of fire. From down below, where the Rhine flows, come the despairing but lovely cries of the Rhinemaidens, still lamenting the loss of their gold.

DIE WALKÜRE

(*The Valkyrie*)

Opera in three acts by Richard Wagner with
libretto in German by the composer

WOTAN, *ruler of the gods*	*Bass-baritone*
SIEGMUND ⎫ *his children*	*Tenor*
SIEGLINDE ⎭	*Soprano*
FRICKA, *his wife*	*Mezzo-soprano*
HUNDING, *Sieglinde's husband*	*Bass*
BRÜNNHILDE, *a Valkyrie*	*Soprano*
GERHILDE	
ORTLINDE	
WALTRAUTE	
SCHWERTLEITE *other Valkyries*	*Sopranos and*
HELMWIGE	*Mezzo-sopranos*
SIEGRUNE	
GRIMGERDE	
ROSSWEISSE	

Time: mythological
Place: Germany
First performance at Munich, June 26, 1870

Without being too specific about it, one must assume an
interval of at least a quarter of a century between *Das Rheingold* and *Die Walküre*, during which Wotan has been populat-
ing the universe with illicit progeny. He has had a lengthy
affair with the earth goddess, Erda, producing nine daughters
who have grown up to be athletic equestriennes with enlisting
commissions. They swoop down on battlefields to bring up to
Valhalla recently deceased heroes who are to form a guard for

the fortress. These girls are known as the Valkyries, and one of
them is the character referred to in the title of the opera.
Wotan has also had an affair with an anonymous mortal
woman, siring a son and daughter with whom he lived, under
the name of Wolfe, until the girl was abducted. Their race is
called the "Wälsungs."

ACT I

Stormy weather is vividly painted in the opening measures
of music; and as the curtain rises, an exhausted young warrior,
fleeing from his enemies, finds shelter in a rude home built
around a huge ash tree. He throws himself on the hearth, and
here a young woman finds him, brings him drink, and comforts him. The tender love themes in the orchestra suggest
the attraction these two feel for each other at once.

When the owner of the house, as rude and rough as his
home, returns, he orders his wife to prepare the evening meal.
His name is Hunding, and during the repast his unexpected
guest tells something about himself. His name, he says, is
Woeful (*Wehwalt*), for his life has been full of woe. His sister
has been stolen by enemies; his father, Wolfe, has disappeared
during a battle; he has since been at odds with everyone.
Hunding, meantime, has been struck by a marked resemblance between his wife and this "Woeful"; and, putting details of the narrative together, he realizes that his guest is one
of the Wälsungs, who are mortal enemies. Gruffly he tells the
man that he may have shelter for the night, but in the morning
he must defend himself. As Hunding has weapons and Woeful does not, the result is foreordained: simple murder.

Hunding then orders his wife to prepare his nightly potion,
and she takes the opportunity to put into it a sleeping draught.
As she does so, she catches her guest's eye and tries to get him
to look at a particular spot in the ash tree; but before he can
understand the message, Hunding notices the exchange of
glances and orders her into the bedroom, where he shortly
follows her.

Left alone by the hearth, the man's thoughts are gloomy.

He longs for a sword to defend himself. His father had promised that one would appear in his hour of need; and just then the dying fire grows briefly brighter and lights up the spot on the tree the woman had looked at. There, buried deep in the ash, is the hilt of a sword. The orchestra sings out the triumphant Sword Motive, but it is not yet understood by the hero.

The woman now slips into the room and tells him about the sword. It had been put there by a stranger who appeared at her wedding, struck the sword into the tree, and said that it would belong to whoever could pull it out. Many warriors had tried and failed, but now she feels that one has come to take it. But as they speak of the sword, their passion for each other also grows. They are soon in each other's arms; the door flies open revealing a beautiful spring night; and the hero sings of love and spring (*Winterstürme wichen dem Wonnemond* —"Winter storms have waned in the winsome moon"). She replies in equally passionate accents (*Du bist der Lenz*—"Thou art the spring"). And suddenly they know who they are: both are children of the stranger who brought the sword—Wolfe, the Wälsung. Let his name no longer be Woeful but Siegmund, as hers, indeed, is Sieglinde.

Now Siegmund rouses himself, seizes the hilt of the sword, and pulls it forth triumphantly, naming it Nothung ("Needful"). Together, they flee into the beautiful spring night.

ACT II

Siegmund and Sieglinde have been fleeing for some time, but Hunding is on their trail, and Wotan (no longer Wolfe) is at a wild, rocky passage, where he expects the battle to be joined. With him is his favorite Valkyrie, Brünnhilde, whom he instructs to favor the Wälsung. The warrior maiden is delighted and, springing from rock to rock (at least, that is what the stage directions demand), utters her famous battle cry: "Ho-yo-to-ho!" But her high spirits are somewhat dampened when she sees Fricka, her father's wife, coming up the mountainside in no amiable mood, and she leaves her elders to have it out.

Hunding, it seems, has come to Fricka for help, and there is no question that she holds all the moral trump cards in the game that is now played. Wotan has rigged the whole sorry situation; he is trying to fool himself if he thinks this is the way to get a hero to solve the difficulty with the lost Ring; the two miserable wretches, Siegmund and Sieglinde, are no better than a pair of incestuous adulterers; and not only will she have nothing to do with them, but she insists that Siegmund be given no supernatural help—either from Brünnhilde's interference or from that magic sword he has. Wotan tries to stand on his dignity and to rationalize all his questionable actions; but he has to recognize that Fricka is unanswerably right in everything she says. Dejectedly he agrees to all Fricka's demands, and she has her brief moment of triumph as she meets the returning Brünnhilde and tells her to ask her honored father who is to win the battle now.

There now ensues a very long scene in which Wotan tells his beloved daughter practically all that has happened in *Das Rheingold* and then goes on still further about Alberich and Fafner. Fafner he cannot attack himself because of his treaty, and his only hope was to raise a hero who could. Now that, it seems, is to be denied him. And as for Alberich—Erda has told him that any son of the dwarf's is destined to destroy the gods. Worst of all, Alberich has, despite forswearing love, impregnated a mortal woman and "grim envy's son now stirs in her womb." Nevertheless, Brünnhilde must see to it that Hunding defeats Wotan's own son, Siegmund. But she flatly refuses, for Wotan himself, she says, has taught her to love Siegmund. Once more he insists that she obey his command; and then he rushes off into the mountains, while Brünnhilde, with heavy heart, picks up the spear and shield she had laid aside and wanders slowly off.

For a few moments the stage is empty, but the orchestra assures us that someone is hurrying toward the rocky crag. It is Siegmund and Sieglinde, the latter exhausted by flight and sorely troubled in her conscience. She loves Siegmund deeply, but she fears she has done wrong, and she wildly dreads the coming battle. Finally, she falls asleep, her head on her brother's knee, and Siegmund bends silently over her and kisses her brow.

Suddenly Brünnhilde stands before him. Solemnly she tells him that he is about to die, that she has come to take him to Valhalla to join the other heroes there. Even his magical sword shall not save him, for its power has been withdrawn. All this he receives with dignified tranquillity; but when he learns that Sieglinde may not be with him, that she must remain on earth to bear his child, which she is already carrying, he bursts out wrathfully. He rejects Valhalla and says he would rather go to the lower regions than be parted from Sieglinde. He even raises his sword to kill the sleeping woman so that they may remain together. This gesture makes Brünnhilde change her mind. She now promises to shield him in battle, and she rides off swiftly.

Off-stage are heard the sounds of Hunding in pursuit. Light begins to fail; and in the semi-darkness Siegmund bids his sleeping sister farewell and hastens up the mountainside to meet the enemy. A moment later she awakens, calling for Siegmund, and is terrified by the sound of Hunding's hunting horn. Up on the mountain a flash of lightning shows Siegmund already in battle. For a moment Brünnhilde hovers over the hero, defending him, but then a red light reveals Wotan, holding his spear between the two men. Siegmund's sword is shattered on that spear, and Hunding drives his own into the body of his enemy.

As Brünnhilde rushes down to take up the body of Sieglinde, who has fainted away, Wotan turns contemptuously to Hunding. With a gesture of his hand he causes the desperate man to fall dead, and then, through the thunder and lightning, he sets off in pursuit of his disobedient child.

ACT III

The last act begins with the exciting *Ride of the Valkyries*, familiar in its orchestral garb to every concert-goer but far more exciting when the curtain goes up and the music is supplemented with the warrior maidens themselves, rushing over the mountain tops, first four, then eight of them calling to each other, "Ho-yo-to-ho!" (The stage directions require that the girls come riding on horseback, each carrying a dead hero on the way to Valhalla. Few if any opera houses have ever assembled so gifted a female choir as to be able to perform this scene literally as horse opera.) Of the nine daughters of Wotan and Erda one, however, is missing. This is Brünnhilde, and when she arrives late on the scene, she brings with her not a warrior but a pregnant woman—Sieglinde. Swiftly she explains to her sisters who Sieglinde is and why Wotan is pursuing her. They are afraid to help her for fear of angering their father; nevertheless, they tell her that in the East, the giant Fafner, changed into the shape of a dragon, is guarding the Ring. There, Brünnhilde knows, Sieglinde will be safe from Wotan as he does not dare go near the place. She gives Sieglinde the pieces of Siegmund's sword, which she has saved, and tells her that someday her son may put them together again. Thrilled with her mission, Sieglinde thanks her savior and hurries away.

Amid thunder and dark clouds Wotan now arrives on the scene. At first her sisters try to hide Brünnhilde and to plead for her, but Wotan is adamant and calls on her to come forth. With great dignity she does so and asks for her sentence. It is that she may no longer serve her father, that henceforth she shall no longer be a Valkyrie, and that she shall serve, one day, a mortal husband. Again her sisters try to plead for her; again he turns on them; and he threatens that anyone who helps her shall share her fate. Then, on his stern command, they ride swiftly off, leaving Brünnhilde alone with Wotan. After a long silence Brünnhilde raises herself from her prostrate position and asks, "Was it so shameful, what I have done?" (*War es so schmählich?*) With fine feminine logic she points out that she did only what he himself wished he might have done. The fire of Wotan's anger goes out of him, but not the steel. At great length, and with great sorrow, he tells her that they must now be forever parted. He must put her to sleep, and she shall belong to the first man who shall come upon her. At least, she begs, let it not be a coward who claims.

Let him build around her sleeping place a fiery flame to guard her.

Deeply moved, Wotan raises her to her feet and sings his noble and heroic farewell, promising the fire that she has requested. Slowly she falls asleep; he lays her on a grassy mound; he kisses her once more, covers her with her shield, and solemnly walks to the center of the stage. Lifting his spear, he commands Loge to appear. This is where the *Magic Fire Music* is played. Fire starts springing up on every side as Wotan directs; and when it is all over the stage, he pronounces a final spell: "Only the man who does not fear my spear may walk through this fire!" Then, after one last look at his beloved daughter, he strides through the fire himself.

SIEGFRIED

Opera in three acts by Richard Wagner with
libretto in German by the composer

WOTAN, *disguised as the "Wanderer"*		*Bass-baritone*
SIEGFRIED, *son of Siegmund and Sieglinde*		*Tenor*
BRÜNNHILDE, *formerly a Valkyrie, now a mortal*		*Soprano*
ERDA, *the earth goddess*		*Contralto*
ALBERICH	} *brother Nibelungs*	*Baritone*
MIME		*Tenor*
FAFNER, *a giant transformed into a dragon*		*Bass*
FOREST BIRD		*Soprano*

Time: mythological
Place: Germany
First performance at Bayreuth, August 16, 1876

Again a number of years have passed between the operas
of the *Ring* cycle, though this time it is easier to estimate
about how many. Sieglinde left the last act of *Die Walküre*
to wander in the direction of the home of the Nibelungs.
There she was found by Mime, Alberich's smithy brother;
there she died giving birth to her son, who, Brünnhilde had
told her, was to be named Siegfried; there he had grown up,
with Mime as his foster father, into a healthy, arrogant, rude
young man, delighting in the creatures of the forest and despis-
ing the dwarf who has raised him.

ACT I

Shortly after the curtain rises, we learn of Mime's motives
in having taken the trouble to rear the child. He sits at his

forge in a forest clearing outside the cave he inhabits, muttering aloud to himself as he works halfheartedly at a sword for Siegfried—halfheartedly because he knows that the powerful youngster will disgustedly smash it to pieces as he has done with all of Mime's other inferior swords. Someday he hopes an invincible sword may be made of the pieces of Nothung, which Sieglinde had left with him, but he is not strong enough to forge them himself. With this sword, Mime believes, Siegfried will be able to slay Fafner and give his foster father the Ring, with all the power it carries. Fafner, for his part, having seized the whole hoard of gold (at the end of *Das Rheingold*), has used the Tarnhelm to change himself into a huge dragon and is so dull-witted that he can find nothing better to do with the gold than to lie on it.

With this much exposition out of the way, Siegfried comes in hallooing and driving before him a young bear which he has brought simply to frighten the dwarf. He insults Mime, wondering why he ever comes home when the animals are so much better company than this ugly fellow. Whiningly (but not without considerable justification, it would seem) Mime complains of the shabby reward he gets for having brought Siegfried up, serving both as father and as mother. Siegfried remains unimpressed by these complaints, which he has doubtless heard often, and finally manages to elicit from Mime what little he knows of his mother, that is, her name and the circumstances of his birth, for Mime professes ignorance of her distinguished paternity. Nor will he tell Siegfried who his father was. But he does tell him about the broken sword that Sieglinde had left and, demanding that Mime forge it for him at once, Siegfried dashes off once more to rejoin his furry and feathered friends.

With Siegfried gone, Mime has a second visitor—a distinguished-looking old gentleman with a staff and a long blue coat, who boasts of his great wisdom and calls himself "Wanderer." Mime is not receiving this afternoon and unceremoniously asks the old fellow to be on his way. Quite unperturbed, the Wanderer seats himself at the hearth and offers to demonstrate his wisdom by answering any three questions put to him. His head shall be the forfeit if he fails. Mime, who has been boasting of his own native intelligence, cannot resist the offer and comes up with three questions in a category on which the Wanderer is the top expert—for, as can be learned from the Cast of Characters, he is Wotan in disguise. The questions are: who inhabits the deepest caverns, who rests on the "back of the earth," and who lives in the cloudy heights? The answers—each given with additional detail—are the Nibelungs, the giants, and the gods.

Admitting the answers to be quite correct, Mime again invites his guest to leave. But Wotan insists that he too now has the right to ask three questions, and his are much harder. The first two are answered without difficulty, the correct answers being "the Wälsungs" and "Nothung." In giving these answers, with added detail, Mime shows that he knows a good deal more about family history than he has yet divulged to Siegfried. But the third question (an unfair one, as it deals with the future) floors the dwarf. It is: who is going to put the pieces of Nothung together again? And when Mime, in great fright, admits he does not know, Wotan tells him that it will be someone who has never experienced fear. However, he will not demand Mime's head: let that be taken, also, by one who knows no fear. And the Wanderer wanders off.

Left alone, Mime is overcome by fright. The orchestra whips up a fury of forest sounds; in the distance the bellowing of the dragon is heard; and, thinking that Fafner is on his trail, he hides, trembling, behind the anvil. When Siegfried returns, demanding his sword, he cannot at first find the dwarf. Finally the little fellow comes out, tells him that Nothung can be fashioned only by one who has not experienced fear, and asks Siegfried whether he knows anything about that emotion. Siegfried does not (Mime blaming himself for never having "taught" it to him) and demands instruction. But no matter how vividly Mime describes the frightening sounds of the forest at night and the reactions they produce in himself, the simple Siegfried cannot make sense of it. Maybe, suggests Mime, Siegfried could learn fear by visiting the cave of the fearsome dragon who lives not very far away. Siegfried, ever eager for instruction, begs to be led there, but first he must have the sword. And, as Mime clearly cannot fashion it himself, Siegfried takes up the pieces and begins to work at the forge. Mime, sitting by, offers professional counsel, but Siegfried, apparently inspired, goes about it eagerly in his own way. Meantime, the dwarf hopes that if Siegfried makes the sword and kills Fafner, he himself will bring him a drink with a sleeping potion in it, kill the youngster, and then make himself master of the gold. Siegfried, pounding away at his work, sings the exciting *Forging Song* (*Nothung! Nothung!*), and when the sword has been plunged into the water trough and the hilt fashioned, he waves it aloft exultingly and crashes it down on the anvil, which splits in two. Mime falls terrified to the ground.

ACT II

Deep in the woods, Alberich squats in the dark outside the cave of Fafner, awaiting the day which shall see the dragon slain. No love is lost between him and Wotan, who comes by and exchanges a number of unpleasant speeches with the dwarf. Wotan tells him of the hero who is coming to fight the dragon, a youngster who knows nothing about the gods or about the Ring, and who is acting wholly without guidance. Together, Wotan and Alberich awaken the dragon, and the latter suggests that a fight with a well-armed enemy can be avoided if he will just give up the Ring. Fafner's laconic answer is a request to leave him alone (*Lasst mich schlafen!*). With a laugh and a suggestion that Alberich keep an eye on his brother Mime, Wotan disappears into the forest.

With Alberich once more in his hiding place, dawn begins to break, and presently Siegfried and Mime arrive on the scene. "This is the place," says Mime, and Siegfried hopes now to learn about fear. Mime describes the terrors of the dragon graphically enough, including the fierce, snapping jaws, the poison that drips from the mouth, the powerful tail that can snap a man's bones as if they were glass; but Siegfried only wants to know whether the beast has a heart which may be pierced by Nothung, and then he drives his mentor away.

Waiting for the dragon to come out for his midday drink, Siegfried lies down under the trees, and the episode known to concert-goers as *Forest Murmurs* (*Waldweben*) ensues. Siegfried wonders about his mother; he listens to the songs of the birds; he tries to converse with them through blowing first on a reed, then on his horn; but he cannot understand what the birdcalls seem to be telling him. His homemade music, however, awakens the dragon, who comes forth to see what is disturbing him. Siegfried—not the least disturbed by the dragon's horrible features or by the bellowing basso whose voice reaches him through a speaking trumpet in the dragon's jaws—asks to be instructed about fear. Annoyed by the young man's brashness, the dragon attacks him; Siegfried wounds him in the tail; and then, when the monster rises in wrath, the opportunity presents itself to stab him to the heart. With a final warning to beware whoever it was who put him up to this murder, Fafner shudders and expires. But as Siegfried draws out his sword, a drop of blood falls on his fingers; he puts them into his mouth to wipe it off; and, lo, he can now understand the birds. The voice of one of them (an off-stage soprano) tells him about the hoard of gold, about the Tarnhelm, and about the omnipotent Ring. With thanks Siegfried enters the cave.

The disappearance of Siegfried is the signal for the two Nibelung brothers to steal in from their respective watching posts. Neither is pleased to see the other, and they engage in a snarling contest probably intended to be funny. Alberich, the more forceful of the two, gets the upper hand, denying Mime even the Tarnhelm from all the hoard, which Alberich fully expects to get for himself.

But when Siegfried emerges from the cave, they see that he already has both the Tarnhelm and the Ring, having taken them on the advice of the bird and passed over all the rest of the gold. The Nibelungs slink away in different directions; and when Siegfried has put the Ring on his finger and stuck the Tarnhelm into his belt, he hears the bird offering further advice. "Don't trust Mime" is what he hears; and he is also told that by the power of the dragon's blood he has drunk he will be able to understand the real meaning of Mime's words no matter what he appears to be saying.

Thus it is that when Mime speaks to him again and tries to wheedle Siegfried into trusting him, the words that come out betray his real intent. He hates Siegfried and his whole race, and he plans to murder him with his own sword as soon as he has got him to sleep. And when he actually offers him the drugged drink, Siegfried, in utter disgust, kills him with one blow of the sword. He wastes no sentiment on the death of his foster father, but throws the body into the cave and then drags the body of the dragon to guard over it. As for Alberich, he emits a peal of laughter from his hiding place when he sees his brother killed.

Once more the hero lies down below the branches and meditates on his aloneness in this world. Once more the bird cheers him up. "Hi, Siegfried," it calls, and proceeds to tell him about the glorious bride that awaits him, asleep and surrounded by fire. Her name is Brünnhilde, and she will belong to one who can go through the fire and who knows no fear. Laughing delightedly, Siegfried cries, "I'm the stupid boy who doesn't know how to be afraid," and he asks the bird to show him the way. By flying overhead before him the bird does just that as the act closes.

ACT III

Scene 1 It is a wild night at the foot of a great mountain, and Wotan calls upon Erda, the nature goddess and the mother of the Valkyries, to aid him once more with her wisdom. Looking very strange in a bluish light, her hair and cloak glowing, she rises through the ground, irritated, in a dignified manner, over being awakened from a long slumber. He tells her what is troubling him, but she is not much help. First she advises him to go to the Norns, the weavers of fate; and when he tells her that they cannot advise him, she suggests that he consult Brünnhilde. Only then does she learn what has happened to her daughter. She thoroughly disapproves of the whole business and only wants to go back to sleep. But before she goes, Wotan tells her that he is now completely resigned to the destruction of the gods, and that his power shall be inherited by young Siegfried, who is full of the joy of love, who knows no malice, and who shall awaken Brünnhilde. And when Brünnhilde awakes, she shall perform a great deed for redeeming the world.

Erda returns to her underground slumbers; the scene grows brighter; and a few moments later Siegfried is led in by the bird, who flies off on sight of Wotan. Siegfried naturally does not recognize his grandfather and demands to know the way to the sleeping maiden. The old man answers him with a great many references to things the boy can scarcely understand (and the audience may be expected to have some difficulties as well.) Finally, however, he makes it clear that it was he who had put the girl to sleep, whereupon Siegfried assumes that the Wanderer must be an enemy of the family. Therefore, when Wotan puts up his spear, barring the way up the mountain to Brünnhilde, Siegfried impatiently shatters it with his sword, Nothung. This is apparently a convincing and not entirely unsatisfactory symbol to Wotan of the waning of his own power and the growing might of the new order. He invites Siegfried to advance and he himself disappears. "The whole stage," to quote the directions, "fills itself with a sea of surging flames," and Siegfried disappears into them, blowing his horn, and crying, "Hoho! . . . Now I shall catch me a darling companion!"

Scene 2 As the orchestra spins out a bright web of significant themes, clouds cover the foreground of the stage, and when they have disappeared, we are once more on the spot where Wotan had put Brünnhilde to sleep at the end of *Die Walküre*. Siegfried climbs down the mountainside, first seeing Brünnhilde's horse, Grane, and then the sleeping girl herself. As she is clothed in armor, her visor down, he takes her to be a man; and even when he lifts the helmet and her bright, yellow hair falls out, he is not enlightened. We must remember that he had probably never before seen a human female in his life. Finally, noting that the "warrior" is breathing heavily, he cuts off the breastplate, staggers back, and cries, "That is no man!" A completely new emotion surges through him; he calls upon his mother for help; he imagines that for the first time he is experiencing fear. But he does know, now, that it is a woman he sees, and his instinct prompts him to implant a long and ardent kiss upon her lips.

This finally awakens Brünnhilde from a sleep that had begun before Siegfried was born. Her first reaction is one of joy at seeing the sun. It is not long, however, before she knows who Siegfried must be. She greets him by name; she tells him of how she had known him and loved him even before his birth; and in the long duet that constitutes the balance of the scene many emotions are gone through. Siegfried's are understandably simple: he is proud of his accomplishment, and he longs to embrace Brünnhilde. Her emotions are rather more complex, for she realizes that now she is no longer a goddess, that no god had ever touched her, and that her rescuer is a mortal, or at best a demigod. At the same time she is deeply attracted to the handsome young fellow (who is her nephew, though that does not cross the mind of either of them); and though she seems to know somehow that the reign of the gods is doomed, she welcomes a life that promises a glowing love and a laughing death. The opera ends as their voices join in a passionate acceptance of their love and their fate.

DIE GÖTTERDÄMMERUNG

(*The Twilight of the Gods*)

Opera in prologue and three acts by Richard Wagner with libretto in German by the composer

FIRST NORN	⎱	*Contralto*
SECOND NORN	⎰ *daughters of Erda*	*Mezzo-soprano*
THIRD NORN		*Soprano*
SIEGFRIED, *grandson of Wotan*		*Tenor*
BRÜNNHILDE, *daughter of Wotan*		*Soprano*
GUNTHER	⎱ *Gibichungs*	*Bass*
GUTRUNE	⎰	*Soprano*
HAGEN, *their half brother*		*Bass*
WALTRAUTE, *a Valkyrie*		*Mezzo-soprano*
ALBERICH, *a Nibelung*		*Baritone*

Time: mythological
Place: Germany
First performance at Bayreuth, April 17, 1876

It will be recalled that one of the bits of gossip retailed to Brünnhilde by her father during Act II of *Die Walküre* was that Alberich had bribed a mortal woman to bear him a child. This child, an almost exact contemporary of Siegfried's, grew up to be a saturnine young fellow named Hagen. His mother was Grimhilde, wife of a respectable Teutonic chieftain named Gibich, and she also had two legitimate children named Gunther and Gutrune. When *Die Götterdämmerung* begins, Gunther is King of the Gibichungs, and Gutrune and Hagen live with him. None of the three is married.

PROLOGUE

It is night, and still so dark that the unwarned spectator does not know till much later that the scene is Brünnhilde's rock, where she was left by Wotan and found by Siegfried. The three Norns (who roughly correspond in Norse mythology to the three Fates or Parcae of Greek and Roman myth) sit upon the ground and tell sad stories of the deaths of gods. One of them tells how Wotan many years ago had traded an eye for a drink of the well of wisdom. Now Wotan, who is always represented as missing one eye, had told Fricka, during the course of their *Rheingold* argument, that he had lost it in wooing her. Whether this inconsistency is owing to forgetfulness on Wagner's part or whether it is a subtle reminder that the ruler of the gods was not above telling a fib when arguing with a lady, no one exactly knows. Either explanation will do.

Wotan, we also learn, had fashioned his spear from a branch of the world tree (i.e., Yggdrasill's ash). Since then the ash has shriveled and the well of wisdom dried up; Wotan has had the Valhalla heroes pile up the boughs of the tree around the fortress of the gods; and heroes and gods now sit in Valhalla, in state, waiting for a fire to consume both them and it. All the time the Norns relate this dismal tale, they are passing a golden rope to each other. But when they ask each other how soon the fire will start and what will become of Alberich's gold, the rope suddenly breaks. Frightened, they tie themselves together with the pieces and run off crying: "To mother!"

This mysterious and somewhat mystifying scene prepares one for the final catastrophe in Act III; but as it is not strictly necessary dramatically and as the opera is extremely long, it is often omitted.

During an orchestral interlude day breaks, and we soon behold Siegfried and Brünnhilde issuing from the cave. They have exchanged pledges of love; he has learned wisdom from her; and now he is being sent forth to do great deeds. Before he goes, however, he gives her his Ring to guard her, and she

gives him Grane, her horse, to ride. After a heroic farewell, he
starts down the mountainside; she looks after him for a while;
and the curtain descends as the orchestra plays the eloquent
music of *Siegfried's Rhine Journey*, a glorious tissue of many
of the most significant motives of the *Ring*.

ACT I

Scene 1 The hall of the Gibichungs is an airy place, and
through the back of it may be seen the river Rhine. Hagen,
obviously a more intelligent, determined, and capable being
than either of his half siblings, is offering some family advice
and a rather tricky plan. It is time for both of them to get
married, he says, and he thinks it can be arranged. Brünnhilde
is the noblest woman in the world and would make Gunther
a fine wife. Unfortunately, she can be won only by a hero who
will fight his way through fire, and Gunther is not quite up to
that. Siegfried, however, is. Now, if Siegfried could be got to
fall in love with Gutrune (and what a fine match that would
be!), he might be persuaded to win Brünnhilde to please a
brother-in-law. And to get Siegfried attracted to Gutrune, all
that may be necessary is a magical potion which is in the wine
closet and which will make Siegfried forget Brünnhilde. Gunther, far from being shocked by Hagen's underhanded scheming, thanks his mother's memory for having produced such a
bastard. As for Gutrune, she can barely wait to see a hero like
Siegfried.

Nor does she have long to wait. Siegfried comes sailing down
the Rhine in a boat (just where he got it is not made clear,
and so most impresarios do not go to the expense of supplying
it), and steps into the Gibichung hall. He is most cordially
welcomed by the family; and Hagen, in the course of the
Gibichung equivalent of small talk, elicits the interesting information from Siegfried that the only portions of Fafner's
gold hoard he had taken were the Tarnhelm, which he has in
his belt, and the Ring, which he has given to a woman.
("Brünnhilde!" cries the villain Hagen, aside.)

Gutrune, who was immediately covered with girlish wonder

on sight of the handsome hero and had retired in confusion, returns with the drink of welcome, the one with the power of making its drinker forget everything; and as soon as Siegfried has drunk it, he falls spang in love with the girl. (Siegfried's easy susceptibility to women makes even Romeo look like a laggard.) He proposes for her at once, and a pact is made whereby he is to win Brünnhilde for Gunther in exchange for Gutrune. The pure and simple hero can no longer recall his recent "marriage." A solemn oath of blood friendship is sworn; Gunther and Siegfried cut their arms with their swords and let some blood drop into a horn; and both drink. Hagen, however, refuses to join in the oath: he says his nature is not so noble as theirs and his blood would poison the drink.

They waste no time. Gunther and Siegfried depart in the boat on their marital mission; Gutrune is enraptured with the idea of her own impending marriage; and Hagen sits down before the door of the house, on guard with spear and shield, muttering to himself about the Ring, and how he will get it through the agency of this merry team of wooers.

Scene 2 During an orchestral interlude the scene changes back to Brünnhilde's rock, where the ex-Valkyrie is admiring the Ring and covering it with kisses. Suddenly she hears a sound she had not heard in some twenty years—the wild riding of one of her sister Valkyries. It is Waltraute who arrives, bearing sinister tidings of Valhalla. In a long passage known as *Waltraute's Narrative*, she tells of the doom that seems to be preparing for the gods and of a remark of Wotan's, made during a dream, to the effect that only the return of the Ring to the Rhinemaidens will lift the curse. On her own initiative Waltraute has made this journey to beg Brünnhilde to avert the doom of the gods by returning the bauble. But Brünnhilde is utterly devoted to Siegfried: she would rather have Valhalla fall into ruins than give up this pledge of love. Waltraute utters a despairing cry and dashes away.

Evening begins to fall, and the surrounding fires grow brighter. Suddenly a frightening figure looms before Brünnhilde. It is Siegfried, but by the magic of the Tarnhelm, he has taken on the form of Gunther and also his lower voice.

He announces that he has come to make her his bride, he, Gunther, the Gibichung. Desperately Brünnhilde tries to defend herself, holding out the Ring in the thought that its power will save her. But the Ring has no power over Siegfried. He chases her across the stage; he seizes her with violence; he roughly tears the Ring from her finger; and when she falls utterly exhausted into his arms, he takes her toward the cave. But before he follows her into it, he draws out his sword and swears, by his oath of brotherhood, to lay it between himself and Gunther's bride.

ACT II

Outside the hall of the Gibichungs, with the flowing Rhine on one side of the stage and the entrance to the hall on the other, sits Hagen, still on guard, and apparently half asleep. Through the night slinks his father, Alberich. He tells him of the absolute necessity to get hold of the Ring before Brünnhilde gives it back to the Rhinemaidens. Hagen, in his own gruff way, tells his father not to worry: he will lay hands on it, all right.

With Alberich gone, the sun begins to rise, and Siegfried comes out of a clump of bushes by the riverside, now once more unmistakably himself. Hagen summons his half sister, and Siegfried reports the success of his expedition, omitting the wrestling with the bride but including his exemplary behavior in the cave. The rest of the party is sighted coming along in a boat, and Hagen summons all the vassals to help celebrate the wedding. Their rough, joyful chorus is the only choral passage in the entire *Ring*.

But when Brünnhilde arrives with Hagen and sees not only Siegfried but the Ring on his finger, she becomes wild with anger and despair. She cries that Siegfried, not Gunther, is her husband; that Gunther, if he is her husband, should take the Ring; and finally that Siegfried's sword did not lie between them when he won her, but that it hung in its sheath on the wall. Finally, when she has succeeded in filling the Gibichungs with doubt as to Siegfried's honorable behavior, he swears a mighty oath on Hagen's spear, offering up his life on that very spear if Brünnhilde's accusation is true. But Brünnhilde steps forward too and swears in the same solemn notes that Siegfried is forsworn; and she goes on to bless the point of the spear so that it may sink into "that man."

Siegfried, honestly bewildered, suggests that Brünnhilde be given time to compose herself, and with all the grace he can summon, he takes Gutrune into the hall to prepare for the wedding. Brünnhilde, Gunther, and Hagen are left alone, and the last develops plans for getting rid of Siegfried. He learns from Brünnhilde that the hero is impregnable in battle, but his back is vulnerable. In giving him this supernatural protection, as she had done, she felt confident that he would never turn his back on an enemy. Gunther has some initial compunctions about murdering Siegfried, both on account of the oath of blood-brotherhood (which Hagen points out has already been broken) and on account of Gutrune's possible reaction. Thereupon Hagen suggests that Siegfried be murdered the next day on a hunt and that Gutrune be told it was a boar that did it.

Barely is the plan agreed to by all three when the wedding procession begins to issue from the hall. Gunther takes Brünnhilde by the hand to join it, and Hagen remains alone outside, no member of the wedding.

ACT III

Scene 1 In a mountain-ringed valley of the Rhine, the three Rhinemaidens sing sweetly about their lost gold and the hero who they hope will give it back. And speaking of the devil, in comes Siegfried, who has wandered away from the hunting despite the identifying horn calls that have been sounding back and forth. First by teasing and then by warning him of the curse that falls on the possessor of the Ring, they try to get it from him. Good-naturedly he laughs at their warnings, telling them how he got it in the first place and also that he has not yet learned the meaning of fear. When they have swum away, giving him up as a bad job, he looks after them admiringly, thinking that if it weren't for Gutrune, he wouldn't mind having one of the charming creatures for himself.

There the rest of the hunting party finds him. Gunther's conscience is apparently bothering him, and, to cheer him up, Siegfried amiably tells the party of his childhood with Mime and the affair of Fafner, the dragon. In the midst of his recital Hagen offers him a drink, which restores the memory he had lost before the expedition to Brünnhilde's rock. He then goes on to tell how he originally won Brünnhilde. At this, Gunther starts up in amazement. Hagen points out two black ravens who are circling over Siegfried's head and asks whether he can understand their language. As the hero turns to look after the birds, Hagen thrusts his spear deep into his back. Siegfried turns and tries to crush Hagen with his shield, but he falls back upon it himself. With his dying breath he calls upon Brünnhilde, the heavenly bride who beckons him now. As for Hagen, with a contemptuous "I have avenged perjury" he stalks off.

With night falling, the vassals take up Siegfried's body on his shield and begin to carry it off. The moon breaks through the clouds; mists rise from the Rhine and cover the stage; and while the scene is changed, the orchestra plays the grand, gruff, and moving *Siegfried's Funeral March*.

Scene 2 Back in the Gibichungs' hall, Gutrune, uneasy, comes from her room and meets Hagen. He is in time to tell her of the procession that is bringing her back her husband, victim, he says, of a wild boar. When the body is brought in, Gutrune, in an agony of grief, throws herself upon it and denounces Gunther. Her brother, however, tells her that Hagen was the boar who destroyed the hero. Hagen admits it, justifies himself, and claims the Ring. This precipitates a most unseemly fight between the two half brothers, which ends with Hagen striking Gunther dead. He turns then to seize the Ring, when the dead arm of Siegfried raises itself menacingly, and they all recoil in horror.

At this moment Brünnhilde enters the hall and commands peace. She now understands what has happened, and she shows

generous pity for Gutrune, who huddles over the body of her
brother. Then she orders a huge funeral pyre to be built by
the side of the river to consume the greatest of heroes. For a
while she stands and muses on the face of Siegfried, and then,
in a long solo, often performed at orchestral concerts, she sings
of the tragic ending of Wotan's plans; she seizes the Ring;
and she takes a firebrand and addresses the two ravens who
fly overhead: Let them know that at last the twilight of the
gods is come. Then she throws the flame onto the pyre; the
ravens fly off; and, mounting her horse, Grane, she rides directly into it.

The fire blazes up and begins to consume the whole hall;
the river Rhine rises in back; the Rhinemaidens appear.
Hagen, suddenly rousing himself, jumps into the river after
the Ring which the Rhinemaidens have seized; but Floss-
hilde bears it away, while the other two twine their arms
around Hagen's neck and drag him down into the depths.

Meantime, the fire from the burning hall of the Gibichungs
has reached up into the clouds, and by its light one can see
the gods and heroes sitting in Valhalla. The flames catch on
there too; and as they cover it, the full orchestra softly sings
the motive of *Redemption by Love*. The whole world, Wagner seems to say, shall have a new birth, a new order, through
Brünnhilde's noble love.

ROMEO AND JULIET

(Roméo et Juliette)

Opera in five acts by Charles Gounod with libretto in French by Jules Barbier and Michel Carré, based on Shakespeare's play

COUNT CAPULET	Bass
JULIET, *his daughter*	Soprano
GERTRUDE, *her nurse*	Mezzo-soprano
TYBALT, *Capulet's nephew*	Tenor
GREGORY, *a Capulet*	Baritone
ROMEO, *a Montague*	Tenor
MERCUTIO, *another*	Baritone
BENVOLIO, *another*	Tenor
STEPHANO, *Romeo's page*	Soprano
THE DUKE OF VERONA	Bass
COUNT PARIS, *engaged to Juliet*	Baritone
FRIAR LAWRENCE	Bass

Time: *14th century*
Place: *Verona*
First performance at Paris, April 27, 1867

Of all the masterpieces of literature on which the team of Barbier & Carré, libretto manufacturers extraordinary, operated, the one they treated with greatest respect was Shakespeare's *Romeo and Juliet*. Though the scenario is considerably condensed, especially in Act I, and though the low-comedy servant Peter is omitted and a charming page boy named Stephano substituted, the outlines of the story are faithfully followed, the principal characters retain their Shakespearean vitality, and even many of the lines are directly translated or

441

at least paraphrased. One major concession to operatic requirements these industrious workmen did have to make: they permitted Juliet to awaken soon enough to indulge in a duet with Romeo before he died of his poison. But even here there was the justification of literary history: Brooke, the author of the poem that was one of Shakespeare's principal sources, had done the same thing.

Adelina Patti, the most famous of Juliets, also followed at least one portion of the story with faithfulness to the spirit of the text. In the 1880's, when she was married to (but separated from) the Marquis de Caux, she sang the role at the Paris Opéra with a French tenor named Nicolini. (His real name was Ernest Nicolas, but he changed it out of respect for Italy, which appreciated his singing more than did his native country.) The principals were as much in love, apparently, as the characters they were representing; and one heartless observer (could he have been a critic?) tallied twenty-nine genuine kisses that passed between them during the balcony scene. When Patti was finally divorced from the Marquis, this operatic couple was married—and lived lyrically together for twelve years, at the end of which the tenor died and the soprano returned to the aristocracy as the Baroness Cederström.

PROLOGUE

Shakespeare's play is prefaced with a prologue in the form of a sonnet spoken by a single actor denominated "Chorus." Its well-known lines begin:

> *Two houses, both alike in dignity,*
> *In fair Verona, where we lay our scene . . .*

and goes on to speak of the "star-cross'd lovers." Gounod's opera begins with the same sonnet, but the lines of "Chorus" are sung by the full chorus.

ACT I

Act I begins with the ballroom scene, which, in Shakespeare's play, is Scene 5. However, the librettists manage to tell us all the important things that happen in the earlier scenes—and even a few that don't! The curtain rises to the music of a waltz being danced to at a party given by the Capulets. Tybalt discusses his cousin Juliet's forthcoming marriage with the Count Paris. (Incidentally, no one has bothered to tell Juliet that she has been betrothed. Parents did things in a rather highhanded way in those days.)

Pretty soon, along comes that pompous old bore Lord Capulet, Juliet's father. He introduces his daughter to the company, and she obliges with a very nice little aria. It shows her to have at least one very marked talent—a fine coloratura.

It appears, however, that there are some unwanted guests at the ball—a group of the hated Montagues. One of them is Romeo, and he naturally has fallen in love with Juliet at first sight. Mercutio teases him about it a bit, and he sings a light baritone aria—a French paraphrase of the famous Queen Mab speech. Next there is a scene between the nurse and Juliet, and when marriage is hinted at to our heroine, she claims she wants none of it. It is then that she has her most famous aria —the well-known *Waltz Song*. Ironically, she meets a moment later the man she is to marry. Juliet and Romeo have the first of the series of love duets that characterize this opera, and at its end Juliet is just as much in love as Romeo is.

But Cousin Tybalt believes he recognizes the voice of a Montague. He is not certain, for the guests are wearing masks. However—hotheaded fellow that he is—he is ready to cause trouble and is restrained with some difficulty by the host, Lord Capulet, who insists that there be no trouble at his party. He urges everyone to dance, and so the act ends as it began —with a waltz chorus.

ACT II

Act II is the familiar balcony scene. It begins—as does Shakespeare's balcony scene—with Romeo escaping from his jolly companions, and finding himself beneath Juliet's balcony. "He jests at scars that never felt a wound," he mutters to himself (in French, of course), and then he sings his big aria,

Ah! lève-toi, soleil! The balance of the act is an exceptionally fine love duet. As in Shakespeare, it is Juliet who proposes marriage—and a very speedy one—and Romeo eagerly agrees. Twice during the course of the long duet they are interrupted. Once it is a party of Capulets who are still searching for the Montagues, and once it is the nurse, who urges Juliet to go to bed. Toward the close there is the famous couplet about "parting is such sweet sorrow"; and then, after Juliet has followed the nurse indoors, Romeo breaths a few more ecstatic phrases.

ACT III

Scene 1 is very brief, consisting largely of the secret marriage of Romeo and Juliet. They come to the cell of the good old Friar Lawrence; Romeo explains that they wish to be married quickly and secretly; the friar decides such a marriage may end the bitter feud between the Montagues and the Capulets; and the ceremony is performed. At the end there is a quartet of rejoicing, in which they are joined by the nurse.

Scene 2 contains a good deal of action and one brand-new, non-Shakespearean character. This is the page Stephano. He is an elegant, gay, and fearless young Montague—so young, in fact, that his part is sung by a soprano. He opens the scene by singing a pert and insulting serenade to the Capulets, *Que fais-tu, blanche tourterelle?* Gregory, a Capulet, starts to attack him with a sword. But a group of Montagues arrives, and very quickly there is serious trouble. Tybalt challenges Romeo, and Romeo, who has just been married to Tybalt's cousin, refuses the challenge. The hotheaded Mercutio takes it up instead, and when he is slain by Tybalt, Romeo can no longer restrain himself. He attacks Tybalt and slays him in turn. Now older and wiser heads appear, Lord Capulet and the Duke of Verona among them. The Duke, properly shocked by the bloodshed, banishes Romeo from the city. This is the worst possible fate for the tragic newlywed, and he leads the ensemble in a fine concerted number bewailing his misfortune.

Act IV begins with the third of the four love duets that melodiously punctuate this sad story. Romeo and Juliet have spent their one night together, and it is now time for Romeo to depart. The Duke has decreed that if he is found within the walls of Verona, he shall forfeit his life. In vain the lovers imagine that it is the nightingale and not the lark who sings (to quote Shakespeare) "so out of tune." Very much *in* tune, the soprano and the tenor take a tragic farewell.

But worse is in store for poor Juliet. Her father comes in to tell her that she must marry the Count Paris at once. She is utterly distraught, and when she is left alone with Friar Lawrence, she begs for advice. She is ready for anything—even death. The friar conveniently produces a phial. In it, he explains, there is a drug. If she drinks it, she will appear to be dead for forty-two hours. At the end of that time, he promises, he will have brought Romeo back to her. Quickly she takes the drink.

Thereupon, oddly enough, there is a ballet in several movements. I say "oddly enough" because it wasn't originally in the score. Gounod obligingly supplied it when the opera was first given at the National Opera, a year after its premiere at the Théâtre Lyrique. The fashionable members of the Jockey Club always insisted on a ballet in the middle of any opera given at the big house, and who was a mere composer to object? The ballet makes no dramatic sense at all, but the music is rather pretty.

Now Lord Capulet reappears to urge on the marriage. Wildly Juliet cries that the grave shall be her marriage bed— and she falls in a dead faint as everyone is horror-struck. The drug, apparently, has done the first part of its work during the ballet.

The last brief and tragic act is devoted largely to the last of the love duets. It opens, however, with a little tone poem supposed to describe Juliet's deathlike sleep in the vault of the Capulets. Romeo (who has heard that she is dead—not that she is only drugged) comes into the vault to sing a last farewell, O *ma femme! o ma bien aimée!* Thereupon he, too, takes a drug—only, his is real poison, not merely a sleeping draught like Juliet's. A moment later Juliet begins to wake and learns to her horror what Romeo has done. One more duet they have, but the poison works too well, and Romeo is dying. Quickly she seizes her dagger—and the two most famous lovers in literature die in each other's arms.

DER ROSENKAVALIER
(The Knight of the Rose)

Opera in three acts by Richard Strauss with libretto in German by Hugo von Hofmannsthal

PRINCESS VON WERDENBERG, the Marschallin	Soprano
BARON OCHS VON LERCHENAU, her cousin	Bass
OCTAVIAN, her lover	Mezzo-soprano
HERR VON FANINAL, a wealthy parvenu	Baritone
SOPHIE, his daughter	Soprano
MARIANNE, his housekeeper	Soprano
VALZACCHI, an Italian intriguer	Tenor
ANNINA, his partner	Contralto
POLICE COMMISSIONER	Bass
MAJOR-DOMO OF THE MARSCHALLIN	Tenor
MAJOR-DOMO OF FANINAL	Tenor
ATTORNEY	Bass
INNKEEPER	Tenor
A SINGER	Tenor
A FLUTE PLAYER	
A HAIRDRESSER	
A SCHOLAR	silent
A NOBLE WIDOW	
MAHOMET, a page	
THREE NOBLE ORPHANS	Soprano, Mezzo-soprano, Contralto
A DRESSMAKER	Soprano
AN ANIMAL TAMER	Tenor

Time: middle of the 18th century
Place: Vienna
First performance at Dresden, January 26, 1911

There is an anecdote about *Der Rosenkavalier* and its composer which, as the Italians say, *si non è vero, è ben trovato*, if not gospel truth, is at least to the point. The opera was produced in 1911, and quite some years later the aging composer was, for the first time, conducting a performance of it himself. In the last act—all the while conducting—he leaned over to his first fiddle and whispered, "Isn't this awfully long?" "Why, maestro," objected the concertmaster, "you composed it yourself." "I know," said Strauss sadly, "but I never thought I'd have to conduct it."

A completely uncut version of the opera, without intermissions, would take almost four hours to perform. All the more remarkable is it that a light comedy can sustain its charm so consistently that its length has not prevented its becoming the most popular of all the operas of Richard Strauss, a staple in the repertoire of almost every great opera house in England, the United States, and Central Europe (Latin countries take to it a little less kindly); and, along with Wagner's *Die Meistersinger*, it is generally regarded as the greatest comic opera to come out of Germany since Mozart. Like *Die Meistersinger*, incidentally, it was originally planned as a very short work, but its composer became so enamored of the idea of reproducing a full-length portrait of a phase in social history, that it gained enormous depth in detail during the writing. No one who loves either of these works wishes to forgo a single one of those details.

ACT I

One of those "details," which the librettist, Von Hofmannsthal, had not even thought of when he wrote his first synopsis, turned out to be the dominant character in the story. This is the Princess von Werdenberg, who is married to a field marshal and is therefore generally referred to as the Marschallin. Although too often represented on the stage by an overripe soprano, Strauss and Von Hofmannsthal thought of her as a very attractive young woman in her early thirties. When the curtain rises, it is midmorning, and she has been entertaining, in her husband's absence on a hunting trip, her current young lover. This is an aristocrat named Octavian, just seventeen years old. With the Marschallin still in bed and Octavian in deshabille, the lovers are bidding each other good-by, a farewell overshadowed with pathos as the Princess realizes that the discrepancy in their ages must soon put an end to the affair.

Before an unwelcome visitor—her cousin, the rather brutish Baron Ochs—can force his way in, Octavian manages to hide behind the bed and disguise himself as a chambermaid. As his part is written for a sylphlike soprano (Hofmannsthal had Geraldine Farrar or Mary Garden in mind), Ochs is quite taken in by the disguise and tries, throughout the scene, to make passes at the "girl" and a date with her. Actually, he has come to request the Marschallin to obtain the services of a Knight of the Rose (a *Rosenkavalier*) to fulfill a traditional custom, that is, to present a silvered rose to his fiancée, who turns out to be Sophie, the daughter of a wealthy *nouveau riche* gentleman named Von Faninal. Ochs also wants the services of an attorney, and his distinguished cousin bids him wait so that he may meet her own man of law, who is expected at her levee that morning.

This levee now begins. Not only the attorney, but a hairdresser, a widow with numerous progeny, a couple of Italian busybodies (of whom we shall hear more later), an Italian tenor, and various other odd characters try to get something from the Princess. The tenor shows his wares in a very handsome Italian aria, which is interrupted at its climax by Ochs's arguing with the attorney about the dowry.

At last the Marschallin is left alone again, and, in the *Mirror* aria, she reflects sadly on the changes wrought in her since the time when she was a blooming young girl like Sophie von Faninal. The return of Octavian, now booted and spurred, does not alter her sadly nostalgic mood. He protests his undying devotion, but the Marschallin knows better. She tells him it must soon be over, and she sends him away. Maybe she will see him later in the day, riding in the park, maybe not. And off the youngster goes. Suddenly she remembers: he has not even kissed her good-by. She sends some servants off to get him back. But it is too late: he has dashed away from the door. And as the act closes, she scans her face in the mirror. She is a sad lady, but a wise one, too.

The second act takes us to the home of Von Faninal. He and his housekeeper, Marianne, are delighted over the prospect of his daughter's marrying a nobleman, however tarnished his reputation may be. Today is the day when Octavian is expected to bring the silvered rose on behalf of Baron Ochs, and the formal presentation takes place soon after the beginning of the act. It is one of the most beautiful passages in the opera. Octavian is suitably dressed in great grandeur, and he and the lovely Sophie fall in love at once. Soon after, the Baron Ochs arrives with his retinue. His behavior is very coarse indeed. He tries to squeeze and to kiss his young bride-to-be, but she repulses him at every step. This only amuses the old roué. He goes off to another room to draw up the marriage contract with Faninal, and he even suggests that, while he is gone, Octavian might teach Sophie a little something about love-making. This instruction has not proceeded very far when they are interrupted by the wildly angry servants. It seems that the Baron's men, taking after their master, have tried to make love to one of the Faninal servant girls, who didn't like it.

Now Octavian and Sophie have a very serious discussion, for both know that the Baron will make her an impossible husband. Meanwhile, as the two fall more and more in love, Octavian promises to save Sophie. The two Italians, briefly met in Act I and named Valzacchi and Annina, suddenly appear from behind a couple of decorative stoves, just in time to discover the lovers in each other's arms. Loudly they call for Baron Ochs in the hope that he may reward their services as spies. A quite colorful and confusing scene then develops. Sophie insists she will not marry Ochs; Ochs is largely amused; Faninal and his housekeeper insist that Sophie *must* go through with the marriage; and Octavian grows more and more outraged. Finally he draws his sword on the Baron, who calls for help from his servants. The Baron is slightly wounded in the arm and loudly demands a doctor. When the physician arrives, he declares the wound slight.

At last Ochs is left alone to recover, and as he sips wine, he gets a message signed, "Mariandel." This is the servant girl he thought he had met in Act I at the Marschallin's, and the note confirms the date he had tried to make with her. "Mariandel" is none other than Octavian himself, who obviously has some useful mischief in mind in sending Ochs this billet-doux. Meantime, the news that he has a date with a new girl cheers him up. Under this influence—not to mention the wine he has been drinking—he starts to sing waltzes. Snatches of the famous *Rosenkavalier* waltzes have punctuated earlier parts of the score, but now, at the end of the act, they are sung and played irresistibly.

ACT III

The Baron's two henchmen, Valzacchi and Annina, have deserted him. He did not pay well enough, and they are now in the employ of Octavian, supervising the preparation of the *chambre séparée* of an inn—that is, a private dining room, complete with bed. Here the Baron is to come for his date with the disguised Octavian, and a pretty horrific surprise is in the making. There are to be windows that open suddenly, revealing strange heads, a trap door, and other devices to drive the evil old fellow crazy.

When the Baron arrives, everything seems to start off well enough. There are Viennese waltzes from an off-stage orchestra, and Mariandel acts coy but not too standoffish. Then things begin to happen. Doors spring open, as planned, and a disguised Annina rushes in with four children. She claims the Baron as her husband, while the children address him as "Papa." The Baron calls for the police, who arrive in due time but fail to be impressed by this pathetic nobleman, who has lost his wig. Next, Faninal is summoned and is duly shocked at the behavior of his son-in-law-to-be. Sophie, too, descends on the party and becomes involved in a real argument with her father. The Marschallin is the last to appear in all her dignity, and she roundly tells off her kinsman.

At last—thoroughly defeated and threatened with huge bills for the entire party—Ochs is glad to escape. Faninal and the rest also retire, and then comes the climax of the whole opera.

In a beautiful trio the Marschallin finally renounces her late lover, Octavian, and bestows him—sadly but graciously—on her young and beautiful rival, Sophie. Then she leaves them, and the final love duet is interrupted only briefly, as the Marschallin brings back Faninal for a fatherly comment on the ways of youth.

"It is a dream . . . it can hardly be true . . . but it will last forever." These are the last lines heard from the two young lovers, but the opera is not quite over. When they have left, the little black page, Mahomet, runs in, finds a handkerchief that Sophie has dropped, and quickly disappears.

SALOME

Opera in one act by Richard Strauss with libretto translated (with a few excisions) into German by Hedwig Lachmann from the French original by Oscar Wilde

HEROD, *Tetrarch of Judea*	*Tenor*
HERODIAS, *his wife*	*Mezzo-soprano*
SALOME, *her daughter*	*Soprano*
JOKANAAN (*John the Baptist*)	*Baritone*
NARRABOTH, *a young Syrian, Captain of the Guard*	*Tenor*
A PAGE	*Alto*
FIVE JEWS	*Four Tenors, One Bass*
TWO NAZARENES	*Tenor, Bass*
TWO SOLDIERS	*Bass*
A CAPPADOCIAN	*Bass*
AN EXECUTIONER	*Silent*

Time: about A.D. *30*
Place: Judea
First performance at Dresden, December 9, 1905

This one-act shocker is sometimes referred to as a "biblical drama" because the bare elements of the story are found in the New Testament. Just how bare those elements are may be discovered by reference to Matthew xiv and Mark vi, where Salome's name is not even mentioned. She is identified simply as the daughter of Herodias, and her motivation in asking for John's head on a charger stems from a request of her mother's. But before Wilde wrote the French drama that serves as the libretto for the opera, the subject of Salome had been treated

453

by a long list of writers, including—to name but a very few—such divergent figures as Eusebius, St. Gregory, Aelfric, Heine, and Flaubert. Some of the versions of the story are even more fantastically different from the Bible's than Wilde's, and one of them—Flaubert's—served as the basis of another opera, Massenet's *Hérodiade*, which was highly successful in its day. Wilde's version, essentially a study in neurasthenia, had an operatic setting written even before Strauss's by the French composer Antoine Mariotte. Its success was local and it is today practically forgotten. Wilde's conception of the character of the psychopathic princess is said to have been inspired as much by Huysmans and by Italian and French artists' treatment of the subject as by anything else.

Be this as it may, there can be little doubt that it was written as a *fin de siècle* shocker. And shock it did. The British censors banned the dramatic version from the London stage for many years; Kaiser Wilhelm II (who, after all, was Queen Victoria's affectionate grandson) banned the operatic version from Berlin; and the directors of the Metropolitan withdrew it after one public rehearsal and one performance on account of protests from the pulpit and press.

When Mary Garden appeared in the opera at the Manhattan Opera house two years later, one of the pulpit protesters was Billy Sunday. After his attack (delivered without hearing or seeing the performance), Miss Garden met Sunday, shared an ice-cream soda with him, and made it all up. Today's public has made it all up analogously with composer and librettist, and it is only a rare and courageous oldster who will dare to admit that he is still shockable by what remains a willfully vivid projection of degeneracy.

Just one technical detail to indicate that this characterization is justified and that the effects were produced with clever deliberateness: In a certain passage the double-bass players are required to pinch their strings tightly with thumb and forefinger as they administer quick, hammerlike strokes of the bow. The purpose—to quote the composer's own instructions —is to produce a noise like "the suppressed, choked moaning of a woman."

THE OPERA

It is a beautiful, warm, moonlight night on the terrace off the banqueting hall of Herod, Tetrarch of Judea. Inside, among the banqueters, is Salome, the Tetrarch's stepdaughter; outside, a handsome young captain of the guards named Narraboth comments passionately on the beauty of the Princess. A well-wishing page tries to warn him against this dangerous mooning, but he is scarcely listened to.

From inside the hall comes the sound of the banqueting; but from below, from a cistern on the right-hand side of the stage, comes the prophetic voice of John the Baptist—or Jokanaan, as he is known in the German libretto—speaking of the coming of Christ. The soldiers are impressed but think their prisoner probably mad.

Into the moonlit night rushes Salome, annoyed by the persistent sex-hungry glances of her stepfather. She is a pretty chit of only fifteen, but it would take no Greek dramatist or psychologically trained social worker to offer an unpromising prognosis from a glance at her case history. Her mother had murdered her father in order to marry Herod; Herod himself is a degenerate pleasure-seeker; she has been brought up in a viciously corrupt court; and Herod's desire to sleep with his stepdaughter has been weakly veiled at the same time that it has been strengthened by her obvious aversion to him.

The voice of Jokanaan strongly attracts her, not only for its natural manliness, but, perversely, because he has cursed out her mother for wickedness and because her stepfather seems to fear him. It does not take her long to seduce the love-struck Narraboth into ordering the prophet to be brought forth; and as he, in rags but with religious passion, denounces her elders, she is more and more physically attracted. Repeatedly, in successively higher keys and with broadened versions of the musical phrase, she cries: "I want to kiss your mouth, Jokanaan!" His advice to try penance instead only inflames her the further; while her shameless behavior disturbs young Narraboth so deeply that he suddenly whips out his sword and commits suicide. The charming girl does not even glance at the body; and Jokanaan, with a final admonition to seek Jesus, retires into his cistern cell.

The banqueting party, headed by the Tetrarch and Herodias, now adjourns to the terrace, with Herod demanding the whereabouts of Salome, and losing his balance as he slips on the blood of Narraboth. He invites her to share a piece of fruit so that he may place his lips where hers have just been. The reaction of Herodias to these undignified goings-on is one of cold contempt; but when she hears Jokanaan denouncing her from his cistern, she turns in fury on her husband and demands why he has not delivered the prisoner up to the Jews. Five Jews now come forward to demand the prisoner; but Herod argues with them at some length, maintaining that Jokanaan is really a man of God. This infuriates the suppliants, whose parts are written for four tenors and a bass and whose complex, chattering music is unflatteringly satirical. The voice of Jokanaan, heard once more from the cistern, silences them all; and then two Nazarenes discuss some of the miracles of the Saviour, whom Jokanaan has been preaching of. Herod is badly frightened once more—as he had been earlier merely of a rising wind—and his peace of mind is not further promoted when Herodias turns on him to demand that Jokanaan, who is once again denouncing her and prophesying a bad end, be silenced.

Turning away from all these unpleasant aspects of his party, Herod asks Salome to dance for him. Herodias forbids it, and Salome herself shows a decided lack of enthusiasm. However, Herod persists, promising her all sorts of things. Finally she agrees on condition that he will give her anything that she demands. Ominous winds frighten Herod further, who superstitiously thinks he hears the flapping of wings. He makes his oath, tearing a chaplet of roses from his head because, he says, they are burning him. He falls back exhausted; and as some slaves prepare Salome for her dance, the voice of Jokanaan continues to prophesy doom.

Then comes the voluptuous music of the *Dance of the*

Seven Veils, during which Salome sheds one veil after another as the dance mounts in intensity. Strauss had originally planned to have a ballerina take the place of the prima donna for this dance and did not hesitate to compose physically taxing music to follow upon it. This is the way it was performed at the premiere, and this is the way it was done most effectively in a televised performance by the NBC Opera Theatre with a dancer who bore a striking resemblance to Elaine Malbin, the Salome of the occasion. Many prima donnas nowadays, however, like to perform their own gyrations. All too seldom can these be called dancing.

Much of the dance is usually performed with the cistern of Jokanaan as a pivotal point of interest; but at its close, Salome throws herself at the feet of Herod and, with an almost childish sweetness, asks for her reward—the head of Jokanaan. Herod is horrified; but Salome, encouraged by her mother, sticks relentlessly to her demand, turning down all of Herod's alternative offers, which include jewels, white peacocks, the mantel of the High Priest, and the veil of the temple. Finally, weary and frightened, he gives in. Herodias takes a ring from his finger as an order for the execution.

As the bloody work goes on below, Salome leans over the mouth of the cistern, demanding that the executioner hurry. Clouds begin to cover the moon, which had previously lighted the scene brightly; and in the gathering gloom the hands of the executioner emerge from the cistern bearing aloft the head of Jokanaan on a platter. Salome seizes it and, in her last powerful and revolting scene, sings of her triumph over the man who repulsed her and slobbers over the dead lips and kisses them.

A ray of moonlight breaks through the clouds, and even the degenerate Herod is revolted at the scene, which Lord Harewood has aptly termed a "psychopathic Liebestod." "Let that woman be killed!" he orders; and the soldiers crush her under their shields.

Postscript for the historically curious: According to more sober historians, Salome did not meet the dramatically apposite end concocted for her by Oscar Wilde. She survived her dance and the execution of John the Baptist to marry, successively, her uncle, Tetrarch Philip of Trachonitus, and her cousin, King Aristobulus of Calchas.

SAMSON ET DALILA

(Samson and Delilah)

Opera in three acts by Camille Saint-Saëns
with libretto in French by Ferdinand Lemaire,
based on the Book of Judges

DELILAH, *a priestess of Dagon*	*Mezzo-soprano*
SAMSON, *leader of the Hebrews*	*Tenor*
HIGH PRIEST OF DAGON	*Baritone*
ABIMELECH, *Satrap of Gaza*	*Bass*
AN OLD HEBREW	*Bass*

Time: biblical
Place: Gaza
First performance (in German) at Weimar, December 2, 1877

Ask any music-lover to name offhand the subject that has inspired the largest number of operas, and he will probably nominate either Faust or Orpheus, or just possibly Romeo. I am not sure what the correct answer should be, never having tabulated the subjects of the scores of the 28,000 operas that lie in the *Bibliothèque Nationale*, not to mention the thousand of operas that never found their way into France in any form. But high on the list, I am sure, would be the subject of Samson. I have found records of eleven treatments antedating Saint-Saëns's; and this does not include, of course, Handel's great setting of Milton's drama, which is an oratorio. Nor were all these by forgotten composers. One of them, for example, was by Rameau, whose librettist was no less a figure than Voltaire, and another was by the German Joachim Raff. Oddly enough, though each of these composers was not only a highly respected musician in his day but also a powerful figure, neither of their Samson operas was ever produced.

Saint-Saëns also had some troubles before he ever got to see a full performance of his work, and even more before he could hear it in his own country. His cousin, Ferdinand Lemaire, delivered the libretto in 1869, and the score was well along when the Franco-Prussian War broke out. This interrupted the completion for two years, after which the score lay idle on the composer's desk for another two. Finally, Liszt heard of the work. Ever enthusiastic about helping younger men, the Abbé took the score and gave it its world premiere in German at Weimar. *Simson und Delila*, it was called. That was in 1877; but it took the natural home for this work, the Paris Opéra, another thirteen years to see its merits. There it has been a staple ever since, being played at least once or twice a month year in year out.

In English-speaking countries it was also slow to make its way. In England there used to be a law (and in America a prejudice) against representing biblical characters on the stage. It was first heard in these countries, therefore, in the form of an oratorio. In England it never received an operatic production till 1909; while in the U.S., despite a few scattered performances in the nineties, it did not enter the regular repertoire of the Metropolitan till 1915. Then, with a cast headed by Caruso and Matzenauer, it made such an impression that it has been a semi-regular in the repertoire for many years. Nowadays, however, there is this interesting difference in standards of production: audiences insist on—and get—a Delilah who can look as well as sing like a dangerous woman.

In 1947, when Saint-Saëns's opera was temporarily out of the repertoire, the Metropolitan produced a one-act version of the story by Bernard Rogers, entitled *The Warrior*. In this opera Samson's eyes are put out very realistically, with a red-hot poker, right on the stage. The management had the happy thought of producing this little horror on a Saturday afternoon bill for moppets, with *Hänsel und Gretel* as the lure. Naturally, poor Mr. Rogers' work failed to win the parents' approval, and Saint-Saëns was subsequently restored.

ACT I

At Gaza the Israelites are in bondage to the Philistines, and even before the curtain rises, they are heard bewailing their misfortunes. On a square in the city, early in the morning, they are gathered, and Samson tries to arouse them to active resistance. They are slow to take fire, but are finally roused to such enthusiasm that Abimelech, Satrap of Gaza, comes with his bodyguard to see what the matter is. His taunts and his invitation to abandon Jehovah in favor of Dagon boomerangs. Samson rouses the Israelites to still stronger feelings of revolt with his vigorous call to revolution (*Israel, burst your bonds*); whereupon Abimelech attacks him; Samson wrenches away the Satrap's sword and slays him; and the whole band scatters into the city to make good the rebellion.

The doors of the temple open, and out comes the High Priest with his attendants. In solemn tones he curses Samson. Yet he cannot bring courage that way to the terror-struck Philistines; and when the Israelites return, High Priest and all make good their escape.

It is Samson's great hour of triumph. Yet, in that very moment, the seductive priestess Delilah issues forth from the Temple of Dagon with her almost equally seductive young ladies' chorus of attendants. They greet the triumphant hero, bringing him garlands, singing a song of spring and dancing enticingly. Delilah tells him that he already reigns in her heart, and, taking the cue from her maidens, also sings a ravishing aria about the spring (*Printemps qui commence*—"The spring is beginning"). One of the old Hebrews warns Samson; but the young hero, who already has a reputation for being quickly attracted by feminine beauty, is utterly fascinated by Delilah.

ACT II

It is going to be a dark and stormy night in the vale of Sorek, but the short prelude to Act II establishes the fact, as well as music can, that the late afternoon is fine. Delilah, clad as seductively as the decencies of grand opera permit, is waiting, in her luxuriant Oriental garden, for her lover. She hates him as an enemy of her people, and in a powerful aria (*Amour! viens aider ma faiblesse!*) she prays that the god of love may help her to render him powerless.

The High Priest comes to her to tell her that things have gone from bad to worse, for the Hebrews, once slaves, are now terrorizing their former masters. Knowing something of the psychology of beautiful women, he reports that Samson has been boasting of her lack of success in dominating him. But Delilah hates the man enough already without such spurring; and later on, when he offers her a rich reward if she can wring from him the secret of his strength, she tells him that bribery is not necessary. She has already tried three times; three times she has failed; but this time she swears that she will succeed. Samson, she believes, has become a slave to sexual passion; and the two sing a duet of triumph over the anticipated victory.

Now a storm starts brewing. The High Priest leaves, and Delilah awaits Samson impatiently. When he finally stumbles in through the growing darkness, he mutters to himself that he has come only to break off with Delilah. He had not reckoned with her determination or her woman's wiles, which include not only love-making but also sentimental references to past pleasures, anger, and tears. As she sees him beginning to weaken, she sings the famous aria *Mon coeur s'ouvre à ta voix* (usually translated "My heart at thy sweet voice"). Heard as a concert aria it is far less effective than in the opera, for Samson's passionate avowal of love at the end of each stanza is tamely given over to the mezzo.

Once again Delilah asks for the secret of his great strength, and once again Samson refuses to reveal it. But when Delilah finally repels him, calls him coward ("*Lâche!*"), and rushes off into the house, Samson is distraught. With the storm raging about him, he raises his hands in despair and slowly follows her inside.

Everyone knows, from the Bible story, what happens inside to Samson and to his hair. On-stage, there is a clap of thunder; then a troop of Philistine soldiers sneaks in and silently sur-

462

rounds the house. Suddenly Delilah appears at the window and calls for help. Samson's voice is heard shouting that he has been betrayed, and the soldiers rush in to take him captive.

Scene 1 Bereft of their powerful leader, the Hebrews have been conquered, and a chorus of them, in an off-stage prison, complains bitterly that Samson has betrayed the god of his fathers. On-stage, the blinded Samson is turning the millstone to which his captors have chained him in the prison yard. In an agony of despair he calls upon Jehovah to take his life so that he may atone for his people's misery. Relentlessly the off-stage chorus continues its denunciation of him. Finally, his jailers lead him away.

Scene 2 In the Temple of Dagon the Philistines are working themselves up into an orgy of worship before a huge statue of their god. The dancing girls sing the victory chorus they had offered, in Act I, to Samson. The ballet performs the *Bacchanale*.

When Samson is led in by a little child, they turn on him in mockery. Delilah takes especial delight in triumphing over him; and the High Priest, with exquisite taste, offers to turn Jew if Jehovah will be so good as to restore Samson's sight. Samson, turning his sightless eyes upward, prays that the Lord of Hosts may avenge such monstrous impiety.

But now the serious part of the sacrificial ceremony begins. Libations are poured before the statue; the altar begins to flame; and as a climax, Samson is to be made to kneel to Dagon. Amid the triumphant singing of the Philistines, the child leads Samson between the two great pillars where he is to make obeisance. Quietly the huge man tells the boy to leave the temple, as the invocation to Dagon rises louder and louder. Finally, Samson grips the two pillars, prays aloud for a last show of strength, and with a shout starts the pillars swaying. The Philistine mob screams in terror and tries to rush from the hall. It is too late: the whole temple crashes down destroying everyone in it, including Samson and Delilah.

THE SECRET OF SUZANNE

(*Il segreto di Susanna*)

Intermezzo in one act by Ermanno Wolf-Ferrari with libretto in Italian by Enrico Golisciani

COUNT GIL } *newlyweds*		*Baritone*
COUNTESS SUZANNE } *newlyweds*		*Soprano*
SANTE, *their mute servant*		*Mute*

Time: early 20th century
Place: Piedmont
First performance at Munich (in German), December 4, 1909

Of all of Wolf-Ferrari's dozen operas this delicate gem is the sturdiest—that is, if we may measure sturdiness by frequency of performance. It requires the services of only two singers and a silent actor; it can be done with the simplest of sets; it can serve as a curtain-raiser for a major work or as an intermezzo between two shorter ones. In fact, its nature is that of the early Italian *intermezzo*. The older *intermezzo* was usually a comic scene between a soprano and a bass thrown in between the more serious business of a tragedy. Much of the comedy was spoken, and it was customary for the audience not to pay too much attention. The comedy of *The Secret of Suzanne*, however, is set to music throughout and is easily worth the delighted attention of everyone within hearing distance.

The overture, often played as a separate concert piece, is admirably suited to set the emotional pace with its light, bustling, tuneful inconsequentiality.

The action takes place some fifty or more years ago, when

nice young women in the upper classes seldom did either of two things—go out in the streets alone, and smoke. But our pretty newlywed, Countess Suzanne, has combined these sins just before the curtain rises by going to the neighborhood tobacconist and purchasing a package of cigarettes. Her husband, who enters the living room of his comfortable home when the curtain rises, has just seen her do this and cannot believe his eyes: it must have been another woman wearing a similar costume. He goes to his own room, and a moment later Suzanne enters wearing precisely the costume he has described, and carrying a wrapped-up little package. This she gives to Sante, the mute servant, and then retires to her own room. And so, when Count Gil returns and listens at her door, he is relieved to think that she has been home all the time. However, he is almost certain that he has detected the odor of tobacco, and his tentative conclusion is that Suzanne must have an admirer. He questions Sante whether he himself smokes and also whether Suzanne does. Both questions are answered by the mute with a negative shake of the head.

When Suzanne enters, he tries to continue the questioning. She looks sad; he asks why; she says it is the first time he has been unkind to her; and the difficulty is temporarily obliterated in the cordial sentiments of a love duet. But the personal proximity with which it closes gives him another whiff of dame nicotine, and he is jealous all over again. Now she believes that he must know of her secret vice, and innocently she suggests that he go to his club, shutting his eyes conveniently, as all reasonable husbands do. Putting a completely different construction on her speech, he works himself up into a fury, throws vases about the room, and drives her out of it for a good, comfortable cry.

Utterly grief-stricken, he throws himself into an easy chair, and this gives the composer a chance to write a charming intermezzo while Sante clears up the debris. Suzanne then comes out, gives him his hat, gloves, and umbrella, and urges him to go to the club. And in a brief little aria (*Via, così non mi lasciate*—"You're not going to leave me like this, are you?")

she begs for a little show of affection, which he delivers in the shape of a stiff peck on the forehead.

Considerably relieved, Suzanne lights one of the wicked little weeds and just has time to put it out before Gil returns, looks for an unwanted visitor, and finds nothing but more traces of tobacco odor. Once more he works himself up into a jealous rage; once more he leaves; once more Suzanne lights up. This time, however, Gil remains away long enough for her to sing a pleasant aria in praise of smoking (*O gioia, la nube leggiera*).

At last she is fortunately caught. Gil suddenly makes a reappearance through the window, sees what she is vainly trying to hide behind her back, and is enormously relieved. So relieved, in fact, that he joins her in the petty vice, and they smoke, dance, and sing together, utterly in love.

As they depart together for her room, old Sante cleans up the room once more, looking very wise and very much pleased with himself and his employers.

LA SERVA PADRONA

(*The Servant Mistress*)

Opera *buffa* in one act by Giovanni Battista
Pergolesi with libretto in Italian by Gennaro
Antonio Federico

UBERTO, *a bachelor*	*Bass*
SERPINA, *his maid*	*Soprano*
VESPONE, *his valet*	*Mute part*

Time: *18th century*
Place: *Naples*
First performance at Naples, August 28, 1733

Between the acts of those frightfully formalized eighteenth-century entertainments known as *opera seria*,* it was
common practice to relieve the monotony of high-mindedness
with *intermezzi†*—short, low-comedy musical acts calling for
the services of two singers—a soprano and a bass—and often a
silent actor. *La serva padrona* was written to serve as *inter-
mezzi* for the composer's three-act *Il prigionier superbo* ("The
Proud Prisoner"), a run-of-the-mill *opera seria* calling for the
services of a castrated male soprano in the leading feminine
part and a genuine female contralto in the role of the King
of the Goths. Like the five other *opere serie* that Pergolesi
composed during his four-year career as opera writer, *Il prigionier* was a failure. But *La serva padrona* was a huge success,
for the two intermission pieces added up to a neat little story.

---

* The only genuine *opera seria* described in this volume is Handel's
Julius Caesar (see p. 236).

† For a description of a modern *intermezzo*, see *The Secret of
Suzanne*, p. 464.

They could be—and were later on—played as a one-act comedy; the tunes were simple and gay; the action and characters, while stemming directly from eighteenth-century comedy, were not only understandable but almost realistic. Thus was born the form known as *opera buffa*, which has had a long and honorable history; and its classic exemplar, *La serva padrona*, has had a career equally honorable and equally long. (Strictly speaking, perhaps, the form was born five years earlier with Johann Adolf Hasse's *La contadina*, the first *intermezzo* to be based on a real play. But Pergolesi's little work was the first one to receive wide circulation.)

Pergolesi died in 1736 at the age of twenty-six, and so he never knew that a dozen years later, when an Italian troupe put on his little work in Paris, it created an opera war known as *La guerre des bouffons*. The vastly respected Rameau and Lully were then composing stately works which earned the disrespect of such advanced intellectuals as Rousseau and Diderot. *La serva padrona* gave them the ammunition for attacking the formal musical entertainments favored by the King, while the Queen favored the musical insurrectionists. Among the results of this war were no fewer than sixty polemical pamphlets on the subject, a successful *opera buffa* composed by Rousseau himself and called *Le devin du village* (which became the model for *Bastien und Bastienne* by Mozart—see p. 66), and almost two hundred performances of Pergolesi's masterpiece.

We cannot credit all this Parisian *brouhaha* with the comedy's long life, for the whims of operatic fashion brushed it right off the stage for a generation or two in the nineteenth century. But its charm and vitality caused it to be revived in the 1860's, since when it has retained its position as the earliest opera regularly revived by practically every opera-producing group in the world, from college workshops to the Metropolitan and other august museums.

INTERMEZZO I

Uberto, a comfortably off Neapolitan bachelor, has two servants, a pretty girl named Serpina and a mute named Vespone. He complains vigorously of the girl's failure to bring him his morning chocolate so that he can go out; and when they come in, he tries reading a lecture to both his servants on their deliberate inattention. But Serpina will have none of his lip. She gives him back everything she gets. The chocolate hasn't been prepared; he'll just have to do without it. This leads to Uberto's first aria (*Sempre in contrasti—*"Always at cross-purposes"), in which he continues to complain but in which he already shows some weaknesses of which Serpina is quick to take advantage. She refuses to let him go out, even threatening to lock the door; and when he complains that she is giving him a headache, she delivers herself of an aria (*Stizzoso, mio stizzoso—*"My own fuss-budget") in which she advises him to take her advice. Thereupon Uberto instructs Vespone to go find him a wife just to spite Serpina. A wife, says she, is just what he needs; and who could be a better one than herself? And the first half of the opera ends with a duet in which Serpina assures him that he really means to marry his beautiful and graceful servant even though he says he won't, while Uberto insists that she is perfectly mad to think it.

INTERMEZZO II

Presumably a short while after, Serpina brings Vespone into the room, dressed as a soldier and wearing a set of horrendous false whiskers. When Uberto enters, she hides her co-conspirator outside the door and proceeds to tell her master that as he refuses to marry her and as she must look after her own interests, she has engaged herself to another. His name, she says, is Captain Tempesta, and he has a frightful temper. This softens Uberto somewhat; and when she sings him a sentimental tune about how one day he shall remember her fondly (*A Serpina penserte*), he begins to feel downright sentimental. He agrees to meet this frightening military man; and while she is gone to fetch him, he admits to the audience that he is more in two minds about this matter than he would like to admit (*Son imbrogliato io già*). Vespone, thoroughly instructed, plays his part beautifully. He fumes all over the place without ever uttering a word, and lets Uberto know, through Serpina, that he demands a dowry of four thousand crowns. If he doesn't get it, he refuses to marry the girl; and, furthermore, Uberto must marry her. When Vespone makes threatening gestures and begins to attack Uberto, the master finally gives in and does what he obviously wanted to do all along: he offers his hand both literally and figuratively. Thereupon Vespone doffs his disguise, but Uberto cannot be angry at him very long. Instead, he joins his fiancée in a darling duet about their delighted hearts (which, they say, beat respectively *tippitì, tippitì* and *tappatà, tappatà*) and which ends with two most elegant and eloquent lines:

Serpina: *Oh, caro, caro, caro!* (Oh darling, darling, darling!)
Uberto: *Oh gioia, gioia, gioia!* (Oh joy, joy, joy!)

SIMON BOCCANEGRA

Opera in prologue and three acts by Giuseppe
Verdi with libretto in Italian by Francesco
Maria Piave, based on a play by Antonio Gar-
cía Gutiérrez

SIMON BOCCANEGRA, *Doge of Genoa*	*Baritone*
AMELIA, *his daughter*	*Soprano*
JACOPO FIESCO, *her grandfather*	*Bass*
GABRIELE ADORNO, *a young patrician*	*Tenor*
PAOLO, *a politician*	*Baritone*
PIETRO, *another*	*Bass*

Time: 1339 to 1363
Place: Genoa
First performance at Venice, March 12, 1857

Except for a few years during the 1930's, when Lawrence
Tibbett starred in the role with a dramatic sense all his own,
Simon Boccanegra has never captured the imagination and
affection of a large public—either here or abroad. It was a
comparative failure in its early years, and the composer was
not only disappointed but also puzzled. By 1881 he had established a fine relationship with the composer-librettist Arrigo Boito, who had collaborated with brilliant skill and taste
on *Otello,* and Verdi turned to him to revise a pretty murky
and static libretto. Boito did his best (which, in this case, was
not too good); Verdi did far better. The revised version—the
only one performed nowadays and the one described below—
includes some of Verdi's most eloquent pages. Even so, the
opera remains much more admired by the critics than loved

by the public. Every once in a while an opera company will revive it for the benefit of a star baritone and the opportunity to exhibit some rich scenery. The critics praise it; the public stays away; the baritone stars in something else; and the scenery goes back to the warehouse for another few years.

PROLOGUE

The rather long prologue takes place in a public square of Genoa of the early fourteenth or fifteenth century. (The libretto says early fifteenth century, but the historical election of Simon Boccanegra as first Doge of Genoa took place in 1339.) Genoa was, at the time, a republic, and the opera begins with the professional dealings of a couple of politicians named Paolo and Pietro. They represent the democratic, or Ghibelline, faction, and they discuss who shall be elected the new Doge—that is, the head of the state. Quickly they agree that it shall be Simon Boccanegra. He is, at the moment, a popular and highly respectable freebooter, who has rid the sea around Genoa of non-European pirates. Simon himself enters at this moment, claims he does not choose to run, but is quickly persuaded to change his mind by Paolo. For Simon wishes to marry Maria, with whom he has had a clandestine love affair—and Maria is the daughter of the nobleman Jacopo Fiesco. Should Simon be elected Doge, he would have the rank of a prince, and Fiesco could not deny his daughter to him.

When Simon has consented, the two conspirators summon a group of voters around them. Their political arguments are rather personal, but nonetheless effective. They argue against Fiesco—who would be Simon's rival of the Guelph party—by claiming that he keeps a beautiful woman mysteriously locked up as a prisoner in his palace. This persuades the populace that Simon will make the best Doge, and they depart, their minds made up. Now, Fiesco, however much a nobleman and a Guelph, is not a villain. The woman he is supposed to be keeping locked up is really his daughter, Maria, the beloved of Simon, and she has just died. In the best-known aria of the opera (*Il lacerato spirito*), Fiesco speaks of his sorrow as an off-stage chorus sings a *miserere*.

Simon, who is the father of Maria's child, begs for the friendship and forgiveness of Fiesco, even offering him his life, by baring his chest. But the patrician Fiesco refuses to be an assassin, and he promises forgiveness only if Simon will turn over to him his grandchild. This, Simon explains, he cannot do. For some time ago the woman to whom the child had been entrusted was found dead, and the child had disappeared. And so Fiesco—without telling Simon that Maria has just died—coldly turns on his heel and leaves his political rival. Simon, however, enters the Fiesco palace, and a minute later comes out again. He has come across the dead body of his beloved Maria!

And at that moment the populace comes into the square to hail their newly elected Doge. As the prologue ends, the crowd cries *Viva Simon!* to the brokenhearted man.

ACT I

Scene 1 Twenty-four years have now passed. Simon Boccanegra is still Doge of Genoa, and his long-lost daughter lives with his old enemy, Fiesco, her grandfather. However, neither the grandfather, the father, nor the girl herself is aware of her true identity, and she goes under the name of Amelia. When the act begins, she is awaiting her lover, Gabriele Adorno, a young nobleman of the party opposed to Simon. She looks out over the sea at dawn, and she sings a lovely aria as she waits for Gabriele. At its end his voice is heard off-stage, singing a love song in the distance. Ecstatically they embrace. But there is a shadow between them, for Amelia does not approve of Gabriele's plotting with her guardian. As they speak together, they are interrupted by Pietro, who announces the imminent arrival of the Doge himself. Amelia hastily explains that the Doge seeks her hand for one of his favorites, and she begs Gabriele to arrange for their immediate marriage. Before the Doge enters, old Fiesco (who now, to hide his identity, goes under the name of Andrea) tells Gabriele that Amelia

Simon Boccanegra

comes of humble stock. This makes no difference to the ardent lover, and so her guardian blesses the union in a duet that strikes a fine religious tone.

Now the Doge enters. The purpose of his visit is to secure Amelia's hand for Paolo, the man who had helped him become Doge and who is now a chief counselor. But in the course of their long and touching duet he learns of her history, and it suddenly becomes obvious to both of them that she is really his long-lost daughter. Their secret must, for the time being, be kept. The Doge decides that Paolo must not have Amelia as she hates him and loves someone else. But as yet Simon does not know that the accepted lover is his bitter enemy, Gabriele Adorno.

Scene 2   A number of things have happened between the scenes. First, Paolo, Simon's villainous counselor, has heard that Simon no longer backs him in his suit for Amelia's hand. Second, he has made an unsuccessful effort to have his henchmen kidnap the girl. And third, the attempt has been foiled by Amelia's lover, Gabriele, who believes that Simon instigated the plot.

As the act opens, Simon is presiding over a meeting of his council, giving sage advice about maintaining peace. Suddenly there is an uproar outside. The people are angered over the attempt to abduct Amelia, and they mistakenly shout, "Death to the Doge!" Simon takes the whole situation in at once. With a scornful majesty he rises over everything, and turns them to his side. But Gabriele rushes to attack Simon with a dagger. Amelia throws herself between the men, and she indicates clearly, without mentioning his name, that Paolo was the villain behind the abduction. A wonderful sextet, with chorus, develops, as everyone expresses his own emotions in connection with this rather complicated situation. At its end Simon turns to Paolo. He knows that Paolo is the unadmitted guilty one, and he tells him that—as guardian of the people's honor—he must curse the man who committed the crime. Horrified, Paolo is forced to curse himself: *Sia maledetto*. And as the act closes, the whole assemblage repeats the curse in whispers: *Sia maledetto!*

474

ACT II

At the beginning of Act II, Paolo swears vengeance on Doge Simon and prepares a cup of poison for him. Then he orders the two prisoners, Fiesco and Gabriele, to be brought before him. First he attempts to persuade Fiesco to murder Simon in his sleep. But the old aristocrat again refuses to stoop to assassination. Next, Paolo turns to the young lover, Gabriele. He tells him that Simon has wicked designs on his beloved Amelia and urges *him* to murder the Doge. Left alone, Gabriele gives vent to his rage—and then, in a lovely melody, begs heaven to restore Amelia to his breast.

Amelia now enters the chamber of the palace where this scene takes place, and in a fine duet begs him to respect the Doge and her own innocent love for him. The entrance of the Doge interrupts their interview, and the young man quickly leaves. In the duet that follows, Simon learns that his daughter's beloved is his enemy, Gabriele. Greatly moved, he promises pardon if Gabriele himself will repent.

And now, the tired Boccanegra sits wearily down, thinks of his troubles—and drinks the poisoned cup that Paolo had left for him. He falls asleep, and Gabriele rushes forth to slay him. But Amelia throws herself between them just in time, and it is only now that Gabriele learns that Simon is Amelia's father —and that he is greathearted enough to pardon the enemy in his power. Outside, the angry shouts of Simon's enemies are heard. He urges Gabriele to join his friends on the other side, but the young man cries that he will never again fight Simon. Side by side, they join the battle.

ACT III

The Doge and young Gabriele have been victorious in their battle against the Guelph aristocrats, and Paolo, who had turned traitor to Simon, is brought into the ducal palace, condemned to be hanged. Before he is led off, he tells old Fiesco that he has poisoned the Doge; and then, to make his own end doubly bitter, he hears, off-stage, the wedding chorus that joins Amelia and Gabriele. Simon—now sick unto death—is led in, preceded by trumpeters. The two old enemies, Fiesco and Boccanegra, are left alone. And as Fiesco learns that Amelia is the long-lost daughter of his own Maria, the two are finally united in friendship.

Amelia and her new husband, Gabriele, then come into the chamber with many others. Only now does she learn that Fiesco, her guardian for many years, is really her grandfather. Everyone is deeply moved by Simon's evident growing weakness. A splendid quartet rises, and then, just before he dies, Simon appoints Gabriele as the next Doge of Genoa.

SUOR ANGELICA

(Sister Angelica)

Opera in one act by Giacomo Puccini with libretto in Italian by Giovacchino Forzano

SISTER ANGELICA	*Soprano*
THE PRINCESS, *her aunt*	*Contralto*
THE ABBESS	*Mezzo-soprano*
THE MONITOR	*Mezzo-soprano*

Time: 17th century
Place: Italy
First performance at New York, December 14, 1918

Puccini's early training was in church music; but by the time he began to compose *Suor Angelica*, which takes place in a convent, he was fifty-eight and had had a long career of writing only for the lyric stage. It was, perhaps, natural for him, then, to try out his score on a preliminary audience which ought to have some special insight into the problems of the opera. His sister Ingina lived in a convent, and there he played his score for the assembled sisters. When his audience dissolved into tears and agreed that the erring heroine deserved forgiveness, he was satisfied.

Lay audiences and professional music critics were less easily pleased. When the opera had its world premiere in New York, at the Metropolitan Opera House, along with *Il tabarro* and *Gianni Schicci*, it was found rather dull—the music all too much alike, male voices entirely lacking. As in *Il tabarro*, the drama really begins only halfway through, the first part of the little work being all atmosphere-building. A reading of the score or a phonograph hearing actually becomes more dra-

matically absorbing if one begins with the fourth of the six
parts into which the opera is divided, each with its subtitle.

The Penance begins with two postulants hurrying through
the cloisters of a little convent, for they are late to prayers.
Sister Angelica, also late, does her own penance by saying a
prayer before entering the church. Then the Monitor of the
order of nuns emerges and delivers penances to several young
nuns and postulates for minor infractions of the rules.

The Recreation is that brief period after prayers when the
sisters gather in the garden to admire the flowers. They also
compare wishes. Sister Angelica, it turns out, seems to have
none. She is a somewhat mysterious figure to the others. All
they know of her is that she has been in the convent for seven
years and it is rumored that she is a princess who has been renounced by her family for some crime or other.

The Return from the Quest brings in two members of the
order who carry a load of supplies on a small donkey. They
also report that a handsome carriage is outside the convent. A
bell announcing a visitor is rung, and the Abbess summons
Sister Angelica. Her aunt, the Princess, is there to visit her.

The Princess, who gives her name to the next section, is an
elderly lady of great dignity and severity, who carries a stick.
Greatly agitated, Sister Angelica kisses her hand and seems to
implore forgiveness. But the Princess has come for only one
thing. It seems that Angelica's sister is about to be married,
and a signature on a document is necessary so that their dead
parents' fortune may be divided. As the parents had died
twenty years earlier and as she has now no use for money,
Angelica readily consents and asks about something that interests her far more: what has happened to her little illegitimate
son, whose birth is the reason that she was hidden away in a
convent. When the Princess tells Angelica that the child died
two years before, she breaks down completely. For a moment
the Princess is almost moved by these tears to say something
kindly. But she regains her control, calls for pen and ink, ob-
tains the necessary signature, and hobbles off in aristocratic
silence.

The Grace. Alone in the garden, with night descending,

Angelica decides to use her knowledge of herbs, gained at the convent, to take her own life. She sings a tender farewell to her sister nuns, prepares a poisonous potion, and swiftly drinks it. Only then does she realize that suicide is a terrible sin, and that she may never see her son in heaven after all. Frantically she prays to Mary for forgiveness.

The Miracle occurs in answer to her prayers. The little church becomes illumined with an unearthly light, and the Madonna herself appears to Sister Angelica, leading a little blond boy by the hand. Angelica dies in peace, as an invisible choir of angels promises her salvation.

IL TABARRO

(*The Cloak*)

Opera in one act by Giacomo Puccini with libretto in Italian by Giuseppe Adami, based on Didier Gold's French play *La houppelande*

MICHELE, *owner of a barge*	*Baritone*
GIORGETTA, *his wife*	*Soprano*
LUIGI, *a stevedore*	*Tenor*
TINCA, *a stevedore*	*Tenor*
TALPA, *a stevedore*	*Bass*
FRUGOLA, *his wife*	*Mezzo-soprano*

Time: *about 1910*
Place: *the Seine River near Paris*
First performance at New York, December 14, 1918

Il *tabarro* is the first of three one-acters that Puccini intended to have produced as one evening's entertainment under the title of Il *trittico* ("The Triptych"). The other two, in order, were *Suor Angelica* and *Gianni Schicchi*; but only the last of the three is often performed these days, for the initial and subsequent receptions of the complete bill almost invariably elicited enthusiasm for *Gianni* and comparative indifference to the other two.

The fact seems to be that the first half of Il *tabarro* is an extraordinary skillful and subtle sketch of barge life on the Seine while the second half is a brutal shocker, and the two parts don't jell too well.

The central story is brief, violent, dramatic. Michele is the skipper of a barge that is tied up in Paris, on the Seine. He has lost the love of his pretty young wife Giorgetta, since their child died in infancy. Now she is secretly in love with Luigi, a longshoreman who works for Michele. When Michele has gone to sleep, she tells Luigi, she will strike a match as a signal for him to come aboard to meet her.

Unfortunately, Michele stays up later than usual. Thinking bitterly about his lost love, he lights a match for his pipe. Luigi, mistaking this for Giorgetta's signal, steals on board. The suspicious Michele surprises Luigi, forces him to confess his love, and then quietly strangles him to death.

Giorgetta, uneasy, comes from the cabin and asks her husband whether he does not wish to have her near him.

"Under my cloak?" asks Michele.

"Yes," she answers. "You said once that everyone carries a cloak: sometimes it hides joy, sometimes sorrow."

"But sometimes it hides a crime!" cries Michele, and he tears the cloak from Luigi's body. As she utters a cry of horror, he seizes her roughly and hurls her forcibly upon the body of her dead lover.

That is the central, dramatic story, most of it occurring in the last few pages. But we are first treated to a whole series of memorable vignettes. There is Tinca, the longshoreman, who drowns his sorrows gaily in wine, and dances drunkenly with Giorgetta. There is Frugola, the wife of Talpa, another longshoreman, who seems to love her cat as much as her husband. There is a song pedlar who passes musically by. There is the idealized picture of life in a small town sung in a duet between Luigi and Giorgetta. And always there is the background of the river Seine itself, suggested by the undulating rhythms of the prelude—rhythms that come in again and again.

THE TALES OF HOFFMANN

(*Les contes d'Hoffmann*)

Opera in prologue, three acts, and epilogue, by
Jacques Offenbach with libretto in French by
Jules Barbier based on a play by him and Mi-
chel Carré, based in turn on three stories by
E. T. A. Hoffmann

LINDORF, *a councilor of Nuremberg*	Bass or Baritone
STELLA, *an opera singer*	Soprano
ANDRÈS, *her servant*	Tenor
LUTHER, *an innkeeper*	Bass
HOFFMANN, *a poet*	Tenor
NICKLAUSSE, *his companion*	Mezzo-soprano
SPALANZANI, *an inventor*	Tenor
COCHENILLE, *his servant*	Tenor
COPPÉLIUS, *a partner of Spalanzani*	Bass or Baritone
OLYMPIA, *a mechanical doll*	Soprano
GIULIETTA, *a courtesan*	Soprano
SCHLÉMIL, *her lover*	Bass
PITTICHINACCIO, *her admirer*	Tenor
DAPERTUTTO, *an evil genius*	Baritone
CRESPEL, *a councilor of Munich*	Baritone
ANTONIA, *his daughter*	Soprano
FRANTZ, *his servant*	Tenor
DR. MIRACLE, *a doctor*	Bass or Baritone
THE VOICE OF ANTONIA'S MOTHER	Mezzo-soprano
THE MUSE OF POETRY	Soprano

Time: early 19th century
Places: Germany and Italy
First performance at Paris, February 10, 1881

The "Hoffmann" of our title was a gifted German author, lawyer, composer, literary critic, and caricaturist who was christened Ernst Theodor Wilhelm Hoffmann. He altered his third name to Amadeus out of love for the works of Mozart, of whose *Don Giovanni* he wrote an influential and highly romantic interpretation. He also wrote the three stories on which this opera is based, though he himself was the hero of none of them and though they are far more macabre and romantic than their familiar transmogrifications in the libretto. (For the curious with a literary bent: the titles of the original tales are *The Sandman, New Year's Eve Adventure,* and *Councillor Crespel.* They are well worth reading.)

Thirty years before the opera was produced, its librettists had had performed, at the Odéon in Paris, a not very successful comedy called *Les contes d'Hoffmann,* in which the three young heroes of these tales were transformed into Hoffmann himself, thus making a kind of pun on the title's preposition: they are tales "of" Hoffmann because they are both by and about him. When the comedy was quite dead, Barbier reworked it into libretto form and offered it successively to Hector Salomon, Charles Gounod, and Jacques Offenbach. Salomon was very much attracted but graciously turned over the opportunity to his colleague, Offenbach.

At the time, Offenbach was the most brilliantly successful composer of French operettas—and no one has begun to rival him since. He had produced almost a hundred of these confections, but never a serious work. He therefore set great store by this effort, worked very hard at it, and, being seriously ill at the time, only prayed that he might live to see it on the stage. He did live to see a private run-through with piano accompaniment, and then went back to work to rewrite the role of Hoffmann, which had been intended for a baritone, into a tenor role. But he did not live to see its immensely successful premiere, or even to complete the orchestration. The first act he did himself; the balance had to be completed for him by Ernest Guiraud, who performed an analogous service for *Carmen* when he composed its recitatives after Bizet's death.

The opera was enormously successful from the beginning,

in Paris, where it received 101 performances in its first season. On its first trip outside of its native country, however, it encountered an ironically tragic fate. During its second performance at the Ringtheater in Vienna, the house burned down and there were many fatalities. This is precisely the same fate that had befallen Hoffmann's own masterpiece *Undine* sixty-five years earlier in Berlin. The parallel, which would have appealed to the imagination of Hoffmann himself, impeded the quick success of the *Tales* in Germany. But eventually it became part of the permanent standard repertoire in that country, as it had meantime everywhere else.

The original intention, seldom carried out today, was to have the roles of Lindorf, Coppélius, Dapertutto, and Dr. Miracle sung by the same baritone, thus showing Hoffmann's series of evil geniuses to be the same person in disguise. Similarly, one soprano was supposed to impersonate Stella, Olympia, Giulietta, and Antonia—all four the loves of Hoffmann. But the vocal requirements for these roles vary so much that few modern baritones or sopranos can be found to cope successfully all evening. However, if one remembers the original intention, it may lend a fresh, if possibly spurious, dramatic perspective to the tales. An analogous intention for the secondary tenor roles of Andrès, Cochenille, Pittichinaccio, and Frantz seems to be inspired more by economical than by dramatic interest.

PROLOGUE

The curtain rises on the empty tavern of one Luther in Nuremberg. Next door a performance of *Don Giovanni* is supposed to be reaching its intermission, but no sounds can be heard excepting an invisible chorus of the "Spirits of Beer" singing in praise of themselves. Presently Councilor Lindorf appears and bribes Andrès, servant to the prima donna Stella, to give him a letter. It is addressed to the poet Hoffmann and contains a key to her room for use later that night. (In many performances this incident is entirely omitted, along with the roles of Lindorf and Stella.)

When the intermission in the imaginary opera house is reached, a chorus of students troops into the wine cellar, demanding refreshment from the good host Luther. Presently they are joined by Hoffmann, who is accompanied by his ever-present friend, Nicklausse. Hoffmann is in a strange mood. He has just run across a drunk in the gutter, and he describes him poetically and realistically. A song is called for, and Hoffmann obliges with *The Legend of Kleinzach*. In the middle of it he falls into rhapsodizing about his beloved Stella; but he finishes the *Legend* and, after making a few unpleasant remarks to Lindorf, proposes to spend the evening telling his boon companions the story of his three loves. (Stella, he says in an aside, symbolizes all three of them—as artist, as courtesan, as young girl.) And as the prologue ends, he announces the name of his first love. It was Olympia. . . .

ACT I

There are two villains in the first of Hoffmann's tales—Spalanzani and Coppélius. Together, these charlatans have built a pretty mechanical doll named Olympia, and they quarrel about ownership. Hoffmann, a young student, wishes to study with the pseudo-scientist, Spalanzani, and, catching a glimpse of the doll Olympia, falls melodiously in love. His friend, Nicklausse, tries to tease him out of his infatuation by singing an apropos ballad, *Une poupil aux yeux d'émail,* but Hoffmann does not understand the warning so gaily delivered. And then Coppélius sells Hoffmann a pair of magic glasses which make Olympia look real.

Now Spalanzani and Coppélius come to an agreement: Spalanzani offers a check of five hundred ducats on the banking house of Elias to buy out Coppélius. The latter, greatly elated, agrees, and he advises Spalanzani to marry off his Olympia to the silly youngster, Hoffmann.

Announced by the stuttering servant Cochenille, a large crowd of guests arrives to see Olympia. She is brought out and, to the accompaniment of a harp, sings a pretty, and very difficult, coloratura aria (*Les oiseaux dans la charmille*). Everybody then goes out to dine, and Hoffmann is left alone to make love to the doll. He wears his magic glasses; he accidentally presses one of Olympia's mechanical buttons; and when she utters the words "yes, yes," he is in heaven, for he thinks she has accepted him. He runs after her, and a moment later Coppélius re-enters. He has discovered that Spalanzani's check was bad, as Elias had failed, and he now vows revenge.

A waltz is heard as the guests return. Olympia, as Hoffmann's partner, dances so hard that her inventor fears she will hurt herself. But nothing can stop this mechanical doll. She even sings the whirling waltz, reaching up to an almost incredible A-flat above high C. Right out of the room she waltzes, and Coppélius steals after her. Before anyone can stop him, he seizes the doll and smashes it to pieces. In the excitement Hoffmann's magical glasses fall off, and he cries despairingly: "It's automatic; it's automatic!" The guests laugh at him; the two villains fight angrily; and everything is in a fine tumult as the act ends.

ACT II

The second act might be called the *Barcarolle Act*. It begins and ends with that familiar, undulating melody—and is dominated by it. (Offenbach borrowed the tune from one of his own operettas, *Die Rheinnixen*.) It is first sung by the courtesan Giulietta, Nicklausse, and the guests assembled at a party in her luxurious home in Venice. Then Hoffmann, one of the guests, sings a song that derides enduring love. But the ever-wise and ever-futile Nicklausse sees trouble ahead. Hoffmann, he believes, is destined soon to be a rival to the evil-looking Schlémil, Giulietta's lover. Hoffmann, for his part, only laughs at the idea of falling in love with a courtesan.

But now a really sinister figure comes on. He is Dapertutto, and he sings his sinuous *Diamond Aria*, extolling the almost supernatural merits of his jewel. He summons Giulietta, and, by playing on her vanity, persuades her to try to capture Hoffmann's reflection—as she has already captured her lover Schlémil's. Dapertutto means "reflection" literally—as in a mirror; but this is the symbol of the soul, and that is what the evil genius wants.

Giulietta goes about her work well. She pleads for the love of Hoffmann, and he gives in with passion and abandon. But as they kiss, the whole company, led by the jealous Schlémil, finds them together. Dapertutto now shows Hoffmann that he no longer has a reflection—or a soul—and a wonderful sextet ensues. Out of the music emerge the various themes of the *Barcarolle*, and then the *Barcarolle* itself is played once more from beginning to end. Only the voices of the off-stage chorus are heard, but the action is very dramatic. Hoffmann demands Schlémil's key to Giulietta's room. A duel ensues in which Hoffmann uses Dapertutto's sword; Schlémil is killed; Hoffmann seizes the key; and at that moment he sees Giulietta sailing by in a gondola—in the arms of the dwarf Pittichinaccio. He has been once more betrayed, and Nicklausse has to hurry him off before he is arrested for the murder of Schlémil.

ACT III

The last act tells the fate of Hoffmann's last great love—Antonia. Antonia is a young, inexperienced singer, the daughter of a great one. She lives in Munich with her father, and when the act opens, she is in the music room, singing of her lost love. This is Hoffmann, whom she has not seen in a year but hopes to see again. Her father, Councilor Crespel, begs her to give up singing, and she promises to do so. For, unknown to herself, Antonia is sick almost to death with consumption.

When Crespel orders Frantz, a deaf servant, to keep all visitors out, he responds with very comic misunderstandings. In fact, he feels rather sorry for himself—as he tells us in a little song concerning his unappreciated musical talents. Of course, he fails to keep out Hoffmann, who comes to see Antonia once more. The two lovers greet each other warmly, and soon are singing together a sweet duet that they had sung together in better times *C'est un chanson d'amour*. Hoffmann is worried by Antonia's unexplained ill-health, and when she leaves, he hides behind a curtain to try to solve this mystery.

Now the evil genius in this act enters in the shape of Dr. Miracle, a charlatan who had caused the death of Antonia's mother. Crespel cannot get him out of the house, and Dr. Miracle proceeds to examine Antonia's health, making believe she is present even though she is in another room. He even forces her to sing off-stage. Hoffmann, listening to this, begins to understand; and as Miracle prescribes for Antonia, as Crespel objects, and as Hoffmann is amazed at the evil he sees, a male trio develops. At last, Miracle is driven out of the house; and when Hoffmann once more meets Antonia, he forces a promise from her never to sing again.

But it is Dr. Miracle who has the last word. He returns miraculously through a wall and tries to persuade Antonia to sing. At first he fails, but then he works a miracle on a picture of Antonia's mother that hangs on the wall. The picture begins to urge Antonia to sing; Dr. Miracle seizes a violin to accompany; and Antonia's voice rises higher and higher. It is finally too much for her; and as she falls back, dying, Hoffmann rushes back into the room and cries out his despair, while Crespel's accusations of Hoffmann prove equally futile.

EPILOGUE

While the scenery is being changed, the orchestra quietly plays a chorus that Hoffman's drinking companions had sung shortly before he began his recital at the end of the prologue. And when the curtain rises, we are back in Luther's tavern, with everyone in the precise position he had occupied when the curtain last went down on it.

"That was the tale of my loves," concludes Hoffmann. "I shall never forget them." At this point Luther breaks the spell the poet has woven by coming in to announce that Stella has been a smashing success in *Don Giovanni*; and Lindorf, unobserved, goes out to meet her. Nicklausse, meantime, explains the meaning of the Tales of Hoffmann: Olympia, Antonia, Giulietta, artist, innocent, and courtesan, are all embodied in one woman—Stella. He proposes a toast to her, but

Hoffmann angrily forbids it and suggests instead that everyone get drunk. As this is the more enticing prospect, the students take up their glasses, sing their drinking song, and file off into the next room.

Only Hoffmann remains behind, dejected and considerably the worse for wine. The Muse of Poetry briefly appears to him and consoles him with the thought that one is made great through love but even greater through tears. Inspired by this elementary tenet of romanticism, Hoffmann bursts into the passionate melody he had sung to Giulietta and then falls back into his chair, quite overcome. There Stella finds him as she passes through the room on the arm of Nicklausse. "Hoffmann asleep?" she asks. "No, just dead drunk," answers his good friend, and he turns her over to her new lover, Councilor Lindorf. But before they go off together, she tosses a rose at the feet of the unconscious Hoffmann. Off-stage, the students repeat their drinking song.

Postscript for the historically curious: On June 25, 1822, at the age of forty-six, the poet and composer E. T. A. Hoffmann, by this time a confirmed drunkard, died of locomotor ataxia in Berlin.

TANNHÄUSER

und der Sängerkrieg auf dem Wartburg
(Tannhäuser and the Song Contest at the Wartburg)

Opera in three acts by Richard Wagner with
libretto in German by the composer based on a
legend related in the medieval German poem
Der Sängerkrieg

HERMANN, *Landgrave of Thuringia*		Bass
HEINRICH TANNHÄUSER		Tenor
WOLFRAM VON ESCHENBACH		Baritone
WALTHER VON DER VOGELWEIDE	*Knights and*	Tenor
BITEROLF	*Minnesingers*	Bass
HEINRICH DER SCHREIBER		Tenor
REINMAR VON ZWETER		Bass
ELISABETH, *niece of Hermann*		Soprano
VENUS		Soprano
A YOUNG SHEPHERD		Soprano

Time: 13*th century*
Place: Thuringia, near Eisenach
First performance at Dresden, October 19, 1845

Tannhäuser has had the not unamusing distinction of receiving both accolades and damnation from most surprising
directions. There was, for example, Vienna's most influential
critic, Eduard Hanslick, who has gained an immortal infamy
in the hearts of thousands of Wagnerians for acute and devas-
tating analyses of Wagner which they have not read. This is
what Wagner's archfoe had, in part, to say about *Tannhäuser*
when it was a brand-new show: "I am of the firm opinion
that it is the finest thing achieved in grand opera in at least
twelve years. . . . Richard Wagner is, I am convinced, the

greatest dramatic talent among all contemporary composers."

This from the last man on earth to be called a Wagner-worshiper. But the greatest Wagner-worshiper of them all utterly disagreed. *"Meine schlechteste Oper"* (my worst opera) is how the composer himself dismissed it late in life.

Less well equipped critics than Hanslick and Wagner also expressed widely divergent opinions. When the opera was first performed in Paris, Wagner gladly (and brilliantly) supplied a ballet, for that was a *sine qua non* of opera nights in the reign of the good Emperor Napoleon III. Unfortunately, the only conceivable spot for the interpolation was in the opening scene, which came much too early for the habits of the young dandies of the Jockey Club; and as these gay blades patronized the opera largely to applaud the ballet girls, they organized a young riot of protest. At the second and third performances their antics were so preposterous that Wagner withdrew the work. But these gentlemen's form of criticism was single-minded (if simple-minded) and, in one respect at least, thoroughly honorable. Wagner himself tells, in his memoirs, of one young fellow who, on being reprimanded for his behavior, riposted: *"Que voulez-vous?* I am myself beginning to like the music. But you see, a man must keep his word. If you will excuse me, I shall return to my work again."

OVERTURE

This is one of the most popular pieces ever written for "pops" concerts. It is based partly on the *Pilgrims' Chorus,* with which it opens and closes, and partly on the contrasting music of the orgies in the court of Venus. It thus summarizes the theme of the whole story—the battle of sacred and profane love for the soul of the hero, Tannhäuser.

ACT I

In the original, or "Dresden," version of the opera, the overture comes to a full close. In the "Paris" version, which was mounted sixteen years later, the curtain rises without interruption for applause, on a scene of great voluptuousness in the court of Venus—a scene that Wagner revised extensively for the occasion, bringing to it the musical powers greatly matured through the composition, in the intervening years, of *Lohengrin*, over half of the *Ring* cycle, and *Tristan und Isolde*. This court of Venus had its being in the Thuringian mountains, where the spring goddess, Holda, was supposed to reign. The poetry of mythology, however, quite rightly disregards the mundane logic of historians, and Holda is easily equated with Venus, the goddess of love.

At the moment, with the amiably distracting assistance of sirens, naiads, nymphs and bacchantes, she is trying to make things attractive for Heinrich Tannhäuser, a more or less historical German knight who was also a singer and composer. Henry has deserted the court of Landgrave Hermann, ruler of Thuringia, to spend some time at the more glamorous spot he is inhabiting now. But he has grown tired of the pagan rites and tells the goddess so. Despite all her pleadings, Tannhäuser calls on Mary, and the whole wicked court vanishes.

The scene is transformed at once into the valley of the Wartburg. Tannhäuser listens to a shepherd boy sing sweetly and innocently (oddly enough, about the goddess Holda, who, in *his* mythology, is a good girl), and he greets a group of pilgrims chanting on their way to Rome. From the distance, then, comes the sound of hunting horns, and presently Tannhäuser is cordially welcomed by the Landgrave himself and a party of hunters, all old friends. They urge him to return, for they miss his singing. At first he refuses. Then his particular old friend and comrade-in-arms-and-song Wolfram tells him that the Landgrave's daughter Elisabeth has been brokenhearted since his departure. In a noble melody Wolfram urges Tannhäuser to return, and he is joined in these hospitable sentiments by the Landgrave himself and all the knights. Warmed by this reception—and by the thought of the beloved Elisabeth —Tannhäuser is won over, and the act closes with hunting calls as the whole party leaves for the castle of the Wartburg.

The second act takes place in the magnificent Hall of the Minstrels, in the Wartburg. Elisabeth has long kept away from the festivals of song held here. After a short prelude, she returns to the hall and rapturously greets it in a brilliant aria (*Dich, theure Hall'*). The reason she has returned is that Tannhäuser, the greatest of the singers, is once more in the court. Soon he is brought in by Wolfram, who discreetly retires. She tells Tannhäuser modestly but frankly how he has been missed, and the two unite in a rapturous duet over their reunion.

Then, enter the Landgrave. He informs Elisabeth that there will be a tournament of song, that she shall crown the winner, and that her hand will go with the prize. Trumpet calls are heard off-stage, and to the familiar "*March from Tannhäuser*" the entire court assembles for the tournament of song. It turns out to be a rather more exciting event than most singing contests. Wolfram begins, conservatively praising a pure and holy love. Tannhäuser—recently returned from that great expert on love, Venus—rashly tells Wolfram he does not know what he is talking about. Biterolf, another contestant, takes up the argument on Wolfram's side. Thereupon Tannhäuser becomes even more violent. To the consternation of everyone, he takes up his harp and sings frankly and vigorously in praise of carnal love. Everyone is deeply shocked. The knights take out their swords to attack the profaner of the Hall; the women start to leave in disorder; and suddenly Elisabeth intervenes. Throwing herself before her beloved, she begs for his forgiveness. The Landgrave consents, provided Tannhäuser makes a pilgrimage to Rome to get a pardon from the Pope. Just at that moment a group of pilgrims conveniently passes by. Filled with contrition, Tannhäuser rushes out to join them.

The prelude describes, mournfully enough, our hero's unhappy pilgrimage to Rome. Elisabeth has been sadly awaiting his return; and at a roadside shrine in the valley of the Wartburg, she silently prays for him as the faithful Wolfram watches and muses over her. In the distance we hear a band of pilgrims approaching. They sing the famous *Pilgrims' Chorus,* and as they pass by the shrine, Elisabeth eagerly searches for her beloved Tannhäuser. He is not to be found among them; and when the pilgrims have departed, she kneels once more to pray to the Virgin Mary that Tannhäuser may yet be saved—and that she herself may leave this unhappy earth. When she arises, Wolfram wishes to accompany her home, but Elisabeth quietly refuses the kind offer: she hopes, now, only to die.

Dusk is gathering; the evening star comes out; and Wolfram sings the famous aria to that heavenly body, accompanying himself on his harp. Now, in the semi-darkness, appears the wretched figure of Tannhäuser. Bitterly he says that he is on his way again to the Venusburg. He recites to Wolfram the long narrative of his journey to Rome. The hardships had been almost incredible; and when he reached the Pope, he had been told there was no forgiveness—not till the staff the Pope held in his hand should burst into bloom. Reasonably enough, Tannhäuser considers this unnatural phenomenon very unlikely. He calls upon the goddess Venus, who appears in the distance, singing seductive music and surrounded by her court of bacchantes. Desperately Wolfram tries to restrain his friend and finally succeeds only through telling him that one angel prays for his soul. Her name is "Elisabeth." Just as Tannhäuser is at last won over again, a cortege passes by bearing the body of Elisabeth, who has at last found the rest she so earnestly desired. Completely broken, Tannhäuser sinks down beside her bier.

The opera closes ironically, but on a joyous tone. A chorus of young pilgrims enters bringing with them the latest miracle from Rome. It is the Pope's staff, which has burst into bloom. God has forgiven the errant Tannhäuser.

THE TELEPHONE

or L'amour à trois

Opera in one act by Gian-Carlo Menotti with libretto in English by the composer

LUCY   *Soprano*
BEN   *Baritone*

Time: the present
Place: practically any country with telephones
First performance at New York, February 18, 1947

Mr. Menotti's *The Medium* is a grim and powerful tragedy but too short for a full bill at the opera house. Therefore, when it was first produced by the Ballet Society at the Heckscher Theater in New York, the composer supplied this short curtain-raiser most admirably contrasted in tone.

The opening measures of the prelude have the tempo marking *Allegro vivace*. Translated literally, this musickese for "fast and lively" means "vivaciously happy"—as good a description of the entire score as anyone could find.

In her apartment Lucy unwraps a present that Ben has just handed her, a bit of crazy sculpture. "Oh! Just what I wanted," she giggles even before she has looked at it. Ben, obviously smitten with the pretty bird-brain and even more obviously shy, manages to say that he is going away by train in an hour, but when he returns he hopes, he hopes . . . He has not yet nerved himself to the proposal, when the telephone rings. It is one of her girl-friends, and for several pages she goes on with the typical inane chatter of girls on the telephone: "Jane and Paul are to get married next July. Don't you think it is the funniest thing? . . . And how are you? And how is John? And how is Jean? . . . And how is Ursula? And how is Natalie? And how is Rosalie? I hope she's gotten over her cold . . ." And so on, including the most *delicious* peals of merry girlish coloratura laughter, till poor Ben begins to show his desperation.

Finally the conversation is through; Ben begins his embarrassed proposal once more; and there is another ring. Wrong number. Oh, but she must dial for the time. It is four-fifteen and three and a half seconds. Once more Ben begins. Once more the telephone. This time it is a friend named George. Apparently Lucy has been repeating some gossip about him, and she tries in vain to defend herself against his tirade. George hangs up on her; Lucy bursts into tears; and Ben tries awkwardly to soothe her. When she goes into the next room to get a handkerchief, Ben seriously considers cutting the telephone wire—but once more it rings, "desperately," says the score. Lucy, running back and taking it from Ben, pouts that he "must have hit it first." Now she must ring Pamela and tell her all about George. This is another real long call, and Ben, first muttering to himself, finally becomes desperate. Lucy barely notices when he leaves: "I have a feeling he had something on his mind," she murmurs after hanging up.

But a moment later one corner of the stage lights up, showing Ben in a telephone booth. He dials Lucy's number, gets an answer, and finally comes through with the proposal. Will she marry him? Of course! And the opera ends with a telephoned duet in which Ben promises never, never to forget her telephone number.

THAÏS

Opera in three acts by Jules Massenet with libretto in French by Louis Gallet based on the
novel of the same name by Anatole France

THAÏS, *a courtesan*	*Soprano*
ATHANAËL, *a young cenobite monk*	*Baritone*
NICIAS, *a young Alexandrian*	*Tenor*
PALEMON, *an old cenobite*	*Bass*
SERVANT OF NICIAS	*Baritone*
CROBYLE, *a slave*	*Soprano*
MYRTALE, *another slave*	*Mezzo-soprano*
ALBINE, *an abbess*	*Contralto*

Time: fourth century A.D.
Place: Alexandria and surrounding desert country
First performance at Paris, March 16, 1894

Thaïs has always been what is called a vehicle opera; that
is, it has been most successful when sung by a spectacular
soprano in the leading role. Massenet composed it for the
glamorous Sybil Sanderson, the American toast of Paris, while
in the United States (and in France, too) the role was practically identified, for many years, with that glorious singing-
actress, Mary Garden.

The story of the opera is based on the novel of the same
name by Anatole France, the great French ironist. It should
not be confused, by the way, with the story of that other Thaïs,
the one for whom Alexander the Great burned Persepolis.
Alexander's Thaïs died as the Queen of Egypt; Anatole
France's heroine had a very different fate.

497

The original tale was written by France two different times, both in prose; but when Louis Gallet came to build a libretto on it, he decided to experiment with something new, something he called *poésie mélique*—a sort of rhythmical prose or unmetered and unrhymed poetry which might fall gracefully into musical phrases. This sounds like a good idea, and it worked out well in this case; yet it inspired no imitations at the time, and it is only recently that librettists have been trying similar ideas once more.

ACT I

Scene 1 takes place in the desert near Thebes, on the banks of the Nile, some time in the fourth century. A group of monks—"cenobites," they were called—is having an evening meal of bread, salt, hyssop leaves, and honey, and their leader, Palemon, is praying. Athanaël, one of their members, comes back, dusty and exhausted, from a trip to Alexandria, his birthplace. There he has seen the corruption amid which he himself was raised. But it is worse now, he reports. The courtesan and actress, Thaïs, has inspired even greater vice, and Athanaël wishes to return and try to save her. Palemon gently tries to tell him he would be doing better to mind his own business; but when everyone leaves the young monk, he sees Thaïs once more in a vision, acting, half naked, before a crowd, as he had seen her in Alexandria.

Terribly excited, he calls back his fellow monks. He tells them he must go at once; and though Palemon repeats his gentle warning, Athanaël sets out on his trip. As the scene closes, he is on his way, and one hears the monks praying for him from ever and ever greater distances.

Scene 2 finds Athanaël once more in Alexandria, and the graceful music of the prelude suggests how much pleasanter this place is than the desert. He stands before the splendid home of his old friend Nicias, but he finds nothing pleasant in the sight of all this cursed wealth. Nicias greets him with complete cordiality, and when Athanaël tells him the reason for his visit, Nicias says: Fine! It happens that Thaïs is his own mistress for the time being, and, in fact, he is giving her a big farewell party that night. Athanaël must come—only he must be dressed properly for the festivities, not like a dirty old monk. And so he summons two pretty slave girls, Crobyle and Myrtale, to bathe and dress him in the highest Alexandrian fashion. The girls are delighted, for they find this monk a most handsome and attractive fellow. In a charming duet, full of laughter, they effect a startling change, finishing just before the guests, in very high spirits, come rushing in. Among them is Thaïs, beloved of all of them as the most glamorous and beautiful girl in town. She is left for a short while alone with Nicias, and in a good-natured but slightly sentimental fashion she tells him it is his last time with her, for he has no more money. Not a cynical note creeps into the expression of this basically cynical attitude, for these are the rules of the game, and Nicias does not question them.

Thaïs is struck, however, by the appearance of Athanaël. Nicias tells her that his friend has come to convert her to Christianity. Thaïs, attracted in spite of herself, tells Athanaël she believes only in the power of love—her kind of love; but Athanaël, almost literally, *threatens* her with salvation. This angers the actress, and before Athanaël's eyes she begins to disrobe to portray the love of Aphrodite. Deeply shocked, he rushes from the scene as Thaïs, ending on a high D-flat, cries: "Only dare to come near—you who defy Venus!"

ACT II

Scene 1 finds Thaïs in her own luxurious home. She is beautiful, but she is tired—tired of her life as actress and as courtesan. Her fear, she tells us in a long scene alone, is that she will grow old, she will lose her loveliness; and she prays for eternal beauty to the one deity she acknowledges—the goddess of love, Venus.

The rest of the scene is a duet between her and Athanaël, as he tries to persuade her to give up her evil life for a holy one. In vain, at first, he tells her of the difference between her love and his—between profane and holy love. To this she replies that she knows only one language of love—kisses. Athanaël, however, persists, and at one point in the duet they pray simultaneously—he to the Christian god, she to Venus.

Suddenly he pulls off the fine robes his rich friend Nicias has given him and stands before her as a monk in a hair-shirt. Now she is afraid, for she feels that eternal life can come only through Athanaël's religion; and when she hears Nicias singing ardently outside her room, she sends him off. Athanaël, too, is ordered to go, for she must be alone to ponder and to learn. She is still confused; she cannot think; and the scene closes as she is driven to hysterical laughter.

Her thoughts, as she is alone, are suggested in music—the music of the familiar and beautiful *Meditation,* which is played while the scenery is changed.

Scene 2 Athanaël has lain quietly at the doorstep of Thaïs's house all night long. Soft sounds of the gay music of Alexandrian festivities are heard at the beginning of the scene. But the conversion of Thaïs has been complete. She comes from her home prepared to go with Athanaël, to lead a holy life. He promises to take her to a convent, but first, he says, she must destroy all her evil wealth. One thing alone she would preserve—a little statue of Eros, Love, and she sings a touching aria about it (*L'amour est une vertu rare*—"Love is a precious virtue"). But Athanaël hurls the little pagan statue to the ground, and, obediently, Thaïs prepares to follow him.

Suddenly Nicias and his whole crowd of revelers bursts in. As Thaïs and Athanaël re-enter the house, this crowd sings and dances, and the orchestra plays the ballet music from *Thaïs.* Just at its close Athanaël comes back and is laughingly greeted by his friends. But when Thaïs follows, now dressed in only a woolen tunic, they grow angry. Athanaël take away their great Queen of Beauty into the desert? Never, never— and they drunkenly attack the monk. Nicias, however, rises to the occasion. He distracts the crowd by tossing gold among them; and as Thaïs steals away with her holy mentor, he cries after her: "Adieu! Your memory will ever be perfume to my soul." He is really a nice, sentimental fellow, this Nicias; and it is only then that he discovers that Thaïs and Athanaël

have put a torch to the house, which starts burning wildly
about him.

ACT III

Scene 1 begins at the end of the dusty trip through the
desert. As Athanaël and Thaïs reach an oasis, she wishes to
rest, for her frail body can take no more punishment. At first
Athanaël is harsh with her: a holy life, in his philosophy, demands punishment of the flesh. But soon he relents, and
leaves her to find some refreshment. As the orchestra plays
some of the music from the *Meditation,* she prays to God,
acknowledging the sweetness of His spirit.

When Athanaël returns with fruit and water, they sing a
gentle duet as they bathe their hands and lips. Refreshed,
they are about to go on, when the nuns come up to meet
them. They are headed by the Abbess Albine, and they chant
the Lord's Prayer in Latin as they come. Tenderly Athanaël
turns his charge over to the Abbess; tenderly Thaïs bids farewell to the man who has saved her soul. "*Adieu, mon père,*"
she says—for never once in the opera does she utter Athanaël's
own name. And suddenly—for the first time—Athanaël realizes
that he loves Thaïs, and that he may never see her again. He
utters a cry of anguish—as the nuns depart, taking Thaïs with
them.

Scene 2 Anatole France was a great satirist, a great ironist.
The neat point of his story is that the great exponent of profane love—Thaïs—becomes a saint, while the great exponent
of self-denying holy love—Athanaël—renounces it for a sinner.
In a scene that is almost always omitted as not really necessary,
Athanaël struggles with his temptation in his solitary hut; but
a vision of Thaïs, dying, makes him rush off to see her one
last time.

Scene 3 Athanaël arrives at the convent, barely in time.
For three months Thaïs has mortified her flesh, and now she
lies dying. Albine and the other nuns mourn her as the most
saintly of them all. Athanaël, in anguish, rushes in. The dying
Thaïs recognizes him, but it is now in vain that he tries to tell

her that the only true love is love between earthly beings. As the strains of the *Meditation* are heard once more, Thaïs believes she sees two angels and God Himself preparing to take her to heaven. The recusant monk, utterly frustrated, sees his convert die a holy death.

TOSCA

Opera in three acts by Giacomo Puccini with libretto in Italian by Luigi Illica and Giuseppe Giacosa, based on Victorien Sardou's play of the same name

FLORIA TOSCA, *a prima donna*	*Soprano*
MARIO CAVARADOSSI, *a painter*	*Tenor*
BARON SCARPIA, *Chief of Police*	*Baritone*
CESARE ANGELOTTI, *a political prisoner*	*Bass*
A SACRISTAN	*Baritone*
SPOLETTA, *a police agent*	*Tenor*
SCIARRONE, *a gendarme*	*Bass*
A JAILER	*Bass*
A SHEPHERD BOY	*Mezzo-soprano*
ROBERTI, *an executioner*	*Silent*

Time: June 1800
Place: Rome
First performance at Rome, January 14, 1900

Victorien Sardou, king of French melodramatists, wrote *Tosca* as a dramatic vehicle for Sarah Bernhardt. It was enormously successful and was given, according to its author, three thousand times. (Maybe that was only a slight exaggeration: he made the statement twenty years after the premiere.) At any rate, it appealed as a possible source for a libretto not only to Puccini but to Verdi and to Franchetti as well. Franchetti, in fact, secured the rights first, and it was only through a fine bit of skulduggery by Tito Ricordi, both Puccini's and Franchetti's publisher, that the rights were transferred from the lesser composer to the greater.

But there were others who thought, and perhaps still think, that the play is just too strong dramatically to serve as an ideal libretto. Some of the opening-night critics said just that. Mascagni thought so too. He said: "I have been victimized by poor librettos. Puccini is the victim of a libretto that is too good."

Whether or not these critics are right, the facts remain that the opera is a huge success, that Sardou's play virtually died after Bernhardt gave it up, and that Puccini's opera continues a vigorous life over sixty years after its premiere, after much more than three thousand performances, after hundreds of sopranos have taken that final jump over the parapet.

Puccini well understood the value of Sardou's drama, its speed and intensity. He objected strongly when his librettist, Illica, wanted to give the tenor a long farewell oration and compromised with the short but extremely moving aria *E lucevan le stelle*. He refused to write an old-fashioned quartet with the tortured tenor off-stage while Scarpia, Tosca, and Spoletta made comments on-stage. He even disliked the famous aria *Vissi d'arte* because it held up the action; and when, one day in rehearsal, Maria Jeritza accidentally rolled off the couch just before the first notes and sang the aria from the floor, the composer said: "That's good. It gives the aria some life." Jeritza always sang it that way thereafter.

Yes, Puccini was very much a man of the theater. Not that he lacked appreciation for a fine voice. One time, when the scheduled tenor was unable to keep an engagement to sing Cavaradossi, Ricordi sent for an audition a young tenor who, said the publisher with no show of originality in phrase, had "a voice of gold." The unknown's name was Enrico Caruso; and after Puccini had accompanied him in a run-through of *Recondita armonia,* he turned around on the piano stool and asked: "Who sent you to me? God?"

ACT I

Three crashing chords, always used to suggest Scarpia, Rome's sinister chief of police, open the opera. He is the grim and elegant figure who epitomizes the reactionary forces of Italy, in 1800, when Napoleon was regarded as an apostle of freedom. Immediately after those opening chords the curtain rises on the interior of the church of Saint'Andrea della Valle. In rushes a disheveled man. He is Angelotti, an escaped political prisoner, and he hides in the chapel of the Attavanti on the right. A moment later comes the sacristan of the church, busily talking to himself and fussing over a painter's dais on the left of the stage. Now enter our hero, Mario Cavaradossi, a painter, who starts working on a portrait of the Magdalen that stands half finished on the easel. He sings the aria *Recondita armonia*, in which he compares the features of his picture with those of his beloved, the celebrated diva, Floria Tosca.

After the sacristan has left, Cavaradossi discovers Angelotti, whom he thrusts back into the chapel as the voice of Tosca is heard outside demanding entrance. Tosca is a strikingly handsome, fashionably dressed prima donna, and, as so many beautiful women are said to be, is easily aroused to jealousy. This time she is jealous of the picture her lover is painting, and he has some difficulty calming her. He succeeds, however; and at the end of their love duet they plan a rendezvous in his villa for that same night, after she has sung a performance at the Farnese Palace. When she has left, Angelotti emerges once more, and Cavaradossi goes off with him, to hide him in his own house.

Now comes news of the defeat of Napoleon in the north. Preparations are made for a special service in the church. But in the midst of these preparations in comes Scarpia, who, as chief of police, is searching for the escaped Angelotti. With his evil-looking assistant Spoletta, he finds a number of clues, including a fan. This he uses cleverly to arouse the jealousy of Tosca, whom he desires for himself.

The services begin. A great procession comes into the church; and while the *Te Deum* of victory is sung, Scarpia stands to one side expressing his hope of disposing of his rival, Cavaradossi, through Tosca's jealousy. If his plot succeeds, Cavaradossi should end on the scaffold and Floria Tosca in

Scarpia's arms. Just before the curtain falls, with these evil thoughts still in his mind, he kneels in prayer with the others.

ACT II

That night, in the Farnese Palace, the victory over Napoleon is being celebrated, and music is heard through the windows of Scarpia's office in that building. Scarpia, alone, ruminates on the events of the day; he sends, via the gendarme Sciarrone, a message to Tosca; and he receives a report from Spoletta. That vulture had searched Cavaradossi's house, failed to find Angelotti, but had seen Tosca there. He had arrested Cavaradossi and brought him to the palace, a prisoner. As Tosca's voice is heard below, singing the solo part in a victory cantata, her lover is brought in and questioned, but to no avail. When Tosca arrives, he manages to whisper to her that Scarpia knows nothing as yet and that she should tell of nothing that she had seen at his villa. He is then ordered into the next room accompanied by guards, including the executioner Roberti.

Scarpia then begins to question Tosca, who maintains a fine poise until she begins to hear Cavaradossi's screams of anguish under torture from the next room. Unable to bear this, she tells Scarpia that Angelotti is hidden in the well in the garden.

Cavaradossi, considerably the worse for wear, is brought in and learns that Tosca has betrayed his friend. A moment later news comes that Napoleon has won a victory at Marengo. The painter sings a triumphant paean to liberty, and is contemptuously ordered out, to be executed in the morning.

Then Scarpia politely and fiendishly recommences his interview with the distraught Tosca, and it is during this very uncomfortable interview that she sings her aria *Vissi d'arte*, passionately apostrophizing love and music, the two great forces to which she has devoted her life. Finally, she agrees to sacrifice herself for her lover's life.

Now Scarpia explains that, as he has already ordered Cavaradossi's execution, a mock execution at least must be arranged. He summons Spoletta to give these orders, and he makes out passes for Tosca and her lover to leave the city. But as he turns to take his victim in his arms, she plunges a knife into him, crying at the same time: "Thus it is that Tosca kisses!" (The orchestra plays those three Scarpia chords—but this time pianissimo.)

Quickly, then, she washes her bloodstained hands, takes the safe-conducts from Scarpia's lifeless fingers, places a lighted candle on either side of his head and a crucifix on his breast, and sweeps from the room as the curtain falls.

ACT III

The final act begins peacefully enough with the very early morning song of a shepherd boy heard off-stage. The scene of the act is the roof of the Castle of Sant'Angelo in Rome, where Cavaradossi has been brought for execution. He is allowed a short time to prepare for death. This he uses to write a farewell to his beloved Tosca, and he sings the heartbreaking aria *E lucevan le stelle*—"The stars were shining brightly." Soon Tosca herself enters. She shows him the safe-conducts she secured from Scarpia; she tells him how she has killed the wicked police chief; and the two lovers sing a passionate duet, anticipating their happy future. Finally, Tosca explains that Cavaradossi still must go through the farce of a mock execution, after which they will fly together.

The execution squad now enters, led by Spoletta. Mario stands up before them; they fire; he falls; the soldiers depart; and Tosca rushes over to the fallen body of her lover. It is only then that she discovers how Scarpia had fooled her. For the bullets used were real, and Cavaradossi lies dead. Even as she gives vent to her grief, the soldiers return, having discovered the murder of Scarpia. Spoletta attempts to seize Tosca but she wrenches herself free, climbs high on the parapet, and flings herself over to certain death. As the orchestra thunders out Mario's farewell, the soldiers stand helpless and horror-struck.

LA TRAVIATA

Opera in three acts by Giuseppe Verdi with
libretto in Italian by Francesco Maria Piave
based on a play by the younger Alexandre
Dumas entitled *La dame aux camélias* (usually
called *Camille* in English), which is in turn
based on his semi-autobiographical novel

VIOLETTA VALERY, *a courtesan*	*Soprano*
FLORA BERVOIX, *another*	*Mezzo-soprano*
ALFREDO GERMONT, *young man from Provence*	*Tenor*
GIORGIO GERMONT, *his father*	*Baritone*
BARON DOUPHOL, *a protector of Violetta's*	*Baritone*
DR. GRENVIL	*Bass*
ANNINA, *Violetta's maid*	*Soprano*

Time: 1846
Place: Paris and the suburb Auteuil
First performance at Venice, March 6, 1853

When *La traviata* was first performed on March 6, 1853,
at Venice, it was an instant failure. Neither the critics nor the
public liked it. One trouble was the singers: there was a too
healthy heroine dying of consumption, and everyone thought
that was funny. Another trouble was costumes: it was played
in modern clothes (that is, of course, modern for 1853), and
no one was used to grand opera in modern clothes.

At a later performance all this was changed, and the opera
was from then on successful in Italy. The public also liked it—
right from the start—in England and America. But not the
critics. They thought the story "foul, hideous, and immoral."

But critics are sometimes wrong at first, and the public is usually right. Today, over a century old, it is one of the most popular of all operas and one finds the story told in books of opera plots intended for children. So much for the morals of critics.

The story, of course, has to do with disease and love. That doesn't sound, offhand, like an attractive combination. Still, when one realizes that the first theme in the famous prelude is related to the heroine's illness and the second to her love, there should be in it a lesson in how beautifully composers can project some rather unbeautiful concepts.

ACT I

Act I takes place during a late evening party at the home of Violetta Valery. Violetta is a delightful young lady of somewhat dubious reputation. (As a matter of fact, the younger Alexandre Dumas, who wrote the original story, based her character on that of a real courtesan he knew and loved in the Paris of the 1840's. Her original name was Alphonsine Plessis, but she changed to Marie Duplessis in order to sound more high-toned.) It's a very gay party, as the opening music attests. Pretty soon Violetta is introduced to a young fellow from the country—Alfredo Germont—an attractive, slightly naïve boy with an excellent tenor voice. He shows it off in the *Brindisi*, or drinking song. Violetta—and later everyone else—joins in the quick-waltz rhythms of the tune. When all the guests go into the next room to dance, Violetta remains behind. She is not feeling well, and she is briefly overcome with a fit of coughing. Alfredo, who has quietly remained in the room, begins to tell her quite seriously how much he loves her, even though he had only seen her from a distance before. His accents are so sincere—so passionate—that Violetta is both moved and embarrassed. In light, laughing phrases she advises him to forget her. She knows that she is not the sort of

girl for this earnest type of young man. Their voices join in a
sort of expressive coloratura at the end of this duet, and just
before the guests return, she promises to see him again the
next day.

It is now late. The guests take their leave, and Violetta is
left alone for her great scene. She sings the aria *Ah, fors' è lui*,
wondering whether this young man from the country can really
represent true love in her life of light loves. She takes up the
passionate tune he had sung a little earlier, but then (in the
so-called *cabaletta* to the aria), she cries, in effect, "Nonsense,
nonsense!" *Sempre libera*—"Ever free"—she sings. Hers must
be a free life. For a moment she is silent, as outside her
window she hears the voice of Alfredo repeating his love music,
but she only grows more feverish and wilder as her voice
mounts, in coloratura runs. Almost all sopranos take these runs
up to an E-flat above high C, even though Verdi did not write
it that way. As the act ends, we know that, despite her protests, the lady *is* for burning.

ACT II

Scene 1 takes place three months later. The love affair begun at Violetta's party has developed, and now she and Alfredo are comfortably ensconced in a suburban cottage outside
Paris. Alfredo, in his opening aria, *De' miei bollenti spiriti*,
tells us how good she is for him, and also how wild she is
about him. But it is Violetta who is paying all the bills for
the establishment; and by questioning the maid, Annina, Alfredo finds out that she is even selling her personal belongings.
The hotheaded young fellow thereupon dashes off to Paris
himself to raise the necessary thousand louis. And so when
Alfredo's father, a few minutes later, calls on Violetta, he
finds the lady alone.

A long and eloquent duet follows. At first he demands that
she give Alfredo up. Slowly he realizes that there is real nobility in Violetta, and then he pleads with her. Alfredo's sister, he says, will never be able to marry well while her brother
maintains so disreputable a connection. He utters this rather

caddish sentiment in more tactful terms—and very mellifluously, too; yet that is what it amounts to. And strangely, Violetta is impressed. Before his rather lengthy farewell-taking, she has promised to give up the love of her life and not even to let him know why. Quickly she pens a farewell note to Alfredo, and also accepts an invitation to a party from Flora Bervoix, one of the old gay crowd.

Before she is finished, Alfredo returns. He is full of confidence, sure that his father will love her as soon as he sees her. Her heart breaking, Violetta begs him always to love her and then secretly leaves for Paris. A moment later a servant brings him the farewell letter. Greatly distraught, he is about to run after her, when his father appears and stops him. Now old Germont has his great aria *Di Provenza il mar,* in which he reminds his son of their home in Provence, and begs him to return. Alfredo's answer is to find Flora's invitation, to decide that that is why she has left, and to dash off (as he says) to avenge the insult.

Scene 2 takes us to a party like the one that opened the opera. This time the hostess is Flora Bervoix, and she has provided sumptuous entertainment for her guests. Gypsy dancers and singers are performing as the scene opens, and pretty soon Alfredo puts in an appearance. Everyone is surprised to see him without Violetta, but he makes it clear that he does not much care what has happened to her. That lady herself arrives shortly after, on the arm of Baron Douphol, one of her friends of the bad old days. The Baron and Alfredo take an almost instant dislike to one another, and they start gambling for pretty high stakes. Alfredo wins repeatedly; and as the orchestra plays a nervous little theme, Violetta sits on one side praying that the men will not come to blows. Fortunately, just when Alfredo has all but wiped out his older opponent, supper is announced. Violetta calls Alfredo to her side and begs him to leave. She fears, otherwise, that there may be fighting. Alfredo says he will leave—but only with her, and then he demands to know whether or not she loves the Baron. Remembering her promise to old Germont, Violetta tells a lie: yes, she says, she loves the Baron. Thereupon Al-

La traviata

fredo summons the entire company, dramatically denounces Violetta, and hurls all his winnings directly at her. It is shocking behavior—even for a hot-blooded young Frenchman of the 1840's. No one is more shocked than Alfredo's own father, who arrives on the scene just in time to denounce him. Even Alfredo is ashamed—ashamed of himself—and the scene ends with a great ensemble number, as the Baron challenges Alfredo to a duel.

ACT III

The last act begins with a very beautiful and very sad prelude. It suggests the sickness that is slowly bringing Violetta's life to a close, and when the curtain rises, the opening strains of the prelude are repeated. The poor girl has retired to a shabby flat in Paris. She is lying, desperately weak, in bed, attended by the faithful Annina. Dr. Grenvil calls to give his patient some professional bedside-manner cheer; but Violetta is not fooled, and a moment later the doctor whispers to Annina that it is now only a matter of hours. Violetta sends the maid out to give half her remaining fortune of twenty louis to the poor and then pulls out a letter to reread. It is from the elder Germont; it had arrived several weeks ago, and it says that Alfredo wounded the Baron in the duel, that he left the country, but that he now knows of Violetta's sacrifice and will come to her. So, too, says Germont, will he come himself. Violetta knows that it is a little late for these fine gentlemen to begin appreciating her merits, and she sings the pathetic aria *Addio del passato*—"Farewell to the past, farewell to smiling dreams." At its close, merrymakers are heard outside her window, for it is carnival time in Paris—a time to which Violetta has just bidden her last farewell.

Suddenly Annina returns, breathless, to announce the arrival of the beloved Alfredo. He rushes in, and the lovers sing their touching duet *Parigi, o cara*. In it they plan to leave the city to revive her strength, to live happily ever after. Feverishly Violetta calls for a dress—but she has not even the strength to get into it. Annina rushes off for the doctor, and Germont enters the room in time to see Violetta make her last, sad sacrifice. She gives Alfredo a miniature portrait of herself and charges that he should give it to his future bride. Let her know that there is an angel praying for them both. Then, for a wild moment, Violetta imagines herself better, and the love music of Act I is heard trembling high in the orchestra. But it is only the euphoria that so often precedes death, and the doctor is on hand to pronounce the fateful *È spental* as Violetta falls back into her remorseful lover's arms.

Postscript for the historically curious: In the cemetery of Montmartre, directly below the white church of the Sacre Coeur, tourists still visit the grave of Marie Duplessis, the original *traviata* (or misguided girl). She died February 2, 1846, just nineteen days after achieving her twenty-second birthday. Among her numerous lovers during her last year had been Alexandre Dumas *fils* and Franz Liszt.

TRISTAN UND ISOLDE

Opera in three acts by Richard Wagner with
libretto in German by the composer, based on
old legends

KING MARKE OF CORNWALL	*Bass*
TRISTAN, *his nephew*	*Tenor*
KURWENAL, *Tristan's faithful follower*	*Baritone*
ISOLDE, *an Irish princess*	*Soprano*
BRANGAENE, *Isolde's attendant*	*Mezzo-soprano*
MELOT, *a Cornish courtier*	*Tenor*
A YOUNG SAILOR	*Tenor*
A HELMSMAN	*Baritone*
A SHEPHERD	*Tenor*

Time: the legendary days of King Arthur
Place: Cornwall, Brittany, and the sea
First performance at Munich, June 10, 1865

Tristan und Isolde is generally rated—and with very good
reason—the greatest paean to pure erotic love ever composed.
Its history is intimately bound up with this passion. During
much of its composition Wagner was living with a wealthy
silk merchant of Zurich, one Otto Wesendonck, and the composer was in love with his host's attractive young wife, Mathilde. Later, when the opera was completed, it was given no
fewer than fifty-four rehearsals at the Court Opera in Vienna—
only to be withdrawn. The reason may have been that it was
too difficult and new in style for the company—at least that
was the published reason. But love and politics (two great
motives in Wagner's life) also had much to do with the with-

drawal. For there were pro-Wagner and anti-Wagner camps in the company, the former led by the soprano scheduled to sing the role of Isolde, Luise Dustmann-Meyer. She, however, withdrew her support when she found the composer carrying on a love affair with her younger sister.

Even before Vienna, Wagner had attempted to secure performances at Strasbourg, Karlsruhe, Paris, Weimar, Prague, Hanover, and, of all places, Rio de Janeiro, where it was to have been done in Italian! Mostly for political reasons none of these worked out. It finally achieved its premiere at Munich, six years after the score was completed, under the patronage of Wagner's great but unbalanced friend, King Ludwig II of Bavaria.

The conductor of the premiere was Hans von Bülow, a fierce champion of Wagner's music. Two months before the performance Frau von Bülow had given birth to a daughter, whom she named Isolde. Very probably the conductor did not realize at this time that the composer, in addition to being the godfather, was also little Isolde's real father. In fact, Cosima von Bülow (an illegitimate daughter of Franz Liszt's) bore Richard Wagner three children before Hans finally divorced her and she married the composer.

One need not find in the opera reflection of Wagner's own series of passions for other men's wives: the love of Tristan and Isolde is a far more idealized and purer thing throughout than any page of the composer's shocking life-story. It is basically a very simple tale; and the score, perhaps more than any other Wagner ever composed, carries out his theories of what a music drama (as opposed to a traditional "opera") should be. Gone are the set pieces of his latest produced opera, *Lohengrin*; and here, for the first time, the world heard a music drama in which the orchestra plays the unquestioned dominant role, commenting on every psychological and dramatic development with an elaborate system of leitmotivs, pursuing its way with the "endless melodizing" that Wagner had substituted for the arias, duets, quartets, and so forth to which everyone was accustomed. It created a violent war of the critics that is still being waged.

Tristan und Isolde

PRELUDE

Gone, too, was the security of knowing what key the music is in. I have decided never to be technical in this book; but perhaps I may be permitted to describe just the first two bars of the prelude harmonically. It bears the signature of C-major (or a-minor); it begins with a fragment of melody that might as well be in F-major (or d-minor); and before the second measure is completed, we have reached the dominant seventh chord of A. We have also been given two of the principal motives of the work by this time, melted so intimately into each other that some commentators have called them respectively the *Tristan* and the *Isolde* motives.

I shall leave the technical commentary at that. The Prelude is, as everyone knows, one of the most eloquent, sensuous, and moving tone poems about love ever written.

ACT I

Isolde is a princess of Ireland, the daughter of a distinguished witch, and herself entirely at home with poisons, drugs, and the medieval arts of healing. When the curtain rises, we find her on a ship. This is taking her, against her will, to become the bride of King Marke of Cornwall. The man taking her to Cornwall, the captain of the ship, is Tristan, nephew of King Marke. And Isolde, in a long and angry narrative, explains her anger to her attendant, Brangaene. She had had a fiancé named Morold. Tristan had fought Morold to decide whether or not Cornwall should continue to pay tribute to Ireland, and Tristan had won. But he had been wounded, and, disguised as a harper, he came to Isolde's castle. Isolde was nursing him back to health, when she found a piece of Morold's sword blade in Tristan's head, and in that way she recognized who he was. She was about to kill him with it, when he looked into her eyes—and she fell in love. But now, on orders from his uncle, he is taking her to be married to the old man. No wonder she is angry!

She sends for Tristan, but, being busy with the ship, he sends his henchman, Kurwenal, instead. Kurwenal is a pretty down-to-earth and rude sort of baritone. He gruffly tells Isolde that Tristan will not come and impolitely sings her a ballad about Tristan's victory over Morold. This makes Isolde angrier than ever, and she decides to kill Tristan and herself rather than be married to Marke—whom, by the way, she has never met. She tells Brangaene to prepare a poisoned drink and again summons Tristan. This time he comes, for it is almost time to land. Brutally she reminds him that he has killed her betrothed and, to atone, he offers her his sword to kill him. Instead, she suggests a drink. Fully expecting to be poisoned, Tristan accepts the cup. But Brangaene—without telling Isolde—has substituted a love philter for the death philter; and when Tristan has taken half the drink and Isolde the other half, there is an unexpected result. For a very, very long moment (while the orchestra plays music from the prelude) the two look into each other's eyes. Hastily they embrace, uttering ecstatic phrases of rapture.

But suddenly the sailors are heard singing, for land has been sighted, and the journey is over. Together the two lovers rush off, utterly unprepared to meet King Marke.

ACT II

There is a quick-moving introduction to Act II, clearly depicting impatience, before the curtain rises on Isolde's garden, outside her chambers in the castle of King Marke. (Whether or not a wedding ceremony has taken place between Acts I and II Wagner never makes clear. It is sufficient that Isolde, like everyone else, regards herself as Marke's bride.) The King has gone hunting, and at the beginning of the act, we may hear the hunting horns off-stage. But while the King hunts, Tristan and Isolde have planned to meet. By the side of the castle there is a burning torch, and when that torch is extinguished, it is the sign for Tristan to come to the garden.

Brangaene, Isolde's maid-in-waiting, fears a plot. She believes that Melot, a Cornish knight who is supposed to be

Tristan und Isolde

Tristan's particular friend, will betray them. She warns Isolde to keep the torch burning till the hunting horns can no longer be heard. But Isolde is impatient. She says she cannot hear the horns, and she refuses to believe that Melot may be treacherous. She extinguishes the torch, climbs some steps, and waves her bright scarf in the moonlight to give Tristan a second signal.

As the orchestra mounts to a feverish climax, Tristan rushes in. "Isolde! Beloved!" he cries; and Isolde echoes him: "Beloved!" It is the beginning of the great love duet known as the *Liebesnacht*—a long, eloquent, moving expression of transfigured love—love that prefers night to day, and love that prefers death to life. At the end of the duet they are singing the familiar and beautiful melody of the *Liebestod*; and just as they reach the climax, Brangaene, who has stood watch, utters a piercing shriek. The King and his hunting party have unexpectedly returned. They have been brought back by Tristan's supposed friend, Melot, who is himself secretly in love with Isolde and therefore acts from rather reprehensible motives. The noble King's principal emotion is sorrow—sorrow that the honor of his dearly beloved nephew, Tristan, is besmirched. He sings of this in a very, very long monologue, while Isolde turns aside in deepest shame.

At its close Tristan asks her whether she will follow him; and when she assents, he denounces Melot and in a brief fight deliberately permits himself to be wounded. Before Melot can kill him, King Marke thrust Melot aside. With Isolde throwing herself on the wounded hero's breast, the long act closes.

ACT III

Tristan has been brought to his castle in Brittany by his faithful henchman, Kurwenal. There he lies, wounded and ill, before the castle. He is waiting for a ship—the ship that bears Isolde, who will come to heal him. Off-stage, a shepherd plays a very doleful tune on his pipe. He is to make it cheerful only when he sees the ship. The doleful tune, the fever of his illness, the tragedy of his life—these all combine to help confuse poor Tristan's mind. It wanders over many things—his friendship for Kurwenal, his hatred of his enemies, his love for Isolde, the death of his parents. All these themes (and others too) go through his agonized brain as he lies there, while poor, simple Kurwenal tries in vain to comfort him.

Suddenly the shepherd's tune changes. It brightens in a major key. The ship has been sighted. It disappears again—and it reappears—and a few moments later, Isolde comes rushing in. She is almost too late to see her lover alive, for in his excitement he has pulled off his bandages. As he embraces his beloved Isolde, he falls and breathes his last.

But another ship is seen. It is the ship bearing King Marke —and the villain, Melot, too. Marke has come to forgive the lovers, but Kurwenal does not know this. He rallies his few men, valiantly disputing the way with Marke's followers, and he manages to kill Melot. But he himself also receives a mortal wound, and he falls, dying, at his hero's feet. Then quietly, in the presence of King Marke and of Brangaene and the few survivors, Isolde takes the dead body of Tristan in her arms. Transfigured by her emotions, she sings the great *Liebestod* —the Love-death—and at its end she herself expires. Marke quietly blesses the dead, as the opera closes on two soft, long B-major chords.

IL TROVATORE

(*The Troubadour*)

Opera in four acts by Giuseppe Verdi with
libretto in Italian by Salvatore Cammarano
based on a play by Antonio García Gutiérrez
which was based, in turn, on some real happenings

LEONORA, *lady-in-waiting to Princess of Aragon*	Soprano
AZUCENA, *a Biscayan gypsy woman*	Mezzo-soprano
MANRICO, *a chieftain under tht Prince of*	
Biscay and reputed son of Azucena	Tenor
COUNT DI LUNA, *a young noble of Aragon*	Baritone
FERRANDO, *Di Luna's Captain of the Guard*	Bass
INEZ, *confidante of Leonora*	Soprano
RUIZ, *a soldier in Manrico's service*	Tenor

Time: 15th century
Place: Biscay and Aragon
First performance at Rome, January 19, 1853

Ever since it was first produced in Rome on an especially
dark and stormy night more than a century ago, *Il trovatore*
has been one of the most popular operas in the world. The
reason for its popularity today must be, at least partly, that
it has so many tunes that everyone has loved from childhood.
The *Miserere, Home to Our Mountains, The Anvil Chorus,
The Tempest of the Heart*—these are only a few of the wonderful melodies that form part of our folk culture, whether
sung by school children or heard on barrel organs. It can
hardly be the storytelling which makes this opera so popular,
for it boasts one of the most puzzling plots that ever graced

a stage. It is based on various events that actually happened in fifteenth-century Spain, but the scenes are so arranged that most of the pivotal actions occur before the opera begins or between the acts. Still, because the music is so eloquent, one can always tell whether the characters are happy or sad, or full of love or full of hate. And everyone in *Il trovatore* is full of some strong emotion all the time.

ACT I ("THE DUEL")

Scene 1   The first act, which bears the subtitle *The Duel*, opens in the vestibule of the palace of Aliaferia, where our heroine Leonora lives. An old soldier named Ferrando tells some servants and soldiers of the Count di Luna (who is outside waiting to court Leonora) a bit of family history. It seems that an old witch had cast a spell on one of the two sons of the old Count. For this she was burned at the stake, but her daughter, another witch, named Azucena, in revenge had stolen the old Count's other son and thrown him into the flames. Everyone wants to catch and burn this younger witch; but meantime the ghost of the older one is supposed to be still flying about in the shape of an owl and frightening people to death. Ferrando's listeners become wildly excited over this tale, and as the midnight bell tolls vigorously, they all curse the witch.

Scene 2   On a moonlight night, outside the castle, Leonora tells her confidante Inez of the mysterious knight she loves. Many years ago she had crowned him the winner of a tournament, but then he had completely disappeared. Suddenly, on a recent night (and here Leonora sings her lovely aria *Tacea la notte*) he serenaded her. Inez warns Leonora against such a love, but her mistress only swears eternal faith to the mysterious troubadour.

When the two girls have returned to the castle, this mysterious singer is heard off-stage accompanying himself on a lute. Leonora rushes out and—mistakenly, of course—throws herself into the arms of Di Luna, who has been lying in wait for her. And when the singer, the troubadour, appears, the Count immediately challenges him to a duel. In a mighty trio Leonora pleads for the troubadour's life, while the two men defy each other. Then, with swords drawn, they rush off to fight.

ACT II ("THE GYPSY")

Scene 1 The gypsy Azucena is in the center of the stage as the curtain goes up, surrounded by other gypsies in their camp in the mountains of Biscay. They break at once into the famous *Anvil Chorus*. Immediately afterwards, in the aria *Stride la vampa*, Azucena describes the terrible day on which she had seen her mother burned at the stake; and as soon as the gypsies have melodiously gone off in search of food, she gives her son Manrico (who is the troubadour of Act I) more details. With great intensity she tells how she had stolen the old Count di Luna's younger son and how, intending to throw *him* into the flames, she had by error picked up her own child and destroyed him instead. Thus we learn that Manrico is really the brother of his rival, the present Count di Luna. As for Manrico's questions as to who he really is, she insists that *he* is her son, for she has saved his life. Manrico, like the audience, remains puzzled. And now, in a lovely aria, *Mal reggendo*, he tells about his duel with Count di Luna. He had had Di Luna on the ground, defenseless, when some mysterious power held his victorious arm and spared Di Luna's life. But the mother and son agree that he never again should show such mercy.

Just then Manrico receives a message from his Prince, urging him to help defend the castle of Castellor against the forces of Di Luna. He also learns that Leonora, thinking him slain, is about to take her vows as a nun in the convent at Castellor. Thrusting aside Azucena and her protestations, Manrico wildly rushes off to the rescue of his Prince and his beloved.

Scene 2 takes us outside the convent. Here we find the Count with his followers ready to abduct Leonora just as she is about to take her vows. While waiting, he sings of the tempest that is raging in his heart in the familiar aria *Il balen*.

An off-stage chorus of nuns tells us the ceremony is about to take place, and when the women come on, Count di Luna attempts to lead Leonora off. As if by magic, Manrico suddenly appears, to Leonora's great joy and surprise, for she had thought him dead. A moment later Manrico's followers also come on the stage. The Count di Luna is overcome, and the act ends with a great ensemble, led by the voice of Leonora expressing her happiness.

ACT III ("THE GYPSY'S SON")

Scene 1 The third act leads us to the military camp of Count di Luna, who is laying siege to Castellor, where Manrico has taken Leonora, expecting to marry her. The soldiers sing a stirring march tune (*Squilli, e cheggi*), and presently Azucena, who has been found wandering near the camp, is brought in. She denies her identity, but the old soldier, Ferrando, recognizes her as the mysterious woman who had burned the Count's younger brother many years before. Desperately she calls on Manrico for help; and the Count, who now has two reasons for hating the old woman, swears a dire vengeance. The soldiers drag her off as the scene ends.

Scene 2 The brief second scene takes place inside the castle, where Manrico is preparing for two great events—the coming attack by Di Luna's forces and his marriage to Leonora. In a soothing aria, he quiets his beloved's fear. A moment later, just after the sound of the organ is heard, Ruiz bursts in. He is Manrico's lieutenant, and he reports that the pyre on which Azucena is to be burned to death is already lighted. Immediately Manrico orders a sortie to rescue his mother, and he sings the stirring aria *Di quella pira*, usually translated, though not very accurately, as "Tremble, ye tyrants!"

ACT IV ("THE ORDEAL.")

Scene 1 Outside the prison tower of the palace of Aliaferia comes Leonora to bewail the loss of Manrico, who has been taken prisoner in battle and is soon to be beheaded. A chorus of monks inside the prison tower intones the *Miserere*, a prayer for those about to depart this earth. Manrico sings his own farewell to life and Leonora, accompanying himself on his lute, and Leonora gives voice to her terror over the dreadful event about to take place. It is one of the most memorable —as well as one of the most hackneyed—numbers in all opera.

The Count now enters, and Leonora pleads for the life of her lover, even offering herself as a sacrifice for him. Overjoyed, the Count agrees to this bargain, but Leonora secretly takes poison from her ring so that she will not fall into the hands of the man she hates.

Scene 2 Inside the prison we find Azucena resting on a pallet of straw, while Manrico tries to comfort her, singing of the mountain home to which they shall return. This is the melodious duet *Ai nostri monti*—"Home to Our Mountains." Now Leonora comes and urges him to flee by himself. Fearing that Leonora has made a dishonorable bargain with the Count, Manrico is at first terribly angry; but as the poison begins to take effect, he understands what has happened. During their duet, Azucena lies quietly on her pallet, half out of her mind, and continues to sing of their old mountain home.

Just as Leonora dies, the Count enters and sees at once that he has been tricked. He orders Manrico's immediate execution and then pulls Azucena to the window to see the death of her supposed son. Turning violently on him, she now cries: *Egli era tuo fratello!*—"He was your brother!" And as she adds a triumphant cry of vengeance, the curtain descends to the crashing of tragic orchestral chords.

LES TROYENS

(The Trojans)

Opera in two parts and six acts (though sometimes divided into seven or even eight) by Hector Berlioz with libretto in French by the composer based on Books I, II, and IV of Virgil's
Aeneid

PART I—The Capture of Troy

PRIAM, *King of Troy*	Bass
HECUBA, *his wife*	Mezzo-soprano
AENEAS	Tenor
HELENUS	Bass
CASSANDRA *their children*	Mezzo-soprano
POLYXENA	Soprano
ASCANIUS, *son of Aeneas*	Soprano
COROEBUS, *fiancé of Cassandra*	Baritone
PANTHUS, *a Trojan priest*	Bass
ANDROMACHE, *widow of Hector*	Mime
ASTYANAX, *her son*	Mime
GHOST OF HECTOR	Bass
A GREEK OFFICER	Bass

PART II—The Trojans at Carthage

DIDO, *Queen of Carthage*	Mezzo-soprano
NARBAL, *her minister*	Bass
ANNA, *her sister*	Contralto
AENEAS, *leader of the Trojans*	Tenor
ASCANIUS, *his son*	Soprano
IOPAS, *a Carthaginian poet*	Tenor
HYLAS, *a young Trojan sailor*	Tenor
THE GHOST OF CASSANDRA	Mezzo-soprano

THE GHOST OF COROEBUS	*Baritone*
THE GHOST OF HECTOR	*Bass*
THE GHOST OF PRIAM	*Bass*
THE GOD MERCURY	*Bass*
FIRST TROJAN SOLDIER	*Baritone*
SECOND TROJAN SOLDIER	*Bass*

Time: Ancient Troy and Carthage
Places: Troy and Carthage
First performance, of Part II only, at Paris, November 4, 1863
First performance of both parts at Karlsruhe (in German)
  December 5 and 6, 1890

One of the great enthusiasms of the French nineteenth-century romanticists was classical literature; and one of the greatest enthusiasms of Hector Berlioz, most romantic of the romanticists, was Virgil, the laureate of Augustan Rome. Accordingly, when the Princess Wittgenstein, mistress of his great and good friend Franz Liszt, suggested the *Aeneid* as the subject of an opera to Berlioz, he embraced it with all the enthusiasm of his romantic heart.

With infinite labor and affection he wrote a vast libretto based on Books I, II, and IV of the epic (with a telling passage from *The Merchant of Venice* thrown in for good measure) and composed a score of imposing dimensions. Then began the still more heartbreaking business of trying to wangle a production. That took five whole years; and even then he might not have succeeded had he accepted an invitation to visit the United States. He turned it down partly because the Civil War was going on, partly because he hated Americans, whom he knew only as tourists. We have—quite foolishly, I feel, but also quite unconsciously—evened the score, for so far as I know, the work has never been staged here in its entirety although concert versions have been given.

The French, however, were not a great deal more perspicacious. When the work was finally given in 1863, only the second half reached the stage—and that was remorselessly cut after a while. Berlioz never lived to see the entire work done anywhere. He wrote bitterly about this defeat; and when, twenty-one years after his death, a complete performance of *Les troyens* was staged, it took place in Germany and in the German language.

When the entire work is given, two evenings must be devoted to it; and as the first part is comparatively static, it has become customary in France to give only the second part, under the title of *The Trojans at Carthage*. The first part is called, then, *The Capture of Troy* and the whole simply *The Trojans*.

Despite its comparatively few productions it is generally regarded as one of the few really great French operas. Even Donald Francis Tovey, one of the great critics of the twentieth century who had, generally, little good to say of Berlioz, wrote: "It is one of the most gigantic and convincing masterpieces of music-drama."

PART I: LA PRISE DE TROIE

(*The Capture of Troy*)

ACT I

Scene 1 The Greeks have apparently abandoned the siege of Troy, and outside the walls of that fabled city, before the empty tent of the once-dreaded Achilles, the people of Troy are celebrating. News comes that the departed enemy has left behind, on the shore, a huge wooden horse as an offering to the goddess Pallas Athene, and they rush off to see the wonder. Only Cassandra is left behind—that beautiful daughter of King Priam who has been cursed by Apollo with the gift of uttering true prophecies which are never to be believed. She has seen the ghost of her brother Hector looking fearfully across the sea, and she knows that Priam is doomed. Yet no one will believe her, and even Coroebus, to whom she is engaged, believes her to be mad. Coroebus comes to her and tenderly asks her to rejoice with the others, but she is still full of gloomy prophecies: the streets of Troy will be running with blood; its virgins will be violated; and Coroebus himself will be killed by a Grecian spear. She implores him to flee the place; but Coroebus is a hero, and in the duet that follows, she speaks lovingly and comfortingly to him. The gloomy girl promises to marry him, but adds that death is already preparing their bridal bed.

Scene 2　Before the citadel of Troy, King Priam and Queen Hecuba hold court, celebrating the victory and giving thanks to the protecting gods. Processions pass by, and a mimic battle is danced. At its close, Andromache comes in with little Astyanax. She is the widow of the great hero of Troy, Prince Hector, who had been slain by Achilles in single combat and dragged around the walls seven times. Mother and child are dressed in white, the symbol of mourning, and everyone receives them with solemn respect. At the back of the stage, however, Cassandra prophesies even greater disaster for Hecuba; and the ensemble develops as a solemn funeral march.

Aeneas, another son of Priam's, comes rushing in with somber news. The priest Laocoön had shared some of Cassandra's misgivings about the wooden horse. "I fear Greeks when they bear gifts," he said, and hurled a javelin at the monster. Immediately two serpents had come across the waters and destroyed him and his sons. The news strikes horror into the Trojan hearts, and an impressive ensemble expresses it. Nevertheless, the advice of Aeneas prevails. He interprets the action of the serpents as revenge of the gods for an act of impiety and orders the horse to be drawn into the city. Only Cassandra warns against this foolhardy act, but no one, as usual, pays any attention to her.

An elaborate scene develops as night falls; off-stage the soldiers begin the *Trojan March of Triumph*; and chorus after chorus comes on. A few of the people are disquieted by a report that weapons have been heard clanking inside the horse, but when it is actually drawn across the scene, joy prevails again. As Cassandra sees it drawn into the city itself, she cries: "It is finished! Death has seized its prey!"

ACT II

Scene 1   Aeneas is asleep, and his little son, Ascanius, disquieted by the ominous sounds he has heard outside, steals in. He does not dare awaken his father, however, and leaves again. He is followed by a bolder and more sinister figure—the ghost of Hector. Hector warns his brother of Troy's impending doom and tells him to save the household gods from the disaster. Then in a most solemn address (which is, musically, nothing but a slow descending chromatic octave) he tells him to seek out Italy and found an empire to rule the world. (This, of course, is to be Rome.)

Hector's warning is already too late. Panthus, a priest, himself badly wounded, brings in the statuettes of the gods and tells Aeneas how Greek soldiers poured out of the wooden horse, slew the guards, and have already massacred many of the people and the King himself. Ascanius, Coroebus, and others follow, and Aeneas rushes out at their head, determined to make a last stand.

Scene 2   The women of Troy are gathered in the Temple of Vesta, which has a high gallery at its back. They sing a wailing prayer to the goddess Cybele (the mother of Zeus), and Cassandra joins them with the report that Aeneas and a band of followers have escaped, that they are on their way to Italy to found a greater Troy. But as for herself, there is nothing left: Coroebus has fallen. She urges all of them to escape a fate worse than death by hurling themselves from the gallery; but a few of the younger girls shrink from the sacrifice, and they are driven from the temple, presumably into the arms of the Greek rapists.

A band of these Greeks invades the temple, looking for treasure rather than girls, and their anonymous leader is struck with awe by the sight of the women, wailing as they play their lyres. Cassandra and her sister Polyxena (once the beloved of the Greek Achilles) stab themselves; most of the others hurl themselves from the gallery; and Cassandra, with her last breath, stretches her arms toward Mount Ida and cries: "Italy!"

Postscript for the mythologically curious: According to other versions of the story, Cassandra was carried home by Agamemnon as his concubine, and his wife, Clytemnestra, murdered both of them, using the beautiful newcomer as one of the excuses for her mariticide. Polyxena is also variantly reported as having been sacrificed at the tomb of Achilles on the demand of that redoubtable warrior's ghost.

PART II: LES TROYENS À CARTHAGE

(*The Trojans at Carthage*)

ACT I

After an overture thoroughly in the spirit of classical tragedy, the action opens as Queen Dido and her Carthaginian subjects are having a thanksgiving festival in the gardens of her palace. Seven years before, Dido's husband murdered, they had all fled to North Africa; and now, through hard work and the blessings of nature, they have established a prosperous city-state. When the subjects leave, Dido is approached by her sister Anna, who thinks it time for Dido to consider marrying again. In the duet that follows, Dido makes it clear that she wishes to remain faithful to the memory of her husband, but she also makes it clear that (like any classical lady in a French libretto) she yearns for love.

At the close of the duet a messenger announces that a storm has forced a fleet into the harbor of Carthage, and the strangers request an audience. In comes a group of sailors with a young boy who offers gifts. This boy turns out to be Ascanius, son of Aeneas, the glamorous leader of the Trojans. The interview is interrupted by Dido's chief adviser Narbal, who announces the imminent invasion of the defenseless Carthaginians by a mighty Numidian force. Immediately one of the sailors throws off his disguise. It is Aeneas offering Dido the use of his army and weapons in defense of Carthage. The offer is at once accepted, and the act ends with a martial call to arms.

ACT II

Between Act I and Act II, Aeneas and his followers have helped Dido throw back the invaders. The opera resumes with the one passage in the work fairly familiar to concert-goers. That is the *Royal Hunt and Storm*, which is a sort of ballet in which Aeneas and Dido are engaged in a hunt. They are overtaken by a storm and driven for shelter into a cave, where their love is consummated. The wild scenery and the hunt are graphically described by the orchestra, and toward the close wild nymphs and fauns are heard crying: "Italy, Italy!" These are reminders of the destiny of Aeneas, who must leave Dido and Carthage to go to Italy and found the great city of Rome.

Act II proper begins with a duet between Dido's sister Anna and Narbal. That wise gentleman is worried because Dido is paying more attention to her beloved guest than to affairs of state. "Why worry?" asks Anna, for no one could make a more suitable King of Carthage than the heroic Aeneas. The only trouble is, counters Narbal, that Aeneas may not marry the girl: he has another future mapped out for him at Rome. At the close of their duet there is a ballet celebrating the victory of Aeneas. Then Dido calls for a song from the court minstrel, Iopas, who obliges with an ode in praise of Ceres, goddess of agriculture.

Now Aeneas relates the fate of Andromache, who married the son of the murderer of her beloved husband, Hector. As he talks, Dido falls more in love with him. Everyone is fascinated by the recital, and the act ends with a love duet based on the poetic exchange between Nerissa and Lorenzo in the last act of *The Merchant of Venice*. Yet, at its very close, comes the voice of Mercury, the messenger of the gods. He must urge Aeneas on his way; and he cries: "Italy, Italy, Italy!" like the nymphs and fauns earlier.

ACT III

We now move down to the harbor of Carthage, where the fleet of Aeneas is ready to sail. A young sailor named Hylas sings a nostalgic song of homesickness, and a group of Trojans comments on a strange phenomenon: the ghosts of various Trojans have been urging Aeneas to leave Carthage and go to Italy.

This somber scene is followed by the one comic scene in the whole opera. Two Trojan sentries talk about the hospitality and lack of race prejudice among their Carthaginian hosts. It has a strangely modern ring to it.

And now Aeneas, in a long monologue, complains of the fate that drives him from the arms of his beloved Dido. He decides to pay her one last visit. But then the shades of his fellow-warriors and relatives urge him to leave. Priam, Hector, Cassandra—their voices all unite in demanding that he go on to Italy. He finally decides to obey and orders everything readied for departure.

But then Dido reappears. Pitifully, reproachfully, she begs him to remain. His fate is ordained by the gods, he says; he must leave, and he must die in founding Rome. He loves her, but the gods are adamant. In a tower of anger she departs, denouncing him as a "monster of piety." With her curses still sounding in his ears, he listens as the sailors make their joyous preparations. "Italy, Italy, Italy!" they shout.

ACT IV

Scene 1 In her palace Dido tries to persuade Anna to plead with Aeneas, but then Narbal brings the news that he is already at sea with his fleet. Now she is forever deserted. First she wishes to pursue him in her own ships and to burn the Trojan fleet; next she gives way to complete despair; and finally, as the scene ends, she sings a long last farewell to her own city of Carthage.

Scene 2 On a terrace overlooking the sea Dido commands

a huge pyre to be built. There she will sacrifice the tokens of her love to the gods. When all is in readiness, she mounts the pyre herself. In an ecstasy of inspiration she foresees the future invasion of Rome by Carthaginians under Hannibal. And then, again, she foresees the ruin of Carthage at the hands of the Romans. Finally, in utter despair, she seizes the sword Aeneas had left behind and stabs herself. As she utters her dying, savage cries, the chorus hurls a series of curses on the race of Aeneas, the race of the Trojans, and the Romans. But the *Trojan March* is played once more, and in the distance, behind the pyre, rises a vision of the Eternal City.

TURANDOT

Opera in three acts by Giacomo Puccini with libretto in Italian by Giuseppe Adami and Renato Simoni, based on Carlo Gozzi's drama of the same name with some hints from Friedrich von Schiller's adaptation of it

PRINCESS TURANDOT	*Soprano*
THE EMPEROR OF CHINA	*Tenor*
TIMUR, *exiled King of Tartary*	*Bass*
CALAF, *his son (the "Unknown Prince")*	*Tenor*
LIÙ, *a slave girl*	*Soprano*
PING, *Grand Chancellor China*	*Baritone*
PANG, *Supreme Lord of Provisions*	*Tenor*
PONG, *Supreme Lord of the Imperial Kitchen*	*Tenor*
A HERALD	*Baritone*

Time: legendary
Place: Pekin.
First performance at Milan, April 25, 1926

Halfway through the final act, at the premiere of *Turandot*, the music stopped, Arturo Toscanini laid down his baton, and he turned to the audience to say: "Here the Maestro laid down his pen."

Suffering from cancer of the throat and finally taken off by a heart attack, Puccini had not lived to complete the score of his last opera. Throughout the readying of the libretto (which was a slow business because one of the writers was a successful dramatist engaged in his own work), and throughout the composition of the score, Puccini was querulously complaining that he might never live to finish it. Yet there is no sign of waning power in the music. It is bolder in its harmonies and orchestration than anything the composer had attempted before; there is a new mastery of choral effect; there is more dramatic power than in anything he had done for twenty years. True, there are some tiresome stretches (something much, one feels, of the philosopher-politicans Ping, Pang, and Pong); but if he had lived not only to complete the work but to revise it, it might well have achieved general popularity along with critical respect.

Franco Alfano, a friend of Puccini's who, twenty years before, had achieved an international reputation with his opera *Resurrection,* completed the score with some help from Puccini's notes for the final duet.

ACT I

In legendary times, in the city of Pekin, there dwelt the Princess Turandot. She was to be won only by a royal suitor who could answer three riddles. If he failed, he was to be executed.

When the opera opens, the Prince of Persia, having failed to answer the three questions, is about to be executed. He is to die at moonrise, and the excited crowd is calling for his death. In the melee an old man is knocked down and then rescued by a young man—the Unknown Prince. The old man is Timur, once King of the Tartars, and the young man is his son, Calaf, whom the King had believed lost since a disastrous battle. The King has been attended in his wanderings by a young slave girl, Liù, who helps the old King because she has been grateful to Calaf since the day that he once smiled at her in his palace.

As the moon begins to rise, the mob has a change of heart and demands pardon for the gallant young Prince of Persia. But Turandot appears in all her cold regal beauty and silently gives the sign for his execution. The crowd follows the death procession.

Calaf, having now seen Turandot, is madly in love with her.

He is warned repeatedly not to try the three riddles which have caused so many deaths. Timur asks him to refrain; Liù begs him not to attempt the enigmas; and so do the three ministers, Ping, Pang, and Pong. Calaf's answer to Liù is the sympathetic aria *Non piangere, Liù*—"Do not weep, Liù." But nothing can persuade him. As the act closes, he strikes the great gong before the palace, and calls out Turandot's name to signify the arrival of one more suitor for her hand.

ACT II

In an introductory scene three ministers of the court at Pekin philosophize. They are Ping (the Grand Chancellor), Pang (Supreme Lord of Provisions), and Pong (Supreme Lord of the Kitchen), and they are based on stock figures from the *commedia dell' arte*. Their commentary is on the trouble caused by Turandot's dangerous game of riddles and on the charms of the quiet life in the homes they came from.

The curtains are drawn to show the full court assembled, and the Emperor, echoing the ministers' sentiments, asks Calaf to retire from the contest. Naturally, he refuses. The Princess herself now warns Calaf in her turn. She explains the reason for the game: it is designed to avenge an ancient ancestress who had been captured by an enemy and who had died in exile. Turandot warns Calaf once more; but at the close of the duet their voices join in agreeing on a brutally brief summary of the rules: the riddles are three in number; the life to be paid is but one.

Thereupon the riddles are propounded and answered:
Question: What phantom is born every night and dies the next day?
Answer (very prompt): Hope.
Question: What blazes like a fever when you think of great deeds but grows cold in death?
Answer (almost as prompt): Blood.
(The crowd encourages Calaf before Turandot silences them and poses the third riddle.)
Question: What is the ice that sets you on fire?

Answer (given after considerable hesitation and some taunts from the Princess): *Turandot!*

The crowd is delighted that the young Prince has correctly answered the fateful riddles, but Turandot is not. She begs the Emperor to be let off the indignity of marrying a foreigner, but he answers that his oath is not to be violated. Calaf, however, is not only in love; he is magnanimous as well. He proposes that Turandot be relieved of this fate and that his own life be given up if she can answer, by the next morning, but a single riddle—his name.

ACT III

Once again, as in Act I, we are in the gardens before the walls of Pekin. The herald explains that no one must sleep in Pekin that night before the name of the Unknown Prince is discovered: the penalty is death. Rather pleased than otherwise, Calaf sings his aria *Nessun dorma*—"No one must sleep." He is confident that he alone will be in a position to reveal his name, and that Turandot shall be his bride.

The three gabby ministers offer Calaf all sorts of inducements to tell them his name, including a guaranteed safe-exit visa from China. He is not interested.

Now Timur and Liù are roughly brought in by the guards. As they have been seen talking to Calaf, they must know his name. Liù boldly claims that she is the only one who knows it, and cruel torture is at once applied; but in vain. Turandot, coming on the scene, asks what gives the girl such powers of resistance. It is love, she says, and in the aria *Tu, che di gel sei cinta*—"You who are encircled by ice"—she prophesies that one day Turandot will love Calaf. At the close of the aria she seizes a dagger from a soldier, and, fearful that she may break under further torture, stabs herself to death. Timur bursts out in anger, but he and the body of Liù are carried out by the crowd, and Turandot is left alone with the Unknown Prince.

It was from this point on that Alfano had to complete the work of Puccini.

The Unknown Prince upbraids Turandot, and then suddenly takes her in his arms. The ice of which Liù had sung is melted; Turandot weeps; and she begs Calaf to leave her, his secret unrevealed. But he knows now that she loves him, and, venturing all, he tells her his name and, so doing, offers her his life.

Once more the scene is swiftly changed to the court as trumpets sound. Turandot speaks before them all. She has learned the stranger's name, she says, and it is Love.

WILLIAM TELL

(*Guillaume Tell*)

Opera in four acts* by Gioacchino Antonio Rossini with libretto in French by Victor Joseph Étienne de Jouy and Hippolyte Louis Florent Bis (with considerable help from the composer and Armand Marrast), based on the play of the same name by Johann Christoph Friedrich von Schiller

WILLIAM TELL, *a Swiss patriot*	Baritone
HEDWIGE, *his wife*	Soprano
JEMMY, *their son*	Soprano
GESSLER, *Austrian Governor of Schwitz and Uri*	Bass
MATHILDE, *his daughter*	Soprano
ARNOLD, *a Swiss patriot*	Tenor
MELCTHAL, *his father*	Bass
WALTER FURST, *another Swiss patriot*	Bass
RUDOLPH, *captain in Gessler's guard*	Tenor
LEUTHOLD, *a shepherd*	Bass

Time: 14th century
Place: Switzerland
First performance at Paris, August 3, 1829

William Tell was Rossini's longest opera—and his last. Maybe it was the writing of so long a work (its original performance took over six hours) that discouraged him from writing more. At any rate, though *William Tell* was a great

* Originally in five acts, later reduced to three by omission of the third and condensation of the last two acts. Current practice is to restore Act III and retain the condensation, thus making four acts.

critical success, he did not write another opera although he lived almost forty years more. Rossini himself authorized a version that was cut from five to three acts, and for a while it was even customary, in Paris, to give Act II alone, with another opera to fill out the bill. The story goes that one time the director of the Opéra told the composer that Act II of *William Tell* was on the bill for that night. "What?" exclaimed the bitter Rossini. "*All* of it?"

For many years it was customary to say that *The Barber of Seville* and *William Tell* were the only Rossini operas which had survived the composer many years in the repertoires of the great opera houses. Whether because of its length or because of the extremely demanding tenor role of Arnold, *Tell* can no longer be called "standard" repertoire, while other Rossini operas, like *La cenerentola* and *The Italian in Algiers*, are being revived with greater frequency. The fact is that *The Barber* has by far the best libretto of the lot. The *William Tell* story is serviceable enough, but little better than that.

In several countries, during the politically sensitive 1830's, it was regarded as dangerously revolutionary. Accordingly, the libretto was revised, and in Milan the opera was called *Guglielmo Vallace* (that is, the Scottish William Wallace), in Rome *Rodolfo di Sterlinga*, in London and Berlin *Andreas Hofer*, and in St. Petersburg *Karl Smily* (Charles the Bold). It seems odd that the censors should have been more frightened of the name of an almost completely mythical revolutionary than of some real ones. But many things that censors do seem odd.

OVERTURE

The overture to *William Tell* is the best-known piece of orchestral music ever to come out of an opera, rivaled, perhaps, only by the *Intermezzo* from *Cavalleria rusticana*. It has survived in the affections of the public—and perhaps even grown in those affections—the satirical use of it in Disney's animated cartoons and as the theme of the Lone Ranger. It begins, boldly, with a quintet for five solo cellos; a soft roll on the kettledrums introduces one of Rossini's pet storms, including realistic raindrops spattered from the piccolo; then comes a pastoral section based on a Swiss alphorn melody played on the French horn; and eventually, after a brilliant fanfare of trumpets, comes the familiar *galop*, which retains its excitement when well played despite the many humorous associations, polite and impolite, that have been attached to it.

ACT I

The story concerns the legendary activities of a legendary fourteenth-century Swiss patriot. The country is under the heel of the Austrian Governor, Gessler, who has shown himself to be a tyrant. High up in the Alps, in Tell's native village, the Swiss are celebrating a traditional festival. The old shepherd Melcthal is to give his blessing to three couples who wish to be married. Two serious voices are slightly out of tune with the happy occasion. One is that of Tell, who bemoans the fate of his country, the other that of Arnold, son of Melcthal, who is involved in a dangerous love affair.

There is a long duet in which Tell urges Arnold to fight for his country, but Arnold at first hesitates as his beloved is Mathilde, daughter of Gessler. Occasionally there is heard the sound of hunting horns—an indication that Gessler's men are in the neighborhood, hunting.

Now the festivities are resumed. There is first a ballet, and in the ensuing games Tell's young son Jemmy distinguishes himself by being a good shot, just as his father is. The celebration is interrupted by Leuthold, a Swiss fugitive from Gessler's men, running in. Tell saves him by spiriting him away on a boat despite great danger on the lake.

When Gessler's men, headed by Rudolph, arrive, no one will tell them who aided in the escape, and in revenge they seize upon old Melcthal and drag him off.

ACT II

The second act begins with a recitative and the brilliant

coloratura aria *Sombre forêt* sung by Mathilde, daughter of the Austrian tyrant Gessler, in which she admits her love for Arnold. He meets her in the Alpine clearing in a forest where she waits, and a fine love duet ensues. Mathilde leaves hastily when she hears the approach of William Tell and Walter Furst. These men have come to persuade Arnold to join them in an uprising against Gessler, but they are suspicious of him because of his meeting with Mathilde. Presently, however, they give him some bad news: Gessler has had Arnold's old father, the shepherd Melcthal, executed. Now there is no longer any hesitation on Arnold's part, and at the close of the fine trio the three men swear to deliver their country from its oppression.

One by one, trusted groups of men arrive from the Swiss cantons of Unterwalden, Schwitz, and Uri. Tell delivers a dramatic address, and a solemn patriotic oath is taken by all present as the act ends.

ACT III

In the market place of the village of Altdorf, the tyrant Gessler has put up the Austrian coat-of-arms and his own hat for every Swiss to bow before. William Tell refuses to bow, and he and his son are at once arrested. Gessler says that Tell must demonstrate his vaunted skill with bow and arrow by shooting an apple off his son's head, and when Tell refuses, Gessler orders the boy to be executed. Now Tell has no choice. The boy, Jemmy, fearlessly expresses complete confidence in Tell's skill, and cheers go up as the arrow splits the apple in two.

But a second arrow falls from Tell's coat; and when Gessler demands to know what that is for, the patriot tells him it would have been for Gessler's own heart if the boy had been hurt. Greatly incensed, Gessler orders the arrest of Tell, but before our hero is dragged off, he manages to send his wife a message through his son. Tell Hedwige, says William, that the lighting of mountain beacons will be the signal for the uprising of the cantons. Gessler's own daughter, Mathilde, flees from the spot with little Jemmy, to deliver the message.

Scene 1 is largely taken up by an aria sung by Arnold. He has returned home, and his father's death at the hands of Gessler continues to haunt him. A group of Swiss patriots reports to him the arrest of William Tell, and, finally roused to action, he leads the men off to rescue their leader.

Scene 2 takes place on a rocky spot off the Lake of the Four Cantons and near Tell's own home. Jemmy, accompanied by Mathilde, rushes in to his mother, Hedwige. The little boy is hopeful that Tell will escape despite the storm that is brewing, when suddenly he remembers his father's message. He himself sets fire to his father's house as a signal for the cantons to rise. As the storm develops, they all pray for Tell's deliverance, and suddenly the hero appears, jumping from a boat. Close behind him come his pursuers, including Gessler. But Tell seizes his bow and arrow from Jemmy, who has rescued them from the burning house. Tell takes careful aim and, with a cry, Gessler tumbles headlong into the lake. At that moment a party of Swiss patriots, led by young Arnold, comes in to announce the taking of Gessler's headquarters in Altdorf. The opera closes with rejoicing on the part of every surviving Swiss member of the dramatis personae.

WOZZECK

Opera in three acts by Alban Berg with libretto
in German by the composer, based on a play of
the same name by Georg Büchner

WOZZECK, *a soldier*	*Baritone*
MARIE, *his mistress*	*Soprano*
THEIR CHILD	*Boy soprano*
ANDRES, *a friend of Wozzeck's*	*Tenor*
MARGRET, *a neighbor*	*Contralto*
THE CAPTAIN	*Tenor*
THE DOCTOR	*Bass*
THE DRUM MAJOR	*Tenor*
FIRST AND SECOND WORKMEN	*Baritone and Bass*
A FOOL	*Tenor*

Time: about 1835
Place: Germany
First performance at Berlin, December 14, 1925

Alban Berg, the most distinguished disciple of Arnold
Schönberg, died at the age of fifty in his native Vienna. The
date was 1935. Usually I have not included such vital statistics about composers in my introductory comments, but this
time I think they are important. For—to me, at least—Berg
and his operas *Wozzeck* and *Lulu* epitomize one aspect of a
certain time and place. *Wozzeck* was conceived during World
War I; its composition was completed immediately after that
war; and it received its first stage performance, in Berlin, in
1925. It deeply stirred all of Middle Europe of that period.
And that period was the period of Dr. Sigmund Freud, the

period of Franz Kafka, the period of the rise of National Socialism. In music it was the period that saw the most violent breakdown of old ideas of melody—and, even more, of harmony. It was revolutionary, it was intellectually curious, it was unstable, and it reflected the sickness of the German soul.

Berg wrote his own libretto for *Wozzeck*, basing it on a hundred-year-old play written by a strange, youthful genius named Georg Büchner. It deals with the psychological torture and breakdown of a dull-witted militiaman named Johann Franz Wozzeck and with the tragic fate of his mistress and their illegitimate child. Charming theme, isn't it? And, possibly excepting these three unfortunates, there is scarcely one amiable person in the whole cast. Nevertheless, its entry into the Metropolitan Opera repertory in 1959 was a surprise popular success.

ACT I

Scene 1 finds Wozzeck shaving his captain, for whom he is a personal servant, while the captain philosophizes in a mildly idiotic way. (The part is written for a very high tenor voice.) Wozzeck answers at first stupidly, mechanically *Jawohl, Herr Hauptmann*—"Certainly, Captain,"—but finally he comes out with an incoherent complaint about his poverty.

Scene 2 Wozzeck shares this scene with another high tenor —his companion-in-arms, Andres. Andres is inclined to be cheerful, but Wozzeck imagines he sees various supernatural things in the field where they are working.

Scene 3 In her room Marie, Wozzeck's mistress, is playing with their child. She sees a parade of soldiers passing and admires the Drum Major; she is jeered at by a neighbor, Margret, for her easy virtue; she sings a lullaby to the child. When Wozzeck passes by, he frightens her with an account of the supernatural things he thinks he has seen. Something dreadful, he feels, is going to happen.

Scene 4 Next day, in the regimental doctor's office, Wozzeck is being examined. The Doctor is a kind of amateur psychiatrist—not to say a bit of a sadist. This crazy, incompetent man implants the idea in Wozzeck's mind that he is bad, that he may be going crazy. As the scene ends, he boasts to himself that he will become famous through what he is doing to poor Wozzeck.

Scene 5   Marie meets the Drum Major in the street. He is a handsome fellow, she notes. He agrees. He starts to make love to her. It is a quick conquest—and they disappear into her house.

ACT II

Scene 1   Marie preens herself on the pair of earrings that the Drum Major has given her. When Wozzeck enters, he notes the new earrings and is suspicious. Yet he is still upset in his mind about other things, and he is sorry for the child, who lies asleep with a slight fever. Almost absent-mindedly he gives Marie his wages. When he has left, she scolds herself for her wickedness.

Scene 2   In the street the Captain meets the Doctor, who frightens his friend by telling him he looks bad. "You might find yourself partially paralyzed one day," he remarks unsympathetically. But a better target for his malice passes by. It is poor Wozzeck. The two officers make unmistakable references to Marie's unfaithfulness, and the Doctor suggests that Wozzeck is also pretty sick.

Scene 3   Encountering Marie in the street, Wozzeck accuses her in wild terms. She begs him not to hit her. Rather, she cries, she would prefer a knife in her heart. And as she runs off, Wozzeck repeats her phrase mutteringly: "Rather a knife . . ."

Scene 4   At the beer garden everyone is in high spirits and slightly boozy. Wozzeck joins the crowd, sees Marie dancing with the Drum Major, and is about to attack him. But the dance stops, and a soldier begins a drunken song. Someone else delivers a crazy sermon. A fool starts talking to Wozzeck. And as he sits there listening, his feeble brain seems to weaken even more.

Scene 5   Wozzeck is moaning in his sleep, in the barracks.

Andres awakens and hears him talk about a knife blade. Then, enter the Drum Major, who boasts about his conquests. Wozzeck, maddened by jealousy, attacks him. But the Drum Major is a big fellow, and Wozzeck is badly beaten up. Having done his job, the Drum Major leaves. The other soldiers heartlessly shrug their shoulders, turn around, and go to sleep.

ACT III

Scene 1 is entirely Marie's. She is alone with her child and full of guilt. She reads from the Bible, first the story of the woman taken in adultery and then the story of Mary Magdalene. And she prays to God for mercy.

Scene 2 takes us to a pool in the forest outside the town at night, where Wozzeck is with Marie. He makes her sit beside him; he kisses her; and he mutters earnestly of love. Then he whispers mysteriously to himself, and there is a long silence. Suddenly Marie notices that the moon is red. "Like a blood-red iron," says Wozzeck, and he draws out his knife. Terrified, Marie tries to escape. But he madly plunges the knife deep into her throat; and when she is dead, he rushes away.

Scene 3 It is to a tavern that he rushes. More than half drunk, he sings madly, and dances with Margret, Marie's neighbor. Suddenly she notices blood on his hand, and she cries out. Everyone crowds around and sees the blood, but Wozzeck runs out as fast as he can.

Scene 4 Back he rushes to the scene of his murder. He *must* get rid of his bloody knife, and when he finds it, he flings it into the pool. But then he fears it may be found after all and the blame pinned on him. Completely befuddled, he wades deep into the pool. He fishes for the knife with his hands; he topples over; and he drowns. The Doctor and the Captain, passing by, think they hear a noise. But they decide it was only the lapping of the water, and they leave the ghostly night scene.

Scene 5 It is bright sunshine the next morning, and outside of Marie's house children are playing ring-around-a-rosy.

Among them is Marie's little boy. Another group of children comes in, bursting with news. One of them shouts to the little boy: "Hey, your mother is dead!" But the child does not hear. He is playing horse. And when the others rush off to see the body, which has been discovered near the pool, the child just goes on riding his hobbyhorse. "Hop-hop, hop-hop!" he cries.

CHRONOLOGY

For anyone who wishes to use this volume as a survey of the
subject of opera, the works described are indexed below,
grouped by composers, in the order of the births of the composers. Reading, in this order, merely the introduction to each
of the works will serve either as an informal history of the
subject or as a supplement to formal studies such as Donald
Jay Grout's A *Short History of Opera*, in two volumes, or the
one-volume *The Opera: 1600–1941*, by Wallace Brockway
and Herbert Weinstock.

Wolfgang Amadeus Mozart (1756–91)
Bastien und Bastienne (1768), 66
Die Entführung aus dem Serail (1782), 11
Le nozze di Figaro (1786), 295
Don Giovanni (1787), 124
Così fan tutte (1790), 110
Die Zauberflöte (1791), 275

Ludwig van Beethoven (1770–1827)
Fidelio (1805), 175

Carl Maria von Weber (1786–1826)
Der Freischütz (1821), 200
Oberon (1826), 346

Giacomo Meyerbeer (1791–1864)
Les Huguenots (1836), 226
L'Africaine (1865), 15

Gioacchino Antonio Rossini (1792–1868)
Il barbiere di Siviglia (1816), 55
La Cenerentola (1817), 95
Guillaume Tell (1829), 539

Gaetano Donizetti (1797–1848)
L'Elisir d'amore (1832), 140
Lucia di Lammermoor (1835), 265
Don Pasquale (1843), 131

Vincenzo Bellini (1801–35)
Norma (1831), 341
I Puritani (1835), 395

Hector Berlioz (1803–69)
Les Troyens (1863, Part II only), 525

Ambroise Thomas (1811–96)
Mignon (1866), 336

Ruggiero Leoncavallo (1858–1919)
  Pagliacci (1892), 362

Giacomo Puccini (1858–1924)
  Manon Lescaut (1893), 290
  La Bohème (1896), 68
  Tosca (1900), 503
  Madama Butterfly (1904), 270
  La fanciulla del West (1910), 215
  Gianni Schicchi (1918), 206
  Suor Angelica (1918), 477
  Il tabarro (1918), 480
  Turandot (1926), 534

Gustave Charpentier (1860–1956)
  Louise (1900), 252

Claude Debussy (1862–1918)
  Pelléas et Mélisande (1902), 371

Pietro Mascagni (1863–1945)
  Cavalleria rusticana (1890), 91

Richard Strauss (1864–1949)
  Salome (1905), 453
  Elektra (1909), 138
  Der Rosenkavalier (1911), 447
  Ariadne auf Naxos (1912), 51
  Arabella (1933), 47
  Capriccio (1942), 83

Umberto Giordano (1867–1948)
  Andrea Chénier (1896), 41

Maurice Ravel (1875–1937)
  L'Heure espagnole (1911), 224

Italo Montemezzi (1875–1952)
  L'Amore dei tre re (1913), 37

Ermanno Wolf-Ferrari (1876–1948)
  Il segreto di Susanna (1909), 464

Igor Stravinsky (1882–   )
  The Rake's Progress (1951), 399

Alban Berg (1885–1935)
  Wozzeck (1925), 544

Sergei Prokofieff (1891–1953)
  The Love for Three Oranges (1921), 257

Virgil Thomson (1896–   )
  Four Saints in Three Acts (1934), 197

George Gershwin (1898–1937)
  Porgy and Bess (1935), 384

Gian-Carlo Menotti (1911–   )
  The Medium (1946), 321
  The Telephone (1947), 495
  The Consul (1950), 100
  Amahl and the Night Visitors (1951), 35

Benjamin Britten (1913–   )
  Peter Grimes (1945), 377

11I